DEFINING THE PEACE

DEFINING

THE PEACE

World War II Veterans,
Race, and the Remaking
of Southern Political
Tradition

Jennifer E. Brooks

The University of North Carolina Press

Chapel Hill and London

© 2004 The University of North Carolina Press
Manufactured in the United States of America

Designed by April Leidig-Higgins
Set in Minion by Copperline Book Services, Inc.

The paper in this book meets the guidelines for
permanence and durability of the Committee on
Production Guidelines for Book Longevity of the
Council on Library Resources.

Frontispiece: Courtesy of Lane Brothers Commercial
Photographic Collection, Photographic Collections,
Special Collections Department, Pullen Library,
Georgia State University, Atlanta, Ga.

Part of this book has been reprinted in revised form
from Jennifer E. Brooks, "Winning the Peace: Georgia
Veterans and the Struggle to Define the Political
Legacy of World War II," *Journal of Southern History*
66, no. 3 (August 2000): 563–604.

Library of Congress Cataloging-in-Publication Data
Brooks, Jennifer E.
Defining the peace: World War II veterans, race, and
the remaking of Southern political tradition /
Jennifer E. Brooks.
p. cm. Includes bibliographical references and index.
ISBN 0-8078-2911-0 (cloth: alk. paper)
ISBN 0-8078-5578-2 (pbk.: alk. paper)
1. World War, 1939–1945—Veterans—Georgia.
2. Veterans—Georgia—Political activity.
3. Georgia—Politics and government—20th
century.   I. Title.
D810.V42U63   2004
305.9'0697'0975809045—dc22   2004011780

cloth   08 07 06 05 04   5 4 3 2 1
paper   08 07 06 05 04   5 4 3 2 1

To the memory of
Donald C. Bogue
1932–1997

Contents

Acknowledgments

ACKNOWLEDGING ALL THOSE good people who helped me along this journey requires more space than is available here. However, a few do stand out. First of all, my deepest gratitude and continued respect go to my mentor and major professor, Dr. James C. Cobb. His simple suggestion to a rather bewildered graduate student casting about for a dissertation topic that World War II veterans might be a subject worth looking into ballooned quickly into a large and rich project that has carried me through the past nine years. More importantly, his support for my work, from the time I entered the graduate program at the University of Tennessee to the publication of this book, has never faltered. Though any mistakes, miscalculations, or wrong turns in this book are solely my own, much of my understanding of the dynamic relationship between political, economic, social, and cultural change in the modern South derives from Dr. Cobb's rich, eloquent, and pioneering work. I was fortunate enough to arrive at the University of Tennessee at just the right time.

I am indebted to Professor Clarence Mohr at the University of Alabama for taking the time to peruse and comment on an earlier version of this manuscript. Many thanks go as well to the University of North Carolina Press reviewers who offered meaningful criticism that helped me to expand this work beyond what I initially envisioned it to be.

I would also like to thank Dr. Dan Pierce at the University of North Carolina, Asheville, for reading and commenting on a chapter and Dr. Donal Sexton of Tusculum College for absolving me of committee duties at opportune moments. Tom Silva, my favorite artist, made the process of obtaining photographs a far less onerous one, and he labored with generous devotion to meet the deadlines I usually forgot to mention until the last possible moment. Dan Jansen and Lydia Reid, my friends in Silver Springs, Maryland, and Rich Felsing, my cousin in Madison, Wisconsin, provided hearth, home, and pets to sustain me on long-distance research trips.

David Perry, at the University of North Carolina Press, offered his invaluable confidence, perseverance, and wise counsel as this work progressed through the rigorous review process. Paula Wald and Bethany Johnson shepherded the manuscript through the copyediting and production phases with inspiring skill and efficiency. The librarians at Tusculum College searched without complaint for my interlibrary loan materials, no matter how odd the request. This proved crucial to completing new chapters for the manuscript, and I am especially thankful to Charles Tunstall for his diligence. The Appalachian College Association graciously provided a Stephenson Fellowship, which allowed me to take off one semester to complete the research for the chapter on union veterans. Tusculum College provided faculty development funds to support research trips to local archives in Georgia and elsewhere.

Though I have heard of archival horror stories from my peers, I have been fortunate to have none to tell myself. Indeed, the archivists I encountered in a myriad of libraries and special collections proved to be unfailingly helpful, cheerful, and interested, and they proved essential to the successful completion of this project. Special thanks go to the staff at the Georgia State University Special Collections and Southern Labor Archives, particularly Peter J. Roberts; the Richard B. Russell Library at the University of Georgia; Special Collections at the Atlanta University Center; the Hoskins Library Special Collections at the University of Tennessee; the National Archives and Records Administration II, in College Park, Maryland; and the State Historical Society in Madison, Wisconsin.

I am especially grateful for the willingness shown by James Mackay, former U.S. congressman from Georgia, to answer the many questions I had, and to his fellow World War II veterans Calvin Kytle, Dave Burgess, George Stoney, and Don McKee for completing survey questionnaires regarding their perspectives on the CIO's postwar organizing drive in Georgia. Their courage in and commitment to working for a better day, both at home and abroad, in peacetime and in war, stand as an inspiring example of good citizenship for us all.

To my brothers and sisters-in-law, nieces and nephews, and friends, I extend my heartfelt thanks for their wisdom in only asking about the book at the right moments. My parents, Charlie R. and Shirley H. Brooks, continued throughout to be a source of inspiration and support. They are the bravest people I know. Most of all, I am grateful for my husband and best friend, John Thaddeus Ellisor. His constant companionship and depth of wisdom and humor saw us both through. I hope I am returning the favor.

Abbreviations

ACRC	All Citizens Registration Committee
ACU	Augusta Citizens Union
AFL	American Federation of Labor
AVC	American Veterans Committee
CIO	Congress of Industrial Organizations
CIO-PAC	Congress of Industrial Organizations Political Action Committee
CPL	Citizens Progressive League
FEPC	Fair Employment Practices Committee
GA-PAC	CIO Political Action Committee in Georgia
GVL	Georgia Veterans League
GVMR	Georgia Veterans for Majority Rule
HB	House Bill
KKK	Ku Klux Klan
NAACP	National Association for the Advancement of Colored People
NLRB	National Labor Relations Board
PACS	political action committees of the CIO
SCHW	Southern Conference for Human Welfare
SOC	Southern Organizing Committee of the CIO
SRC	Southern Regional Council
TWUA	Textile Workers Union of America
USES	United States Employment Service
USO	United Service Organizations
WAVES	Women Accepted for Volunteer Emergency Service
WWII-VA	World War II–Veterans Association

DEFINING THE PEACE

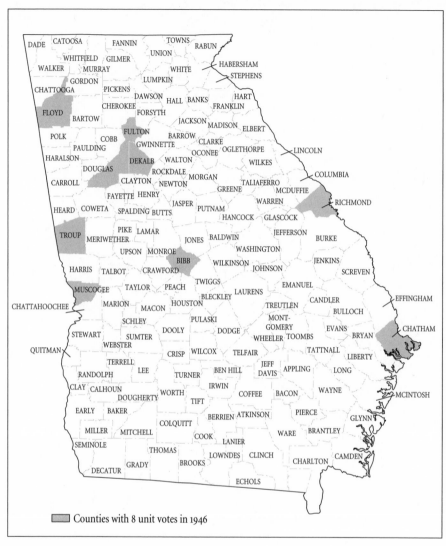

Counties with 8 unit votes in 1946

Georgia's 159 Counties
Source: U.S. Census Bureau, 2000.

1 : Introduction

World War II Veterans and the Politics of Postwar Change in Georgia

WHEN GEORGIA'S servicemen left for the combat theaters of World War II, few anticipated how profound an impact this experience would have on their lives. By the war's end, however, many of Georgia's veterans felt sure they knew exactly what their military service had meant. The extreme personal sacrifice made by Doyle Combs, a black veteran, fueled a deep determination to seize the political rights that he had just fought in a Jim Crow army to defend. "I went in combat, and I lost a portion of my body for this country," Combs declared, "when I didn't have no right to fight whatsoever cause I didn't have no rights in the United States of America, as a black man." Thus, "I was going to vote regardless [of] what it take." Putting his life on the line—literally—to defend the American way of life earned Combs the right to at least some measure of political freedom when he returned.[1]

For white veteran John Sammons Bell, survival itself created a civic and political obligation he could not ignore. After making it through the horrific invasion of Guadalcanal in 1942, Bell and his buddies made a pledge as the next deadly phase of island-hopping operations against the Japanese loomed: "everyone of those four soldiers said when we get back home," Bell explained, "we are going to do our best to make America a better America." This simple pledge became a serious covenant. None of Bell's comrades made it home alive. As a result, Bell explained at a local Georgia political rally in 1946, "I feel it a bounden duty to carry on their fight for good government." Veterans such as himself, Bell explained, "are determined to continue in peace to fight for the things we fought for in war."[2]

On American and overseas military bases, in combat units, engineering battalions, and quartermaster depots, and in both the Pacific and European theaters, southern veterans such as Doyle Combs and John Sammons Bell found their sense of manhood and citizenship magnified by meeting the challenges of military service and war.[3] Fulfilling this duty heightened veterans' sense of themselves—of who they were and where they fit into postwar political life. In putting a premium on the role of men as citizens—as soldiers performing the highest of civic duties—the war tended to strengthen the historic connection between male identity and political rights.[4] Thus, both black *and* white veterans believed that they had earned the right to participate in determining the state's future. That veterans of both races registered the war's impact in such similar fashion made for a particularly volatile postwar climate. The Jim Crow South wove political, racial, and gender identities tightly together, making the question of expanded civic participation a highly racialized one.[5]

The structures and institutions that constituted southern political tradition, such as all-white primaries, literacy tests, and poll taxes, sustained the notion that only certain white men were fit to rule. Indeed, southern Democratic conservatives had maintained their domination of state and regional political life for so long by posing any other model of "majority rule" as threatening to pollute the sanctity of the domestic sphere, and white women, with racial amalgamation.[6] The war generated postwar political turmoil by destabilizing the political, gender, and racial identities of both black and white veterans. To returning black veterans, the political and racial manhood they derived from their war experiences mandated that they resist Jim Crow "normalcy" and lead the drive to develop a black political voice. To reactionary white veterans, black activism itself threatened their own notion that white men enjoyed the exclusive entitlement to rule. They reacted accordingly, interpreting black voting as the harbinger of a racial assault on white womanhood and domestic security.

In strengthening, rather than undermining, these complex connections between military service and citizenship, the war produced a politics of change fraught with contradiction. If black veterans wanted racial equality, progressive white veterans prioritized majority rule over desegregation. If white union veterans wanted an organized voice on the shop floor with the political influence to match it, white pro-modernization veterans believed that the importance of recruiting new industry to the state precluded unionization.

Nonetheless, Georgia's black and white veterans did share a deep conviction that military service had a meaning that extended beyond the war itself. It made them uniquely suited, they believed, to play a role in shaping postwar political life. It gave them a special claim, they were certain, upon the American democratic conscience, especially in the notoriously undemocratic South. Thus, returning veterans proved to be the most politicized and ubiquitous of organized citizen groups throughout the South and Georgia in the first years after the war.

Georgia's veterans, however, shared more than a sense of agency born in the war. They also felt a keen disappointment with what the end of the war had wrought: a persistent lack of economic and political opportunity in communities throughout the state. The economic development touched off by the war proceeded unevenly in Georgia, boosting economic growth and populations in urban communities such as Atlanta and Columbus, but also undermining the stability of rural life. Moreover, the end of the war and the trials of reconversion, as military contracts ended, war jobs disappeared, and veterans began returning home, fueled fears of a renewed era of depression and want. Amid this turmoil, Georgians struggled to maintain control over whatever they believed would secure their future. Thus, far from making a smooth transition into postwar civilian life, veterans collided at every turn with persistent racial, class, and political barriers. Black veterans encountered white Georgians who denied the value of their service in the war by fighting to maintain segregation and disfranchisement at all costs. Veteran workers faced antagonistic employers anxious to roll back organized labor's wartime gains and showing little compunction in impeding the right of workers to organize. All activist veterans confronted county seat politicians and mossbacked conservatives who interpreted veterans' political claims as an affront to their own state and local hegemony. These conflicts all took place within a broader context of political stagnation sustained by discriminatory institutions and practices that worked to maintain the prewar status quo, such as disfranchisement and legislative malapportionment.

These conditions stoked the flames of a political disenchantment that sparked a wave of postwar veteran activism across the state, one that represented an unusually broad-based attack on southern political tradition. Black veterans who believed their service in the war should bring the rewards of full citizenship at home, progressive white veterans who took from the destruction and inhumanity of the war a lesson for majority rule and democracy, white union veterans who found in fighting for survival overseas the self-efficacy to stand up to management at home, and white veterans who found Georgia's poor reputation abroad to be a badge of shame they were determined to throw off all represented a diverse array of protagonists. They staged the most significant electoral challenges many of the state's mossbacked incumbents had ever faced.[7]

Nor did these insurgencies remain an abstraction—little dramas played out between competing factions in the chambers of state power and largely removed from the lives most Georgians, black or white, lived. All southern states experienced a degree of political turmoil after the war, but the county unit system in Georgia dispersed this instability all the way down to the local level.

Legislated by the Neill Primary Act of 1917, Georgia's county unit system apportioned the vote in state elections by county population, awarding six unit votes to the eight most populous counties, four unit votes to the next thirty most populous counties, and two unit votes to each of 121 smaller counties.[8] On its face, it appeared to be a democratic mechanism for proportional representation of the vote in gubernatorial and other elections. However, as its many critics charged, given Georgia's abundance of small counties, this system always allowed the less populous rural counties to dominate politics in the state. A gubernatorial candidate, for example, could secure enough unit votes among the smaller and medium sized counties alone to win an election without any unit votes in the largest urban and populous counties. A candidate with the right connections in the state's myriad rural county seats could thereby capture the governor's office without a popular majority of votes. Thus, the unit system of voting meant a candidate had to literally campaign in every single county in the state in hopes of winning over the local politicos who could deliver a county's unit votes. Political controversies at the state level played out, in this sense, at the local level as candidates vied for the favor of each local courthouse gang or opposing faction.[9]

In postwar Georgia the county unit system ensured that political conflict over the ultimate consequences of the war erupted in local communities throughout the state. Thus, in virtually every county courthouse, rural crossroads, city hall, and polling place, returning veterans emerged to challenge incumbents' desire to keep power and policy-making to themselves. The veterans' activism prompted an historic surge in black and white voter registration that threw many local political machines into disarray.[10] Veteran campaigns produced some surprising results, including new faces in the General Assembly and in local governments throughout the state. The veteran programs that prevailed, however, prioritized economic growth, anti-unionism, and racial stability over the racial or industrial democracy many progressives had hoped to implement. Thus, Georgia's veterans offered an apt, if peculiar, portent of change for the future.

Georgia's postwar political drama ultimately played out in three grand acts. The curtains first parted on the campaign season of 1946, as the political insurgencies mounted by veterans electrified the state's first postwar campaign season. Much controversy revolved around the question of black voting. In 1944 the United States Supreme Court had ruled in *Smith v. Allwright* that the practice of holding all-white Democratic primary elections in Texas violated the federal Constitution and had to end. This decision sent shock waves throughout the Democratic South. A federal court decision in the *Primus King* case only two years later overturned the all-white Democratic primary in Georgia, driving home the political implications of the earlier *Smith* decision. The door to black participation in the state's Democratic primary elections opened for the first time ever.[11] In Georgia progressive southerners and national liberal organizations seized this opportunity to implement a progressive reconstruction of the political South by initiating campaigns to enfranchise new black and white voters and to target reactionary incumbents for defeat. Black veterans, liberal groups, and the Georgia Congress of Industrial Organizations (CIO) launched unprecedented drives to register black and white voters for the state and local races of 1946.[12] To maximize their influence, these progressive campaigns often collaborated with civic groups led by other white veterans seeking to oust complacent, provincial, and corrupt local dynasties. "Good government" veterans forged these often uneasy alliances in order to boost voter turnout to a level beyond what local courthouse gangs could control, opening the way to electing white officials who would support programs for governmental accountability, fiscal prudence, and active industrial recruitment.

Campaigns in Augusta, Savannah, and the statewide gubernatorial race soon took center stage.[13] Black and white veterans fought to overturn conservative and long incumbent political machines in these cities and to challenge the bid of former governor and inveterate race-baiter Eugene Talmadge to retake the gubernatorial office. This activism enlivened Georgia's postwar political scene, turning out droves of black and white voters across the state, defeating entrenched urban rings in Augusta and Savannah, and electing pro-modernization white veterans to local and statewide offices in communities throughout the state.

Antagonists with a very different agenda, however, waited in the wings. Reactionary white veterans were greatly alarmed by the scores of black southerners registering to vote and collaborating with white insurgents to challenge conservative rule. Inspired by Eugene Talmadge's race-baiting bid for governor in 1946, they led the charge to defend all the prerogatives and privileges of white male supremacy. They condemned any campaign for change, however conventional, as a scheme for integration, joined hate groups such as the Ku Klux Klan (KKK), campaigned for Talmadge and other reactionaries, and sometimes terrorized black voters. Even good government crusades, in which white veterans often went to great lengths to proclaim their southern white loyalties, suffered the sting of their opposition's racial wrath. Black voters, however, bore the brunt of this postwar racial tirade aimed at circumscribing their ambitions for change by any means necessary.[14]

Eugene Talmadge's victory in the gubernatorial race of 1946 under the aegis of the county unit system appeared to be a disappointing setback to the hopes Georgia's insurgent veterans had for the future. His sudden death that fall before assuming office, however, threw his entire program into question. Focus then shifted to the chambers of the Georgia General Assembly, as the white veterans elected through the insurgent campaigns of 1946 took their seats in the Georgia statehouse. How would the conservative Talmadge program, which revolved around restoring the white primary, fare under good government veterans' program for change?

The curtains to Act Two parted on the convening of the Georgia General Assembly of 1947, one of the most controversial sessions in Georgia's modern political history. This opening scene began when Herman Talmadge, Eugene's son and also a World War II veteran, seized the governor's office and ousted incumbent governor Ellis G. Arnall by force.[15] This strong-arm approach to the unsettled question of gubernatorial succession provoked a wave of mass protest meetings by angry citizens across the state. Thus, Georgia's newly elected good government veterans faced a daunting task: they were charged with defining what their state's postwar priorities were to be in the midst of political chaos and controversy. They wasted little time before demonstrating what the limits to their notion of progress would be.

In this racially charged climate, good government veterans abandoned the collaboration with blacks and unionists that often had helped elect them to office. Most endorsed Herman Talmadge's bid for governor, advocated measures to further the disfranchisement of Georgia's black citizenry, stood largely mute in the face of the violence and terror directed against the state's black citizens, and strongly supported two anti-union "right-to-work" bills. They fought tirelessly not to implement any notion of racial or industrial democracy, but to elect leaders and to enact policies that would integrate Georgia into the national economic mainstream. They wanted modernized government capable of responding to the dynamic economic potential unleashed by the war. They strove to break Georgia away, permanently, from the morass of the underdevelopment and poverty of the past and propel the state toward a developed and prosperous future.[16]

In the postwar 1940s, good government veterans did not see these goals as irreconcilable with segregation, especially given that most regarded integration as undesirable and unimaginable anyway. They did see overturning segregation and allowing an expansive unionism to take root in Georgia as direct threats to the political, racial, and economic stability that new industries and investors allegedly wanted.[17] In an increasingly conservative climate, the imperatives of Cold War liberalism displaced the mandates of New Deal reform, while the developing national focus on southern segregation rapidly polarized politics in the region. Good government advocates proved more able than progressive reformers to traverse this difficult thicket of postwar political conflict, electing officials in Georgia who established a conservative foundation to the state's postwar agenda for change.[18]

The price this program exacted for blacks and unionists in Georgia immediately became evident. The third and final act in Georgia's postwar political drama opened on the campaign season of 1948, amid the tumultuous national controversy over the Truman civil rights program and the developing Dixiecrat revolt from the national Democratic Party. Removed from the governorship by judicial fiat in 1947, Herman Talmadge mounted a successful bid for governor in 1948, campaigning on a white supremacy platform that combined terrorism against black citizens with calls for economic modernization. Meanwhile, unionists struggled to sustain their locals and organizing campaigns in a climate rendered increasingly hostile by the right-to-work laws Georgia's good government veterans had just helped to enact. It was a bitter end for black and progressive white veterans. Their highest hopes about the war's mandate for postwar change dissipated quickly under the weight of conservative modernization—a politics of "progress" that good government veterans deftly shaped into the war's contradictory political legacy.

VETERAN ACTIVISM IN Georgia clearly establishes World War II as a pivotal moment in the South's transition to the modern era.[19] The diversity in the programs veterans pursued reflected how complex the war's political impact on the region proved to be. On the one hand, the immense infusion of capital and the dislocation of blacks and whites, men and women, wrought by the war accelerated and expanded the economic, social, and demographic trends of the prior decade.[20] In altering a region long mired in the muck of endemic poverty, underdevelopment, and national neglect, World War II stood second only to the Civil War as a watershed of change for the region, as many historians have noted. Indeed, the South looked so different in so many ways by 1945 that at least one scholar has suggested that it might even have eclipsed the Civil War as the region's paramount historical event.[21]

Yet, on the other hand, the South's political and racial landscape in 1945 appeared to have weathered the "winds of war" remarkably well. In the Deep South, especially, conservative white Democrats still dominated politics and policy at all levels of government; corruption, exclusion, and fraud still marred most elections; and blacks and many whites still remained outside the perimeters of southern political life.

What can reconcile this apparent paradox between the war as a purveyor of lasting change versus the war as a promulgator of tradition? As early as George Brown Tindall in 1967, many historians have answered by noting that the changes in the social and economic realm induced by war mobilization generated a hardened defense of white supremacy that sustained the one-party South and effectively stalled the momentum for progressive reform for at least another decade. In this view, World War II stands as a period of retrenchment from the currents of New Deal liberalism of the 1930s, not unlike the reactionary backlash that followed the end of World War I.[22]

This emphasis on political continuity does help to explain some of the limits to the war's immediate impact, but it also leaves much out. As more recent studies have found, more exists in the story of the early postwar era than the conventional change-versus-continuity framework allows.[23] Beneath the image of a Solid South that survived the war largely intact, a troubled political South most certainly was brewing. This reality escapes notice unless we consider the era in its own context and especially at the state and local level. From this vantage point, everything about the war in the South raised questions that local, state, and regional leaders were hard-pressed to answer: questions about the meaning of black men in military uniform; about what the northerners flooding into regional ports, cantonments, and towns would think about the southern way of life; about why local and state leaders had never worked to attract the kind of investment and opportunity that now appeared to pour into every southern community, or at least into the next town over; about how things could seem to change so quickly when southerners had been told for so long that southern life would never, ever, change, nor should; and especially about what would happen when the war was over, and the soldiers came home, and the federal spending dried up.

The war failed to wholly transform the southern political and racial landscape in the short term, but it did challenge fundamental notions about the static nature of the southern way of life. Most of all, it altered southerners' understanding of themselves, their opportunities, and the region's place in the nation. It put economic, social, racial, and political relations in flux, generating a political instability that permeated the postwar era at every level.

Using this instability as the true measure of the war's impact, the South looked anything but solid in the immediate postwar years, when a broad spectrum of southerners—namely, veterans—challenged the fitness of the southern old guard to rule. Liberal veterans, pro-modernization veterans, and reactionary veterans, black and white, all believed that they best understood what the war's meaning should be. All were equally determined to see their own interpretation prevail, whether that meant expanding black southerners' and workers' political participation, implementing agendas for economic modernization and governmental reform, or defending southern political and economic tradition from the war-born contaminants of change. Surely this ferment reflected not a political culture unchanged by the war, but one in transition, evolving beyond the certainties of an older era toward a different and undefined future—moving out of the past, but not wholly escaping it, either.

What the war generated, above all, was debate about the South's future in a nation transformed by war, a debate that proved to be both acrimonious and comprehensive. Returning veterans played a key role in shaping the South's postwar political deliberations on the future, yet few historians have explored their significance thoroughly.[24] Measuring the war's political effects by the gauge of veteran activism deepens our understanding of the postwar era. Resistance to the conservative domination of southern political life emerges as a continuity between the pre–World War II and post–World War II eras that was just as significant as the persistence of the southern old guard's overweening power.[25] The clash between change and tradition heightened by the war took place not just in the halls of Congress or in state assemblies, but at the local level as well. It reflected the struggle of a people poised on the cusp of a new era, uncertain but determined in the face of an often bewildering array of challenges and opportunities, a struggle undeniably generated by going to—and returning from—a world war.

Placing returning veterans at the core of this struggle reveals not only how destabilizing the war really was, but also how pivotal it ended up being to the emergence of the modern political era. World War II made the politics of white supremacy and of modernization the key features of the postwar era, sowing the seeds of the movements that eventually transformed politics in the region. Reactionary white veterans presaged the scorched-earth opposition to *Brown v. Board of Education* in 1954, which ballooned quickly into massive resistance to integration.[26] Black veterans were an early vanguard of the grassroots leaders who waged the black freedom struggle throughout the South in the 1950s and 1960s.[27] And good government veterans foreshadowed the rise of the neo-Whig leaders who eventually put the "chamber of commerce" ethos of dynamic development, social conservatism, and racial moderation at the core of Sunbelt prosperity.[28]

World War II exerted a complex and dual influence on Georgia and the South. It widened the already developing fissures in the foundations of political stability that would rupture into permanent breaches in later decades. But it also generated a renewed resistance to racial reform and a conservative ethos of growth and development that limited how far any immediate departure from the past ultimately would be. As such, the Second World War proved to be an engine of change for Georgia and the South, but one that traveled along a quintessentially southern track. It bypassed racial and industrial democracy in favor of the politics of race, anti-unionism, and modernization. Returning veterans were its political conductors, striking a Faustian bargain between change and tradition at the crossroads to the modern South that would define and, in fact, bedevil the state and region's political life for decades to come.

2: The Ballot Must Be Our Weapon

Black Veterans and the Politics of Racial Change

ON MARCH 31, 1946, C. W. Greenlea, director of a black United Service Organizations (USO) center in Atlanta, Georgia, announced the imminent deployment of almost one thousand black veterans of the Second World War to the doorsteps of the city's black citizenry. Their mission was to encourage black registration and voting in preparation for the upcoming Fifth District congressional and gubernatorial primaries in Georgia. Sponsored by a new organization of recently returned black veterans named the Georgia Veterans League (GVL), the door-to-door canvass promised to be a historic civic event. "A huge 'task force' of Negro ex-servicemen" in partial service uniforms, reported the *Atlanta Daily World*, would be "mustered" out for "a unique 'war' mission." In talking to local reporters, veterans made clear the connection between this activity and their recent participation in World War II. "Veterans feel that the democracy they fought for is worth working for here at home," declared one John B. Turner, and "registering and voting are essential to getting democracy."[1] Veterans in the GVL organized this "arm for democracy" drive, explained the chairman of the GVL's Civic Action Committee, to "defeat" the "enemy" of "ignorance, laziness, fear or any other excuses people might have for not being real citizens."[2] Above all, veterans were staking a claim to Georgia's future: "We love Georgia and we are going to stay here and live in peace in spite of what the Ku Klux Klan, Talmadge, or any other un-Christian Georgia fa[s]cists boast about it."[3]

The highly motivated black veterans who led the GVL's "arm for democracy" voter drive appeared not only in Atlanta but in nearly every town, city, and rural crossroads in Georgia after the war. In organizing to defend their access to veteran benefits, to protest racial discrimination and hatred, but especially to expand black political influence, Georgia's black veterans voiced a strong moral claim as veterans and as citizens to the political rights, opportunities, and justice they felt should reward their military service. That claim was born in the crucible of war.

Georgia's black veterans were well aware of the irony in fighting for democracy through the vehicle of a segregated military. Their experiences with segregation and discrimination within the armed forces heightened their frustration with southern racial practices even as the skills and experience afforded by military training instilled ambitions for a better life after the war. Together, these influences produced a powerful sense of civic and economic entitlement. Yet black veterans returned home to find that few white southerners were as convinced of the value of black participation in the war as they were. This reality could be a painful realization, for veterans and for their families. "Out of all this Your Boy and my Boy when call on to go an die on the Battle field we never hesistate [sic] on Sendin Him," noted R. B. Dunham of Surrency, Georgia, the father of a black veteran; "when we are call on we are ready to help them to defend the good name of our country." But, "as soon as the battle is fought and the victory is won and we return back home," he bitterly lamented, "we are denied our rights as citizens and all manner of punishment is put upon us and nothin much done about it [sic]." After all this, he concluded, "It is hard to stand what we Negroes has to stand."[4]

Southern white intransigence and the lure of opportunities elsewhere convinced many black veterans to abandon what they knew in Georgia for what might be in the North and West. Many chose, however, to remain in the South, where they quickly realized that fulfilling their postwar dreams of economic security and full citizenship meant first waging another battle, this time against the enemies of democracy in their own backyard. A federal district court decision overturning the all-white Democratic primary in Georgia in early 1946 seemed to provide a ready avenue. Motivated both by their experiences in the war and by the harsh reality of homefront conditions, these veterans made black voting in Georgia's first postwar elections their primary weapon in storming the citadels of southern racial tradition.

In registering voters and in supporting moderate or progressive white candidates for office, black veterans pursued a politics of issues unusual for Georgia and the one-party South. Their activism helped to produce a record-breaking voter turnout in several Georgia communities in 1946, even poising black voters as a balance of power in several hotly contested local races. Indeed, black voters helped to defeat some key incumbents in Georgia, including one of the state's longest surviving political machines, the John Bouhan organization in Savannah, which never recovered from this defeat.

Thus, black veterans in Georgia played a key role in shaping what the political legacy of the Second World War would be. Their activism helped to ensure that the end of the war brought no automatic transition to prewar "normalcy." Instead, the war inaugurated a period of racial uncertainty and political turmoil that destabilized Georgia's postwar political landscape. Real change would come slowly, and the activism of black veterans in the postwar 1940s would not, alone, be enough to bring the walls of southern racial tradition tumbling down, in Georgia or elsewhere. Even such a gradualist and conventional approach to racial reform as voter registration spurred a devastating white backlash that effectively stalled much of the postwar momentum for expanding black civil rights in Georgia.

Nonetheless, black veterans' activism—from organizing to ensure they received the federal and state benefits that were their due and unleashing individual acts of rebellion against Jim Crow to calling on black citizens to register and vote—marked the postwar 1940s as a period of significant black civic ferment well before the *Brown v. Board of Education* decision of 1954. Black veterans ultimately failed to implement what they understood as the war's mandate for racial change in the postwar 1940s. Their efforts, however, did expose the cracks developing in the edifices of the Jim Crow South, fissures later irreparably widened by massive resistance to integration and the black civil rights movement in the 1950s and 1960s.

Alexander Heard, a native white Georgian and a political researcher in the South immediately after the war, remembered this time as a period of unusual "political agitation and volatility" in which "the impact of black soldiers coming back from the war was very important."[5] Indeed, he explained, "these fellows came back and, well they had risked their lives," and their confidence and determination encouraged "a lot of other people who felt these things . . . to speak up."[6] Robert Flanagan, a black youth in Atlanta in the postwar 1940s, agreed. When "the GI's came out . . . [they expressed] kind of an activist [attitude of] I don't want to take [it] anymore." And their efforts, he noted, "did make a difference."[7] Thus, concluded Heard, "it wasn't in my observation of it, a placid period at all, and it wasn't a period with an assured progress at all. It was a period in which the race issue was front and center . . . and it was stimulated by World War II."[8]

GEORGIA'S AFRICAN AMERICAN men answered the call to military duty in World War II for a variety of reasons, including patriotism. More often, though, service in the war offered an escape from the dead-end lot most black men faced in the Depression-era South.[9] Nevertheless, black veterans found that participation in the war tended to magnify the importance of individual citizenship, strengthening the connection between political, racial, and male identity. On the one hand, the highest act of citizenship was to fulfill the call to military duty in defense of the nation, an act that put a premium on one's identity as a male and as a citizen. This service earned a veteran, at least in theory, the right to civic participation at home, which, in turn, underscored the importance of exercising the rights of citizenship.[10] Thus, southern black veterans returned with a new moral claim on the American democratic conscience, a claim they readily used to justify their activism after the war. Unlike the many whites who disputed the worth of the military service of African Americans, black soldiers believed that their contribution to American victory had value, not only to the nation as a whole, but particularly to their state and region. They had served the country well. Who could now legitimately deny them at least a voice in postwar political affairs and the chance to establish the economic independence and family security that they believed men and veterans had a duty to provide?[11]

Yet, on the other hand, political, racial, and gender identities in the Jim Crow South were enmeshed so thoroughly that no single thread could be altered without disrupting the overall pattern to the fabric of southern political life.[12] Being a veteran, for example, was not a status that remained separate from being black. The rights of citizenship could not be invoked by black men, especially veterans, without also inducing the age-old political-racial-sexual anxiety of many southern whites, who remained as wedded as ever to the notion that majority rule meant whites only. Anything less threatened white supremacy and the very sanctity of white womanhood.[13]

Thus, black veterans also confronted a strong phalanx of resistance in postwar Georgia, as fearful and resentful whites worked hard to circumscribe the veterans' economic and political ambitions. Taken together, service in the war *and* this persistent discrimination served to heighten both black veterans' expectations for a new day and their frustration with the racial barriers and injustices that still kept that day from dawning. Thus, as several scholars have recently confirmed, many black GIs found military service to be an experience that nurtured both their sense of personal efficacy as well as their racial consciousness.[14]

Whether in the United States or overseas, military service provided skills and training to which few black southerners had ever had access. The army's Quartermaster, Transportation, and Engineering Corps in which many black GIs served (three-fourths were in these branches by mid-1945, and most were serving overseas), for example, proved to be schools of occupational education. Even though most black GIs labored in semi- and unskilled jobs in these outfits, including stevedoring, road building, laundering, fumigation, and truck driving, it would be misleading to assume that they gained little in the way of useful training.[15] Truck driving, for example, was a new skill transferable to civilian life and a definite improvement over the hard physical labor that had been the lot of most black men before the war. Not surprisingly, black soldiers anticipated parlaying this wartime training into better jobs when they returned home. Sixty-one percent of black soldiers interviewed by the Army Research Branch during the war believed that military training would help them find a better job than they had held before the war. Only 39 percent of white soldiers proved to be as optimistic.[16] Moreover, just one-fifth of black enlisted men planned to return to their prewar jobs or employers, and two-thirds planned to find a new postwar occupation.[17]

Black veteran and Georgian Horace Bohannon, a field agent for the Southern Regional Council's (SRC) postwar Veteran Services Project, confirmed these findings in the course of his interviews with other black veterans in Georgia. What most black ex-servicemen wanted, he discovered, was "a decent job. They wanted to work. They wanted to make it." After all, "they had lived, they'd seen other circumstances, they'd seen other peoples. And by now they knew that all every man wants is a job, and security for his family, and so forth . . . . That's all these guys wanted."[18] In a period in which a black man "couldn't even apply [to be] the guy who drives the telephone truck," Bohannon explained, "these guys . . . would at least like to be able to get those [type of] jobs," or to be a "cashier [or] loan officer, etcetera."[19]

Nor were black soldiers' aspirations purely economic. The army's wartime research data, for example, indicated that "there was a tendency among Negro soldiers to expect or hope for an increase in rights and privileges, improved treatment, or better economic status after the war," with southern black soldiers tending to be more optimistic than those from the North.[20] Forty-three percent of black GIs questioned believed that they would "have more rights and privileges" after the war, and 42 percent believed that "in the long run Negro soldiers [would] be better off . . . after they got out of the Army than they were before they went into the Army."[21] Even those black GIs who made the war against the Axis powers a priority over the fight for civil rights at home explained their choices in similar terms. "If we lose, the Negroes lot can't improve," one soldier argued, but "if we win there is a chance." Another agreed, noting that "by virtue of our valor, courage, and patriotism, things will be better for the Negro." "We are helping win the war," declared one soldier, "so we will be treated better." Thus, concluded Samuel A. Stouffer and his associates at the Army Research Branch, "one cannot overlook the fact that Negro support of the war derived in part from special 'racial' hopes for the future."[22]

Such hopes, recently defined by one scholar as a "special moral claim to fairness and justice," confronted significant obstacles during and after the war.[23] In fact, service in the armed forces exposed black soldiers and sailors to daily lessons in the persistent vitality of segregation and discrimination. W. W. Law, for example, a black veteran from Savannah, Georgia, found military service to be a disheartening series of racial humiliations. When drafted, Law recalled, "I asked for frontline duty as an infantry soldier. But they assigned me to the quartermaster, as was typical." Finally, he received an assignment to go overseas as part of Keesler Army Airfield's aviation battalion, having risen to first sergeant for his company. However, he never made it. "I ran into difficulty with my . . . company commander," Law recalled. "I believe that he was a Mississippi white man[;] . . . we were being assigned chores on the base of picking up matchstems and cigarette butts. And I objected and was called before my commander, and we had a discussion on leadership." At the time, "I was young [and] I told him that I felt . . . a proper leader, would be a person who could inspire his people into formation, and this was not inspirational work." After this discussion, the commander "found a way to transfer me out because I did not go with the proceedings."[24]

Experiences such as these, combined with the occasional exposure to more equitable and freer conditions overseas, intensified both consciousness of and frustration with the racial injustices that persisted.[25] In questioning black soldiers near the end of the war about their own contribution to the war effort and about Allied war aims, the Army Research Branch found that black responses often focused on homefront conditions and postwar treatment. When asked what question one would most like to ask the president of the United States, most white soldiers wanted to know about the progress of the war effort or how much longer the war would last. Black soldiers, however, responded differently. Over 50 percent of their answers mentioned a specific question about racial discrimination or exhibited a definite but less direct racial emphasis. Almost 30 percent drew an explicit connection between the war and postwar conditions. Black soldiers wanted to ask questions such as "Will I as a Negro share in this so-called democracy after the war?"; "Will the South treat Negroes as human beings?"; and "After the Negro men go and fight to their best, would they have equal rights?"[26]

Doyle Combs, who later became a leader of the Toccoa, Georgia, chapter of the National Association for the Advancement of Colored People (NAACP), aptly illustrated the direct influence that the expectations, ambitions, and racial consciousness born in the war exerted on the political and racial identity of many black veterans.[27] Combs did not take lightly the cruel irony of being seriously wounded while fighting to defeat an intolerant and undemocratic enemy in defense of an unjust and unequal country: "Since I lost a portion of my body to protect my own rights," Combs declared, "I would die for my rights, and I would kill for my rights. And I was going to vote if I had to kill somebody to vote."[28]

A clearer sense of the dynamic relationship between service in the war and postwar activism could hardly be stated. The war tended to create highly motivated black men cognizant of their own rights, conscious of the barriers that impeded their full citizenship, and determined to establish for themselves the freedom, opportunity, and political participation they felt they had earned. What they discovered when they returned, however, was that few white southerners valued black servicemen's contribution to American victory. The burning ambitions and civic righteousness that drove black veterans clashed immediately with the determination of many white southerners to maintain all the edifices of Jim Crow. Rather than the improved opportunities, full citizenship, and respect black veterans had hoped to find, they encountered a level of discrimination and violence that seemed all too familiar.

Even during the war, there had been plenty of indication that white southerners would resist the social and demographic changes accelerated by war mobilization.[29] Whispered rumors reminiscent of antebellum fears of slave revolt conspiracies, for example, told of African American men using the absence of white "bosses" to stockpile weapons in preparation for a general uprising. In Georgia, the story went, these men were even hoping for an Axis victory to boost their own chances of success.[30] Far-fetched as most of these rumors were, they nonetheless reflected a real sense of white vulnerability. Planters and employers struggled to maintain a paternalistic and coercive caste system in the face of a growing black exodus off the farm and out of the South.[31] During the war, for example, local "fight-or-work" laws in Georgia required black laborers to carry proof of employment or risk arrest for vagrancy. In Sandersville, black workers over sixteen years of age had to wear identification badges exhibiting an employer's name and a work schedule. In Macon, police raided pool halls, diners, and beer parlors to round up and arrest two hundred African American men without such badges, exacting from them a hundred dollar fine or sixty days of hard labor. Police in Atlanta assisted local industrialists in tracking down and arresting black absentees for "idling and loitering."[32]

White southerners who adamantly defended Jim Crow during the war steeled themselves for the return of black soldiers, whose uniforms alone were a testament to the threatening consequences of the war. From Fort Valley, Georgia, field agent Horace Bohannon reported to the SRC that some white citizens anticipated that the "returning Negro veteran is dissatisfied with conditions and will inevitabl[y] be a troublemaker." Others similarly predicted that "the white southerner is going to 'pick on' the returning veteran to try and steer him 'back into his place.'"[33]

They were right. As soon as the war ended, white southerners initiated a widespread campaign of discrimination aimed at impeding black veterans' utilization of their wartime skills and GI Bill benefits.[34] Black teachers, principals, and administrators attending a summer seminar at Atlanta University in 1946 thus reported employment difficulties as the paramount problem confronting black veterans in communities throughout Georgia and the South.[35] "I believe that the single greatest problem confronting the returning Negro veteran," stated a Bibb County, Georgia, teacher and minister, "is that of obtaining employment." While a large number of veterans had found jobs in the county, "for the most part this employment has been largely common labor." An Atlanta student agreed: "The veterans in my community are having difficulty getting suitable job placement in newly acquired skills. In most cases," he stated, "these men were in a low income bracket prior to the war, but while in service they learned how to do better jobs." Now, veterans "are unwilling to accept the old job as before."[36]

Readjustment to low-wage work troubled veterans in Jackson and Rome, while school officials in Macon and Fort Gaines cited the "difficulty in getting skilled work." In Rome, one teacher noted, "veterans are not able to find any white collar jobs. Jobs with small salaries are always given to the Negro veteran. It is hard for the veteran to find the type of work they would like to do." "For myself I was not able to find a job because I was not able to do the kind of work they wanted done," lamented a student and veteran from Hogansville, Georgia; "I can operate any kind of office equipment but I was refused a job in this line of work." Thus, he concluded, "The Negro veterans are merely being pushed around."[37] In Cordele, related one teacher, "insinuative insults occur frequently. A demand is made that they go to work at certain low salaries," but when veterans refused, "cruel treatment" prevailed, often spurring "race trouble." In fact, "there are a few cases where shooting, wounding and even killing of soldiers occurs." And, the teacher added bitterly, "of course nothing is done about it . . . . [T]his section is one of plantation owners."[38]

In their travels across the region, SRC field agents found that these difficulties often stemmed from the collusion of white employers with veteran services officials.[39] Local United States Employment Service (USES) officials often refused to refer black veterans to prospective employers, which prompted a bitter complaint from Reuben H. Thomas, a disabled black army veteran of Rome, Georgia. "About two years before I went into the Army I was a dishwasher in a cafe," Thomas wrote, "but [during] my time in the Army I trained for truck driving and that is all I did." Having been out of the service about five months, Thomas went to the USES office "to apply for a job of truck driving but I couldn't get one." Instead, "they wanted to give me a job washing dishes but I didn't except [*sic*] because cafe jobs here don't pay enough and I have a mother to support." Nor would Thomas accept a job working in a foundry because "I have not done anything like that and I am not able to." "I am not asking them to give me anything," Thomas declared, just "the kind of job I am capable of doing." When he put in for unemployment compensation, however, Thomas failed "to get it," though "most of the white boys get the unemployment with ease."[40]

At the veteran services center in Macon, Horace Bohannon discovered "for the first time . . . someone who already knew of job-training" as a part of the GI Bill. This official not only was familiar with the provision, he had also "been using it to the disadvantage of nearly every Negro veteran who applied." Inquiries at that office only prompted "rough treatment" for Bohannon, but other sources, probably local veterans, described to him the service center's usual procedure. A black veteran entered the office in search of a job with little knowledge about the GI Bill's job-training program. A service official would suggest the program, and the veteran would receive a referral to a participating firm, which then would give him "the dirtiest, the most difficult work to do and scheme to keep him at that particular work." When the disillusioned and frustrated veteran complained, "the V.A. [was] advised by the local agency to strip him of his benefits."[41]

In Savannah a local service official informed Bohannon of a "very sad state of affairs" in which "few or no white shops admitted Negro workers"; moreover, "in cases where Negroes were in white shops, they were only being exploited." He then cited the example of "a veteran in a furniture shop, supposedly taking upholstering. However, a visit to the shop proved that the boy was unloading and uncrating furniture."[42] In Augusta, Bohannon met J. W. Bassett, a recently discharged black veteran whose former railroad employer had refused to rehire him to his old position when he returned from the war. Having been a fireman on the railroad for ten years, including ten months in the service, Bassett found his postwar position ambiguous and unfavorable. Though his former employer violated federal law by refusing to rehire Bassett, "strangely enough, the Georgia railroad has taken on at the Augusta shop some twenty-five (25) new men (white) in his same job." Bassett related similar stories of three other black veterans.[43]

Of the 246 approved on-the-job training programs in Georgia in March 1946, the American Council on Race Relations observed, black veterans participated in only 6. According to SRC estimates, only 7 to 8 percent of all southern black veterans were enrolled in such programs after the war, even though they constituted about one-third of the southern veteran population. Such discrimination, wrote "L.M.S." of Atlanta, was "a big slap in the face" to veterans who had gone "to the front for the right of the pursuit of liberty and happiness."[44] As far as whites were concerned, a black veteran's war service counted for little in the postwar South. "Just because a Negro boy served his country and fought and died or drove trucks or cooked or anything the Army told him to do," remarked William B. Twitty, another black ex-soldier and SRC field agent, "he is a Negro veteran. . . . [T]hat means he is first a Negro and secondly a veteran."[45] Not surprisingly, noted a Warm Springs, Georgia, school principal, "For the most part, the returning soldiers seem not to be able to adjust themselves."[46]

Difficulty in readjusting to the traditional parameters of southern race relations was a dangerous thing. Indeed, racial violence permeated the immediate postwar years, as one scholar concluded, "cast[ing] a shadow of dread over the postwar South."[47] The murders of black veteran George Dorsey and his three companions in Walton County, Georgia, in the summer of 1946 exemplified what could happen when the expectations that black veterans brought home collided with the racial defensiveness many southern whites displayed.

The changes in southern rural life accelerated by the war formed the backdrop to the Walton County lynching. On the heels of the Great Depression and the New Deal, war mobilization hastened the decline of plantation agriculture, and many areas of the black belt South embarked on a chaotic and uneven transition to a new system that was more dependent on capital and machines than on black tenants and sharecroppers. This shift proved to be a gradual one, however, and in 1946 the ability of Walton County's white farmers to capitalize on the postwar market for cotton-bale lint still depended on access to a steadily dwindling supply of black labor. Opportunities created by war mobilization had lured many black Georgians away from plantations and farms, and the trend continued in the postwar era. Black Georgians particularly fled from areas such as the Blassingame District in Walton County where white farmers had a reputation for "oppressing their Negroes even more than usual." As local white farmers struggled to adjust to these shifting circumstances, blacks in the county seat of Monroe initiated a controversial voter registration drive in anticipation of the summer's Democratic primaries.[48]

What began as a private quarrel on the afternoon of July 14, as one scholar has concluded, gained new import in the racially charged atmosphere of the summer political campaign season of 1946, as gubernatorial candidate and noted racist Eugene Talmadge made his final race-baiting romp across the state in the face of an unprecedented surge in black voter registration. A dispute between George Dorsey's brother-in-law, Roger Malcolm, and his white landlord's son,

Barney Hester, ended badly when Malcolm stabbed Hester. Although Hester survived, whites subsequently beat Malcolm then jailed him in Monroe, where he languished throughout the volatile campaign season. Concerned for his safety, Malcolm's wife, Dorothy, convinced her brother, George, and his wife, Mae Murray Dorsey, to intervene. The Dorseys persuaded their white landlord, Loy Harrison, to bail Malcolm out of jail and to let him work off the favor on the farm until his trial.[49]

Harrison subsequently drove the Dorseys and Dorothy Malcolm to the Monroe jail by way of the Athens-to-Atlanta highway. After a delay of several hours, the party, now including Malcolm, headed home. This time, however, Harrison drove along isolated back roads. At Moore's Ford Crossing, in the outlying part of the county, a group of armed white men waylaid Harrison's car and removed both George Dorsey and Roger Malcolm. In a desperate attempt to save the men, one of the women called out and identified a member of the mob. The lynchers then removed the women from the car as well, lined up both couples by the creek, and summarily executed them. All four bodies were riddled with bullets and maimed beyond recognition.[50]

At first glance, George Dorsey's murder (and certainly that of the two women) appears to be a case of being in the wrong place at the wrong time, as angry whites finally caught up to Roger Malcolm to exact revenge for the Hester stabbing. Some evidence suggests, however, that Dorsey himself—because of his status as a recently returned veteran—was also a target. With five years of service in the Army Air Force, including campaigns in the Pacific for which he earned several medals and honors, Dorsey was able to use his army discharge pay to free himself of debt once he returned home. To local whites accustomed to employing perpetual debt as a means of labor control, such independence of spirit and means seemed "biggety." Moreover, Dorsey apparently had a troubled relationship with his white landlord, Loy Harrison. After the lynchings, rumors circulated that Harrison previously had tried to drive Dorsey away in order to take his "fine crop of cotton," but, apparently, "Dorsey did not scare easily." In fact, Dorsey reportedly "boasted that he had survived far worse in the Pacific than any punishment his landlord could mete out."[51] Though Harrison publicly denied any role in the lynching and cast himself as an innocent victim, a ten-year-old white boy named Clinton Adams allegedly witnessed the murders while hiding in the nearby woods. Adams claimed years later that Harrison himself had enthusiastically joined in shooting both couples, though his accusation remains unverified.[52]

The brutal Monroe lynching provoked a national outcry and directed an intense media spotlight on both Monroe and Georgia. Public outrage, nonetheless, did not produce a single conviction.[53] To black veterans in Walton County, in

Georgia, and throughout the South, the message was clear. "They're exterminating us," a black Monroe veteran told NAACP investigator Ollie Harrington; "They're killing negro veterans, and we don't have nothing to fight back with but our bare hands. In Italy and Germany we knew which way they were coming, but [not] here."[54] As Loy Harrison explained years later: "Up until George went into the army he was a good nigger, but when he came out, they thought they were as good as any white people."[55] George Dorsey, an individual, went into the army, but *they* —black veterans—returned with attitudes unbecoming to their "proper" place in southern society. And *they*—Dorsey and countless others—had to be stopped.

This repressive racial climate continued to plague black life in postwar Georgia, offering a bitter reward to ex-servicemen who had hoped for something much better. "During the time I was in the Army I tried to uphold the name of Georgia when the boys started talking about it," a veteran sardonically recalled in 1946, and "this is what they would always say: If I had a home in hell and a plantation in Georgia I would sell the plantation and go back home." Now, however, he agreed: "I jumped out of the frying pan into the fire when I left New Guinea and came back to Georgia."[56]

Not surprisingly, many black veterans beat a fast track out of their communities and region to the North and West in search of safer conditions and better economic and educational opportunities.[57] In Georgia, Horace Bohannon found a virtual veteran exodus out of some areas of the state. "Well, I tell you," black veterans often told Bohannon, "I'm gonna save my money and I'm going to Los Angeles." Indeed, in the area surrounding Augusta, "the practice has been for a veteran to come home, say hello to all kin, far and nigh, pick up his bags and away to New York, California or somewhere." In numerous black-owned barbershops, diners, and drugstores in Brunswick, he heard the same story. African American ex-servicemen were either migrating elsewhere, reenlisting in the service, or subsisting on unemployment compensation since "almost no effort was being put forth for Negro veterans." Thus, "one of the chief fears . . . was this: the people are afraid the veterans are not going to remain in Georgia and certainly not on a farm . . . unless they can make better than a 'hand to mouth' living."[58] Indeed, within five years of the war's end, over one-half of black ex-soldiers who had been in their twenties during their wartime service were living in a different region from where they had been born. In Georgia, where the black population had declined 12 percent between 1920 and 1950, 36 percent of African Americans born in the Empire State lived somewhere else in 1950.[59]

Not all black ex-servicemen, however, chose to leave. For those who stayed, the injustices they continued to encounter in Georgia added a critical dimension to the impact of the war on their postwar political activism.[60] Although most scholars agree that military service had an important influence on the lives black veterans led after the war, not all are convinced that a direct link existed between participation in the war and later civil rights activities.[61] Certainly, scores of black veterans fled the South after the war, and many others chose pursuing personal opportunity over community or political action.[62] Yet examples of black veterans organizing for change and engaging in political activism immediately upon their return home are ubiquitous throughout the postwar South, particularly in Georgia. And black veterans such as Doyle Combs routinely explained their political activities as a direct outgrowth of participation in the Second World War. An important part of the story of the war's impact on the South, then, was the determination of Georgia's black veterans to resist white racial control. This did much, as Alexander Heard remembered, to put the "race issue" at the "front and center" of the region's postwar political transition.

This activism appears even more widespread if the meaning of what constitutes "political" confrontation is expanded to include personal and indirect acts of individual or unorganized rebellion.[63] As soon as the war ended, for example, racial incidents between rebellious black ex-GIs and testy southern whites erupted throughout the region. A popular story that circulated among southern black communities in the 1940s indicated a recognition that at least some of the black men who returned from the war seemed different. "A group of rural Negroes . . . were having a heated argument," the story went, "over the difference between the old Negro and the new Negro. 'Well, as I sees it,'" drawled one old man, "'when the old Negro was insulted he shed a tear; today, when these young ones is insulted, they sheds blood.'"[64] Indeed, black veterans clashed with southern whites in a variety of realms after the war, not just at the polls. In the charged racial atmosphere that clouded the period, the personal quickly escalated into the political.

In the wake of federal court decisions striking down segregation in interstate bus travel, for example, the Jim Crow practices that still regulated public transportation in the South especially offended black servicemen and veterans.[65] Tensions flared between bus drivers who were determined to maintain segregated seating and black veterans who refused to abide by traditional racial codes. One of the most infamous incidents involved Isaac Woodward of South Carolina, a young black serviceman blinded by police officers in Columbia after an altercation with a Greyhound bus driver.[66] A similar incident in Palmetto, Georgia, when two black veterans refused to comply with a driver's request to give up their seats to white passengers, failed to end as tragically. A Reverend Hall intervened and the veterans agreed to move, averting an escalation of the conflict.[67] Thus, as Georgian, World War II veteran, and actor Ossie Davis later recalled in an interview about his wartime service with an overseas medical unit, "Oh, I didn't do any fighting in Liberia. I did all of my fighting down South."[68]

Although black veterans sometimes chose to wage these individual battles, most recognized the obvious wisdom in organized group action.[69] In Georgia this political mobilization started with the establishment of all-black veteran services organizations, which aimed "to aid returning veterans in adjusting themselves to community life."[70] Groups such as the GVL, a statewide association headquartered in Atlanta, assisted black veterans in cutting through the inevitable red tape that applying for any government benefits entailed. "Whether you were seeking jobs, houses or services," Bohannon recalled, "you got a much better ear . . . if you had credential as a representative of a veterans' group . . . than if you were somebody that [just] got off the train."[71]

Right from the beginning, however, veterans quickly learned that "there was no need of applying for [certain jobs] . . . . You weren't going to get [them] . . . . You had to stay within these artificial barriers."[72] And these barriers would never begin to crumble, veterans surmised, without the pressure of black political influence. Regulatory measures passed throughout the southern states in the late nineteenth and early twentieth centuries and enforced by electoral fraud, intimidation, and even violence had effectively disfranchised southern blacks for decades. Along with literacy tests, the grandfather clause, and other creative and legal tools of disfranchisement, one of the most effective and widespread practices to bar black voting had been to maintain a lily-white membership in state Democratic parties.[73]

In the one-party South, the only elections that had real meaning were the Democratic primaries. Each state had laws on the books that limited participation in primary elections to the members of the respective parties. Since southern Democratic parties barred black members, black citizens generally could not vote in Democratic primary elections, which meant, effectively, that they could not participate in the electoral process. Although progressives within and outside the South often condemned this practice as a violation of the Fifteenth Amendment to the Constitution, state primary elections remained under the purview of state power. That is, until the *Smith v. Allwright* decision in 1944.

In the *Smith* decision, the U.S. Supreme Court overturned the all-white primary in Texas as a violation of the Fifteenth Amendment, which prohibited infringing on a citizen's right to vote because of race or color. As V. O. Key explained in his assessment of southern politics after the war, state laws regulated the primaries in Texas, making them "an integral part of the machinery of the state." By law, for example, the state certified primary nominees for the general elections. This meant that "discrimination by the party" in choosing its nominees for state and federal offices was, in effect, "discrimination by the state."[74] This decision galvanized black civil rights activists in the postwar 1940s, heartened progressives within and outside the South, and unnerved many southern whites. Southern Democrats, particularly in the Deep South, with its large black population, rushed to remove all state regulation of primary elections. Their strategy was to subvert the *Smith* ruling by claiming that the Democratic Party had the status of a private club that could determine its own membership and was independent of state regulation.[75]

At the same time, black activists also took immediate action, developing voter registration campaigns and attempting to vote in the first Democratic primaries that followed the *Smith* decision. When black citizens were still denied the right to vote, these individuals and groups brought suit against the state Democratic parties for these violations, which led to a series of related cases that went before the Supreme Court.[76] In Georgia the Reverend Primus E. King of Columbus attempted to vote in the July 1944 primary, immediately after the *Smith* decision came down, but recalcitrant whites turned him away.[77] With the assistance of the NAACP, King sued in federal court. In early 1946 the U.S. Supreme Court refused to overturn federal district court judge T. Hoyt Davis's decision in the *King v. Chapman* case that the *Smith* decision outlawing an all-white primary did apply to Georgia. Governor Ellis Arnall, who could not run for reelection in 1946, then refused to call a special session of the state legislature to find a way to subvert this decision. As a result, blacks could vote in Georgia's 1946 primary elections.[78]

The *King* ruling and Arnall's subsequent stance underscored the value of adopting a conventional political strategy that was aimed at expanding black voter registration. The demise of the all-white primary provided at least the potential opportunity for black participation in southern Democratic politics for the first time since the disfranchising period of the late nineteenth and early twentieth centuries. Southern white resistance, combined with a lack of federal enforcement of black voting rights, ultimately would negate this potential in the postwar 1940s. That outcome, however, was not apparent at the time. Moreover, the *Smith* and *King* decisions instilled hope that change might be initiated within the regular channels of conventional electoral politics. Given the rhetoric of democratic victory against the totalitarian Axis powers, along with the developing anticommunist sentiment that infused the postwar era, conventional political activism probably had more ideological and pragmatic appeal immediately after the war than the sort of militant direct action tactics more common in the civil rights movement of later decades. Moreover, voter registration and electoral politics conformed with the reform strategy adopted by the national NAACP, its many local community branches, the national and state CIO, and other progressive reform organizations.[79] Finally, veterans had just fought a war that had emphasized the importance of the processes and values of American democracy versus the exclusivity and intolerance of totalitarian regimes. It made sense to at least try those processes as a means of initiating reform, given veterans' special claim to having earned a right to that participation through their war service.

For all of these reasons, voter registration drives in support of moderate or progressive candidates, or against reactionary ones, became a primary goal of black veteran organizations, in cooperation with other civic groups such as the Urban League and local NAACP chapters.[80] Thus, the GVL promised to "work for every Negro of age becoming a registered voter." In fact, to "encourage democracy for all American citizens," membership in the GVL required being registered to vote.[81]

The most successful of these initiatives occurred in Savannah, Augusta, and Atlanta.[82] All were responses to unusual opportunities in 1946 to elect candidates with more moderate racial views and to defeat Eugene Talmadge in the state gubernatorial race. Black World War II veterans played pivotal roles in turning out a historic number of black citizens to register and vote in all three cities.

Savannah's voter registration drive emerged in the context of a developing reformist campaign of businessmen, labor, and white veterans against the corrupt urban machine headed by John Bouhan, Savannah's county attorney and long incumbent Democratic political boss.[83] The insurgent campaign launched by the Citizens Progressive League (CPL) in the spring of 1946 immediately attracted black veterans who seized the chance to augment black political influence by helping to defeat the Bouhan-supported candidates for the state legislature.[84] A new organization called the World War II–Veterans Association (WWII-VA) announced its formation as a "non-partisan" association that, nonetheless, also promised to "take a leading role in politics" in order to improve "the political and economical positions of all of its colored citizens."[85] The WWII-VA immediately launched an enthusiastic voter registration drive.[86]

In May 1946 the Civic Action Committee of the WWII-VA kicked off a series of mass meetings, rallies, and house-to-house canvasses to encourage registration and voting. In June veterans joined the Usher Board of the Central Baptist Church to sponsor a final rally. Speakers informed citizens on the duties of citizenship, updated them on the candidates, and instructed them in the proper manner of casting a ballot. A youth named Alfonso Simmons recited the Gettysburg Address, and a representative from the International Longshoremen's Union emphasized the importance of registering 20,000 black citizens. Calling on all registered voters and every organization and citizen, including pastors, to give their "whole-hearted" support to the drive by taking at least one person to register, the WWII-VA hoped to close out its effort by swelling black voter rolls in the last few days before the registration deadline.[87]

Meanwhile, black veterans in the GVL in Atlanta joined an equally vigorous registration campaign for the gubernatorial and Fifth District congressional primaries. A new umbrella civic organization called the All Citizens Registration Committee (ACRC) initially had registered black voters earlier in the year in support of the candidacy of moderately liberal Helen Douglas Mankin in a special election to fill the Fifth District congressional seat.[88] When that effort succeeded, ACRC leaders decided to expand the registration drive. They planned to support both Mankin's reelection in the regular primary and the gubernatorial candidacy of James V. Carmichael, who was perceived as being a racial moderate, against Eugene Talmadge, known to be a racial reactionary. Black veterans in the GVL assumed a leading role in organizing and carrying out this effort.[89]

The ACRC devised a highly organized structure of campaign workers at the street block, census tract, ward, and precinct levels.[90] David Watson, a black ex-serviceman, served as director of ACRC headquarters and executive secretary of the voter drive. Veterans on the GVL's Civic Action Committee, as well as others, canvassed homes along the streets of Atlanta's black neighborhoods. Watson circulated instructions to these volunteers detailing how to organize blocks and wards and how to approach prospective registrants.[91] GVL veterans drew both on their status as ex-soldiers and on the principles stated in the wartime "Four Freedoms" to legitimate their call for political participation, which they hoped would dispel black fear and civic apathy.[92] A special ACRC "veterans division" scripted the specific appeal veteran workers used when approaching a prospective registrant:

> I spent over two years, a part of which was served overseas, in the armed services. I had hopes that my services would provide YOU with freedom from want and fear. Above all else I wanted to maintain YOUR freedom of speech.

> Now that the war has been won, the most difficult job ahead of us is to win the PEACE here at home. "PEACE IS NOT THE ABSENCE OF WAR, BUT THE PRESENCE OF JUSTICE" which may be obtained, first, by your becoming a citizen— A REGISTERED VOTER. If you will become a REGISTERED VOTER we may be able to win the PEACE.[93]

Clarence Stephens, an Atlanta University student who chaired the GVL's Civic Action Committee, explained to local reporters that "the time has far passed when Negroes in our state can afford to sit back and let others control their well being." "If we are to be treated fairly in this state, if we want to stop police brutality, get justice in the courts, Negro policemen, equal educational, health and recreational facilities," Stephens argued, "then we must have a voice in our government. The ballot must be our weapon against the enemies of democracy here at home in Georgia." Free exercise of the vote, veterans believed, was the key to overcoming the barriers to black opportunity and freedom.[94]

The activism this conviction generated produced some surprising political results in Georgia, serving to destabilize the local political environment in several communities. Black voting—and the potential for change it represented—became an issue where it rarely had existed before the war. Both Savannah and Atlanta, as well as numerous other Georgia communities, saw more black citizens vote in the first postwar primaries than in any prior election in the state's history. In Savannah black citizens overwhelmed the county courthouse as the deadline to register approached. On the last day, local pastors took their parishioners to register in hearses donated by black undertakers, and black citizens stood in lines that extended around the courthouse and down the street well before registration even opened.[95] Loaded down with box lunches and children, black Savannah settled in for a long wait, determined to remain all day if necessary; as one elderly gentlemen told a local reporter, "It's the will of the Lord that us colored folks vote."[96]

As total black registration approached the WWII-VA goal of 20,000, local politicos and the press speculated on what role these newly registered voters would play in the coming elections. With white support divided between the legislative incumbents supported by the Bouhan machine and those candidates put forth by the reformist CPL, the black vote promised to be poised as a historic balance of power.[97] Since the Bouhan machine had a poor reputation among Savannah's black citizens, most observers expected the new registrants to vote for the insurgent CPL candidates. That expectation prompted attempts by the incumbent party to limit black voting through deliberate delays. Poll watchers later recalled the scene that developed at many black polling stations:

> The sun would be beating down sometimes as much as a hundred degrees. And the places where blacks voted, with few exceptions, were all outdoors. So it meant that only one or two people could stand inside the voting place, and all of the others had to stand out on the streets. And there were long lines because they had made no provisions for [that number] . . . . Thousands of blacks were being handled . . . by white poll watchers who . . . had no interest in seeing that the black vote came through because they knew, to a large extent, the black vote was for change. The people who had control of the voting up until that time . . . were satisfied with things as they were because they

were benefiting from it and were not willing to allow too many new voters to enter the situation who would have different views from their own.[98]

Only half of the 20,000 black citizens registered actually voted on election day. Nonetheless, the CPL swept all offices, electing three new state legislative delegates and twenty-four members to the county Democratic Executive Committee. Around 85 percent of the 9,719 or so black voters who did manage to cast ballots voted for the CPL, which won by a 10,000-vote margin of victory. Black veterans, and the citizens and organizations that supported them, thus helped to overturn one of Georgia's longest-lived and strongest mossback political machines. Having gambled that supporting the CPL would pay off, black citizens seemed pleased with the new city administration shortly after the election. It immediately appointed a "Negro Advisory Committee" as promised, hired nine black officers, two black matrons, and one jail attendant, paved the road leading to a black cemetery, and eventually built a new recreation center and high school in a black neighborhood.[99]

In Atlanta the ACRC drive had mixed success. The campaign registered almost 22,000 black voters who did become the core of a new and lasting black political strength in Georgia's largest city. And black voters in the Fifth District and Atlanta helped to give Helen Douglas Mankin and James V. Carmichael popular majorities in their respective races. The county unit system, however, nullified those results by delivering the winning number of county units to James C. Davis in the congressional race and to Eugene Talmadge in the gubernatorial race. Yet, black voting made an impression in Atlanta, as it had in Savannah. Mayor William B. Hartsfield conceded shortly thereafter to demands for black city officers, and a biracial coalition eventually developed that wielded significant political influence in Atlanta in the following years.[100]

The determination of southern black veterans to increase black registration and voting, and their success in doing so, drew national, state, and local attention not only to the potential of an organized and enfranchised black citizenry, but also to consideration of what the racial impact of the war had been. In expanding local electorates beyond what incumbent factions or machines could control and in encouraging insurgent candidates to actually court the black vote in some communities, black veteran activism shook up the political and racial status quo in Georgia. Black voters, as local journalists repeatedly explained, had played a critical role in defeating one of Georgia's oldest political machines in Savannah, contributed to the defeat of the incumbent and corrupt political gang in Augusta, and challenged the claim to power made by Georgia's most infamous and successful reactionary, Eugene Talmadge.[101] Black veterans had fired a shot heard round the state as Georgians, black and white, mulled over what the transition to peacetime might bring to their state and region. The question of black equality now appeared as more than just a blip on the radar screen of the region's postwar political agenda. What might happen next was open to anyone's speculation.

The voter registration drives in which these veterans participated did produce significant results, registering between 135,000 and 150,000 black voters in Georgia in 1946 alone. Between 85,000 and 100,000 of these actually managed to vote that year, 98 percent for gubernatorial candidate James V. Carmichael against Eugene Talmadge.[102] Black voters helped to defeat entrenched political machines in Savannah and Augusta and to elect a new mayor in Macon in 1947. Around 200,000 black citizens registered statewide for the gubernatorial race between Melvin E. Thompson and Herman Talmadge the following year.[103]

Other southern states made significant, if less striking, progress. In Mississippi, for example, black veterans' efforts to oust Senator Theodore G. Bilbo failed to get rid of that state's most noted reactionary, but their courage in testifying against "The Man" at a later congressional hearing encouraged other black Mississippians to take action. By 1950, some 20,000 African Americans had registered to vote in Mississippi, a significant start in a state known for its rabid racism.[104] By the time of the *Brown v. the Board of Education* decision in 1954, over one million African Americans were registered to vote in the South.[105]

These successes, however, hardly tell the whole story. Ultimately, the voter registration drives of the postwar 1940s failed to evolve into ongoing grassroots movements. The initial flurry of activity during and after the war soon subsided. Harry Ashmore, a journalist, southern editor, and white World War II veteran, for example, recalled that the "big voter registration drive of blacks that was throughout the South . . . fell far short of expectations." In fact, "it seemed to me," he explained, "that all the middle class, fairly literate blacks, flocked in and registered and the poor folks didn't show up. They weren't interested . . . . [T]hey didn't think it made any difference whether they voted or not." And, he added, "in fact, it probably didn't."[106]

Thus, the potential for progressive racial change that seemed so promising within the first couple of years after the war quickly dissipated. Leading civil rights organizations generally remained wedded to gradualist strategies emphasizing conventional legal and political avenues for change, but these channels narrowed considerably as the developing Cold War complicated the postwar political context for progressive campaigns of all sorts.[107] The new war on communism sapped the momentum for reform, in part, by redefining progressive social causes as inherently un-American and even communistic. Moreover, the international fight for the "Free World" paradoxically drew national and world attention to the southern system of apartheid *and* made federal officials and national party leaders, anxious to secure broad support for Cold War policies, reluctant to challenge the southern white defensiveness that resulted. The national postwar climate for progressive racial change in the South thus quickly soured.[108]

Scholars also have emphasized the lack of commitment to the cause exhibited by many black southerners, including veterans, who, like many Americans, chose to focus on personal advancement over political mobilization after the war.[109] Much like the veterans who told Horace Bohannon of their plans to hop the first bus or train out of the South, many black veterans found the lure of new opportunities created by the war outside of the region to be irresistible.

Certainly, all of these factors help to explain why the modern direct action phase of the black freedom struggle took at least a decade to develop after World War II ended. The intensity of the white backlash that black activists faced in states like Georgia in the postwar 1940s, however, also undermined black political participation. Each protest against Jim Crow and each black citizen who registered and voted weakened the confidence many white southerners had in the immutability of southern racial tradition. They responded accordingly. From purging registration lists of black voters to outright acts of violence such as the Walton County lynching, racial conservatives reacted to the political activism that black veterans encouraged with a stalwart defense of white supremacy.

Even as thousands of African Americans throughout Georgia managed to register and vote in the first postwar elections, many others failed to do so. The obstructionism of registrars and election officials turned away scores of black veterans and citizens, doubtlessly convincing many others that there was little point in even trying. The NAACP's "Division of Research and Information," for example, published a report on the "Negro Vote in the Southern States" late in 1946, which detailed the disfranchisement that continued to occur. Noting that the county unit system in Georgia constituted a "unique way of minimizing the effectiveness of the popular vote" by offsetting any urban-oriented plurality with rural county unit votes, the report concluded that "it was the county-unit system which re-elected Eugene Talmadge as governor in spite of the effective showing of Negro voters in large urban areas." Election officials estimated that over 80 percent of the approximately 150,000 black Georgians who registered actually voted in the July 17 primaries. Reports to the national NAACP office "indicated that in several towns Negroes outnumbered whites." Yet, this fact had prompted "an organized campaign to purge registrants from county lists," centered in Talmadge's campaign headquarters. "In 31 counties of the state," reported the NAACP, "more than 20,000 names are known to have been challenged."[110]

Georgia's black citizens protested this wholesale usurpation of their voting rights.[111] "We are writing you concerning Our Rights to Vote in Blacksheare [sic] Georgia Pierce County," wrote E. J. Jacobs to the national NAACP. "We have been challenge [sic] and we answered to the Challenge." Jacobs and others hired a Savannah attorney to defend the suffrage rights of over three hundred of Pierce County's African American citizens. A federal judge ordered that all names of qualified voters be put back on the voting lists. Nonetheless, Jacobs reported, "When we appeared at polls we were told that our names were not on the list [sic]." Of 385 black citizens registered to vote, registrars turned away nearly all, including "Several Ex Service Men whom was turned down [sic]." "Please Take note of this and take the matter up for us If you Can," Jacobs wrote, adding that "We have a live NAACP Branch here and are trying to Carry on."[112] In Appling County, R. B. Dunham, who had written so eloquently and bitterly of the hypocrisy in asking black Georgians to send their sons to die overseas, noted that when "me and my wife went to our precinct where we was told we had to go to vote and was denied the right . . . . They claim our name was not on the voting list." Election officials then told the Dunhams "if we still [wanted] to vote we would have to [go] 12 miles to our county seat and . . . ask permission to please let us vote as they would not find our names on the voting list in . . . our precinct." Given these obstacles, not surprisingly, the Dunhams "failed to vote at all," but "if we had of got the chance to vote that would have been two more votes against Talmadge." Thus, he lamented, "you know when a man is denied his rights he can't do anything much."[113]

In the event that the prospect of public humiliation in being turned away by a registrar or election official was not enough to forestall black voting, white Georgians readily turned to harsher methods. In Greenville, Georgia, for example, "it has been reported that . . . seven white men burned crosses on the eve of the election." Black veterans and others registering in Fitzgerald found warning notices posted on church doors promising that "the first Negro to vote in the White Primary in Fitzgerald, July 17, will never vote again."[114] In the summer of 1946 a black church burned in Soperton, the KKK rallied and burned crosses across the state, whites drove through black sections of town in Grady County firing guns, and picketed the polls in Manchester to warn black citizens to stay away. Similar reports came from counties throughout Georgia, but particularly from the rural black belt. Fear of white retaliation and a lack of federal protection diminished black citizens' willingness to put their lives on the line. "Most Negroes in rural districts were either disqualified," concluded the NAACP, "or heeding Talmadge's warning to stay away from the polls, failed to register and vote."[115]

The spate of racial violence that permeated postwar Georgia and the South gave intimidation and threats a convincing ring of truth. In Walton County, for example, many cited the atmosphere created by Talmadge's race-baiting campaign of 1946 as directly contributing to the lynching of the Dorseys and the Malcolms. As one "courthouse lounger" in Monroe put it, "the sight of that long line of niggers waiting to vote put the finishing touches to it," while another added "This thing's got to be done to keep Mister Nigger in his place. Since the state said he could vote, there ain't been any holding him . . . . Gene told us what was happening."[116] In Taylor County, Georgia, not far from Columbus, only Maceo Snipes, another black World War II veteran, dared to cast a vote in the county's Democratic primary in 1946. This act of courage prompted four white men, including, ironically, a white veteran, to shoot Snipes to death on his front porch within hours of casting his ballot.[117] Not surprisingly, after writing to the NAACP to describe voter purges in Wilkes County during the "recent primary in Georgia," M. O. Smith pleaded to remain anonymous: "Now get me straight. I simply cannot be quoted. Dont by any possible means let me be brought into this. It will get me in trouble . . . . Dont mention my name. Dont even write back to me. That might be a give away." In fact, Smith added, "burn my letter. I dont want it traced."[118]

Despite veterans' bravery and determination, this backlash caused black voting in the immediate postwar years to fall below expectations. Although the number of African Americans who registered quadrupled between 1945 and 1950, 80 percent of eligible black citizens in the South remained unregistered. The NAACP hoped to enroll two million black citizens for the presidential election of 1952 but managed to meet only half of that goal. A SRC survey in 1953 found that the registration of African Americans of voting age in the entire South amounted to only 50 percent of white registration. Such statistics led historian Steven F. Lawson to conclude that the voter drives of the 1940s "had skimmed the cream off the top and succeeded with those most receptive to their message," namely, African Americans in the urban South. Enfranchisement proved slowest in the rural black belt where African Americans outnumbered whites and, consequently, met the stiffest white resistance. In many areas, Lawson concluded, black registration slowed considerably after 1947.[119]

In Georgia the turbulent gubernatorial campaign of 1946 saw seven whites register for every single new black voter, and a University of Georgia study found that local politicos had so padded voter lists in thirty counties that the number of white registrants exceeded the number of white residents. Talmadge supporters purged some 16,000 or more black citizens from the rolls in 1946 and denied thousands more the right to vote in 1948 during a gubernatorial campaign dominated by racial terror and intimidation.[120] In postwar Georgia, historian Donald Grant has concluded, "the black vote was large enough to throw fear into whites but not large enough to be courted, which encouraged [a] politics of negativism."[121]

Defining the postwar era in the South only in terms of lost opportunities, nevertheless, neglects taking the events of the period—and the black and white southerners who lived through them—on their own terms. Indeed, the story of black veteran activism in Georgia compels us to understand the postwar 1940s not as an era of failure alone, but as one of significant ferment touched off, at least in part, by the Second World War. If black veterans and citizens had not challenged and threatened the political and racial status quo in Georgia after the war, whites would not have found it so necessary to mount a reactionary backlash. The intensity of their efforts to repel black veterans' advancement testified to the level of racial instability induced by the war. Although this backlash effectively stalled the momentum for progressive racial reform at the time, black veteran activism signaled the real racial discomfort that would only grow for southerners of both races as the twentieth century progressed. The willingness of black veterans to confront the racial injustices that denied them the dignity and freedom they had earned exposed the racial fault line in the foundations of the one-party South, a structural weakness from which massive resistance to integration *and* the black civil rights movement would subsequently emerge.

Black veterans had disturbed the complacency of southern racial conservatives not only because of their own political activism, however, but also because they were not alone in their fight to realize a democratic imperative drawn from the war. A small but vocal minority of southern white veterans also defined the war's meaning and their own participation in it as a mandate to implement a political freedom that applied to all Georgians. They joined black veterans in voter registration campaigns and in interracial veteran organizations that challenged racial intolerance and discrimination. They also spearheaded a controversial legal challenge to Georgia's county unit system as the primary impediment to democratic and inclusive majority rule. This dual assault on the postwar political status quo in Georgia—from both black *and* white veterans and their supporters who wanted a progressive and democratic future—provoked an immediate backlash from other white veterans determined to sustain all the power and prerogatives of white supremacy. It is to the story of these polar opposite reactions among Georgia's white veterans to the war's racial impact that we now turn.

3: The Question of Majority Rule

White Veterans and the Politics of Progressive Reform

EARLY IN 1947, a white ex-Marine chaplain from south Georgia named Joseph Rabun made a ringing declaration for democracy in the halls of the Georgia state capitol. A Baptist minister from McRae in Telfair County, Rabun had served in some of the worst battles of the Pacific war. Now he found himself at a public hearing testifying against a bill to reinstate an all-white Democratic primary in Georgia. His cause, as he made abundantly clear, was a moral one directly connected to the meaning of World War II. "If I remained silent when my Negro neighbors were being politically beaten, robbed, and left for dead," he explained to an Atlanta reporter, "I would immediately forfeit all I have of virtue."[1] Though Rabun had been a fervent believer in American democracy since his religious conversion years earlier, now he had "faced 100 days of battle-fire [and] four years of war" for that conviction. Thus, he explained, "I can never forget the great price we so recently paid for the freedom from the same basic threat."[2] Nor did Rabun take this responsibility lightly: "My stand might place my position in the community where I live in jeopardy," he conceded, "but cost me what it will, I cannot consent to silence against a threat to the welfare of my state." Indeed, he added, "the real issue is not a white primary, it is democracy."[3]

A few months later, with the question of a revived white primary still hanging in the balance, three members of the Georgia General Assembly—white men who were also veterans of World War II—issued their own manifesto that resonated with all the shibboleths of white supremacy. As "veterans of long service in World War II," representatives J. Julian Bennett (Barrow County), Garland T. Byrd (Taylor County), and J. E. Briscoe (Walton County) condemned the fall of the white primary as the first step on the road to racial amalgamation. "Some would have us believe that by Negroes voting our way of life and time honored Southern traditions would still remain intact," but they argued that the opposite was true. Black voters and political influence "in the East and other sections" had tried "ramming down our throats" such "totally unacceptable" federal legislation as the Fair Employment Practices Committee (FEPC), antilynching laws, and interracial education. Declaring it a "crucial period in our history," these veterans called on "the white people" of the South and Georgia to "continue the fight for segregation of the races in all our public institutions and utilities." Southern racial traditions were essential, these veterans maintained, "if we are to continue to have peace and harmony among the negroes and whites."[4]

Joseph Rabun and the three state representatives exhibited polar reactions to black participation in Georgia's postwar political life. Indeed, two more antithetical responses to the war's racial impact could hardly be found. To Rabun, black voting fulfilled an obligation of American democracy written in blood on island beaches throughout the Pacific theater. To Bennett, Byrd, and Briscoe, black voting represented a betrayal of the principles and values on which hallowed southern institutions were built.

This spectrum of response by Georgia's white veterans exemplified the central contradiction at the heart of the war's political impact in the South, namely, its capacity to generate both momentum for and resistance to change. For some white veterans in Georgia, the discrepancy between the rhetoric of freedom that had explained American war aims overseas and the reality of undemocratic practices at home posed a disturbing contradiction they could not ignore. Progressive white veterans returned to wage their own battles for the political democracy and freedom they believed the war had mandated.[5] They worked to reelect liberal congresswoman Helen Douglas Mankin to the Fifth District congressional seat in 1946, then orchestrated a legal attack on the county unit system after Mankin failed to win despite having received a majority of the popular vote. Progressive white veterans also tried to forestall the Georgia General Assembly from reinstating the white primary in 1947.

The immediate objective in these activities was to break the conservative stranglehold on political democracy in Georgia by registering and mobilizing the votes of southern blacks and workers in the postwar Democratic primary elections. This would be an important first step in reorienting Georgia's political priorities toward a more progressive and just agenda, inclusive of the interests of all. This goal also aimed at ending the domination of southern Democratic conservatives in Congress, which was a major obstacle to rebuilding the national momentum for an expansion of New Deal liberalism in the postwar era, the primary aim of key national liberal organizations at the time.[6]

This activism, which attacked the citadels of southern political tradition from without and from within the ranks of white solidarity, provided an important interracial dimension to the progressive political insurgencies of the postwar 1940s in Georgia. This destabilizing potential of the war's impact, however, greatly alarmed many other southern whites, including veterans, who thought that fighting to defend the American way of life abroad also meant upholding the southern way of segregation and white rule at home. Such veterans tended to experience the economic, demographic, and social changes accelerated by the war for the South and Georgia—personified by black veterans determined to claim the political equality and economic opportunity that was their due—as a profound disruption of their confidence in the durability of white supremacy. The war's subversive potential, reactionary veterans believed, undermined their own political prerogatives as white men, and thereby invoked their civic and male duty to defend the racial sanctity of the domestic and political sphere.[7]

Some of these veterans returned to join racist hate groups, such as the Georgia Klan and the neo-fascist Columbians of Atlanta, both of which assaulted black veterans and citizens after the war. Contrary to the political activities of their progressive counterparts, reactionary veterans attacked Helen Douglas Mankin's campaign for reelection to Congress and supported Eugene Talmadge's race-baiting bid for governor. The postwar movement for racial and industrial democracy provoked their hostility, while the white primary and the county unit system inspired their praise and support.

The passion and determination both sides brought to this fight made for a rocky transition to peacetime for Georgia, along a road pitted with the potholes of political conflict and racial controversy. Where that journey would end weighed heavily on Georgians, and the battle of both progressive and reactionary white veterans to determine that outcome raised the stakes in the state's first postwar political primaries.

Veterans' leadership in both challenging *and* defending the postwar political and racial status quo clearly disrupted the generally static nature of southern political life.[8] Their activism ensured that both the politics of racial reform and the politics of racial defense would be an important part of the war's legacy for Georgia and the South. And it would be the twin descendants of the legacy— the black civil rights movement and massive resistance to integration—that did much to finally transform the southern political landscape in the following years.

WHEN JOSEPH RABUN decided to risk his own pulpit in order to defend black political participation in Georgia, he articulated an inclusive understanding of majority rule shared by a small but vocal minority of the state's white veterans.[9] This vision reflected a rejuvenated popular front and New Deal liberalism that had emerged from the war with its eye on Dixie. Born much earlier in the notion of cooperation across ideological divisions in the war against fascism, this variant of postwar liberalism now aimed to bring together "radicals, liberals, and moderates" in support of a broad postwar reform program.[10] This spirit was embodied during the war, according to a recent study, by President Roosevelt's declaration of a "second Bill of Rights" in 1944, aimed at reviving the New Deal reform spirit that had languished under the pressures for consensus during the war. In essence, Roosevelt provided a vision for the postwar future premised on implementing the "Four Freedoms" at home, particularly "the rights to a job, to decent housing, to adequate medical care, and to a good education" —essentially, that which was "fundamental to the rights of citizenship" and which applied to all Americans "regardless of station, race, or creed."[11] This vision inspired progressives who hoped to restart the stalled democratic momentum of New Deal reformism after its wartime hiatus.[12]

This revitalization seemed especially important given that a conservative resurgence in Congress, which had really begun in the late 1930s, threatened the postwar expansion of the New Deal and the gains that organized labor had made during the course of the war. This conservative block consisted primarily of southern Democratic congressmen and their northern Republican counterparts, the same alliance that had played a pivotal role in overturning key New Deal programs in the 1930s. It now took aim at efforts to extend and build on the New Deal legacy in the postwar era, such as establishing a permanent FEPC and guaranteeing full employment.[13] Sustained by a truncated electorate and winning office, time and again, by methods that reeked of fraud and corruption, southern Democratic conservatives comprised a formidable obstacle to any national or regional agenda for progressive economic, social, or racial reform. Thus, popular front and New Deal liberals naturally looked to political events in the South as critical to furthering their goals. National progressive organizations adopted a "southern strategy," devoting personnel and resources to boosting progressive fortunes in the region. The NAACP, for example, increased its local and state membership in the South, supported southern voter registration drives, and continued to attack disfranchisement and segregation through the courts. The CIO formed the Southern Organizing Committee (SOC) and began a monumental organizing drive focused on key southern industries, such as textiles, that still largely remained outside the community of organized labor. It also directed its Political Action Committee (CIO-PAC), formed during the war, to develop an "aggressive voter-registration effort" especially for the South.[14]

The Southern Conference for Human Welfare (SCHW), in particular, played an important role. As the southern wing of the national liberal crusade, the SCHW sought to organize the diversity of progressive interests across the region, from the American Federation of Labor (AFL) and the CIO, to the Highlander Folk School, the NAACP, the Southern Negro Youth Congress, and others, into a more unified effort to implement a progressive postwar program. Most of all, the SCHW stressed the importance of establishing "actual majority rule in the South" as the foundation of a progressive "political movement that would materially benefit" both blacks and whites in the region.[15]

In their focus on an inclusive vision of majority rule, on enfranchising both blacks and whites, and on political change as the avenue for economic and social reform to benefit all southerners, Georgia's progressive white veterans were the local complement of this national and regional progressive drive. Progressive white veterans in Georgia usually were college-educated, and many had been involved at some level in New Deal reform activities before the war.[16] Their commitment to change, however, derived not just from these factors, but especially from the formative influence of military service in World War II. Quite contrary to their initial expectations, these veterans discovered that military service challenged preconceived racial notions, undermined any loyalty to the homefront status quo, and raised serious questions about what the meaning of the war really was. All of these contributed to a disenchantment with the character of southern political life that complicated their reintegration into the civilian homefront.

For whites who often had little direct knowledge of black southerners beyond the facile stereotypes with which they had been raised, service in the war proved, at times, to be an unexpected racial education that few of these men ever forgot. Despite an official policy of segregation, the exigencies of war provided opportunities for black and white GIs to interact, sometimes on very close terms. A barrage of propaganda and slurs against the capabilities of black soldiers circulated among white troops and on the homefront throughout the war, but real contact with these men in the realm of battle tended to undermine, at least for some white southerners, long-held notions of black inferiority. As black soldiers and sailors performed their duties ably despite the discrimination and mistreatment meted out to them by white troops and officers, the view that African Americans deserved unequal treatment grew less convincing as the war progressed. Southern white veterans from across the region expressed dismay at the discrimination and injustice black servicemen and women encountered during and after the war.

The courteous treatment that German POWs received in cafés and diners in the Deep South while black servicemen were refused service, for example, angered many white soldiers, who often commented on this hypocrisy over the course of the war. Corporal Henry S. Wooten described himself as "a southern rebel" who was disgusted at an incident in Louisiana that made him "none the more proud of my southern heritage!" Wooten was outraged when local restaurant owners preferred serving German prisoners over black American GIS. "Frankly," he declared, "this incident is a disgrace to a democratic nation"; and he wondered, "are we fighting for such a thing as this?" Moreover, "what [will] the 'Aryan supermen' think when they get a first-hand glimpse of our racial discrimination. Are we not waging a war, in part, for this fundamental of democracy?" Finally, he concluded, "a lot of us, especially in the South, should cast the beam out of our own eyes before we try to do so in others, across the seas."[17]

This sort of discrimination seemed especially galling given the able performance of black soldiers overseas. This could be a revelation to white southerners steeped in the culture of racial difference. Harry Ashmore, a white veteran and southern newspaper editor after the war, for example, recalled his first encounter with black combat troops in Germany. Ashmore's division commander in the Ninety-fifth Infantry complained loudly when replacements for a final assault on the Rhine included the European theater's only all-black tank battalion. He expected these troops to be hindered both by poor equipment and low morale. Although the commander proved "right about the equipment," Ashmore recalled, he was wrong about the battalion's commitment to the fight. "The white Virginian who commanded the battalion had passed from despair to outrage at the way his men were being treated," Ashmore wrote, and "his anger was communicated to his tank crews." Galvanized by a desire to prove their worth, "the black men in those battered old Shermans performed as well as any armored troopers we saw in action in the bloody campaigns that took us from Normandy to Ruhr."[18]

A white sergeant from Texas agreed. Never concerned with the plight of African Americans before the war, he now felt that white southerners should not continue to "abuse the colored people any more" because "blacks as well as whites had given their lives for this country." Captain Thomas W. Murrell Jr., scion of a prominent Richmond, Virginia, family, returned from the war determined to begin rectifying the injustices that whites had long perpetrated on blacks. Watching black Americans "dying of battle wounds in France," had convinced him that the time for "dramatic change on the racial front" had arrived.[19]

White veterans in Georgia expressed similar sentiments when commenting on the political and racial developments of the postwar years. Henry C. Rivers of Griffin, Georgia, for example, appreciated the contribution African Americans had made to winning the war and saw little reason to mistreat black veterans when they returned. "I have spent four and a half years in the army, twenty months overseas," Rivers remarked, and "I have been around and fought with Negro soldiers and I have nothing to hold against them."[20] Another veteran who served in eight different army posts in Great Britain noted that the "first LSTs [landing ship, tank] back from Normandy on D-Day brought cargoes of dead and wounded—including many Negroes, some burned to a crisp." Thus, he asked, "how can an Army condemn part of its men because the color of their skin is darker than some others?"[21]

The capability and commitment black troops had exhibited in the war challenged the notion of black inferiority. Harold Fleming, a white army officer from Georgia and later a civil rights activist, vividly recalled just how transformative an impact this could be. Although he attended Harvard just prior to the war, Fleming admitted to still being "pretty much a victim of my own upbringing," though he had always looked "with disdain on redneck stuff and on the crasser forms of prejudice [and] discrimination." Still, he remembered, "I didn't know any blacks" and remained "pretty damn unenlightened" on the racial issues of the day. After he graduated from Officer Candidate School, however, Fleming ended up commanding black troops in the Quartermaster Corps on Okinawa. This experience "was critical" in transforming him from a relatively "unenlightened" southern moderate into an outright racial liberal. "It was a very traumatic kind of experience," he reflected; "I don't think anybody could have been prepared for that. You were a white straw boss in a very discriminatory segregated Army, and you felt discriminated against." Indeed, "you lived where they lived. Even though you were an officer and you were white," he recalled, "you were a second class soldier because your privates were black."[22]

What being second class meant really struck home when Fleming's outfit received orders to guard Japanese prisoners on work details. "The big fear of the brass, who were mostly southern," he remembered, "was fraternization between the black soldiers and the POWs. They didn't trust them worth a damn." Although Japanese guerrillas still roamed the island and white soldiers were allowed to keep their arms and ammunition, "they [the leaders] blatantly . . . made us turn in every round. I protested about it . . . . I asked, 'Why?'" When another white officer replied, "dammit, you know why," Fleming proclaimed, "I think I do, but I don't think it's fair." Such conditions made a tremendous impression on Fleming. "It was just the sheer human experience of 'good God, how can these men stand it, why do they do it?,'" Fleming recalled: "here they are being called on to follow the rules, shape up, be a good soldier, work your ass off, be ready to die for your country and then they would crap all over you without apology. 'Not a single one of you black bastards is good enough to be an officer even with your own people. You don't get the Quonset huts, you stay in the tents and mud. All the Quonset huts go to a white unit that landed yesterday even though you have been here six months.'"[23] "I understood why [black soldiers] were bitter," Fleming continued; "the amazing thing is that they functioned at all." While some of his men were "very nice guys," Fleming also became aware of those "who were so alienated or so coarsened by life that they . . . would kill you if they thought they could get away with it." In the end, "it was a very good way to learn about race relations . . . . [Y]ou could really see it plain if you had any sense of fairness and if you weren't just under the total mercy of your prejudices."[24]

For other white veterans, the most unsettling aspect of military service derived not from their encounters with black GIs but from the nature of the war itself. The sheer scale of the war's destruction and inhumanity made it imperative to find a meaning that could justify such a monumental cost in human life and property. In this sense, the war could magnify the value of the freedoms and opportunities most white southerners took for granted. James Mackay, a Georgia veteran and postwar liberal politician, told one interviewer that his fifty-two months aboard a Coast Guard cutter during the war "taught [him] what freedom is." As a first lieutenant on a destroyer escort, Mackay saw several shipmates die. "My life has been terribl[y] wounded by war," he recalled; "I lost thirty-one shipmates and I had to hose down the brains of my buddies on my own ship." Mackay had been at sea with them long enough to recognize "who they were by looking at their shoes, covered with blankets." Before his time in the service, "I had taken freedom for granted"; but when his executive officer despaired if there was "anything, anything worth the death of these guys," the war's meaning to him suddenly grew crystal clear. Mackay found himself explaining that "there's only one thing . . . . [I]t is clear that they died to secure the right of all of us to go behind the curtain and cast our ballot without anybody knowing how we voted or having anything to do with how we voted."[25]

Joseph Rabun, the Baptist preacher who spoke out against the white primary bill in 1947, served in the war as a Marine Corps chaplain, ministering to the wounded and dying under enemy fire on Guadalcanal, Bougainville, Saipan, and Guam. After an interview with Rabun in 1946, a reporter for the *Atlanta Con-*

stitution described the impact this experience had made on Rabun. "He believed then, as now," the reporter explained, "that the war was fought against the anti-Christ, that the war was fought against forces that would shackle and ground men down instead of set him free; that the war was fought against an ideology which held that because of race one man was better than another."[26] For Mackay, Rabun, and countless others, the death and destruction that American soldiers witnessed, endured, and perpetrated had to be vindicated.

Their postwar search for this meaning often began by joining one of the only national veterans' organizations willing to confront the question of racial injustice and to work to provide a progressive voice for veterans on any number of regional, national, and international issues. Like all ex-GIs, progressive white veterans in Georgia also wanted an organization that could facilitate their access to GI Bill benefits and veteran services. But they usually shunned the segregated and reactionary American Legion and Veterans of Foreign Wars in favor of the new national American Veterans Committee (AVC).[27] Described by historian George B. Tindall, a former member, as a "New Dealish liberal answer to the American Legion," the AVC endeavored to be a voice for progressive change throughout the country. With a slogan of "Citizens First, Veterans Second," the AVC pledged "To Achieve A More Democratic And Prosperous America And A More Stable World" and to "associate ourselves regardless of national origin, creed, or color to preserve the Constitution of the United States; to insure the rights of free speech, free press, free worship, free assembly, and free elections."[28] Moreover, the national AVC condemned racial segregation and discrimination, declaring "war 'against the whole idea' that some people are superior 'merely because their ancestors did not have the foresight to get their skins tanned against the rays of the sun.'" The AVC's national charter specifically forbade the formation of racially exclusive chapters.[29]

Membership in the AVC in Georgia did, in fact, reflect a new flexibility toward black-white relations that progressive veterans felt it was important to express. In 1947, for example, the interracial Atlanta AVC sponsored three meetings with the black Wheat Street Baptist Church to advocate improved race relations. At two of the meetings, "several veterans from various theaters in the recent war spoke of their experiences with particular reference to race relations in the Armed Services."[30] Interracial membership, in fact, attracted veterans of both races to the AVC in Georgia, and they cited it as a key influence on their decision to join. Elizabeth Kytle, white activist and wife of white veteran Calvin Kytle, remembered the AVC as "the only interracial veterans' group in the country." Moreover, she recalled, "That's the only reason people like Harold Fleming and Calvin joined a veterans' group."[31]

Nor did black participation represent merely token membership. Black veterans were founding members of the Atlanta AVC and prominent in the chapter's leadership. The all-black GVL, for example, had a "direct relationship with" the AVC, Horace Bohannon pointed out, "because it was from the GVL that these other groups" recruited black members. "Right off the bat," he mused, "I can think of a half-dozen of us [who] were charter members of the AVC in Atlanta . . . and we were also officials in the Georgia Veterans League."[32] In Bohannon's memory, the importance of his AVC experience with integration could not be overstated: "I can't quite express, I guess, what a new experience [it was] . . . . [T]here were no similar experiences, very few. . . . You didn't have it in Church, you didn't have it *anywhere* in Georgia."[33] Membership in the AVC presented a new dynamic of "you come to my house, I come to your house . . . . [W]e're on the same footing. You're not mister and I'm not boy." It was an experience that Bohannon recalled as "fresh and exciting."[34]

Interracial organizing in the Jim Crow South, however, was also risky. Not surprisingly, Georgia AVC chapters developed primarily in larger urban areas and smaller university and college towns. With approximately twelve chapters scattered throughout the state, membership ranged from 125 to 250 in the Atlanta chapter to around 500 statewide.[35] Atlanta AVC president Johnnie Glustrom described this group as "a focal point for crystallizing liberal opinion and action"; the chapter's activities confirmed his assessment.[36] Along with raffling appliances to raise money, conducting membership drives, and petitioning local, state and federal authorities on behalf of veterans' issues, the Atlanta-area AVC attacked racial hatred and discrimination. These veterans wrote to Governor Ellis Arnall in the spring of 1946, for example, to support his crusade against the Georgia Klan. "The basic concepts and principles of the Ku Klux Klan are characteristic of fascism and contrary to the principles for which we fought," AVC veterans declared, and they called on Arnall to "unsheet" the "evil force" that threatened Georgia's progress.[37] "We constantly work for civil rights in close cooperation with other groups," proclaimed President Glustrom, and AVC member Robert Thompson remembered a crusade to desegregate the public library in Atlanta.[38] By 1950, the Atlanta chapter's activities had attracted enough attention to win the national AVC's new George W. Norris Award for "outstanding work" on behalf of "the civil rights of the people of the United States." In particular, the national AVC leadership cited the group's efforts to improve housing for black Atlantans, its support of litigation to "eliminate discrimination" in Atlanta schools, and its success in persuading a "leading Atlanta firm" to hire the "first Negro salesman."[39]

Joining with other white and black veterans in the AVC provided a positive outlet for white veterans anxious to express a sense of social justice and democratic fair play that was derived, at least in part, from their experiences in the war. Yet events soon dictated the development of a more direct and political response to sustain any chance that Georgia could move in a progressive direction after the war. Indeed, these white veterans viewed Georgia's postwar political landscape with ambivalence. They were at first encouraged by the potential for progressive change that appeared to have been burgeoning even before the war ended, represented in Georgia by the moderately liberal administration of Governor Ellis Arnall. But they were also disturbed by the readiness of Georgia's old guard, namely, Eugene Talmadge and the racial reactionaries and economic conservatives who supported him, to resort to the age-old politics of racial division and exclusion to deflect this momentum for liberal reform.

The activities of the CIO, SRC, SCHW, and the NAACP in Georgia, for example, generated a resurgent Ku Klux Klan, reactionary campaigns for local and state offices, and a wave of racial violence and anti-unionism.[40] At the same time, the racial antagonism that attended Eugene Talmadge's postwar reelection campaign and that produced the likes of the Walton County lynching crystallized the disenchantment many of Georgia's progressive white veterans felt toward the character of southern political life at home.

Joseph Rabun, for example, grew distressed by the wave of political race-baiting that emerged during the state's first postwar campaign season. He convinced the Southern Baptist Convention of Georgia to condemn Eugene Talmadge's white supremacy gubernatorial campaign in the fall of 1946. Rabun was no ordinary south Georgia pastor. His pulpit was in the McRae church in which Eugene Talmadge "kept his letter of baptism," a fact that facilitated his ouster from the church for his acts of conscience.[41]

For Harold Fleming, the violence and turmoil of the postwar years intensified a bitterness that had sprouted overseas. "When I came back I was sick of the whole goddamn business," Fleming later recalled. "I was mad at the Army and mad at the system." Then, much to his disbelief and chagrin, "Talmadge came back in." The final straw, however, was the Monroe lynching in the summer of 1946. This event "laid the base for total disgust that built up over the succeeding year," Fleming reflected, although he "wasn't even thinking about any kind of reform or crusading at that point." Still, "the idea of settling and having a normal life in that setting when that kind of thing could take place and where you could have a guy saying the things that Talmadge said, reelected governor after all that," seemed more than he could bear. His initial reaction was to flee the South in disgust—"I just felt I had to get out." As a result, Fleming went back to Harvard that fall.[42] When he returned to Georgia in June 1947 to visit family,

however, Ralph McGill's columns in the *Atlanta Constitution* caught his attention because in "about one out of every five columns he was saying something
quite startling on race." "I was naturally amazed," Fleming remembered, because
"I didn't realize . . . that anybody was doing that [or] that anybody could get
away with it." Consumed with curiosity, Fleming visited McGill, who introduced him to the Southern Regional Council. After meeting with src director
George Mitchell, Fleming accepted a job as Director of Information, a temporary position that turned into a fifteen-year tenure with the src, including a
stint as executive director. "I was ripe for this work," Fleming later mused; "I
didn't know there was anybody in the South, anybody white, who had any egal-
itarian values or wanted to see society move away from segregation and discrimination." The disenchantment that began with his racial experiences during
the war led Fleming to embark on a lifelong commitment to the cause of black
civil rights and racial harmony.[43]

Progressive white veterans such as Fleming, Mackay, Rabun, and others found
events in postwar Georgia to be a disquieting reminder of how tenuous the wartime victory abroad over racial intolerance and undemocratic politics seemed
to be. The realities of life at home conflicted with what they believed the war had
been or should have been about. They believed that fighting globally in the name
of American democracy and freedom, at great cost to human life and suffering,
had created a mandate for democratic change at home, one that they felt obligated to help implement in Georgia. Their conviction in the moral and practical necessity of majority rule added a democratic thread to the fabric of postwar
southern liberalism. National and regional organizations provided the experience, a program, and funds. Veterans offered their passion, commitment, and
moral legitimacy. Both looked to Georgia, especially, as a good place to start.[44]

The popularity of Governor Arnall, who had advocated democratic electoral
policies during his administration, such as ending the state poll tax and refusing
to call a special legislative session to reinstate a white primary, had encouraged
liberals and moderates of all stripes.[45] By 1946, the political opening represented
by the *Smith v. Allwright* decision, Arnall's ultimate refusal to subvert it, and the
pending *Primus King* case, along with the rapid political mobilization of black
citizens in Georgia that followed the end of the all-white Democratic primary,
made Georgia an ideal platform to apply this postwar southern strategy. Although motivated first by an immediate and emotional experience connected to
the war, progressive white veterans also reflected this currency of liberal thought
at the time. Like their black comrades in the Georgia Veterans League, these white
veterans believed it was crucial to take immediate advantage of the demise of

the white primary in Georgia in 1946 to register black and white voters who could instill a more progressive force in statewide politics.

White veterans assisted the GVL and the ACRC in their crusade to increase black voter turnout in the 1946 Democratic primaries, and they drew support, in turn, from the SCHW, the CIO-PAC, and the SOC staff.[46] Alexander Heard, for example, returned to Savannah in 1946 after his discharge from the navy and immediately joined a black voter registration drive, serving as an "election helper" in a black precinct.[47] Progressive white veterans joined the campaign to reelect Helen Douglas Mankin to the House of Representatives. George Stoney, a Georgia native and member of the Atlanta AVC, headed up Mankin's reelection campaign at the urging of friends in the SCHW. Although he lacked political experience, Stoney was nonetheless excited by the opportunity. He soon recruited several volunteers from his peers in the AVC, who became an important core of support for Mankin throughout the difficulties of her campaign.[48]

Progressive white veterans liked Mankin because her reputation as a maverick southern liberal meshed with their own desire to see Georgia move in a progressive direction. "While I was cooling my heels in Pearl Harbor, awaiting return to the states," wrote Robert T. Brooke, "I was pleased to read . . . of the election to Congress of Mrs. Helen Douglas Mankin." Citing her record in the state legislature as an advocate for "more money for schools, child labor laws, and state welfare legislation," Brooke concluded that Mankin was "a representative from our state for whom we would not have to apologize." Her brief term in Congress, he added, "has made me doubly proud of our state," and "we must continue to send our best to Congress, so we MUST re-elect Mrs. Mankin."[49] Returning after "three years service overseas," Calvin Kytle, also of the Atlanta AVC, agreed with Brooke that Mankin had amassed an impressive record of "constructive representation" in only "three months' time." She "fought valiantly" to retain price controls, supported President Truman's veto of the antilabor Case Bill, and "fought consistently for federal aid to education, for veterans' housing, and for better relations between labor and management." "Since March," Kytle believed, "Mrs. Mankin has represented the one cause for cheer in Georgia's otherwise depressing political situation." Thus, he announced, "I'm voting for Mrs. Mankin on July 17."[50]

These combined efforts turned out enough voters to help Mankin win the majority of the popular vote in the Fifth District primary on July 17. Crucial votes in smaller outlying counties, however, went to her reactionary opponent, James C. Davis, who captured the Fifth District seat by way of the counties' unit votes. Defeat at the hands of the county unit system in the face of an unprecedented popular majority proved especially galling. This archaic and discriminatory political system clearly stood as the primary obstacle to implementing the war's progressive democratic mandate. "The simple force of rural domination of Georgia politics [promulgated by the county unit system] had to be attacked," James Mackay later recalled, because "it appeared we had been locked in a room without a key."[51]

The outcome of the 1946 primaries aroused suspicions among reformers within and outside of Georgia. Convinced that "sinister forces might be back of all this," a coterie of Atlanta liberals affiliated with the SCHW, the SRC, and the Urban League obtained a Rosenwald Fund grant to ferret out the "hidden influences" that ostensibly ran the state. White Georgia veterans James Mackay and Calvin Kytle carried out the research to discover "Who Runs Georgia?"[52] After interviewing numerous politicians, editors, writers, and community leaders throughout the state, Mackay and Kytle concluded that the county unit system sustained the dominance of a cabal of large economic interests, namely, the Georgia Power Company and the railroads, which essentially controlled politics in the state via the connections their Atlanta law firms maintained with county courthouse gangs. This control pulled in crucial county unit votes for the candidate that "big business" deemed preferable.[53] Thus, breaking up the county unit system, progressive veterans came to believe, was critical to establishing majority rule in Georgia.

An interracial coalition of veterans, urban citizens, and progressives—all of whom felt disfranchised by the discriminatory nature of the county unit system —subsequently filed two federal lawsuits attacking the system's constitutionality. The coalition also sought an injunction against the certification of Eugene Talmadge as governor and James C. Davis as the Fifth District representative in Congress. Within a few days, veterans had formed a statewide organization, the Georgia Veterans for Majority Rule (GVMR), to raise money to finance these lawsuits and to carry the case all the way to the Supreme Court, if necessary.[54] The support of personnel and funds from organizations such as the SCHW and the CIO provided a foundation for local political mobilization and legal action.

Josephine Wilkins of the Georgia Fact-Finding Committee, Margaret Fisher, the director of the SCHW's Georgia Committee, and Lucy Randolph Mason of the CIO's Southern Organizing Committee served as advisors to the GVMR.[55] Mostly white veterans, both men and women, many of whom also belonged to the AVC, staffed the GVMR headquarters in Atlanta and headed up a structure of committees throughout the state to coordinate these efforts.[56] The GVMR central committee included chairman James A. Mackay, veteran of fifty-two months' service in the Coast Guard Reserve during the war and holder of a Bronze Star;

Calvin Kytle, veteran of forty months' service as an enlisted man and officer in the army and also a recipient of the Bronze Star; James M. Crawford, veteran of seventeen months' service as an enlisted man in the infantry and in the Tenth Armored Division; Elizabeth Penn Hammond, veteran of forty months' service as an enlisted woman and officer in the navy's Women Accepted for Volunteer Emergency Service (WAVES); and Richard T. Brooke, veteran of seventeen months' service as an enlisted man in the navy. Veterans headed committees in each congressional district (such as Alexander Heard in the First District of Savannah) and on each college or university campus in Georgia (such as George Doss Jr. of the Student League for Good Government at the University of Georgia).[57]

The lawsuits filed on behalf of plaintiffs Mrs. Robert Turman of the League of Women Voters, Mr. Cullen Gosnell, head of the Department of Political Science at Emory University, and Mr. Earl P. Cooke, Georgia Tech student and war veteran, claimed that the county unit system violated the Fourteenth Amendment's equal protection clause. The unit system of voting, the plaintiffs alleged, deprived citizens of more populous counties of their right to have their votes counted on the same effective basis as the votes of residents in less populous counties. Under the system, 106 votes in Georgia's largest county were equal to 1 vote in the smallest. As such, the plaintiffs argued, the county unit system constituted "a deliberate, express, and unreasonable discrimination in varying degrees against all voters residing in any but the smallest counties."[58]

Organizing as veterans, however, allowed the GVMR to employ a moral advantage in attacking Georgia's most hallowed—and vilified—political institution. "We had people survive the war who had a great sense of the fact [that] we needed to have representative government in Georgia," James Mackay later explained, and "we took the veteran line . . . to say that we had learned that life was real and life was earnest and this needed to be done."[59]

In solicitation letters sent to prospective donors, veterans in the GVMR explained their current cause in reference to their participation in the recent war. "We are a group of Georgia men and women who served in World War II," they stated, "and who are now fighting for a better state. We need your support." Pointing out that the July primary had allowed less than 45 percent of the population to elect a governor and a congressional representative, GVMR then identified the county unit system as the culprit in perpetuating corrupt minority rule. "For years [this system] has virtually disfranchised the citizens of our urban areas," GVMR members claimed, "and by dividing the state into many distinct political segments, [this] had made it possible for corrupt politicians to control the votes in our rural areas." Although "Progressive Georgians" had labored to end this system for years, "heretofore no relief has been feasible through the courts for lack of specific grievance." Now, however, that situation had changed. When the county unit system nullified the popular majorities that candidates Carmichael and Mankin had earned, "we veterans" decided to challenge its constitutionality.[60]

After all, "as servicemen we saw in other countries the poverty, corruption, and disease that were the product of minority rule," one letter explained. "Now as citizen-veterans we mean to do everything we can to wipe out minority rule back here home in Georgia." In fact, declared another, "the question of majority rule is the fundamental issue facing the world today . . . . It is the basic principle upon which this nation is founded. It is man's one guarantee against oppression. In defense of majority rule the world has just passed through the greatest conflict in the history of man." Thus, the GVMR veterans concluded, "We feel strongly that as long as this system persists Georgia is in danger of the same sort of dictatorship we went to war to defeat."[61]

As the GVMR soon discovered, however, most Georgians, as well as state and federal justices, remained unconvinced that the county unit system posed a truly imminent threat of dictatorship. The U.S. Supreme Court eventually refused to overturn a lower state court decision upholding the constitutionality of the county unit system. The GVMR subsequently spent much of its time raising funds to pay back a personal loan of $15,000 that had been borrowed to finance the lawsuits. The organization appears to have disappeared by 1950, although the fight against the county unit system did not. Throughout the 1950s a coalition of moderates, liberals, veterans, and the state CIO continued, unsuccessfully, to pursue legal action. The U.S. Supreme Court did not invalidate the county unit system in Georgia until 1962.[62]

Georgia's progressive white veterans clearly believed that democracy meant the political participation by all citizens, black and white, rich and poor, urban and rural. This principle of "one man, one vote" fulfilled the war's democratic mandate as these veterans understood it. Certainly, black veterans and citizens were the primary motivating force in Georgia behind this push to broaden the state's electorate after the war, but progressive white veterans played an important role as well. In the AVC, in Helen Douglas Mankin's reelection campaign, in the ACRC registration drive, and in the GVMR, white veterans helped to make the voter registration drives of 1946 and the attack on the county unit system that followed the central progressive achievement of Georgia's early postwar years.[63] For a short time, at least, progressive reform appeared to be alive and well in Georgia after the war.

Despite the racial revelations that came with service in the war, despite their conviction that black citizens deserved equal political rights, and despite their interracial comradeship, progressive white veterans generally refrained from attacking racial segregation itself. The GVMR adopted a careful political strategy that condemned institutions such as the county unit system as undemocratic and discriminatory but that avoided the racial implications of this attack by emphasizing its dangers to the political rights of all Georgians, black and white. And while the AVC in Georgia had an interracial membership and condemned public displays of racial intolerance and blatant discrimination, the segregated institutions it tended to challenge were the less controversial ones, such as the public library. It never approached, publicly, the question of public school segregation, the real linchpin of Jim Crow.

In their focus on political reform as the primary means for achieving democratic and racial justice, rather than a direct attack on segregation, Georgia's progressive white veterans reflected the nature of southern white liberalism at the time.[64] Most southern liberals in the postwar 1940s were gradualists, advocating racial reform through political action within established Democratic electoral channels or through legal action to invoke the Fourteenth and Fifteenth Amendments to the Constitution. They were not racial militants, committed to an all-out and immediate assault on segregation, even though many believed this system of southern apartheid ultimately was incompatible with true democracy and their vision of a progressive future for Georgia and the South.[65] Moreover, southern white liberals in this period often were not comfortable with the notion of black social equality, and few could imagine an easy end to segregation.[66]

Sidestepping the question of segregation also reflected the reform priorities of popular front and New Deal liberalism after the war.[67] Like these reformers, Georgia's progressive white veterans held to the notion that the southern masses could be united across the division of race by emphasizing broad political enfranchisement to achieve shared social and economic interests, not by addressing the question of segregation directly. From the vantage point of a Deep South state, where almost any campaign for change at the time confronted outright hostility, attacking segregation and advocating full racial equality seemed surely destructive of any hope of achieving even a modicum of what progressives wanted.

Thus, progressive white veterans (except for Joseph Rabun) usually argued for the political participation of all Georgians, blacks included, not on the grounds of their complete equality, but because this fulfilled the American democratic values they had just fought to defend. They justified their call to end the county unit system not because it had always been aimed specifically to bar blacks from political life, but because its undemocratic nature disfranchised the majority of

all citizens in Georgia, black and white, and thereby impeded economic and social progress for all. Nor did the regional and national climate encourage white
southern liberals to adopt a more radical stance. The increasingly tense postwar
atmosphere, characterized by the politics of anticommunism and racial reaction, made any campaign for progressive change in the South vulnerable to
being tarnished with the smear of racial and communist militancy, no matter
how circumspect its actual utterances on the question of black social equality
really were.

Thus, Georgia's progressive white veterans adopted a contradictory approach,
at times defending their call for democratic majority rule, but also vacillating, at
other times, between what sounded like racial progressivism on the one hand
and what smacked of racial stereotyping on the other. War veteran R. W. Hayes,
for example, like Joseph Rabun, testified against the white primary bill. "It is
thoroughly undemocratic, and it is tyranny," he argued, because it "deprives the
Negro of the right to vote in a primary, which is tantamount to an election."
After all, "if the Negro was good enough to carry a gun in the war and pay taxes,
he should vote." Thus, he pleaded with the committee, "don't sink back to the
period of 1865. Free Georgia of its Reconstruction complex." In case this argument was not compelling enough, Hayes also fell back on long-standing southern racial stereotypes to reiterate his position. The white primary bill, he warned,
also posed "the imminent danger of forcing colored citizens into a colored bloc
due to present antagonism."[68]

Such equivocation reflected the complicated reality that southern liberalism
faced after the war. Increasing attention to the cause of black civil rights at the
national level in the Truman administration and in the Democratic Party—
however limited it might have been—narrowed the space in which southern
progressives could maneuver by heightening the racial defensiveness of conservatives in the region. In 1946 President Truman sent a new package of civil rights
proposals to Congress, endorsed by the national Democratic Party. Many of
these proposals, which included desegregation of the armed forces and federal
antilynching legislation, struck at the heart of southern race relations.[69] Thus, as
the question of racial reform loomed ever larger nationally, an absolute defense
of white supremacy became much more important to southern political dis-
course regionally.[70] Moreover, in the postwar 1940s both Congress and President
Truman proved more concerned with successfully waging the Cold War than
with intervening in the state electoral prerogatives of southern Democrats, who
freely employed electoral fraud, intimidation, and violence in their own defense.[71] Finally, the anticommunist ideology that developed alongside the Cold
War increasingly targeted all progressive causes as un-American.[72] Thus, all

reformers operated within the political and racial parameters of the day, and that landscape grew increasingly difficult to navigate as the end of the decade approached.

The Georgia AVC, for example, quickly earned a reputation as a "Communist-front organization," according to the Third Army Command, which conducted domestic intelligence operations in the South in the postwar 1940s. Noting that four AVC branches were active in the Atlanta area in 1947, one report explained that "through the subterfuge of a veterans group, the Communists use the AVC to further the Party line," which, apparently, included a "'get-out-the-vote' drive" as the "top project" for 1948.[73]

Not surprisingly, few southern whites, including progressive veterans, were willing to pay the price for standing up as true racial liberals in an increasingly hostile postwar climate.[74] "It was a terrible price to pay to cut yourself off from your society, your tradition, and to be ostracized," recalled Georgia veteran Harold Fleming. "Everybody knew that was what was involved. To be a pariah. To have people shun you." Nor did these fears represent idle anxiety. "The most awful example of it was J. Waties Waring," Fleming recalled—the federal district judge who felt forced to leave South Carolina and the South after refusing to reinstate the white primary in that state. "This was the awful specter that haunted people like that," Fleming mused; "To be cut off and renounced and a pariah in their society."[75]

Beyond the likelihood of social ostracism lay the threat of real personal injury. The climate that produced the Monroe lynching in the summer of 1946 did not encourage anyone, black or white, to rebel against the established racial order. The difficulties Lucy Randolph Mason of the CIO encountered in assisting veterans in raising funds for the GVMR lawsuits, for example, confirmed that a cloud of fear and anxiety hung over the state after Eugene Talmadge's gubernatorial victory in 1946. In writing to Eleanor Roosevelt, Mason praised the efforts of Margaret Fisher and Josephine Wilkins of the SCHW in getting out the black vote in 1946 and in advising veterans in the GVMR. Mason also emphasized the need to keep this information confidential. "It is important that neither woman be identified with the court cases," she wrote, "that is not to be mentioned—nor Margaret's work in the primary." Indeed, Mason worried, "I would literally fear for [their] lives if Talmadge knew what they have promoted, or what Margaret had done to protect the Negro vote." Indeed, as she wrote to other friends, "a pall of fear hangs over this state," and the "fear of reprisals, personal and institutional[,] . . . is very real."[76]

This climate of fear and suspicion impeded the ability of veterans in the GVMR to marshal the support they needed, even among citizens who were sympathetic to their cause. While Mason "risked making the appeal on Talmadge" in her out-of-state efforts, "in Georgia the Veterans Committee can only talk about the county unit system." "It is proving very hard to raise money for the suits . . . within Georgia," Mason concluded, because "there can not be any reference to defeating Talmadge." Instead, the veterans had to emphasize "a plea for eliminating the utterly unfair and undemocratic county unit system of voting," a rather dry approach, as "it is hard to fire people with democracy or court cases."[77]

As progressive veterans of both races soon discovered, Lucy Randolph Mason was quite right. "Firing" people with democracy could be a hard sell when it involved the question of black rights in postwar Georgia. Moreover, internecine warfare among national organizations over the proper direction of American liberalism after the war dissipated the financial support for the local and state-wide campaigns connected to the SCHW, the CIO-PAC, and Operation Dixie. Antiradical and pro-growth Cold War liberals smeared the social and economic progressivism of the popular front and New Dealers with the brush of anticommunism.[78] These conflicts proved critical, since southern liberalism always depended on the support of like minds outside the South to sustain any progressive drive in such a hostile region.[79]

Along with the Great Depression and the New Deal, World War II had cracked open the door to progressive political and racial reform in Georgia, but it also generated the reactionary racial and anticommunist dynamic that quickly slammed it shut.[80] Thus, progressive white veterans failed to make an immediate difference in the lives of most black and white Georgians, in part because they still labored under the burden of their own conventional racial attitudes. They stopped short of directly attacking segregation, the institution that still defined southern daily life. But they really failed because they could not eradicate the key political institutions that still structured southern political power.

Yet, progressive white veterans had dared to read a democratic meaning into the war, to join black veterans in interracial reform crusades, and to challenge the principles and institutions of political exclusion in Georgia. They were as much a part of the war's contradictory racial impact in Georgia as their black counterparts in the GVL or the ACRC. They helped to infuse postwar southern liberalism with a democratic ideology drawn from the war, one that connected these events on the ground in postwar Georgia to the national and regional drive to sustain and expand New Deal liberalism. Together, these streams of postwar progressivism further disrupted Georgia's postwar political and racial stability.

Thus, at least in Georgia, southern whites were not as unified at the war's end on the political and racial questions of the day as they would later become. There were whites in Georgia, particularly veterans, who did interpret majority rule to include black political participation, although they stopped far short of advocating full equality. This was apostasy enough, however, since any division at all in white ranks alarmed southern reactionaries, who grew even more convinced that the lines of racial separation in Georgia were in imminent danger of being permanently breached. Ironically, the troops marshaled to close those gaps and to deflect this threat were also veterans of the Second World War.

GEORGIA'S REACTIONARY veterans were just as disturbed by what they found at home after the war as their progressive counterparts, but not at all for the same reasons. In fact, after months and years spent eagerly anticipating the end of the war, many veterans found coming home to be an unsettling experience. James Covert, for example, who was thirteen years old at the war's end, remembered how different his father and brother seemed when they returned from the Pacific theater. They were not only older, he recalled, but quieter and sad. "They were the winners, the victors," he reflected, "they had fought the war bravely, yet they were disillusioned." Grateful to have survived the war and to be reunited with families and friends, World War II veterans often were disappointed initially with what they found at home. "They had been out there on the front lines [and] had made great sacrifices," Covert stated, "then coming back they found there were not enough houses, and the jobs weren't as plentiful as they thought." As a result, "a period of disenchantment set in."[81]

Part of that disillusionment may have derived from the inflated expectation that immediate prosperity was in store for returning veterans. American corporations bombarded civilians and GIs during the war with advertisements designed to build up postwar consumer demand, fueling the "public's dreams" of the "consumers' paradise" that only awaited the war's end. This promise of postwar affluence became the "obsession" of Americans who anticipated a "pursuit of individual prosperity in the midst of apparently endless economic growth."[82] At the same time, American servicemen and women, particularly from the South, entered the military with the memory of the Depression still fresh in their minds. Many came from communities that had not benefited immediately from the military spending that came with war mobilization. As a result, soldiers and sailors anticipated the end of the war and their subsequent return to civilian life with a mixture of both optimism and anxiety. This emotion formed an important backdrop to the reactionary response some southern white veterans exhibited to the social, demographic, and racial changes accelerated by the war at home.

During the war, researchers for the Army Research Branch discovered that jobs and employment security were the primary concerns servicemen expressed about returning home. A survey of overseas returnees and soldiers stationed in the United States in May 1945, for example, found that one-fifth "worried a lot" about what kind of work they would do after the war, and almost 50 percent "worried a little." Yet, while almost 80 percent thought "most soldiers" would find it "very hard" or "fairly hard" to obtain the kind of jobs they wanted, only 46 percent felt that they personally would have that difficulty. And out of 27,000 officers and enlisted men, 64 percent in 1944 had definite job or educational plans for the future, with a majority expecting to improve their status. Like most civilians, soldiers were concerned about the possibility of a postwar depression (56 percent expected one), but they also hoped to achieve a better standard of living when they returned.[83]

In the first year after the war, however, veterans returning to Georgia found plenty of reason to be disappointed. Economic observers, industrial developers, and the media nervously predicted in 1945 that the state would weather the trials of reconversion easily. "While it is important to not be too optimistic," stated the *Atlanta Constitution* in June 1945, "many practical Atlantans feel sure that this area will meet the shock of transition from war to peace with less pain than many other areas." Specifically, "there will be some sort of job . . . available to everyone wanting to work."[84] Soon after v-j Day, however, such perky optimism evolved quickly into anxious hand-wringing. In September 1946 the State War Manpower Commission announced that there were over 36,016 displaced war workers in Georgia, most of whom were seeking work comparable in pay, skill, and training to what they had done during the war. Governor Herman Talmadge told the Georgia General Assembly in January 1947 that "more than 60,000 workers lost their jobs in Georgia when war plants closed and many other workers have suffered temporary unemployment." In addition, "about 350,000 Georgia veterans have been discharged."[85] Nor did most returning veterans want to take jobs in traditional low-wage industries in Georgia, such as textiles, garment production, and lumbering, even if those openings were more plentiful. Thus, reported a local newspaper in Douglas County in 1946, "the volume of unemployed ex-servicemen . . . is still unusually high."[86]

Most white war workers and veterans eventually would find suitable jobs once the economy reconverted, either in Georgia or elsewhere, but in 1946 that outcome was not apparent. The initial months of reconversion proved to be uncertain and turbulent for many Georgians as canceled war contracts displaced thousands of workers just as servicemen and women returned home. Not surprisingly, veterans throughout the state and region worried about their prospects for the future in communities struggling to make an uneasy transition to peacetime.[87]

The scarcity of housing that plagued even small towns proved especially frustrating. A sailor from Hapeville, Georgia, noted in April 1946 while on leave that "since returning to the States I've been in quite a few states to find prosperity in all but Georgia." In other states, he grumbled, "wages are triple and prices are under the best of control." Yet, housing in Georgia cost far more than elsewhere. W. F. Powers voiced similar disappointment, asking "isn't there anyone in our Federal, State, County or City forms of government who can do something constructive about the deplorable housing shortage?" During the next war, he warned, "a great many ex-GIs ... might stay at home and make a lot of money, or at least provide themselves with a roof over their heads, and let Congress find others to do the fighting and dying."[88]

Difficulty in readjusting to civilian life was hardly unique to southern white veterans. Ex-servicemen and women throughout the United States experienced problems, at least initially, in reintegrating into postwar society.[89] Conditions that could be found elsewhere, however, had special racial implications in the Deep South. White veterans encountered these challenges just as campaigns for progressive reform were adding to the destabilization of the state's economic, political, and social environment. In this context, many white veterans were quick to construe the problems ex-servicemen and women everywhere experienced in specifically racial terms. This interpretation had important implications for the state's postwar politics.

Georgia's veterans returned to a South buffeted by the many changes of the past two decades. A wave of labor strikes crippled important sectors of the national and regional economy in 1945 and 1946. Meanwhile, black citizens throughout Georgia organized well-publicized campaigns to register black voters and to defend their rights to equal economic opportunity. State and U.S. Supreme Court decisions brought down the white primary in Georgia, overturned segregation in interstate travel, and targeted discriminatory registrars for denying African Americans the right to register and vote, all in 1946. National liberal organizations and commentators, from the B'nai B'rith Anti-Defamation League to the American Veterans Committee, kept up a steady barrage of criticism attacking southern economic, racial, and political practices and calling for a permanent FEPC. Meanwhile, the CIO mounted an energetic postwar campaign to organize over a million southern workers.[90]

Georgia's reactionary veterans interpreted these currents of change as a dangerous threat to the inviolability of white supremacy. If the war tended to foster among progressive veterans a universalized definition of citizenship, it had the opposite effect on many others. Many white southern veterans took into the war a gendered and racialized sense of citizenship that intensified, rather than weakened, under the onslaught of the war. Combined with the postwar turmoil that highlighted black and progressive challenges to conservative white rule in Georgia, this notion of racialized citizenship led these veterans in a reactionary direction. They mounted a postwar racial tirade that expressed a matrix of social fears, economic and political anxiety, and their own sense of civic entitlement.[91]

The understanding of citizenship that motivated these reactionary veterans evolved from a notion of white manhood that had emerged in the late nineteenth century, particularly in the South. This notion defined "manhood" as the capability and duty of white men to assert white male authority. It understood "citizenship" as the assertion of this authority—of the ability of white men to rule the domestic and public spheres and to defend both from incursions by black men and their presumed craving for social equality as an avenue of access to white women.[92] This conglomerate of white prejudice, hatred, anxiety, and conjecture provided a foundation for the system of segregation that evolved after Reconstruction to sustain the formal separation of whites from blacks and to maintain white dominance and black subordination. Challenges to this system, whether merely perceived or actually real, constituted a threat to the entire structure of political and domestic relations premised on the predominance of white male authority.[93] Black claims for voting rights, for example, or any assertion of independence represented an attack on southern domestic and political security that, in turn, called upon southern white men—as the key citizens in this structure of power—to respond. Thus, many southern white men were predisposed to view black assertiveness as a threat to the racial sanctity of the domestic and political spheres on which their very understanding of themselves as men, as whites, and as citizens depended. Southern white servicemen took into the war a complicated mixture of male, racial, and political identities.

For many of Georgia's veterans, World War II strengthened, rather than undermined, this notion of racialized male citizenship. First, military service tended to augment their sense of maleness. Although women did serve in the military during the war, including in overseas duty, going to war still constituted a largely masculine endeavor, particularly because combat remained the prerogative and duty of men. Second, the war accentuated the importance of citizenship—of the willingness and obligation to fulfill this civic duty in a time of national need. Meeting this obligation by joining the service and going to war, by potentially risking one's own physical well-being to defend the nation and assert its interests, became a source of pride for men, who often returned with an enhanced sense of personal self-esteem and their own importance as citizens. Third, in putting this premium on citizenship, service in the war also inflated servicemen's expectations of what their participation should mean when the war was over. If one proved willing to put his life on the line for the country, then it followed that recognition and reward for this service would come when a veteran returned home.[94] All of these elements underscored the racialized definition of citizenship that these men had carried off to war. White men were citizens, they believed; black men were not. White men executed the duties of citizenship—asserting male and racial authority in the domestic and political spheres; black men could not.

Thus, the war turned out a bevy of southern white servicemen with an enhanced sense of their own importance as white men and as veterans, as white citizens and as southerners. However, the war also challenged this exclusive understanding of citizenship. After all, white men were not the only Americans serving in the war. Although they remained in segregated units, thousands of black men served in the war as well, often providing critical support to white troops and even participating in combat in some key engagements. Naturally, this service challenged the notion that only white men could fulfill the obligations of citizenship. Moreover, since blacks did join the effort, they would also have a claim on the national conscience to reward that service upon their return, which created quite a conundrum for the Jim Crow South. Finally, black servicemen also found their own sense of manhood and citizenship enhanced by participation in the war, and they regularly expressed a racial assertiveness that intensified southern white veterans' anxiety about what the postwar racial implications of the war would be.[95]

That the war both strengthened the notion of racialized citizenship and challenged its meaningfulness was evident in the tensions that erupted between blacks and whites overseas and at home for the duration of the war. Black troops suffered a barrage of discrimination and mistreatment from whites in a Jim Crow military; white soldiers and sailors, particularly from the South, attacked black troops overseas over fraternization with European women; and rioting and fighting between black and white servicemen at home frequently broke out on military bases and in the towns that surrounded them throughout the South from the beginning of the war right to the very end.[96] Thus, as one scholar has found in her study of the participation of white veterans in the Columbia, Tennessee, race riot in 1946, military service itself could heighten white veterans' hostility toward blacks after the war.[97] The war accentuated the racial, male, and political identities of both white and black veterans who served. They were bound to clash when they returned home.

The war thus primed the pump for reactionary veterans' postwar racial tirades. The homefront, however, provided the context for their political expression. Disillusioned by their own difficulties in reintegrating to civilian life and disturbed by the mounting black and progressive challenge to the political and racial status quo, Georgia's reactionary veterans were more than ready to register their anger, anxiety, and sense of racial and civic entitlement on the postwar southern landscape.

Georgia's reactionary veterans joined hate groups and supported political candidates who were quite willing to explain veterans' postwar predicament in specifically racial terms, both provoking their racial anxiety and invoking their sense of civic obligation to defend the ramparts of white privilege and power. African Americans and their alleged "Yankee-Jewish-scalawag" allies made handy scapegoats. More than one white veteran came to believe that suitable jobs were scarce because the NAACP and the FEPC allegedly gave blacks priority in employment. Housing shortages reportedly grew from the scheming of black families to take over white neighborhoods. In fact, hate groups moved speedily to capitalize on these postwar anxieties. Samuel Green, Grand Dragon of the newly revived Ku Klux Klan in Georgia, boasted of having around "25,000 Klansmen in good standing right now," many of whom "seem to be men returning from the war."[98] This was more than a public relations stunt. According to one scholar, postwar Georgia quickly emerged as the "stronghold" of the 1940s Klan, with a klavern in each one of the state's 159 counties by 1949.[99] Veterans appeared in a number of these chapters.

Stetson Kennedy, an investigative reporter who infiltrated the Georgia Klan after the war, found veterans to be active members. One Klansman told Kennedy in February 1946 that "about a fourth" of the thirty Klansmen at a recent meeting of Atlanta Klavern #297 "wore veterans insignia"; and Kennedy estimated that from one-half to two-thirds of the members in Klaverns #1 and #297 were veterans, "judging from the amount of insignia displayed." In fact, "according to the application reports read at (a) recent meeting," a member informed Kennedy, "approximately one half of those to be initiated at Stone Mountain are veterans of World War II."[100]

Nor was the Klan the only hate group hoping to cash in on white veterans' postwar disenchantment. The neo-fascist Columbians, Inc., sprang up in Atlanta around 1946 as the twisted creation of Homer Loomis, a northerner, veteran, and inveterate hatemonger. Dedicated to promoting white Protestant Americanism by denouncing blacks, Jews, communists, unionists, and foreigners, the Columbians attracted around two hundred members, including a "handful" of World War II veterans. This prompted the AVC in Atlanta to offer a blistering condemnation of the Columbians, directed specifically to those members who had fought in the recent war. "There are veterans in the Columbians. Men who fought as we did; men who fired guns and learned fear, as we did," exclaimed the

AVC. "Did these men, all through the long battles, think they were on the wrong side? What did they think they were doing in the trenches? What reason did they give themselves for being on a large, lonely and tormented ocean?" "Fundamental errors exist in our system and in our education policies," the AVC concluded, "when men who have fought in a war for freedom can become, overnight, zealots in the cause of tyranny."[101]

Stetson Kennedy also infiltrated the Columbians organization and confirmed the active participation of recently returned war veterans. Columbian Bill Couch, reported Kennedy, was an army officer on terminal leave "drawing the $20 per week allotted unemployed war veterans by the federal government." Often appearing at meetings "in full uniform wearing the Columbians lightning bolt silver emblem on his shirt pocket," Couch told Kennedy that "if the Columbians could afford his services full time, he would like nothing better than to work for them." In fact, Kennedy concluded in October 1946, Couch worked "virtually fulltime on the movement." A Columbian named Zimmerlee, a drafting student at Georgia Tech and a former officer bombardier in the Eighth Army Air Force, also wore a "G.I. shirt and trousers" at Columbian events. At one October meeting, several Columbians appeared in GI uniforms with armbands sporting the group's trademark thunderbolt emblem. Other active southern veterans included R. I. Whitman and Lanier Waller, both arrested by Atlanta police in the fall of 1946 for inciting racial disturbances.[102]

The reactionary organizations that white veterans joined especially ranted about apparent transgressions of the domestic racial divide, namely, any threat to the social and sexual prerogatives of white men by black men. According to Klan Grand Dragon Green, for example, the new Klan of Georgia was built on four basic principles that included the duty to "protect the home and the chastity of our white womanhood."[103] Stetson Kennedy concluded that "the Negro vote," tension "between Negroes and whites, heightened by the postwar era," "returning Negro veterans, and [the] reported sale of 'white' property to Negroes" brought veterans and civilians into the Klan rank and file.[104] In April 1946, moreover, a Klansman reported to Klavern #1 "that British war brides were living with their American Negro husbands in the Queensferry section of Atlanta." Another told of "whites and Negroes . . . living under the same roof in the 300 block of Piedmont Avenue," and at a subsequent meeting a Grand Klaliff heard a report that "Negroes had moved into 8-unit apartment building occupied by whites on Pulliam Street." In each case, the presiding officer directed the members present to investigate and take "appropriate action."[105]

Similarly, though the Columbians railed against anyone they deemed to be un-American, much of their rhetoric and all of their activities targeted black

and white southerners who allegedly transgressed the color line.[106] When joining, members signed pledge cards promising to contribute an amount each
week "to continue the fight for the American white working man" and to "effectively separate the white and black races."[107] At meetings and rallies, commented
one writer, the Columbians shouted "keep this a white man's country." When
leader and co-founder Emory Burke spoke at such a rally in Fairburn, Georgia,
an informant reported that "his thesis was the necessity for a white Anglo-Saxon
organization to maintain white supremacy in the South, Nation, and world."
"Our heroes didn't die in Europe to give Negroes the right to marry our wives,"
Burke reportedly trumpeted, then he boasted that "we [the Columbians] have
grown because we have helped you with your problem niggers."[108]

The Columbians' message appeared to resonate particularly in white neighborhoods that bordered on expanding black communities, reflecting the racial
tensions that attended the postwar housing scarcity. Based on an informant's reports, one writer concluded that many of the two hundred or so Atlantans in
the Columbians were mill employees who "lived on streets adjacent to Negro
communities." The Columbians inflamed tensions in these areas by parading
with sound trucks publicizing upcoming meetings and rallies. One such effort
turned out around two hundred citizens. "The fact that the Columbians were
able to rally 200 persons," an informant known as "Ned" concluded, "is an indication of the reality of the issue of interracial housing friction which they are
exploiting." At one meeting, "Ned" overheard a newly recruited member urge a
prospective signee to join by explaining, "It's to keep the niggers down."[109]

Thus, the Columbians specialized in policing the lines of residential segregation.[110] From a truck flying both the Columbian and American flags at an outdoor rally in early September 1946, Hoke Gewinner "charged specifically that
the reason veterans cannot find housing is that unscrupulous real estate dealers are selling white property to Negroes, thus forcing all whites in the neighborhood to move."[111] In an interview with Tom Ham of the *Atlanta Journal*,
Columbian leader Homer Loomis revealed plans to bisect the city into racial
zones. On a large map, Loomis pointed out the houses and sections targeted by
the Columbians. "Here on Ashby street the negroes are driving a wedge toward
Bankhead Avenue," Loomis showed Ham, "and here on Chestnut they're getting
another wedge started." In fact, Loomis declared, "the objective of the enemy
here is to cut off this Western Heights section—and make it an 'island' of whites
surrounded by Negroes." In response, Loomis explained, "our mission is to cut
off those wedges." Indicating a red line that cut across the map, Loomis noted
"we've drawn the color line here . . . . [T]hat's the line we're going to hold." After
putting up posters designating the areas as zoned for whites only, Loomis

claimed, "we've called on Negroes . . . explaining that they're not wanted there."
The Columbians would buy back property "sold by greedy indiscriminate, real
estate operators" and arrange to sell it to white families. Thus, Loomis boasted,
"we have block leaders, community leaders in the areas we are working on.
We're organized to the last degree."[112] Moreover, the Columbians planned to cir-
culate a list of white real estate dealers and homeowners who had ostensibly "sold
out." One list announced that "the following is a group of real estate men . . .
destroying white sections by selling to the nigro [sic]. They betray their own race
and lay the foundation for serious racial trouble for the sake of money." Another
declared that "the following is a list of white men and women who sold out to
negroes forgetting obligations to their white community." "What they did once,"
the Columbians warned, "they might do again when they have moved into your
neighborhood."[113]

This pledge to enforce the lines of racial separation was no idle threat. "In all
of his years of experience," an informant reported, "he had never seen an outfit
as radical and potentially dangerous as the Columbians." Noting their general
belligerence, thuggishness, and propensity for weapons, he concluded that the
Columbians were "a dangerous bunch of hoodlums who will stop at nothing in
order to gain publicity and win adherents."[114]

In the fall of 1946, members of the Columbians, including veterans, engaged
in a brief but intense campaign of intimidation and violence against African
Americans living on the fringes of declining white neighborhoods. The first of
these "terrorist activities" occurred on October 28 when three Columbians black-
jacked a young man named Clifford Hines. Police arrested James Ralph Childers
when they discovered the Columbian insignia in his pocket. They also arrested
the black victim even though white bystanders swore the attack had been un-
provoked. Once in custody, Childers told police that he had been assigned to the
area to "protect" a white family from "Negroes." Homer Loomis admitted charg-
ing Childers with "guarding" the home of a white family and to "hold off" any
"Negroes" trying to move in until the police arrived, but he denied telling him
to attack Hines or anyone else. Nevertheless, the Columbians rewarded Childers
with a ceremony and a "Medal of Honor."[115]

A few days later, Frank Jones, a black Atlantan, encountered these neo-fascist
regulators when he and his family attempted to move into a recently purchased
home on Garibaldi Street in the Ashby Street section of town. Bordered on one
side by a vacant lot and on the other by a white family's home, the house was located in a neighborhood that was already 50 percent black. When Jones arrived,
he found a sticker on the front door sporting the Columbians' thunderbolt em-
blem that demarcated his new home for the "White Community only." Accord-

ing to various reports, veterans James Akins and R. I. Whitman, along with other Columbians, picketed in front with signs that read "White Community only" and "Zoned for Whites" and prevented Jones from entering the house. At the same time, several cars of Columbians paraded up and down the street. At one point, someone telephoned Loomis at Columbian headquarters for instructions while he was meeting with a reporter from the *Atlanta Journal.* "Just stand around," Loomis apparently directed them, and "if the negro tries to move in, just stand there on the doorstep and don't give ground." If the police arrived, however, Loomis advised them to give way because "that will put the burden on the police." Shortly thereafter, Loomis left the headquarters and appeared on Garibaldi Street as the conflict escalated. When the police did arrive, they arrested several Columbians, including Loomis, Akins, and Whitman for disorderly conduct and inciting to riot.[116] Authorities later charged Whitman and Loomis with illegal possession of explosives and usurping police power.[117] Columbian veteran Zimmerlee, however, flatly denied that any member had tried to start a riot. "The nigger had been told not to move in, and he wasn't going to," Zimmerlee explained, but "the police forced them to move on in."[118]

Georgia's reactionary veterans also feared the prospect of competing with blacks for jobs amid the uncertainties of postwar reconversion. A study of the Klan in Athens, Georgia, in the 1920s defines the membership as mostly men and women in transition from the working class into the lower middle class. This group proved to be exceptionally jealous of the privileges and status that only recently separated their station in life from the lot of most blacks in Athens.[119] In post–World War II Georgia, the Klan and the Columbians similarly appeared to draw largely on urban whites who were in close contact and even competition with blacks for economic opportunity and housing.

The Columbians reportedly found their "ready prey among the dispossessed, the displaced, the disadvantaged," particularly those "yearning to break the fetters of a drab world into which a neglectful society has thrust them." Working as a cook in a small diner after drifting from job to job since the age of thirteen, seventeen-year-old James Childers admired the "Nazi-like regalia" of the Columbians who frequented his restaurant. "I liked their uniform so I asked about joining up," he recalled, and he was told "[you] have to be three things to join: hate the nigger, hate the Jew, and have $3." "I didn't have anything against the Jews until I got in the Columbians," Childers admitted; "I never really did hate them." African Americans, however, were a different matter: "I just don't like niggers. I don't want them moving next door."[120] Police reporter Keeler McCartney found that many members came from workers' communities near the Exposition Cotton and Fulton Bag and Cotton Mills in Atlanta.[121] R. I. Whitman, a member of the Columbians and an ex-serviceman, worked as a truck driver and a mill worker but, as McCartney concluded, "his family has never been very far from starvation."[122]

"Klavalier Klubs" carried out the Georgia Klan's racist postwar agenda. Stetson Kennedy gained access to this "inner circle," which he described as the Klan's "storm trooper arm" where "frustration, cruelty, and alcoholism showed on every face."[123] Most important, Kennedy reported in May 1946 that around "half of the applicants" to join this "inner circle" were "said to be veterans of World War II." These veterans were particularly disturbed by the economic competition that developed with the growth of the urban black population.[124] In Atlanta, as the city's infrastructure, business community, and public services struggled to catch up with the war-induced population boom, a sometimes vicious contest emerged between the city's only licensed taxi company and new "fly-by-night" car-for-hire services, which employed both black and white drivers. As the Yellow Cab Company struggled to maintain a legal monopoly over taxi services, sixty-six of its white drivers in the local Klan applied in May 1946 to join the Klavalier Klub.[125]

In her assessment of the Willie Earle lynching in South Carolina after the war, Kari Frederickson identifies direct economic competition with blacks to explain the participation of white taxicab drivers and veterans in Earle's murder. A slump in the taxicab industry in 1946 and 1947 made it especially difficult for cabbies to "avoid black patrons," Frederickson argues, because it was "not economically feasible to do so." Moreover, "the instability inherent in this type of employment, compounded by the fact that many of these cab drivers were veterans returning to a tight labor market and a tense racial atmosphere, heightened their propensity to wield force to maintain the color line."[126]

The same dynamic made black cab drivers in Atlanta a target of the Klavalier Klub. The explanations these Klansmen gave for their activities, however, also reflected the usual bugaboo of racial-sexual fear. In late April 1946, for example, the Klavaliers claimed to have assisted "county and city police" in arresting "a number of Negro cab drivers who were hauling white passengers, contrary to law." At one meeting, a Klavalier leader described the alleged kidnapping and murder of a black cab driver for "molesting" white women at a downtown bus terminal. Members of the Atlanta police department who also belonged to Klavern #1 reportedly cleaned the taxicab after the murder to wipe out incriminating fingerprints. At another klavern meeting, Klansmen applauded when an Atlanta policeman proudly told of recently killing his "thirteenth nigger in the line of duty."[127]

As the extent of these activities indicated, a fear of racial reform, of black competition, and of black social equality motivated many white veterans in Georgia far more than did any conviction in a war-induced democratic imperative. If progressive veterans held a notion that political citizenship applied to all Americans, reactionary veterans countered with a sense of civic entitlement that construed political participation as the prerogative of whites only. Georgia's reactionary veterans thus regarded black incursions into the political realm as a direct challenge to their own personal status and power, thereby undermining the racialized citizenship on which white male identity rested. This was a threat these veterans felt entitled and obligated to combat.

The event that first sparked their political reaction was the election of Helen Douglas Mankin in February 1946 to Atlanta's Fifth District seat in the U.S. House of Representatives. As a special election to fill an unexpired term, this election took place under the auspices of federal electoral rules rather than the county unit system. This enabled a coalition of blacks, progressives, and workers in Fulton County—the precursor to the All Citizens Registration Committee—to elect New Deal liberal Mankin over Thomas Camp, a conservative railroad lobbyist.[128] For conservatives, the role played by Atlanta's black citizens in the Ashby Street district in affording Mankin this victory rang "like a firebell in the night," announcing the potential power of a black electorate no longer circumscribed by a racially exclusive primary.[129] This fear of the black vote grew as Mankin's election immediately produced the ACRC and the efforts of black and white veterans to increase black registration in time for the summer Democratic primaries.[130]

While conservative Democrats in DeKalb County schemed to defeat Mankin by placing the Fifth District election back under the county unit system, Eugene Talmadge seized the opportunity to run for a fourth term as governor of Georgia.[131] Campaigning largely on a white supremacy platform, Talmadge promised to reinstate the white primary, preserve the county unit system, and generally keep black Georgians "in their place." Shortly before the July primary, Talmadge made a live radio address before a crowd at an outdoor rally that demonstrated his typical demagoguery. "I want to thank the *Atlanta Journal* for comin' out about two months ago and statin' it plainly that Talmadge was the only candidate for governor in this race that was champion' [*sic*] the restoration of a Democratic white primary in Georgia," he announced, adding that "it's the law this year [that] some of the nigras [*sic*] will vote . . . [but] if I'm your governor, they won't vote in our white primary the next four years."[132]

Talmadge's race-baiting campaign attracted veterans who were uncomfortable with the direction in which Georgia appeared to be heading after the war. Organizations in which reactionary white veterans were active participants named

Talmadge as their candidate of choice. Both the Columbians and the Ku Klux Klan called on members to get out the vote in order to defend white power from the incursions of a Yankee-liberal-black coalition. Ironically, this response meant that both progressive *and* reactionary veterans worked to boost voter turnout in the 1946 elections.

While the Columbians disclaimed any formal "political alliance" with Eugene Talmadge or James C. Davis, Helen Douglas Mankin's opponent, they announced their support by repeating their social and racial fears, promising to "fight with them against the forces that are seeking to break down all seggregation [*sic*] barriers that should be maintained to prevent mongrelization of the white Caucasian race." In fact, "the Columbian Party is going to act within the framework of the Democratic Party and bring these issues to a vote," declared one Columbian leader, "and the niggers and Jews will pay the check." Pointing out that "a Negro block vote elected Helen Douglas Mankin to Congress," Hoke Gewinner "urged everyone to join the Columbians and organize on a precinct basis to fight the Negro block vote." "There are only two ways to fight this thing," he pronounced, "with ballots and with bullets. We are going to try the ballots first."[133]

The Atlanta Klan agreed, reported Stetson Kennedy, who concluded that "Talmadge is definitely the candidate for Governor who is supported by the Klan." James V. Carmichael, his main opponent, "has been condemned for his condoning things in favor [of] the Negro" during the war as manager of the Bell bomber plant in Marietta. Indeed, the KKK wanted to "wake up the people to their need of a klan and to recognize their fight politically for candidates who stand for white supremacy [and] to encourage their fight against social equality and the FEPC."[134]

In direct response to the unprecedented voter registration and turnout of black citizens in Atlanta and other areas, a "desperate effort is being made in every local to get the [white] ones not registered to a registering place." Klansmen "have pledged to haul unregistered members and their families to the registrars and also to get them to the polls on election day." At one meeting, the Grand Cyclops of Atlanta Klavern #297 read "a request that was sent by Talmadge to the different Klans to get out and get the people registered so they can vote to save Georgia and white Supremacy." Grand Dragon Green warned members that "'Negroes, Jews, unions, Communists, and businessmen' are supporting James Carmichael for governor, and the KKK will have to exert every effort to elect Gene Talmadge."[135] In fact, according to Kennedy, "the Talmadge forces have been busy setting up 'White Supremacy Clubs' in many counties, which are tantamount to Klan klaverns." Club members pledged that "my political disposition is that of an aroused white citizen of Georgia, which means that I breathe no ill winds of hatred against any race, color, or religious creed, but believe that the rule of our government should be left entirely in the hands of white citizens."[136]

Individual veterans publicly avowed their political allegiance to Talmadge and their hostility to Mankin. "I am glad I live in Georgia and not in Fulton County," proclaimed Guy Alford, a combat veteran from Emmanuel County; "Helen Douglas Mankin is the biggest political freak or fraud in Georgia [and] certainly has never added or reflected any credit on the Democratic party in Fulton County."[137] J. M. Jones of Ellaville, Georgia, wrote to the Muscogee County Talmadge Club in June 1946 to announce, "I am a disabled veteran and I will be working hard for Gene untill [sic] all the votes are counted."[138] Wimbric Walker, a war veteran from Talmadge's home county of Telfair, appeared regularly with Talmadge on the stump, and other veterans voiced their support of the "Red-Gallused Man" on the pages of state and local newspapers.[139]

In response to an Atlanta columnist's condemnation of Talmadge, Jimmy Gaston of Atlanta declared, "I have awakened while in Guam, Iwo Jima, and Okinawa. I was there fighting the same as you." Pronouncing that many veteran organizations were "behind Mr. Talmadge," Gaston went on to voice his own support. "I saw men die and I know what it means to lose buddies and friends," he wrote; "I am a veteran of many South Pacific invasions and I and all of my friends are for Mr. Talmadge."[140] Still in the navy in Norfolk, Virginia, J. D. Dickens "watched the recent gubernatorial race with considerable interest" and decided that "the only man in the race that could qualify in a real Southern Democratic primary was Eugene Talmadge." As a sailor for the past 5 ½ years, Dickens hoped "to come back to Georgia in the Spring and I'm glad that Old Gene will be around for the next four years."[141] William Tyson of Nashville, Georgia, agreed. Taking issue with a claim in an *Atlanta Journal* editorial that "'the boys from Georgia who gave their lives in World War II would not approve of such men as Ed Rivers and Eugene Talmadge,'" Tyson proclaimed that "these boys died so we could be free to go to the polls and vote for the man we think most worthy of holding office!" Tyson, who served in the army, had "lost many friends in this war," and his two brothers were wounded in the European theater. "We three brothers will go to the polls and vote for Eugene Talmadge!" he promised, and "we will also talk to our many good friends and pull every vote for Mr. Talmadge possible." After all, "we feel its our duty because we believe Mr. Talmadge is the only man in the race worthy of being governor of Georgia."[142]

These veterans made it very clear what kind of "worthiness" they meant. "I am a veteran of World War One and Two," wrote Christopher De Mendoza to Prince Preston, a Georgia congressional candidate and fellow veteran. "Before I vote . . . I want to write to you . . . to open an outlet in my chest to let out what is in it." Mendoza hoped to vote for Preston "because you are a veteran as I am," but he refrained from avowing his unconditional support. Admitting that Preston's opponent in the First Congressional District race, incumbent Hugh Peterson, had done little for veterans over the years, Mendoza also noted that "one sure thing I know is that Peterson has been fighting in Washington against the F.E.P.C. and social equality." And that, he explained to Preston, "is exactly what I want you to do." To Mendoza, Georgia "was the best state in the Union [until] the influence coming down here from the North" turned the state into a haven for "Negroes lovers." "It seems to me that the white people are tired and disgusted of been [sic] white and now they want to turn into Negroes." Yet, he charitably conceded, "this filth is not from Georgia but this filth come down from the North." "Today we are not living in a democratic country," he continued, "but under a dictatorship like Germany, Russia, Italy, and Japan." In fact, "we are slaves under the dictatorship of a bunch of fools in the Congress and 'Negroes lovers' in the Supreme Court." While "in the First World War we used to sing 'The Yanks Are Coming,'" Mendoza bitterly concluded, "now we are going to sing 'The negroes are coming.'"[143]

All of the candidates in Georgia's 1946 elections campaigned on platforms that covered a variety of issues, from road improvements to teacher pay raises.[144] Veterans' support of the "Red-Gallused Man," however, largely hinged on Talmadge's defense of Georgia's racially exclusive political traditions. "Eugene Talmadge will be elected governor of Georgia," predicted Don Prince of Atlanta, "because the veterans who hail from this state will vote almost in a bloc for the man who has kept faith with them." In fact, he concluded, "a person must be very naive to believe that the white primary is not the main and vital issue in this present campaign."[145]

A group of eighteen World War II veterans, all students at the University of Georgia, accompanied Talmadge when he formally entered the gubernatorial race. The group even paid his $500 entrance fee. Veteran Frank Flanders, the treasurer of a veterans' political group at the university, issued a formal statement in support of Talmadge. "We know that if Talmadge is elected governor," Flanders explained, "the Democratic White Primary will be restored and preserved." If Talmadge lost, however, his opponents would turn the state over "to the Political Action Committee (of the CIO), Negroes, and carpetbaggers."[146] At one Talmadge rally in East Point near downtown Atlanta, W. W. Yergin, a U.S. Marine veteran of the Wake Island detachment, spoke to the Fulton County Talmadge Club. He introduced Talmadge as "a truly great Georgian" who "today is fighting the good fight for all Georgia against a vicious, insidious, sinister combination of outside subversive influences . . . striving to sabotage our time-hallowed southern institutions, beginning with the assault on our white primary."[147]

A group of ex-servicemen in Coffee County ran campaign advertisements in the local newspaper with a picture of Talmadge alongside a large headline that read "Georgia Can Restore the Democratic White Primary and Retain the County-Unit System." "Talmadge leads the fight to keep outsiders from running Georgia," these "Ex-GIS of Coffee County" declared. They went on to explain that if Talmadge were elected governor, recent court rulings could not defeat the white primary in Georgia because he had promised to remove all primary regulations from state jurisdiction.[148] As an added precaution, they also advocated writing the county unit system into the state constitution, where it could not be abolished without the approval of three-fourths of the state Democratic convention, an assembly generally dominated by rural conservatives. And in case these arguments were not compelling enough, these veterans spelled out the consequences of a Talmadge defeat. "Here is what will happen if our Democratic white primary is not restored and preserved," the ad read. "The Negroes will vote in a block" and dictate to white citizens who should be elected. "Proof of this was shown in the recent election in the Fifth Congressional District," they proclaimed, "where the vote of one Negro ward carried the election." "The same thing can happen all over Georgia," they argued, "if Negroes are allowed to vote in the Democratic White Primary and if the [C]ounty Unit System is abolished." Remember, the veterans warned, "there are forty-seven counties in Georgia in which the Negroes out number the whites!" "One thing is certain," another veteran-sponsored advertisement declared, "if Georgia, now feeling progressive tremblors that could shake the entire South, elects Talmadge Governor again, not even a Supreme Court ruling will prevent a return to 'White Supremacy' as only Talmadge can support it." Thus, "Preserve our Southern Traditions and Heritage . . . . Vote for Talmadge and a White Primary!"[149]

Nor did these veterans retire their efforts once the 1946 election season ended, moving quickly to voice their public support of Herman Talmadge's controversial bids for governor in both 1947 and 1948. "We the undersigned voters and citizens of Paulding County, Georgia, wish you to know that we are heartily in favor of the white primary law and the County Unit System for the State of Georgia," wrote a group of citizens, including veterans Cecil Wells, Roland Denton, and William Dodd, to the Honorable Fred Hand, Speaker of the Georgia House. The petitioners endorsed Herman Talmadge for governor because "he is the man to carry out the policies upon which his lamented father was elected . . . by a majority of the WHITE voters of this state."[150] W. C. Plott agreed: "I am an ex-soldier of World War II and also was reared on a farm [and] I am a strong defender of both Herman Talmadge and his father, Eugene."[151] In Floyd County, Georgia, over three hundred veterans signed a petition endorsing Herman Talmadge's moral and legal right to the governorship in 1947, explaining that "we ... who fought for fairness and justice in the world have a firm determination to bring about fairness and justice in Georgia."[152]

In the end, reactionary veterans proved much more successful in postwar Georgia than their progressive counterparts. As the national political climate after 1946 grew increasingly charged by the Cold War politics of anticommunism and increasing national criticism of southern segregation, political events in the South revolved more and more around the defense of white supremacy. In 1946 and 1947, for example, the Talmadge faction won control of state government, and the white primary bill passed in the Georgia General Assembly. In 1948 Herman Talmadge captured the governor's seat by waging a campaign premised, by and large, on a race-baiting attack reminiscent of his father.

Such divergent responses, however, testified to just how contradictory the war's impact in Georgia ultimately proved to be. Veterans such as Joseph Rabun, Harold Fleming, and those in the AVC or GVMR reflected dissent in the ranks of white solidarity that derived, at least in part, from the war's democratic rhetoric and the influence of military service. The veterans who eagerly followed Eugene Talmadge's lead, however, symbolized just how resistant many other white southerners still were to the notion of black equality—political, social, or otherwise. The politics of race that ensued confounded campaigns for racial democracy and complicated the political context for anyone who advocated change, in the postwar 1940s and beyond.

Yet, in creating militant black veterans, in galvanizing local progressive activism, and in moving some white southerners to fight against any democratic racial mandate, the war clearly stood as a pivotal event for the postwar future, destabilizing the political environment and pointing to the likelihood of great changes yet to come.[153] In both building up a momentum for progressive change and then putting brakes on its implementation, the war undermined any certainty about where postwar Georgia was headed. And it was this struggle among southern veterans of both races to determine what that direction would be—to define the political and racial legacy of the war—that provided the bridge between the progressive ferment of the New Deal era and the politics of massive resistance and the black civil rights movement that ultimately transformed the region. In pursuing their conflicting notions of the war's meaning, Georgia's veterans, black and white, liberal and reactionary, ensured that both the politics of racial reform *and* of racial defense would define the war's immediate political aftermath for Georgia and the South. This legacy would, in turn, provide a foundation for the conflicts and controversies that characterized politics in Georgia and the South in the ensuing years. Black veterans would play important roles in leading the grassroots black civil rights movement in the South in the 1950s and 1960s.[154] Many southern white liberals would continue to founder in the face of imminent and comprehensive racial change.[155] And reactionary veterans would lead the region in mounting massive resistance to integration.[156]

As black, progressive, and reactionary white veterans fought over the political and racial meaning of the war, other veterans were asserting their rights to organize union locals and to join the CIO. Their postwar activism disrupted the stability of political and economic relations in Georgia's many textile mill towns and provided another element to the progressive campaign to remake the postwar political South. Like black veterans in the GVL or white veterans in the AVC, Georgia's white union veterans connected their postwar activism to their wartime military service, demonstrating yet another understanding of the war's mandate for postwar political change in Georgia and the South.

Eugene Talmadge formally enters the gubernatorial race of 1946, observed by a group of young World War II veterans who paid his $500 entrance fee. Photo courtesy of Lane Brothers Commercial Photographic Collection, Photographic Collections, Special Collections Department, Pullen Library, Georgia State University, Atlanta, Ga.

James V. Carmichael, gubernatorial candidate and manager of the Bell bomber plant in Marietta, speaking on the stump in Moultrie, Georgia, during the campaign of 1946. Photo courtesy of Lane Brothers Commercial Photographic Collection, Photographic Collections, Special Collections Department, Pullen Library, Georgia State University, Atlanta, Ga.

Campaign vehicle for James V. Carmichael parked in front of the courthouse in Rome, Georgia, during the gubernatorial race of 1946. Carmichael's good government platform appealed to a wide variety of Georgians across the state. Photo courtesy of Lane Brothers Commercial Photographic Collection, Photographic Collections, Special Collections Department, Pullen Library, Georgia State University, Atlanta, Ga.

Black citizens in Georgia responded enthusiastically to the opportunity to register and vote in the Democratic primaries of 1946, a historic first for black participation. The black registration lines at county courthouses in many Georgia communities often extended down the street for several blocks, such as in Fulton County, Atlanta, on May 3, 1946. Photo courtesy of Lane Brothers Commercial Photographic Collection, Photographic Collections, Special Collections Department, Pullen Library, Georgia State University, Atlanta, Ga.

The Eugene Talmadge campaign commissioned photographs of black registration lines, then circulated these among white working-class communities. While waiting their turn to register, the citizens in this photograph appear to challenge the photographer, expressing their disapproval of such tactics. Photo courtesy of Lane Brothers Commercial Photographic Collection, Photographic Collections, Special Collections Department, Pullen Library, Georgia State University, Atlanta, Ga.

Interracial strike by union veterans at a meatpacking factory in Moultrie, Georgia, circa 1947. Both black and white veterans wear portions of their service uniforms on the picket line. Photo courtesy of Lane Brothers Commercial Photographic Collection, Photographic Collections, Special Collections Department, Pullen Library, Georgia State University, Atlanta, Ga.

Herman Talmadge, interviewed by WGST Radio on September 8, 1948, the day of the special election to fill the gubernatorial seat. Combining his father's race-baiting tactics with his own pro-modernization style, the younger Talmadge won the election, defeating incumbent governor Melvin Thompson. Photo courtesy of Lane Brothers Commercial Photographic Collection, Photographic Collections, Special Collections Department, Pullen Library, Georgia State University, Atlanta, Ga.

 **Is This What We Fought the War For?**
Union Veterans and the Politics of Labor

IN 1946 WILLIAM SHIFLETT returned from a two-year stint in the army during World War II to the textile mill in Rome, Georgia, where he had previously worked for five years. Anchor Rome Mill, however, was not the same place it had been, nor was Shiflett the same man. During the war, workers in the plant had organized Local 787 of the Textile Workers Union of America, CIO (TWUA), and Shiflett returned just as new contract negotiations with Anchor Rome management reached a critical point. He promptly joined the union and won immediate election as shop steward for the spooling department's second shift. Soon thereafter, Shiflett became an officer of the local.[1]

During Shiflett's term of office, Anchor Rome management embarked on a vigorous campaign to break Local 787, focusing particularly on persuading workers to withdraw their union membership.[2] Shop floor supervisors, for example, regularly harassed Shiflett, warning him against signing up new members among employees, laying him off for brief periods, and even accusing him of obscene behavior.[3] This campaign of intimidation, however, served to strengthen, not weaken, Shiflett's commitment to Local 787, which he repeatedly defended. He explained to one supervisor, for example, that "the union was responsible for us having the eight-hour shift and wage increases." Shiflett maintained his faith in industrial democracy because, as he later explained, "I honestly believed in it."[4]

If the hostile climate within the mill was not enough to discourage Shiflett, the lack of federal support for Local 787's subsequent strike against Anchor Rome in 1948 certainly was. As president of the local, Shiflett called the strike after Anchor Rome's refusal to cooperate stalled contract negotiations. Shiflett assumed a leading role, including organizing the picket line at the plant's front gates. A local injunction aimed at the strikers soon secured Shiflett's arrest and brief incarceration.[5] But the worst was yet to come.

Although Local 787 eventually filed charges of unfair labor practices against Anchor Rome with the National Labor Relations Board (NLRB), it had to end its strike, unsuccessfully, early in 1949. On top of this disheartening turn of events, the NLRB shortly overturned an earlier order that had directed Anchor Rome to rehire all of the striking workers. As a result, the company refused to reinstate four hundred union members to their prior jobs. Shiflett was outraged, not so much by the actions of Anchor Rome, from which he doubtlessly expected no better, but by the equivocation of the NLRB in the face of these violations.[6] It represented a betrayal that called into question the whole purpose of the recent war. "I can not understand the ruling handed down by the board," a perplexed Shiflett explained to the chairman of the NLRB. After all, he noted, "there [are] still 405 people walking the streets of this city blackballed in every cotton mill in the south by the adverse ruling of the board." As "an ex serviceman," Shiflett bitterly wondered: "is this what we fought the war for?"[7]

In postwar Georgia William Shiflett was not alone in thinking that service in the war should guarantee working-class veterans and the unions they joined a voice in the community's economic, political, and civic affairs. World War II produced a sense of personal efficacy and civic entitlement among a coterie of returning veterans, who expressed a newfound identity as workers and citizens by joining the ranks of the CIO. These veterans became committed and steadfast unionists, who worked hard to sustain both their locals and the CIO's southern organizing drive. The vision of industrial democracy they held—a conviction in the rights of veterans, workers, and unionists to actively participate in the economic, civic, and political affairs of their community and state—challenged the paternalistic pattern of labor relations that had long characterized southern mill towns. In communities throughout the state, but particularly in the textile belt of the Piedmont and northwest, veterans signed union cards, organized fellow workers, and walked picket lines. Their union locals also worked with the CIO Political Action Committee in Georgia (GA-PAC) to register voters, to educate the electorate on the candidates, and, at times, to support or oppose particular campaigns. This activism created a third strand in the thread of southern veteran insurgencies that disrupted the political and racial stability of the postwar South. Along with black veterans in the GVL and white veterans in the AVC, union veterans demonstrated the war's power to destabilize the foundations of the one-party South, which fueled the hopes of liberals within and outside the South that a progressive reconstruction of politics in the region might actually be at hand.[8]

However, William Shiflett was also not alone in reaching the disappointing conclusion that organized labor's promise as a vehicle for industrial democracy and majority rule after the war would not be realized anytime soon in postwar Georgia. The war also unleashed a politics of race, anti-unionism, and growth that undermined the unity of interest among blacks and whites, unionists and workers, and middle-class and working-class southerners that progressives needed to build. In this context, the self-confidence and agency of some white veterans in Georgia's textile mills would not be enough to make the southern organizing drive by the CIO a success. Nor would they prove capable of developing the necessary political influence to move postwar Georgia in a direction favorable to the interests of organized labor or progressive reform.

Thus, World War II once again proved to be a contradictory force, both building up the momentum for political change by destabilizing political, racial, and economic relations in Georgia and the South and generating the conservative resurgence and internal divisions that delayed any progressive postwar dawning. As a broadly inclusive and progressive social movement, organized labor in the South never really emerged from the cloud of this disappointing postwar defeat. The politics of race, anti-unionism, and modernization—not industrial democracy—would be the war's most lasting political legacy for the state and region. Small wonder, then, that William Shiflett ended up questioning the whole purpose of the recent war.

WELL BEFORE THE END of World War II, progressives recognized the importance of organized labor and the South to their plans to rejuvenate and expand New Deal reformism in the postwar era. On the one hand, organized labor, particularly the CIO and its industrial union affiliates, had played an important role in the formation of the new Democratic coalition and had proven to be stalwarts behind President Roosevelt and the New Deal agenda. Moreover, although the imperatives of war production tended to mitigate labor's radicalism during the war, they also enhanced its role as a partner in the war government's economic and political councils.[9] Both through its organized constituencies at the grassroots level and its large bureaucratic organizations that could compete with management for governmental attention and influence, organized labor provided an essential vehicle to carry forth the progressive agenda that New Deal and popular front liberals envisioned for the postwar era.

On the other hand, considerable evidence existed that conservative resistance to any expansion of the New Deal and to organized labor's newfound power was far from broken. During the war, Republicans and southern Democrats in Congress dismantled key New Deal programs, including the Farm Security Administration, the Civilian Conservation Corps, and the Works Progress Administration.[10] Such actions put a premium on expanding the ranks of unionists to create a mobilized constituency that could counter any postwar conservative backlash. That expansion especially needed to happen in the postwar South.

The CIO developed its southern focus for a variety of reasons. Like the NAACP, the SCHW, and other national liberal organizations, the CIO, particularly, regarded organizing the South as critical to sustaining the accomplishments of the past decade and to expanding that record in the postwar era.[11] With a long history of anti-unionism and a predominantly low wage and perpetually unorganized labor force, the South posed a perennial problem to national unionization. Industries based in the North but with production lines also in the South, for example, could hold wage rates at southern, not northern, standards or use southern plants to maintain production in the event of labor conflicts in northern branches. Moreover, the domination of key congressional committees by southern conservatives created a constant political threat.[12] Sustained by a truncated electorate and discriminatory political traditions and practices, southern politicos generally felt no obligation to any constituency of organized labor or workers at home, and they usually opposed even the basic notion of collective bargaining as a right protected by federal legislation.

Naturally, such politicians condemned the progressive racial, economic, and political principles heralded by the national CIO. In 1941, for example, a national convention of the CIO had specifically censured discriminatory hiring practices. The national CIO also strongly backed the permanent establishment of the FEPC, in keeping with a stated commitment to work for "industrial and political civil rights" in the United States.[13] Such policies especially alarmed southern white Democrats as a direct threat to white supremacy, the foundation of southern political, economic, and social life. Thus, southern Democrats consistently supported the repeal of key New Deal programs, continually attacked the pro-labor Wagner Act, constantly opposed any expansion of the social welfare state, and vehemently fought against any movement for civil rights reform. In short, southern Democrats were the biggest thorn in the side of American liberals and organized labor before, during, and after the Second World War. Defeating this regional cabal of conservatism by organizing and enfranchising southern workers became organized labor's primary postwar political goal.[14]

At the war's end, the national CIO regarded the potential for union growth in the postwar South with great optimism. The region had a large labor force, numbering around 14 million, that included a significant industrial sector, from mining and lumber to tobacco and food processing. Textiles, concentrated in the Piedmont areas of Tennessee, Georgia, Alabama, Virginia, and North and South Carolina, employed the single largest segment of the industrial workforce, approximately 500,000 workers. As a result of the war, the overall industrial workforce in the South, textiles included, grew substantially in the 1940s. Although organizing in the South before and during the war did not pay the dividends it did in other regions of the country, still the Second World War "brought dramatic gains" to the South, where CIO membership increased from around 150,000 members at the beginning of the war to around 225,000 by the war's end.[15]

Thus, by targeting the largely unorganized South, the CIO intended particularly to "unionize low-wage southern workers, to protect the contract gains made by CIO affiliates in other sections of the country, and to transform the region's political climate."[16] The SOC, chaired by Van Bittner and headquartered in Atlanta, appointed regional and state directors to oversee the progress of the drive. Operation Dixie, as this southern organizational campaign came to be known, proved to be one of the most important and controversial movements in the postwar South.[17] Only the black voter registration drives that enlivened local, state, and regional politics in this era received more attention and comment. As V. O. Key noted in 1949, the postwar southern labor movement especially "frightened the southern old guard" because "almost everywhere labor groups, Negro organizers, and progressive societies collaborated not only in trying to break down suffrage restrictions and in exciting the political interests of the habitual nonvoter but also in supporting candidates against southern Bourbons."[18]

That collaboration arose from a shared interest among a diversity of postwar progressives. From national organizations such as the NAACP to regional groups such as the SRC and the SCHW, postwar progressives wanted to reform the political and economic structures of power that kept the majority of southerners, black and white, alienated from political participation and made the region as a whole distinct from the national political and economic mainstream. Operation Dixie became crucial to the liberal coalition that aimed to remake the postwar political South.

The SOC adopted a largely conservative strategy to meet the daunting task of organizing in such a hostile region.[19] Rather than relying on the more militant tactics of walk-outs, sit-downs, and strikes that animated the organizing drives of the 1930s, Operation Dixie worked largely through legally sanctioned channels, to pursue a "straight organizing campaign" premised on the "steady recruitment" of potential members and on the execution of "carefully planned NLRB elections" in targeted plants and mills.[20] The SOC also soft-pedaled any connection to the national CIO's more progressive principles, particularly regarding the question of black workers' place in the industrial union movement in the South and the CIO-PAC's stated goal of "reconstructing" the southern political landscape.[21] Bittner and the SOC generally marginalized the participation of black organizers and unionists and eschewed the training and experience of leftist-oriented southern affiliates that had already proven their success in organizing both black and white workers.[22]

According to at least one scholar, this approach reflected, in part, how the more conservative leaders within the CIO and the SOC perceived the peculiarities of organizing in the South. Race strictly divided the southern workforce, with blacks and whites mutually suspicious of one another, and white workers had a reputation for being especially hostile to the notion of black participation and advancement.[23] Moreover, no strong historical tradition of union activism existed to legitimize organizers' efforts and to bolster community support in the face of the certain opposition of local economic and civic leaders.[24] If any lesson could be drawn from efforts to unionize Dixie in the past, it was that organizers could surely count on the antagonism of employers and their political and civic allies.

The SOC tried to finesse these obstacles in a variety of ways, namely by working to solicit community support and to avoid upsetting local social and racial standards. The SOC enlisted the assistance of liberals such as Lucy Randolph Mason, a genteel Virginia blueblood and deeply devoted labor activist, who preceded local organizing campaigns by working to develop positive community relations between civic leaders and union operatives.[25] Operation Dixie also generally bypassed industries with largely black workforces, such as tobacco, timber, and food processing, and relegated to the backburner the strong biracial unions that already existed, such as the International Union of Mine, Mill, and Smelter Workers. In focusing most of its organizational effort and resources on the textile sector, with its predominantly white workforce, organizers could skirt, in theory, uncomfortable questions about the implications of the national CIO's stated racial progressivism.[26] CIO and SOC leaders also regarded textiles, as the region's largest industrial sector, as the necessary foundation for any successful mass organizing drive in the South. And, despite recent gains made by the TWUA south of the Mason-Dixon line during the war, the southern textile industry remained largely unorganized.[27]

An important part of this cautious strategy involved recruiting the participation of the South's returning veterans. From the outset, CIO and SOC officials regarded this constituency as essential to any postwar organizing plans. Early on, CIO leadership appreciated the potential represented by the return of millions of servicemen and women who were anxious to reclaim their place in American life. Many veterans had been unemployed at the time that they entered the service, however, and had little direct experience with collective bargaining or unions. Moreover, few union leaders had forgotten the disturbing lesson of World War I, when returning veterans had participated enthusiastically in the red-baiting and anti-union backlash that devastated the labor movement immediately after that war ended. "C.I.O. officers and Labor Union members are well aware," declared the CIO Veterans Committee, "of the anti-labor, isolationist, red-baiting activities in the name of 'Americanism' [that] characterized several of the veterans organizations of the last war."[28] No unionist wanted to repeat that past, especially given that far more Americans were in uniform during the Second World War than in the first one.

These concerns grew as a barrage of anti-union propaganda circulated both on the homefront and among American troops overseas as several major strikes erupted in the United States during the war.[29] "During the 25 months I served overseas with an infantry outfit, and especially during 7 months in New Guinea," noted a member of the International Association of Machinists, "unionism was maligned by the press and radio until we wondered just what the future of the service men and the unions would be after the war."[30] Corporal Odom Fanning agreed, remarking in June 1945 on the "idle chatter in the press and radio these days 'warning' organized labor not to antagonize further the serviceman, and predicting dire consequences when Johnny comes home." Although Fanning dismissed such stories as "poppycock," rumors alone could be damaging enough.[31] George Mitchell, director of the Southern Regional Council's Veteran Services Project, for example, identified a prevalent misconception among many southerners in 1945 that unions charged high initiation fees for ex-servicemen to join. This rumor persisted despite the well-publicized fact that all CIO affiliates waived such fees for recently returned veterans. "The opinion is still widespread in the South," noted Mitchell, "that unions generally are gouging the returning veterans for initiation fees."[32]

As a result, the CIO developed programs to reintegrate veteran members back into the workforce, to solicit their support of organizing campaigns, and to dispel the impact anti-union propaganda might have had.[33] CIO leaders recommended that all nationals and industrial union councils organize veterans' committees in every local as an "organization of our resources to make our ideas effective."[34] Such committees kept union members informed regarding issues of particular importance to ex-servicemen and women and aided union members in applying for veteran benefits. In Moultrie, Georgia, for example, a United Packinghouse Workers of America local resolved "that all returning veterans of the armed services be made especially welcome by our Union members and that our Union members spend an all out effort to bring returning veterans into the Union to the extent that they may be better protected in acquiring their rights and benefits."[35]

Emphasizing the importance of veterans set a precedent for viewing them as a special population within mills and plants, crucial to the success of any postwar union drive.[36] Enlisting their support also would neutralize veterans as a potential source on which management could draw to oppose organizing drives. Moreover, their active participation added legitimacy to what might easily be construed as a multitude of insurgencies against the economic and political status quo in local communities. Finally, utilizing a devoted group of veterans as Operation Dixie's core organizers allowed Bittner and the soc to avoid using staff already tainted by their leftist or radical associations. Few Americans, the soc surmised, would easily accuse veterans of a recent war against totalitarianism of harboring any communist proclivities. Service in the war made veterans' patriotic credentials impeccable.

Thus, when Bittner kicked off the southern organizing drive in the spring of 1946, he announced that the vast majority of the organizers hired for the effort would be both veterans and southerners. "Our enemies," he explained, "are going to have a hard time convincing people that these boys are out to destroy the government or spread subversive doctrines."[37] Local soc staff recommended several veterans for Bittner's approval as prospective leading organizers, including Clarence Jackson and James H. Perry, both navy veterans with textile experience, L. S. Graham and William G. Dempsey, both Marine Corps veterans, and Walter L. Yates, an army veteran and active TWUA member, all from South Carolina.[38] Truman Henderson of Dalton, Georgia, joined the organizing staff for his state, after serving as an air force lieutenant during the war, spending two weeks stranded behind Japanese lines, and receiving a Purple Heart.[39] Thus, recalled former southern CIO-PAC organizer David Burgess, "several of my best fellow organizers in South Carolina, North Carolina and Georgia . . . were recently returned veterans." In fact, Burgess noted, "most of the recent college graduates employed by . . . [the soc] in 1946 and 1947 and later were veterans."[40]

The soc also directed its field representatives to recruit mill workers who were veterans into local organizing campaigns. This tactic derived from a general strategy of relying on in-plant organizing committees, comprised of "dedicated union sympathizers," to prepare the ground for an eventual NLRB union certification election.[41] North Carolina director, William Smith, for example, stressed the importance of establishing "active, operating committees inside of the plant with special emphasis placed on Veterans committees." "Make a real effort," he repeated, "to get the Veterans interested and active in the drive."[42] Acting on this advice, Draper D. Wood, a southern area director, reported to Smith in June 1946 that efforts to organize in the large Firestone plant in Gastonia, North Carolina, focused particularly on "trying to get the best and most influential people in the plants, particularly veterans" enlisted as in-plant organizers.[43]

World War II veterans, then, not only joined new textile unions but also actively supported and often led local organizing drives and strikes. This kind of participation emerged throughout the southern states targeted by the SOC, creating a pattern of regional involvement by veterans in Operation Dixie from which Georgia's story can be extrapolated.[44] Field staff for the TWUA and the SOC submitted weekly reports to state directors to account for their activities. These reports included the names of newly recruited members, and whether or not each had paid an initiation fee. CIO affiliates exempted ex-servicemen from paying initiation fees (usually one dollar), which meant that membership records differentiated between veteran and nonveteran members. Such records are scarce for the Deep South but do indicate that veterans in other mill areas, including those that bordered Georgia, flocked to sign union cards as a result of these organizing campaigns. Most of these veterans were white, but black veterans joined as well when campaigns or strikes targeted largely black or biracial industries, such as meatpacking.

For example, veterans readily enlisted at the Standard-Coosa-Thatcher Mills in Chattanooga, located within the belt of textile mills targeted by the TWUA in northwestern Georgia, middle Tennessee, and northeastern Alabama. Shortly after the campaign at the Thatcher plant began, organizer John Neal notified Paul Christopher, the CIO state director for Tennessee, that he had signed up 193 members, 63 of whom were veterans. Less than a month later, Neal had signed up an additional 281 members, of whom 51 were veterans. Thus, roughly 24 percent of the members Neal recruited within the first month of the drive were World War II veterans.[45] Operation Dixie organizers enjoyed even more success at Consolidated Vultee in Nashville, Tennessee, a stove manufacturer under the jurisdiction of the United Steelworkers of America. This drive began in November 1946 with one staff member. Within three days, 62 workers had signed up, including 56 veterans. A week yielded 58 more members, of whom 52 were veterans. One week in January 1947 saw 110 workers enlist, including 100 veterans. In these weeks of the campaign, 90 percent of members who signed, on the average, were veterans of World War II.[46]

The same activism characterized organizing campaigns in the eastern third of the state. At the Alcoa aluminum plant just outside Knoxville, Tennessee, for example, some 3,200 members of Local 309 of the United Steelworkers were World War II veterans.[47] By November 2, 1946, one CIO organizer had signed 160 workers at the E. I. DuPont Company, in Old Hickory, Tennessee, 55 of whom were veterans. A little over a week later he reported bringing in 204 more workers, 74 of whom were veterans. Over 35 percent of the new members who signed into the TWUA in these two weeks were veterans. In Knoxville, organizers signed up 50 regular members and 27 veterans into the International Woodworkers of America at the Vestal Lumber Company and 24 veterans of 68 total new members at the Miller Brothers Company by August 21, 1946. Seventy-two miles to the northeast, 48 veterans at the L. B. Jenkins Company in Greeneville, Tennessee, joined 60 other workers in signing with the Food, Tobacco, and Agricultural Workers, CIO.[48]

The same story of active veteran membership emerges from anecdotal evidence in Georgia. Mills and workplaces with established or developing CIO locals, to which veterans belonged, included the Anchor Rome Mill and Celanese (Tubize) Mill in Rome; the Goodyear-Clearwater Mill in Rockmart; Cedartown Textiles, Cedartown Yarn Mill, the Metasap Chemical Company, and the Edward J. Dugan Grocers in Cedartown; the Athens Manufacturing Company in Athens; the Thurman Manufacturing Company in Madison; the *Columbus Ledger* plant in Columbus; the Dundee-Bleachery Mill in Griffin; and the Swift Manufacturing Company in Moultrie. Organizers targeted plants and mills throughout Georgia, but the most active organizing occurred in the northwest region of the state where the majority of textile mills operated. Soon after Operation Dixie's launch in 1946, in fact, the Georgia CIO and TWUA organized the Northwest Georgia Joint Board, made up of eight TWUA locals along the Dalton-Rome axis. This area, along with the Chattahoochee Valley region bordering Alabama to the west, bustled with labor activity during the postwar years, although communities in other parts of the state and other industries were involved as well.[49] Thus, Georgia, from larger cities such as Atlanta and Savannah to small country towns and rural hamlets such as La Grange, Gainesville, and Moultrie, witnessed an upsurge in labor activism as part of a highly publicized, regional organizing drive. Industrial unionism seemed poised to emerge as a significant political and economic force in many southern postwar communities, and the leaders of Operation Dixie recognized veterans as critical to accomplishing their goals.

Indeed, white veterans in Georgia not only signed union cards, they also served as in-plant organizers. Scott B. Dollar, for example, a native Georgian and veteran who served in both the army and the navy during the war, worked as a loom fixer at Cedartown Textiles, belonged to TWUA Local 830 at that mill, and organized for the union at the Aragon, Cedartown, Goodyear, and Berryton mills as part of the southern organizing drive.[50] Doyle Powell worked at the Ceartown Yarn Mill from the time he was eighteen years old until 1942 when he was inducted into the military. Upon his discharge in 1945, Powell returned to the mill and assisted in organizing a TWUA local there. Powell was so active, in fact, that management fired him, an act that eventually prompted an investigation by the NLRB and a reinstatement order. Similarly, Eugene Parks, employed as a GI trainee at the Thurman Manufacturing Company in Madison, Georgia, signed up a majority of the workers in the cutting department for the TWUA. According to a NLRB field examiner investigating the discharge of several Thurman workers, "Parks rode with union organizers, introduced them to prospective members, and had conferences with [union representatives] and other organizers." "Clearly," he concluded, Parks "was the most active union adherent in the cutting room."[51] During yet another TWUA drive at the Dundee-Bleachery Mill in Griffin, Georgia, H. D. Lisk, a TWUA staffer, reported that though the situation in the mill had progressed slowly, "there are signs it will develop much faster than it has in the past." After all, "we have been able to get several good veterans on the organizing committee which will help the situation a good deal."[52]

Recently returned veterans quickly emerged as leaders within many locals. Local 787 in Rome elected William Shiflett as vice president soon after he became a member; he also served a pivotal term as president.[53] At least 150 World War II veterans belonged to TWUA Local 689 in the Celanese Corporation Mill in Rome. Union veterans such as Walter Brooks and H. O. Yarbrough, according to one scholar, "sustained and strengthened the union" by providing leadership "as stewards and elected officials."[54]

Thus, union veterans were on the front lines of the labor-management disputes that accompanied the Operation Dixie drive, marching on picket lines, staffing strike commissaries, and organizing strike activities. Union officials naturally welcomed this participation, reasoning that the appearance of ex-soldiers decked out in military uniforms, medals, and campaign ribbons on picket lines might boost the strikers' community image, deflect charges of un-Americanism, and make any company retaliation appear downright unpatriotic.

Indeed, throughout the South as well as in Georgia, veterans figured prominently in numerous postwar strikes. One such dispute erupted in the fall of 1945 at the Erwin Mills near Durham, North Carolina. "Ervin King and Odell Browning are two of the many union members home on furlough," reported the local TWUA in *Picket Line News*, a strike newsletter, "who have been visiting their friends and fellow members on the picket lines and in the Union Hall." Moreover, Cecil Poe, "another staunch union member" having returned after his discharge, "is in there fighting for the union as always," along with Ellis Emery, "who left his two-year fight in the South Pacific to join in the homefront fight for democracy and justice, on the picket line!" In fact, veterans such as King, Browning, Emery, and Poe also staffed the union commissary that provided food and other supplies to striking workers. A photograph in a Durham newspaper in December 1945 shows several soldiers and veterans in uniform handing out flour and cornmeal to women strikers from the commissary shelves.[55]

Union veterans in Georgia followed suit, joining in and, in some cases, leading strikes against hostile employers. The longest running postwar textile strike in Georgia began at the Athens Manufacturing Company in 1945. The dispute developed when mill management refused to bargain with the TWUA local regarding wages and working conditions in the plant. After the company refused to comply with a National War Labor Board order settling the issues at hand, workers engaged in a legal strike that began on August 29, 1945. "We have worked for you, some of us, for longer than 25 years," explained the Athens local, and "our wages have been among the lowest in textiles in the state." Moreover, "our working and living conditions have been bad. Only 8 of the 219 company mill village houses have bathtubs; only 35 have any water at all inside the house." Thus, the local continued, "we formed the union to try to help ourselves. We wanted a little less poverty, a little more freedom, a chance to live as other people do."[56]

When veterans employed in the mill before this period returned during the strike, they not only refused to cross the picket line but also actively joined in the protest. After a favorable ruling by the NLRB regarding the causes of the dispute, the company's refusal to arbitrate, and its behavior toward picketing workers, the TWUA local called off the strike on March 11, 1947. Reinstatement of workers under the NLRB order, however, ultimately required a circuit court decision, specifying the reemployment of World War II veterans Willie Christian, Ira Crowe, Jewel Lee, Carl Mann, and Local 940 secretary John Crawford. The TWUA local won several thousand dollars in back pay for striking workers, including the "group of veterans who were also involved in the strike."[57]

Veterans also assumed leading roles in two labor disputes in the textile community of Rome in northwest Georgia. TWUA Local 787 in the Anchor Rome Mill organized in 1945 after a hard campaign, in which management retaliated against union members and enlisted in race-baiting to discourage membership. Despite such tactics, organizers signed over two-thirds of the production workers by the end of the summer of 1945, and a NLRB certification election resulted in 518 votes for the TWUA and 251 against it. The TWUA had organized the second largest mill in Rome.[58]

Anchor Rome management, however, never really accepted this outcome. From the time the organizing campaign began to the signing of the first contract with the local and thereafter, management and anti-union employees kept up a steady barrage of attacks meant to undermine Local 787's legitimacy.[59] Throughout the term of the first contract, signed in March 1946, for example, the company continued to engage in practices that prompted the local to file charges with the NLRB. In March 1947 company officials and sympathetic workers began a withdrawal campaign to encourage union members to drop their membership. Local 787 procured a new contract in April 1947, but under new right-to-work laws passed in the state, it did not include any maintenance of membership or check-off provisions (These provisions protected union security by establishing a closed shop in which all workers hired had to join the union and maintain dues payments).[60] After that point, Anchor Rome management refused to settle shop floor grievances through established procedures, to consult the local regarding changing wage rates from hourly to piece work, or to negotiate on employee insurance programs. Moreover, the company resorted to arbitration in many of these disputes, which absorbed the time, energy, and funds of the local and the TWUA's Northwest Georgia Joint Board. All of these factors together, the local believed, forced it into a strike that began on March 18, 1948.

William Shiflett, of course, played a key role in the events leading up to and during the strike. As shop steward, Shiflett submitted written grievances to the personnel director, who told him in September 1947 that "he didn't want me signing up men at the mill," warning that "you know what will happen if you do."[61] Sometime thereafter, management laid off Shiflett for allegedly posting an obscene drawing that lampooned scabs. Throughout these difficulties, however, Shiflett continued to support the union and to advocate its benefits to his fellow workers. He reported a conversation with Hubert Kemp, a low-level shop floor supervisor, for example, in which he extolled "the good the union had done" and asked Kemp "why he did not like the union." Kemp, according to Shiflett, "never missed a chance to make dirty, disrespectful, remarks about the officers of our local union," dismissing it as a "negro loving, communistic organization."[62] At a later union meeting, Shiflett argued against allowing two workers to withdraw their membership. "I took to the floor and objected to letting these people withdraw," Shiflett explained, "and pointed out the benefits the union had gained for Anchor Rome employees and that I thought each employee should support the union."[63] In a later meeting with Will Scott, a mill supervisor, the two workers who had wanted to withdraw from the union took exception to Shiflett's position. The two angry women, a Mrs. Rampley and Mrs. Leonard, threatened to strike Shiflett in the head with a spool of yarn. Meanwhile, "Mr. Scott just looked on and enjoyed the show." Shiflett concluded from this incident that Scott "wanted the women to strike me and hoped I would slap one of them so he could fire me."[64]

A few months later, Scott once again called Shiflett in to tell him "he could hardly believe it when he first heard that I was mixed up with the CIO and that he thought I had better sense than to have anything to do with an outfit like that." Once again, however, Shiflett stood his ground. "I told him that the union had done a lot for me," he recalled, "and that I was going to do all I could for the union."[65]

When contract negotiations deteriorated further, Local 787 went out on strike in 1948.[66] Right from the beginning, Shiflett assumed a leading role. Following the advice of Joseph Pedigo and the Northwest Georgia Joint Board, Shiflett called the strike and then organized the pickets marching at the mill gate. He set up two pickets at each end of the gate, kept them moving back and forth in front of the gate in groups of ten to twenty, and instructed them "not to block gate or put hand on anyone." Shiflett's job, apparently, was "to keep gates clear" and "avoid fights and conduct a lawful strike." Nonetheless, Shiflett reported, "one of the company's men tried to run him down."[67] Despite his efforts, Shiflett, three other strikers, and four nonstriking workers ended up arrested and jailed for ten to twenty days by a superior court judge for allegedly violating an injunction restraining both parties from interfering in the legal rights of the other.[68]

The price paid by Shiflett and the other veterans and workers who struck at the Anchor Rome Mill proved to be high. Serious violence broke out on the picket line and in the mill village during the course of the strike.[69] For example, a non-striking employee named Elmer Adams shot Hubert Wilkey, a nineteen-year-old striker, in the chest in April 1948. A month earlier a mob of seventy-five to a hundred men armed with hammers, wrenches, and blackjacks accosted picketers, assaulting one woman and throwing a man down a steep embankment. In April gunshots fired by unknown parties ripped through the mill village, wounding one nonstriker. This conflict reportedly began when around twenty men threatened picketers with sticks and shotguns during a shift change.[70]

Amid these occasional outbursts of violence, nonunion workers continued to cross the picket line, which further demoralized the strikers. With the dispute essentially still unresolved and the mill resuming full production in late 1948, Local 787 called off the strike in January 1949, after first filing unfair labor practice charges against Anchor Rome with the NLRB. The following month a trial examiner for the board ordered the reinstatement of four hundred strikers, prompting a celebratory parade down the streets of Rome by several hundred workers. Subsequent delays in handing down the final NLRB decision, ongoing eviction proceedings against strikers still in company housing, and the company's ultimate refusal to rehire the workers quickly deflated this euphoria. "We the union feel we have been let down by not learning any thing about our case," wrote Eugene Ingram, an Anchor Rome striker, to the NLRB. "We are asking you to Please give it attenshion [sic] at once if possible because the people is in need of work and money." Ingram explained: "As you know we have asked to go back to work and they wont let us. So the people is in need."[71] The NLRB eventually overturned the trial examiner's order to reinstate the Anchor Rome strikers, which prompted William Shiflett's bitter recrimination.

Although veterans in Local 787 lost their hard-fought strike, those in TWUA Local 689 at the Celanese Corporation in Rome fared much better. From the start of the TWUA campaign of 1944 that organized the plant, Local 689 had more success obtaining and maintaining members than its neighboring local at Anchor Rome and ultimately formed a closely knit union that included roughly 80 to 90 percent of the eligible workforce. Thus, while approximately 400 workers walked out on strike at Anchor Rome in 1948, and 350 nonunion workers continued to report to work, 1,600 workers, all members of Local 689, struck the Celanese mill the same year.[72] The Celanese strike lasted seventeen weeks, and veterans provided critical leadership here as well.

Veterans such as Walter Brooks and H. O. Yarbrough, according to Michelle Brattain in her detailed study of the Celanese conflict, had returned to the mill from service in the war "with a perspective of the world and the nation beyond Floyd County," one that ultimately led them into Local 689. Their leadership strengthened the union. Brooks, in particular, recalled how the self-confidence and empowerment he derived from his service in the war led him into the TWUA when he returned. Before the union came, Brooks recalled, "management thought you were theirs." After the war, however, "I was older and . . . I'd learned better. I came back and I wasn't going to let them talk to me that way, no way." H. O. Yarbrough agreed that having a union made "all the difference in the world."[73] Such veterans brought to Local 689 "a new sense of their rights as American workers" that sustained the union in its dispute with the company.[74] Thus, reported the *Rome News-Tribune* in October 1948, two months into the strike, "union members turned out full strength early this morning for the fourth straight day." In fact, "over 200 marching pickets, including an estimated 150 ex-servicemen in full uniform, paraded past the plant's main gate."[75] After seventeen weeks on the picket line, Local 689 won wage equity with northern Celanese rayon workers.[76]

Veterans in Georgia joined unions and marched on picket lines for a variety of reasons. Certainly, some veterans joined CIO locals because it was a requirement in order to work in a unionized plant before the Taft-Hartley Act of 1947 made the closed shop illegal. This type of motivation to join a local could be problematic during labor disputes since success against an intransigent employer necessitated presenting a committed and united front among union members. A CIO field representative in Georgia, for example, attributed the waning of participation in picket duty during the Anchor Rome strike to the local's non-activist members. Often, he noted, "the workers in the mills are not the ones who fought to make the union." Rather, they "have joined the union because they had to [and] have never really been sold on its necessity and will have to learn the hard way."[77]

Many other veterans, however, stuck by their unions despite continuous harassment by fellow workers and management. Shiflett, for example, could have withdrawn from Local 787, but instead he defended its right to represent Anchor Rome workers. More than one veteran discharged for union activities, in fact, ended up employed by a CIO affiliate as an organizer. Veteran Scott Dollar, for example, who had worked at Cedartown Textile Mills since 1936 and had organized that and several other mills for the TWUA, was arrested for violating an injunction during a Cedartown strike. In 1952, when he could have dropped his union membership, he applied to be an international representative for the TWUA.[78]

Veterans also chose union membership because it offered concrete benefits. Shiflett, for example, often defended Local 787 by extolling the wage increases and other benefits it had brought to workers at Anchor Rome. "I honestly believed in it," Shiflett testified in an affidavit, and other veterans agreed. As Celanese worker and veteran Walter Brooks explained, union membership afforded an opportunity to express one's right to self-determination, respect, and dignity. "People were ready" when TWUA organizers arrived in Rome toward the end of the war, Brooks recalled, "because of the way they were treated, and the way they were working." "The best thing I ever got out of a union," he declared, "wasn't money," but rather "my right to stand up and tell the boss that I was not going to [be pushed around]."[79]

The sense of self-efficacy that drew veterans like Walter Brooks into industrial unionism derived, at least in part, from military service in the war. Indeed, few things served to enhance a sense of personal manhood and civic entitlement more than carrying arms in a victorious war against a widely condemned enemy.[80] SOC staff organizing at Cannon Mills in Kannapolis, North Carolina, for example, counted on returning veterans to be "less influenced by the Cannon myth" of paternalism and more willing to assert their rights against management. Organizers surmised that recently returned veterans "have had sufficient experience, and have only recently arrived back under the influence of the popular opinion, so that these generalizations [about workers' bonds with or fears of Cannon management] are not entirely valid when applied to them." After months and years away from home and mill, Cannon Mills' veterans were "not yet 'reintegrated into the Kannapolic pattern.'"[81]

Indeed, union veterans rarely missed an opportunity to connect what they had done for the country to their postwar actions against recalcitrant employers. "We Fought and Won the War," read a placard in a line of uniformed white and black veterans picketing a Swift meatpacker in Georgia immediately after the war, and "Swift Won the Profits." "We Whipped Tojo, Mussolini and Hitler and We'll Whip Swift," read a sign held by another veteran, who also held up a large American flag.[82] These claims and symbols were more than a public relations ploy. Service in the war strengthened union veterans' identities as workers and citizens who were independent of the paternalistic structures of economic and political power characteristic of southern mill towns. Joining unions and leading organizing drives and strike activities provided a vehicle to express a new claim to participation in the economic and political life of the mill and the community.

Picketing in particular, with its need for slogans, signs, and positive publicity, generated statements steeped in wartime rhetoric. When over nine hundred workers in TWUA Local 246 struck the Erwin Mills near Durham, North Carolina, white strikers picketed at the Erwin civic auditorium during a meeting of the Southern Textile Association. One child carried a sign that declared, "My daddy fought for freedom from want. Raise wages."[83] Workers at the Edward J. Dugan Grocers in Cedartown, Georgia, walked out on strike when the company fired two veterans who were actively engaged in a CIO organizing drive. Stanley Womack and C. D. Stephens, stated the union local, "are veterans of World War II who feel that they fought for the right to join or not join an organization of their own choosing."[84]

The statements veterans made during a strike at the Safie textile mill in Rockingham, South Carolina, in 1947 exemplified all of the elements that drew returning veterans into the postwar labor movement. In a leaflet directed to the "People of Rockingham" entitled "All We Ask Is Fair Play," TWUA Local 930 sought to explain the conflict in its own terms. The strike erupted, it declared, because of "the treatment given us when we exercised our rights as free American citizens" in voting for the TWUA. After all, this was "the same kind of union we Americans established for the people of other countries, after we defeated Hitler and

Mussolini and abolished dictatorship!" Next, the leaflet outlined the harassment that union members encountered due to their membership and activities as well as the company's refusal to negotiate a contract. In a "deliberate attempt" to "destroy our union," the local management not only refused to settle the dispute but also fired sixteen more workers. That proved to be the final straw. "Many of us are veterans and all of us are Americans," the local trumpeted, "who fought for freedom and human dignity and the right of people everywhere to be secure in their jobs and in their homes." While "we veterans need our jobs," they did not want them "on terms dictated to us by the would-be little Hitlers." Moreover, the local protested the company's use of scabs, deploring that "the Company's 'G.I. Bill of Rights' for its returned veterans is to bring in strangers to take our jobs." Yet, "these same people didn't volunteer to take our jobs on Okinawa or Saipan, and on all the battle fronts of the world." Thus, the local concluded, "Our cause is just," and "We intend to fight this battle for Democracy through just as we fought the battle against dictatorship and oppression over there."[85]

Whether in the Safie TWUA local in Rockingham, South Carolina, in Dugan Grocers in Cedartown, or in the Celanese and Anchor Rome locals in Rome, southern white union veterans understood their struggles with management as part of a broader fight for industrial democracy that both gave meaning to and drew meaning from their service in the war. Military service had heightened veterans' sense of patriotic sacrifice—of their realization that they had been the ones to answer the nation's call to civic duty. Service in the war separated veterans, as a whole, from the civilians who had stayed at home, particularly the corporate managers and mill bosses who, veterans believed, had reaped the profits of war mobilization while soldiers and sailors had labored in service and combat units overseas. So long as mill bosses respected veterans' newfound prerogative to participate in the administration of their own jobs or to join and organize unions if they chose, this sense of difference and entitlement need not be invoked. However, the traditionally paternalistic nature of southern labor relations, in which employers often took their workers' unquestioning obedience for granted, naturally challenged veterans' expectations for their role in the community as well as the sense of self-efficacy many drew from the war. In joining unions, organizing workers, and leading strikes, veterans such as Walter Brooks and William Shiflett articulated a new understanding of themselves as veterans, workers, and citizens that initially boosted the southern organizational campaign, further testifying to the war's disruptive impact.

Returning veterans infused Operation Dixie with an enthusiasm and commitment that seemed to justify the optimism that Bittner and SOC officials worked to maintain throughout the campaign's first year. Weekly reports logged the daily

progress that organizers made in southern mills: making contact with likely re-
cruits, establishing in-plant organizing committees, signing up new members,
and preparing the ground for NLRB certification elections to establish new locals.[86] Thus, in June 1947 Bittner and the soc tried to make the case for the southern organizational drive's accomplishments, citing the recruitment of 280,000
workers and victories in over two hundred NLRB elections. In fact, V. O. Key concluded in 1949 that though the southern labor movement remained weak, Operation Dixie had successfully increased "the political consciousness of its members and won victories here and there."[87]

Public claims of victory notwithstanding, soc officials privately conceded
what sounded very much like defeat.[88] As Paul Christopher, the Tennessee director for the soc, noted in 1951, "I am rapidly coming to the conclusion . . . that we
are going to have to resign ourselves to a lot of legwork, that is not going to pay
off in the first campaigns."[89] The number of workers who joined the ranks of the
CIO in the South during Operation Dixie's brief tenure fell far short of the pro-
jected one million members the CIO and TWUA had initially imagined. And most
of the gains made occurred in industries other than textiles, in branches of
northern plants, or in mills where organizing and NLRB involvement had preceded the postwar organizing drive.[90] The initiative in textiles proved especially
disappointing.[91] The victories covered only a few thousand workers, and most
other efforts, particularly in the larger, pivotal plants such as the Pepperell Mill
in Lindale, Georgia, or Cannon Mills in Kannapolis, North Carolina, met with
bitter defeat.[92] In 1949 the southern membership of the CIO had not increased
much since the day the southern organizing campaign began.[93]

In Georgia the case of Local 689 at the Celanese Corporation in Rome, and
those of a few other locals in strongly industrial or urban centers such as Dalton
and Atlanta, seemed to fulfill Operation Dixie's aims to establish strong locals with
significant community legitimacy. The defeat of Local 787 at Anchor Rome, however, proved far more typical. As the leading wave of a progressive reconstruction of the region, the CIO's southern organizing drive proved to be a dismal
failure. It never created a durable foundation of industrial unionism on which a
progressive reform of the political South could build. This failure demonstrated
how contradictory World War II's impact in Georgia really was. The experience
of war not only drew veterans into the postwar labor movement in the South,
feeding the impetus for a progressive politics of change, it also generated a conservative backlash that did much to make the campaign for industrial democracy an early victim.

Organizers at the time and many scholars since have not agreed on what accounted for this disappointing outcome.[94] Most, however, apportion blame to

both the flawed strategies the SOC adopted and to the southern and national postwar contexts that kept this campaign largely on the defensive. The local organizers and unionists, such as William Shiflett, who did much to keep the Operation Dixie campaign alive on the ground, ended up trapped between conflicting imperatives within the CIO and a hostile national and regional environment that undermined their best efforts.

High expectations accompanied the opening of the southern organizing campaign, but the harsh realities of the postwar climate for progressive causes of any sort quickly deflated that optimism. A conservative backlash against the New Deal, which had begun nationally at the end of the 1930s and emerged briefly during the war, reemerged with renewed vigor as soon as the war was over. And the wildcat strikes that erupted during the war, despite the AFL and CIO no-strike pledge, eroded organized labor's popular credibility. In 1943 Congress passed the Smith-Connally Act, which, among other things, allowed the president to seize striking war plants and made union contributions to political campaigns illegal. In 1946 Republicans won a majority in both houses of Congress for the first time since 1930. The culmination of that session was the Taft-Hartley Act of 1947, which eviscerated the pro-labor Wagner Act. Taft-Hartley effectively ended the role of the federal government as an ardent defender of the rights of organized labor.[95] Taken together, these trends indicated the "drastically changed social and political climate prevailing in postwar America," a climate that made labor organizing everywhere all the more difficult.[96] The CIO, and organized labor generally, ended up on the defensive, as conservative Republicans and southern Democrats in Congress mobilized against the legislative gains labor had made in the past decade.

Moreover, as the global war on communism heated up under the Democratic Truman administration, so too did domestic anticommunist fervor, which cast suspicion on progressive social and economic reform as associated with the principles of international communism.[97] An emerging conservative faction within the councils of the CIO grew increasingly concerned with organized labor's public fortunes in this climate and accommodated the conservative and anticommunist impulse by purging left-oriented affiliates and organizers known for or suspected of harboring Communists and "fellow travelers."[98]

This internal battle within the national CIO refracted down to the SOC, with "right-wing stalwarts" such as Van Bittner and George Baldanzi appointed to administer the southern organizing campaign.[99] Bittner in particular, sensitive to the potential of red-baiting to undermine what Operation Dixie hoped to accomplish, quickly picked up this anticommunist thread. He formally distanced the SOC from other progressive campaigns in the South and sidelined the leftist affiliates with proven track records in organizing in the region, such as the Mine, Mill and Smelter Workers Union and the Food, Tobacco, and Allied Workers Union.[100]

At the very least, this decision deprived the southern campaign of its most experienced organizers.[101] In his zealousness to limit any association with leftists in the labor and progressive movement, Bittner even turned down an offer by the Highlander Folk School—highly regarded for its successful labor training and educational programs—to train the organizers hired for the Operation Dixie campaign.[102] This may have deprived new organizers of the means to be more effective at the task they were given and certainly multiplied the many constraints under which they already labored. Returning veterans may have been enthusiastic and committed organizers, but that did not mean they were skilled in the methods needed to surmount the sort of obstacles that labor organizing in the postwar South presented. In fact, one scholar of the southern organizing drive has concluded that "the inexperience of southern organizers was a constantly recurring problem" that plagued Operation Dixie right from the beginning. William Smith, the SOC director for North Carolina, for example, noted that he had to constantly remind his own organizing staff of "the most basic rules of organizing."[103]

One reason that Bittner and the SOC marginalized the participation of the labor movement's left-wing was because of the left's vision of industrial unionism as a foundation for a progressive biracial society.[104] The national CIO endorsed the principles of workplace equality and civil rights as a foundation of industrial unionism, which lent all of the labor movement, rightly or not, an air of racial progressivism that conservative CIO leaders did not anticipate selling well in Dixie. Bittner, in fact, regarded any association with progressive principles on issues such as a permanent FEPC as a death knell for Operation Dixie's fortunes in a region hypersensitive on the question of racial reform. The increasing focus on southern race relations among Cold War liberals nationally, who were anxious to sustain the image of American justice, freedom, and democracy abroad, intensified the South's racial sensitivity.[105]

All of these factors put southern progressives, especially in the labor movement, in a difficult position.[106] They were dependent on outside resources and support to advance the southern organizing campaign, but this reliance made them even more vulnerable to red-baiting, race-baiting, and charges of "outside agitation." To offset these problems, the SOC focused most of its resources and attention on largely white industries, especially textiles. The SOC also never embraced biracial unionism, never really enlisted the broad participation of black unionists and workers, and never elevated black southerners who did join the southern organizational campaign to anything other than a distinctly subordinate position.[107] Instead of marginalizing black workers, critics have argued, the SOC might have employed them as an enthusiastic and steadfast core of support.[108] In this view, Operation Dixie would have been better served by devoting more resources and attention to areas other than the textile industry, which was highly dispersed, predominantly white, and historically very difficult to organize.[109]

Ultimately, Operation Dixie operatives received conflicting imperatives: organize "everything in sight" in a given community, but do not embrace the black workers who often were the ones most likely and eager to respond. This contradictory decree created a delicate balancing act for organizers and unionists, who felt compelled both to organize any worker who expressed an interest and to impose constraints when black workers responded. The composition and structure of a biracial picket line at the Swift meatpacking plant in Moultrie, Georgia, reflected the ambiguity of this situation. Only white veterans held the American flag and displayed the most provocative placards, with messages that clearly asserted their power as veterans and as workers—"We Fought and Won the War," and "We'll Whip Swift." Black veterans, however, held a sign with a message obviously meant not to justify their participation in the strike, but to warn other blacks, not whites, from inflaming racial tensions: "Be A Man—Don't Scab."[110]

Despite the effort of Bittner and the SOC to avoid making race a central feature of the southern organizing campaign, the politics of race defined the political context anyway.[111] The racial progressivism of the national CIO was a well-publicized fact. And even if the SOC had succeeded in distancing itself from those principles, World War II had destabilized racial and political relations sufficiently to alarm many southern whites already. This apprehension helped to make organized labor a ready scapegoat for calculating political incumbents and reactionaries intent on preserving their own claims to power. The politics of race became a useful tool with which to rally the state's white citizens against organized labor's challenge to the economic and political status quo.

Regardless of Bittner's and the SOC's stated hostility to a racially progressive agenda, plenty of others in every Georgia community targeted by Operation Dixie said otherwise.[112] And plenty of evidence existed at the time that race relations in Georgia and the South were, indeed, in flux, which lent credence to charges that organizing the state's workers would upset the hierarchy of white over black. Returning black veterans asserted their claims to political rights and economic opportunity, black and liberal organizations actively registered black voters, and the question of racial reform in the South increasingly preoccupied national postwar political debate. The inflating membership of the postwar Georgia Klan, the violence meted out to black veterans and politically active citizens, and the controversy that attended Eugene Talmadge's race-baiting gubernatorial campaign in 1946 indicated that a number of southern whites had found their racial identity strengthened by this disruptive impact of the war. They would not be inclined to overlook the charges of racial amalgamation levied at Operation Dixie by the southern old guard.

Indeed, local politicos and state legislators quickly marshaled a bevy of red- and race-baiting tactics to undermine the legitimacy of the southern organizing drive.[113] From free subscriptions for workers to the rabidly racist and bitterly anti-union rag, *Militant Truth*, to publicly conflating unionism with integration, mill owners and their allies in Georgia routinely played the race card to undermine a union's credibility.[114] In the midst of the TWUA organizing campaign in 1945 at the Anchor Rome Mill, for example, white worker Ottie Argo recalled that mill officials "played the race issue to the limit," even telling him that a union would "put negro help on any job in the plant" and "have negroes living side by side with us in company owned village housing." Anchor Rome used race, recalled another worker, to "keep the people confused about the real issues in the [union] campaign."[115]

Certainly, hate groups worked hard after the war to recruit members from the ranks of the white working class, particularly in textile mill villages. Chapters of the Ku Klux Klan and the Columbians, including veterans, attacked organized labor and targeted their appeals to mill workers.[116] One informant reported that the Columbians played a pivotal role in breaking a CIO strike at the Exposition Cotton Mills in Atlanta in the spring of 1946. The Columbians held two meetings in the Exposition mill village and apparently provided "special security" to the mill management during the strike.[117] A young veteran at a meeting of Atlanta Klavern #1 in September 1946 "arose and declared that he was working in the Chevrolet plant in Atlanta and that he was proud that 76 fellow workers were members of the Klan." In fact, "he stated that he and his fellows planned to keep on organizing until they had a majority of workmen in Chevrolet in the Klan."[118] A flyer announcing a joint meeting of the Klan and Columbians in Columbus, Georgia, declared that "The White Working People Must Fight to Help Themselves . . . . They Must Learn to Vote and Take the Country Back Out of the Hands of Grafting Politicians." Stetson Kennedy, who had infiltrated the Georgia Klan after the war, concluded that the KKK played a significant role in defeating union drives at the Bibb Mills in Macon and Porterdale, Georgia.[119]

It would be a mistake, however, to assume that white workers in Georgia always responded the way anti-union reactionaries intended. As Michelle Brattain points out in her studies of the labor movement in postwar Georgia, white workers did not always buy into these arguments. During the TWUA organizing campaign at Anchor Rome in 1945, for example, workers generally dismissed management's warnings that the CIO represented racial amalgamation as "empty threats." Similarly, while conducting research for V. O. Key's seminal study of southern politics in the postwar 1940s, Georgia veteran Calvin Kytle found that white workers in the Mary Leila Cotton Mills in Greensboro adamantly refused to allow management to remove from a union contract a nondiscrimination wage clause that applied to the eleven black workers in the mill.[120]

A variety of factors, particularly local conditions and history, influenced whether these tactics worked in a given campaign or mill. Nevertheless, mill magnates and local conservatives gambled that the racial identities of white workers would outweigh the actual reality of the immediate situation. Any movement that aimed to empower ordinary Georgians, as black and progressive white veterans had also learned, proved vulnerable to being charged with advocating racial integration. And in some instances, these tactics did prove to be effective. In Macon, Georgia, Kytle recalled, "we were told that the Bibb Mills would have been organized a year ago if management hadn't exploited the negro issue so skillfully."[121] David Burgess, who worked as an Operation Dixie organizer in South Carolina, cited "lawyers and the employers [who] successfully appealed to the racial prejudices of both blacks and whites—prejudices which divided the workers along racial lines," as one reason for the southern organizing drive's ultimate failure. Don McKee, who organized textile mills in the Carolinas and in Alabama, agreed, noting that the "race issue, played up by Mgn [management]," undermined organizing campaigns.[122]

Just as important, workers were not the only ones, or even the most likely ones, to respond to such tactics. Invoking the specter of racial integration may have resonated with a number of white workers, but it also spoke to middle-class citizens who sustained a community's structures of political, economic, and social power. Workers might be the ones in the mills to defeat an organizing drive by voting against certification in a NLRB election, but shopkeepers, sheriffs, judges, lawyers, teachers, pastors, newspaper editors, bankers, and aldermen were the ones who kept the community's resources arrayed against organizing drives. Moreover, they shared the same racial identity and economic self-interest that made southern textile communities such hard nuts to crack for union organizing campaigns.

Thus, all of these elements, and not one single factor alone, explained why the southern organizing drive that so many labor leaders and other progressives hailed with great optimism at first should fail so dismally soon after it was launched in May 1946. The CIO and the SOC had counted on returning white veterans to be a core of support on which organizing drives and progressive political campaigns could build. Veterans did play a pivotal role in Operation Dixie. The union locals they helped to organize and lead worked hard to develop organized labor's political and economic influence in local communities and across the state. However, these veteran activists were not enough. Not all veterans who returned to mills in Georgia joined union locals, and many veterans probably used their GI Bill benefits, which included job training, to take higher skill, higher wage jobs somewhere else. No less damaging to unionization efforts were the wage increases employed by textile mills to offset organizers' appeal and the consumerist revolution unleashed by the war. The opportunity to purchase homes from mill owners, to buy a car, and to upgrade plumbing and electrical capabilities captured many textile workers' imaginations after the war far more readily than the call to organize. Having paid for these items on installment, one scholar argues, workers proved reluctant to risk losing their jobs due to union or strike activities.[123] Finally, a lack of federal support, the withdrawal of CIO resources from the southern organizing drive, the flawed strategy and conflicting imperatives issued by the SOC, and especially the vigor of local and regional hostility confounded the struggle of union veterans such as William Shiflett to carry on Operation Dixie's mandate after its initial moment had passed. The unity of political and economic interests among the state and region's blacks and whites, working class and middle class, workers and unionists, proved impossible to build.

Beset by a confusing array of external obstacles and internal problems, Operation Dixie ended up being, in many ways, more of a lesson in "the techniques of union-busting than union-building."[124] Employers, civic leaders, pastors, newspaper editors, local politicos, law firms, and manufacturers' associations enlisted all the tools at their disposal to undermine the CIO drive, including wiretaps, race-baiting, red-baiting, injunctions, arrests, discriminatory sentencing, lock-outs, firings, evictions, beatings, shootings, and threats to close mills permanently.

But the impunity with which southern employers, lawyers, and civic leaders attacked the southern organizing drive reflected yet another reason for Operation Dixie's ultimate demise. The postwar drive of the CIO to create a more favorable regional political climate in which unionism could take root and flourish also failed. And that failure further demonstrated the impact that the politics of race and the politics of modernization had on the hopes of Georgia's progressives that industrial democracy would be the legacy of World War II for the South.

Community hostility proved to be one of the biggest problems organizers routinely encountered. The discriminatory treatment that unionists and organizers consistently received in the local and state judicial systems in Georgia highlighted organized labor's political vulnerability. Judges' and prosecutors' ties to mill magnates, who financially supported local political campaigns, provided an incentive to rule against workers during local labor disputes. Organizers and local unions thus usually ended up on the losing end of struggles with local judicial and law enforcement institutions, which hostile local town councils, assemblies and state legislators sustained.[125]

Weakening this wall of opposition became imperative to accomplishing the CIO's postwar organizing goals for the region. "Winning the peace" for organized labor, one scholar has concluded, would have to mean directing "successful political action against . . . the political elite of Georgia's textile towns."[126] The key to this kind of challenge would be to empower the bulk of ordinary black and white citizens, who had been generally excluded from meaningful political participation through mechanisms such as poll taxes, all-white primaries, and the county unit system. Thus, the second arm of the postwar labor movement in Georgia became a political drive to enfranchise the state's black and white citizens, especially workers and unionists. Through its regional, state, and local political action committees (PACs), the CIO worked to forge a reliable voting constituency out of a coalition of diverse interests—one that could strengthen organized labor's political voice and influence in the state and region.[127] Operation Dixie relied on this political drive to weaken the local and state politicos and institutions arrayed against organized labor's interests. The failure of the CIO-PAC to accomplish this goal seriously hampered the success of the southern organizational drive in Georgia.

In at least two important elections in 1946—Helen Douglas Mankin's election in the Fifth Congressional District surrounding Atlanta and Henderson Lanham's election in the Seventh Congressional District around Rome—the southern PAC's strategy appeared to work. Voter registration campaigns and an alliance with other progressives and moderates succeeded in electing these two progressive candidates and defeating two reactionaries. The gubernatorial race that same year, however, proved to be a better indication of what organized labor's political fortunes in Georgia would be. GA-PAC privately endorsed James V. Carmichael as the lesser of evils compared to the reactionary Eugene Talmadge and the unelectable Eurith D. Rivers. The pro-modernization Carmichael, however, turned out to be barely lukewarm for organized labor and incapable of surmounting the continued strength of the state's discriminatory political institutions and practices. Carmichael's defeat, together with the election of a rash of pro-modernization, "good government" veterans to the state legislature in 1946, thwarted the Georgia CIO's political ambitions, further undermining Operation Dixie's chances for success.

THE NATIONAL CIO created the Political Action Committee (CIO-PAC) in 1943 to mobilize the votes of unionists, workers, and others for the 1944 presidential and congressional elections.[128] Specifically, the CIO-PAC maintained an officially nonpartisan stance, not formally endorsing candidates but building a network of local PACs. These groups worked to register voters, to inform the electorate on candidates and issues, and to promote civic responsibility and voter turnout, all of which aimed to carry forth a "progressive agenda into the postwar period."[129] Local PACs often took an active role in primary elections—from distributing literature to orchestrating voter registration drives—in order to "generally alert the membership to the importance of the forthcoming election" and to "lay [the] groundwork for a revitalized postwar New Deal."[130] The CIO-PAC, according to one scholar, heralded voter participation in 1944 as a "crusade for social justice and common decency," rejected "racial and ethnic prejudice," and made outright appeals to blacks and women as well.[131] Not surprisingly, southern political and civic leaders responded in kind, by condemning the CIO-PAC's meddling in southern electoral affairs and predicting that dire racial consequences would flow from any attempt to mobilize the black and white working class.[132]

In 1946 the CIO-PAC especially wanted to defeat conservatives in Congress and state legislatures who clearly wanted to overturn the gains organized labor had made before and during the war. That same year, for example, southern congressmen led a Senate filibuster that defeated an effort by organized labor and other New Deal progressives to enact a permanent FEPC.[133] This renewal of conservative strength made defeating the regional reactionaries who dominated key congressional committees, as well as politics in their home states, a top priority for southern and national progressives.

Much as in 1944, the CIO planned to use local PACs to organize and assist voter registration drives, to distribute literature on candidates, issues, and voting, and to mobilize turnout at the state, ward, and precinct levels.[134] The opportunity to expand the southern working-class electorate seemed especially promising because the *Smith v. Allwright* decision in 1944 had abolished, at least temporarily, the all-white Democratic primary. Thus, the CIO-PAC moved quickly to take advantage of this "critical opportunity."[135]

The southern PAC complemented the efforts of other black and white veterans and citizens to use the southern primaries of 1946 to register a strong progressive voice in the South.[136] The CIO-PAC's emphasis on black political participation as one of the foundations of this drive, along with its stated allegiance to progressive racial reform, however, contradicted the strategy adopted by the CIO's other arm of the postwar labor movement, the SOC. Under Van Bittner, the SOC downplayed any association with the CIO's progressive racial principles in

order to court southern white workers and to avoid community backlash.[137] Bittner had once described the CIO-PAC movement as "the greatest crusade," essential to a "rededication of our lives to the fundamental objectives of the New Deal."
Now, as director of the southern organizational drive, he initially prohibited
SOC organizers from cooperating with the southern PAC campaign, declaring
that "no crowd, whether Communist, Socialist, or anyone else will be permitted to mix up in this campaign," including "the Southern Conference for Human
Welfare or any other organization living off the CIO."[138] Any focus at all on the
question of race, Bittner explained, "is hurting our drive and I am not going to
allow anything to interfere with the organization of workers into CIO unions."[139]

Expedience soon dictated otherwise. Forbidding any alliance between Operation Dixie organizers and the southern PAC movement proved to be impracti-
cal. It simply did not make sense to take an already small coterie of progressives,
labor organizers, and activists and divide it into artificial categories that really
only had meaning at the higher levels of SOC and CIO leadership. According to
one account, Bittner soon put the differences in intent and strategy between
these dual threads of the CIO's postwar labor movement in the South on the
backburner, at least temporarily, in the interest of taking mutual advantage of
the political opportunity to defeat the region's worst anti-union reactionaries.
Thus, in 1946, organizers, staff, and members of both Operation Dixie and the
southern PAC movement worked much more closely on accomplishing the CIO's
southern political agenda than they later would, as a "fragile truce prevailed" in
order to focus all progressives' "energies and attention on the southern primary
races."[140]

Georgia emerged as one of the "most promising arenas" to launch this postwar political agenda. In the wake of the abolition of the poll tax during the war
and the *Primus King* decision overturning the all-white primary in Georgia in
1946, the southern PACs joined the SCHW, black citizen groups, and progressive
veterans in targeting the state's first postwar primary elections.[141] GA-PAC aided
the SCHW and the NAACP campaigns to increase the black vote but focused
much of its energy on enfranchising union members, black and white.[142] "We
are touching the taproots of democracy in this state," proclaimed Lucy Randolph Mason, an official of both the SOC and the SCHW, and "[we] are going to
release new forces for good and right."[143] In 1947 Daniel Powell, the regional director of the CIO-PAC, described the citizens of Georgia as "politicized as not since
the days of [Tom] Watson and the Populist movement" at the turn of the twentieth century.[144]

The Fifth and Seventh Congressional Districts, in the central and northwest
part of the state, represented two of the strongest pockets of CIO strength in Geor-

gia. The successful effort by Georgia's coalition of liberals to "politicize" citizens in these districts testified to the potential of the southern PAC strategy to forge an alliance of interests among a diversity of ordinary black and white Georgians.

In the Fifth Congressional District, centered around Atlanta, a special election to fill a vacant congressional seat in February 1946—an election that would not occur under the county unit system—offered the first opportunity for GA-PAC and other progressives to apply their postwar southern strategy. Like black citizens and veterans in Atlanta's Ashby Street district and white veterans in the American Veterans Committee, the Georgia CIO liked candidate Helen Douglas Mankin for her liberal record of support in the state for labor and child welfare legislation. She was certainly preferable to her opponent, Thomas Camp, a lobbyist for the powerful Georgia Railway Company, who had earned the support of the Talmadge camp.[145] Though endorsing Mankin's candidacy, the CIO-PAC made no direct financial contribution to her campaign, according to one CIO-PAC director, but did spend around $1,000 to register voters who were expected to support her in the election. Like the later ACRC drive, the GA-PAC also distributed literature and canvassed the district, with twenty-five PAC workers blanketing the five wards two days before the election with around 25,000 pamphlets. They also went door-to-door and made individual phone calls to encourage voters to turn out on election day.[146]

After a close and controversial race, Mankin won the election, particularly on the strength of black votes in the Ashby Street district, marking the first postwar success of Georgia's progressive coalition of union members, blacks, and veterans. However, Mankin subsequently lost her bid for reelection in the regular primary later that year because that election occurred under the county unit system.[147]

In the Seventh Congressional District, centered around the textile mill communities of Rome and Dalton, organized labor represented a larger segment of the electorate. Here, the GA-PAC met more lasting success, helping to defeat the incumbent anti-union conservative Malcolm Tarver and to elect Henderson Lanham, who promised to be much more sympathetic to labor and to a postwar New Deal agenda.[148] At the center of this coalition of progressives, unionists, blacks, and middle-class citizens stood a core of black and white World War II veterans who were anxious to direct their communities toward a different future than what Tarver had represented.

As a network of textile communities from the north Georgia hills down into the Chattahoochee Valley to the west, the Seventh Congressional District had drawn much attention from Operation Dixie organizers. It also included TWUA

Local 787 at Anchor Rome and Local 689 at the Celanese Mill, with their active veteran membership. Winning the Seventh District congressional seat, the Georgia CIO calculated, would demonstrate labor's burgeoning political potential, be a significant step in accomplishing CIO-PAC's postwar program in Georgia, and by extension, improve Operation Dixie's chances of organizing the state.[149]

As early as 1944, GA-PAC had leafleted area mills and plants to encourage voter registration and to spread the message of activism and education on behalf of organized labor. That activity increased with the poll tax's demise. "As you know, the poll tax was just eliminated in Georgia," wrote Charles Gillman, GA-PAC chairman, to Paul Christopher, a CIO national representative, in late 1945. "We hope to have our complete committee established before very long," he explained, "in order to put on a concerted drive towards the registering of our people."[150] The Georgia CIO soon held a convention to establish the Seventh Congressional District Political Action Committee. Delegates from locals throughout the district listened to CIO and PAC representatives explain labor's political agenda, elected officers for the Seventh District PAC, and outlined their own plan of action. Celanese Local 689 contributed organizer Hugh Gammon as director of the district PAC, and Georgia's CIO officials sent out a call to action to the delegates and locals in attendance. "We are part of the community," declared Kenneth Douty, Georgia's TWUA director, "and must see that the people's representatives in the legislature vote for the interests of the people and not for special interests." Thus, announced Charles Gillman, "We want to see PAC go further in Georgia than in any other state in the South. We've got a job to do and we must get busy."[151] TWUA locals in northwest Georgia—especially those with the most active veteran members—often took the lead in carrying out these political efforts.

The primary goal in 1946 was to defeat the district's reactionary incumbent, Malcolm Tarver, who had sat in Congress for twenty years and been undefeated in politics for twenty more.[152] Tarver had a well-deserved reputation for impugning any New Deal program that smacked of progressive social reform. He played a pivotal role in launching the conservative attack on the Farm Security Administration in Congress in 1940 and in limiting its subsequent operations. His reputation as a "classic southern anti–New Dealer" stretched far and wide, and he represented exactly the sort of antilabor reactionary that postwar progressives and organized labor especially wanted to see removed.[153]

Henderson Lanham, the solicitor general of Floyd County, represented the type of candidate the CIO-PAC hoped to elect. Lanham adopted a moderately progressive stance and solicited support from "every forward looking person," rather than relying on the usual coterie of courthouse loungers and politicos. Although he opposed the sort of strikes that "could paralyze the industries of the entire country," still he endorsed organized labor's right to strike and bargain collectively.[154]

To avoid provoking outright antilabor attacks by Tarver supporters that might tarnish Lanham, the Seventh District PAC maintained official neutrality in the congressional primary, focusing publicly only on voter registration. However, the district PAC scarcely concealed its opposition to Tarver and its support of his opponent. In late March, for example, PAC field organizer Robert Hodges reported accompanying GA-PAC director Charles Gillman to a meeting with Henderson Lanham. After the men discussed Lanham's probable candidacy, Hodges concluded that "Mr. Lanham in my opinion is the best man in the district to make the race."[155] To facilitate Lanham's success, the Seventh District PAC worked to register as many union members and families as possible and sent Robert Hodges to meet regularly with CIO locals in the district to explain the PAC's purpose and program. Of twelve meetings with different locals or organizing committees in one week, for example, Hodges noted receiving a good to enthusiastic reception in at least eight. In particular, Hodges had a "very good meeting" with Celanese (Tubize) Local 689, which had established its own PAC already, and enjoyed a "very fine reception" from about one hundred members of Anchor Rome Local 787. Both were locals with a significant veteran membership.[156] To coordinate much of this work, the GA-PAC also maintained a list of union members, union officers, and local legislative committees for each congressional district in the state; the Seventh Congressional District had 13,170 CIO members in twenty locals in 1946.[157]

Each CIO local in the district, including those with veteran members at the Celanese, Anchor Rome, and Cedartown Textile Mills, contributed funds to help along Lanham's election. GA-PAC assigned sixteen men to work in Floyd (Rome), Polk (Cedartown), Paulding (Dallas), Whitfield (Dalton), and Walker (LaFayette) Counties on Lanham's behalf, focusing particularly on increasing voter registration and turnout. District PAC workers assigned to the counties worked full-time for the ten days preceding the election, and GA-PAC contributed four sets of sound equipment for two weeks and the gasoline for fifty cars to haul workers to the polls on election day.[158]

Nonetheless, GA-PAC remained publicly mum concerning specific candidates, except in Tarver's home county of Polk, where organizers directly attacked his anti-union record, in response to Tarver's own labor-baiting. As Michelle Brattain found in her excellent analysis of the Seventh District PAC and Lanham's election, however, at least one group of white veterans in Rome showed no such reluctance. They mounted a public campaign against Tarver from the pages of the *Floyd County Herald*, the newspaper they owned and operated. They regularly scored Tarver's congressional voting record, particularly on veterans' issues, and offered their opinions on any other campaign question that arose. Moreover, black veterans proved to be key participants in a voter registration drive initiated by black citizens and the local branch of the NAACP in anticipation of the elections.[159] "When [these] fellows began to come back from the war," remembered one participant, they joined this progressive campaign out of a conviction that "I served my country. I deserve more freedom, I deserve more rights." This activism ultimately tripled local black registration, which prompted county Talmadgites, concerned about the implications for the gubernatorial race, to orchestrate a purge of black names from the voter rolls. This effort failed, but it provoked even some white citizens in the community to come to black voters' defense. "I shudder to think of the circumstances we might now be living under," noted white veteran Glen McCullough, had the notion behind this purge "been applied to Negroes when the Draft law was effected."[160]

A coalition of moderate and progressive citizens in the Seventh Congressional District gave Lanham a two-to-one popular majority, handing the incumbent Tarver his first electoral defeat in forty years.[161] This outcome had been accomplished by the coalescing of opposition to Tarver among a diverse group of working-class and middle-class citizens, unionists and not, blacks and whites, veterans and civilians, who wanted an alternative candidate more sympathetic to working people and organized labor and more willing to court the support of a cross-section of the community's ordinary citizens. Michelle Brattain has concluded that this election offered "a glimmer of what the CIO had envisioned for the postwar South—an organized, informed, active electorate of black and white Georgians supporting change, even if they supported candidates independently and for different reasons."[162]

However, whether in the Fifth District race or in the Seventh, as Michelle Brattain points out, these victories did not always come about because of the southern PAC, which often felt compelled to take a public backseat in these races, even as it supplied funds and manpower to expand the electorate. Nor did it mean that all those who joined this coalition at the time had internalized the progressive principles of the CIO-PAC, particularly regarding the question of black equality. In the Seventh District, according to Brattain, white unionists who had joined black citizens in opposing Tarver in 1946 later endorsed Vaughan Terrell, the Talmadge functionary who had led the earlier efforts to purge black voters in Floyd County.[163]

The mixed results that came from the CIO-PAC drive against Eugene Talmadge's gubernatorial campaign the same year in the Seventh District further demonstrated the extent to which the CIO-PAC's white constituency in Georgia "remained a part of the white South."[164] Ultimately, the strength of racial loyalties, which only intensified for many white Georgians as the postwar decade progressed, undermined what the CIO-PAC had hoped to achieve. An empowered and broad-based political constituency that could unite behind the southern organizational drive across the state failed to develop.

The congressional election in the Seventh District had revolved more around the nature of Tarver's anti–New Deal record and the postwar political role of organized labor. Race, however, emerged as the central feature of the gubernatorial election throughout the state, creating a difficult climate for any campaign that advocated a politics of change. Eugene Talmadge had seized the opportunity presented by the *Smith* and *Primus King* decisions to mount a reelection bid based almost entirely on the restoration of the white primary and a reassertion of white supremacy in Georgia. His primary opponent, James V. Carmichael, a Marietta businessman, confronted a continual race-baiting assault from the Talmadge camp throughout the campaign, despite Carmichael's attempt to proclaim his own southern white credentials. Organized labor, particularly the CIO, found itself besieged by the Talmadge camp as well, as the progressive racial agenda of the national body combined with the interracial electoral strategy of the southern PAC to make it an easy target. Moreover, both Talmadge and Carmichael attacked the CIO for working hand-in-hand with international communism, as allegedly evidenced by the CIO-PAC's racially progressive and socially radical agenda for change.

Nonetheless, the rapid expansion of voter registration rolls proved to be the signal feature of the 1946 gubernatorial election, including large numbers of citizens who were not previously registered to vote. Both camps were sensitive to the need to somehow court this new constituency, whose political proclivities were up for anyone's speculation. Thus, both Talmadge and Carmichael tried to play it safe, in a sense, by forgoing direct attacks on the southern organizational drive, verbally endorsing the right to organize *and* to work, and leveling their real anti-union attacks at the national CIO-PAC. This attack often came in the form of race-baiting, by condemning organized labor's political arm as an "outside agitator" bent on controlling politics in the state and undermining Georgia's most hallowed political and racial traditions. Thus, Eugene Talmadge, according to one account, did not "personally attack PAC," but he berated Carmichael as the "CIO-PAC candidate" and the "Niggers candidate." For his part, Carmichael launched a direct assault on the GA-PAC as an "outside influence" seeking to undermine democracy in Georgia.[165]

The nature of the gubernatorial campaign created a ticklish situation for the GA-PAC. On the one hand, Eugene Talmadge represented precisely the type of

racial, anti-union, and anti–New Deal reactionary that labor and liberal reformers most wanted to see defeated in 1946. After all, one of Talmadge's most
infamous acts as Georgia's governor during the great textile strikes of 1934 had
been to round up striking workers, including women and children, and incar-
cerate them in a barbed wire–enclosed encampment—essentially treating Georgia's own working-class citizenry like national enemies. Because of this record,
most political pundits in Georgia and elsewhere expected the votes of unionists
and workers to go to James V. Carmichael.[166]

On the other hand, Carmichael presented a problem, too.[167] An organizing
campaign underway shortly before the election at a Marietta furniture plant
owned by Carmichael resulted in the filing of unfair labor practice charges against
him with the NLRB in 1946.[168] Already besieged in a difficult race, this action did
not sit well with Carmichael, who promptly launched his first blistering attack
on GA-PAC in response. Yet, the Georgia CIO recognized that Carmichael was the
candidate endorsed by most moderates and progressives in the state, including
Governor Ellis Arnall, and was the man in the race most likely to attract a broad
base of support sufficient to defeat Talmadge. In any event, Carmichael certainly
offered a more modern, respectable, and potentially moderate approach to governing Georgia than his opponents, and he had promised to uphold the decision overturning the white primary. Thus, while GA-PAC publicly endorsed no
candidate, it pledged to defeat Talmadge "at any cost," conducted voter registration drives, and privately assisted the Carmichael campaign. This activism had
a definite impact, convincing Carmichael to abandon his initial attacks on the
CIO-PAC.

Carmichael declared in May 1946, for example, that "I resent [the CIO-PAC's]
entrance into Georgia's political and economic life," and he called on supporters
to help "win this fight by an overwhelming majority."[169] However, shortly before
election day, Carmichael suddenly switched tactics, delivering speeches in Americus, Dalton, and other communities that now embraced labor's right to bargain
collectively, promised to leave the question of the closed shop to workers and
employers, and pledged to not enlist force against legal and peaceful union operations.[170] Not long before this apparent about-face, Daniel Powell, the regional
PAC director, received a letter from Tilford Dudley, assistant to the CIO-PAC chairman, which included the layout for a pamphlet prepared specifically for the
Carmichael campaign. Dudley directed Powell to deliver the pamphlet to Maynard Smith, Carmichael's campaign manager, for distribution among CIO plants
because it offered a good explanation of the "choices" for workers in the upcoming gubernatorial election.[171]

The threat posed by the state's mobilized black and white working-class voters prompted the Talmadge campaign to resort to tried-and-true tactics. As early as June 2, rumors swirled that the Talmadge campaign had blanketed Troup County mill districts with pictures of black foremen "lording it" over white female workers, a blatant scare tactic meant to connect the CIO and the GA-PAC to black social equality, thereby provoking white citizens' sense of racial identity.[172] In late June, Herman Talmadge telegrammed C. L. Foster, a Talmadge functionary, regarding a speech to be delivered in Columbus by Georgia politico Roy V. Harris on Eugene Talmadge's behalf. Herman requested sound machines, noting that he "would like for him to speak right there in the middle of textile mill section primarily on white primary and FEPC bill," another obvious racial ploy. The following day, Herman mailed a batch of circulars to Foster and asked him to ensure their distribution "from door to door in the mill section." In fact, Herman advised, "try and get someone favorable to our cause in the mill section to handle this distribution." This was important, he explained, because "I feel sure that a wide distribution of this circular will make the difference in carrying or losing a number of counties in which mills are located."[173]

Despite Herman's prediction, the outcome of this election in Floyd County at first seemed a replication of what had happened in the Seventh District congressional race. Although Carmichael ultimately lost the gubernatorial race through the county unit system in the state as a whole, he did win a popular majority of votes, and in Floyd County, where the GA-PAC had directed most of its efforts, he won a clear victory. This included a strong showing in the Tubize district, the core of union strength for Celanese Local 689.

However, Eugene Talmadge still won the gubernatorial election, particularly by attracting whites in enough smaller rural counties to capture the unit votes, by purging a significant number of black citizens from the registration rolls, and by enlisting intimidation, fraud, and even violence to scare others away from the polls on election day.[174] His election, in particular, pointed to the strength of the political opposition that progressive campaigns still confronted in the early postwar South. In generating political activism among black and white progressive veterans in Georgia, including unionists, the war made the question of racial reform and organized labor's place in the state prominent issues in the first postwar elections. That, in turn, provoked a reactionary backlash in defense of the status quo that Georgia's progressives, including organized labor, could not overcome.[175] The politics of race and anti-unionism sharply circumscribed the potential of the CIO's postwar political agenda for Georgia.[176] This failure to build the broad coalition of interests among the state's ordinary black and white citizens, in turn, undermined the southern organizational drive and the ability of organizers and union veterans such as William Shiflett to carry on in the face of growing state, regional, and national hostility.

Though many counties with a strong labor presence, such as those in the Seventh District, went to Carmichael, many outlying counties throughout the state did not. Even in the Celanese mill village district, where the Floyd County PAC had increased the rate of voter turnout in the gubernatorial race by 51 percent over the 1942 election, labor votes still split between Talmadge and Carmichael.[177] Indeed, though white unionists and workers in Georgia sometimes staunchly resisted such tactics, race increasingly poisoned the surrounding climate. As the question of black civil rights grew ever more prominent on the national Democratic agenda, the white union rank and file in Georgia, according to Brattain, eventually grew as "preoccupied with race" as Georgia politicians. Even as the GA-PAC continued to register more unionists and workers to vote in Georgia, its influence over how those votes were cast slipped over time. In the Celanese district, for example, where voter registration had grown enormously since 1942, voters ignored the GA-PAC's recommendations and supported Herman Talmadge's race-baiting gubernatorial campaign in 1950.[178] The political direction that Georgia unionists would take in a given race at any particular time remained hard to predict, which also did not bode well for the southern labor movement's need for a stable constituency that could be relied upon to vote in a particular way.

Finally, the "fragile truce" between the SOC and the GA-PAC that prevailed in 1946 soon disintegrated. Division among union officials and organizers in Georgia grew quickly apparent. State PAC leaders and organizers, for example, split over which candidate to support in the 1948 gubernatorial campaign in Georgia. While the leadership apparently tended to favor moderate governor Melvin Thompson over racial reactionary Herman Talmadge, rank-and-file organizers tended to support the progressive candidate and World War II veteran Joseph Rabun. J. P. Mooney, a TWUA-PAC representative in Georgia, for example, wrote to his director, Al Barkan, that "in contacting the key people of some of TWUA and other CIO locals, also staff members, I find a very strong feeling against both Talmadge and Thompson." Noting that Kenneth Douty, Georgia TWUA director, had endorsed Thompson, Mooney also pointed out the support of the GA-PAC executive board and the Second District PAC for Rabun. "I consider that any attempt to change this course of action now," he explained, "would only weaken or possibly destroy any hope for a unified PAC movement for a very long time."[179] And this prediction did not even take into consideration the shift among ordinary white unionists toward the Talmadge camp. The unity of interest among blacks, whites, unionists, workers, and middle-class citizens that the southern PAC had hoped to build never really coalesced in any lasting fashion in the early postwar era.[180] This shortcoming weakened organized labor's voice in the state's postwar political councils, as citizens of every political stripe competed to define what Georgia's future would be. It also further undermined Operation Dixie's chances of success in a state and region notoriously hostile to the notion of industrial democracy.

Along with the activism of Georgia's other progressives, union veterans reflected the disruptive impact of the war on the political, racial, and economic stability that sustained the one-party South. Their failure to make a lasting difference for organized labor, however, also exposed what the limits to the political redirection of the postwar South would be. A progressive reconstruction of the state's politics on a foundation of enfranchised white and black unionists would not happen anytime soon. In part, race remained too central a feature on the southern political landscape for the broad coalition organized labor wanted to build to succeed.

But race was not the only obstacle that organized labor faced in postwar Georgia. Union veterans not only confronted the hostility of the southern old guard in their fight to reform their state and region. They also faced a largely successful campaign to define economic growth and "good government"—the other watchwords of the postwar era—as the politics of change to emerge from the war. That vision of Georgia's future also had no place for organized labor or any notion of progress premised on the empowerment of Georgia's black and white workers. White veterans, again, would be the key players in the good government campaigns, which proved to be the most successful of the postwar insurgencies generated by the war. Yet the vision of industrial or racial democracy that their progressive comrades-in-arms regarded as the war's democratic mandate would pay the price for this fateful accommodation of change and tradition that became the Second World War's most lasting political legacy for Georgia and the South.

We Are Not Radicals, Neither Are We Reactionaries

Good Government Veterans and the Politics of Modernization

LIEUTENANT COLONEL John J. Flynt wasted little time when he returned to his home in Griffin, Georgia, in 1945 after many months overseas. Having earned a Bronze Star in the European theater, he resumed his former position as assistant U.S. district attorney for north Georgia. Within a few short months, Flynt won the Spalding County seat in the Georgia statehouse. Shortly after this electoral victory, he appeared as a guest columnist in the *Atlanta Constitution,* an opportunity Flynt used to explain what Georgia's veterans wanted and why people should listen to them.

Over 60 percent of Georgia's World War I veterans, Flynt began, never returned to their home state or left it soon after the war's end because they found "better places to live, or places that were more in keeping with the progressive age in which they lived." Now, he warned, "unless Georgia keeps abreast of other states, the same thing will happen again." Those men and women who survived the war "have returned to Georgia because of all the places we have seen we like Georgia best." Veterans like himself—and Flynt meant white veterans—"have all come back with a determination to make Georgia a better place and to do our part of that job." Thus, he announced, "the veterans of this, our Georgia, expect and demand the enactment of . . . legislation that will make possible the advancement and progress to which we feel that all Georgians are entitled." This program included improving public health services, since "during our war service we have seen the results of both healthful and unhealthful living conditions in all parts of the world." Moreover, veterans wanted access to twelve years of public school education for their children, to improve and expand the Georgia university system, and to place vocational and trade schools in all parts of the state. Georgia's veterans "gave up our civilian jobs and professions . . . to fight on all continents and on all oceans," Flynt explained; now they saw the need for "sound and progressive legislation" for the betterment of Georgia. Above all, he emphasized, "we are not radicals, neither are we reactionaries."[1]

The vision of progress painted by Flynt derived from a keen determination that many returning white veterans shared to modernize Georgia's economy and government. The experience of the war had served as a mirror, in a sense, reflecting back all of Georgia's social, economic, and political ills to white veterans who rarely, if ever, had traveled outside their state, region, or country before. Traveling throughout the United States and overseas exposed them to levels of development unheard of at home, from modern road systems and public health services to sophisticated educational facilities. All of this underscored Georgia's apparent backwardness. Moreover, the war against Germany and Japan, and the rhetoric that surrounded it, intimately acquainted veterans with the cost of an extreme politics of corruption, exclusion, and reactionism. Together, these influences prompted often uncomfortable revelations about the causes of Georgia's obvious economic and political deficiencies.

Indeed, the pattern of Georgia's postwar political life, characterized by inadequate tax revenues, limited public services, civic apathy, political cronyism, and a reactionary resistance to federal economic intervention, met significant challenges as mobilizing for war and then reconverting to peace became top priorities throughout the nation. The usual excuses for spending as little as possible to maintain streets, schools, and sewage systems, to regulate the proliferation of vice and crime, to build public housing, or to develop plans to recruit industry fell flat in the wake of the development and spending that came with the war, undermining popular faith in the fitness of incumbents to rule. The structures of southern political life, particularly a truncated electorate, perpetuated economic and political conservatism even though the challenges and opportunities of the postwar era seemed to demand change. Georgia's returning white veterans quickly discovered that achieving the prosperity and progress they wanted depended first on winning a homefront battle against the political incumbency, civic complacency, and electoral fraud that had long sustained Bourbon rule.

In response, Georgia's white veterans, riding a wave of civic insurgency that fed on the instability in political, economic, and race relations generated by the war and its aftermath, organized political reform leagues to challenge the conservative political establishment in communities throughout the state. Good government veterans, as they often labeled themselves, organized voter registration drives, rallied popular support behind moderate candidates, and blasted local incumbents as impediments to progress. Their agitation generated political shock waves that reverberated throughout Georgia's cities, towns, and rural communities and helped draw a historic number of citizens into local and statewide politics after the war.[2] In 1946 alone, white veterans' pro-modernization campaigns nearly defeated Eugene Talmadge's reactionary bid to recapture the governorship and succeeded in toppling Georgia's longest-lived urban political machines in Augusta and Savannah.

As Flynt noted, however, good government veterans were neither radicals nor reactionaries. This characterization reflected the political middle of the road that the majority of Georgia's white veterans believed would lead their state into a modernized new day. Conservative local regimes were objectionable not because they routinely denied civic and economic rights to black southerners and workers. Rather, their habits of electoral fraud, civic intimidation, and political corruption impeded creating programs of industrial recruitment and economic development that these veterans believed to be the foundation of real progress.

Thus, good government veterans thought of themselves as "modernizers," as offering a new and positive program of progress and growth beneficial to all Georgians. The reality, however, was quite different. In fact, they remained wedded to the racial traditions and anti-unionism that continued to constrain Georgia's political options. A diversity of veterans fought for substantive political change in postwar Georgia. Their shared antipathy to provincial reactionary conservatives sometimes encouraged cooperation across racial and class lines. In Savannah, for example, black veterans supported white veterans in the reformist Citizens Progressive League in 1946 as a better political option for African Americans than the incumbents bolstered by the local machine. When it came to what the defeat of Georgia's conservative political establishment would mean for the postwar future, however, veterans' agendas for change completely diverged. Desegregation still seemed largely unimaginable and undesirable to good government veterans, the politics of race increasingly constrained everyone's political options, and ambitions for development and growth seemed to dictate the defeat of organized labor.

Far from charting a path to racial and economic justice—which would have meant a comprehensive break with the past for Georgia—good government veterans melded their call for economic development, honest elections, and efficient administrations with the maintenance of white supremacy and opposition to unionization. This program of "conservative modernization" proved remarkably successful in postwar Georgia. It resonated with white citizens anxious to leave the days of the Great Depression behind them, yet who were unwilling to enter into a new era of truly reformed social, economic, or racial relations. Thus, good government campaigns succeeded in defeating local incumbents, toppling some key political machines, and electing veterans to at least one-fifth of the seats in the Georgia General Assembly in 1946. The contradictory politics of change they pursued, however, ensured that economic development, racial stability, and anti-unionism—not racial or industrial democracy—would define the war's political legacy for Georgia.

FOR MANY OF GEORGIA'S white soldiers and sailors, service in World War II was a disconcerting experience, but not simply because of its inherent inhumanity and destructiveness. Traveling to new and often exotic places, far and wide, broadened the horizons of southerners who very often had never before been outside the region. This exposure to different cultures and worlds promised to have significant ramifications for the homefront. "You were exposed to the world . . . and you had different ideas than the parochial world you had lived before you went into the military," recalled Griffin Bell, a Georgia war veteran and later U.S. attorney general. J. H. Bottoms, a U.S. Navy boatswain's mate, echoed this sentiment: "I was born and reared in Georgia and never realized what a place it really was until I got out of it."[3]

Discovering what kind of place Georgia "really was" often served to generate a newly critical perspective. Entering the military while Georgia still struggled to overcome the burden of the Great Depression, veterans at times were amazed at the level of development and prosperity that existed in other states and nations. Flynt explained during his 1946 campaign for a seat in the Georgia state legislature, for example, that in "comparison with some of the places he had seen . . . there was much to be done back home . . . in health, education, housing, and roads."[4] George T. Bennett agreed, remarking that after seeing conditions in "Florida and California, in Maine and Texas," veterans returning to Gainesville, Georgia, "will notice as I did just how far Gainesville is behind in this modern world." After attending a concert by the Nippon Philharmonic Orchestra, Private James Moffett marveled at the cultural sophistication he saw in Tokyo and wondered why Atlanta paled in comparison: "It's generally believed in various sections of the country . . . that the South is backward in every respect," he noted. Yet, "less than a year after v-j day," the Japanese "have mustered an orchestra capable of giving a concert comparable to many heard in the United States." Sadly,

Atlanta "can't compare insofar as culture . . . is concerned, with a city that has been the objective of bombing and foreign occupation."[5]

What seemed to impress Georgia's white servicemen as much as what they saw during the war, however, was what they heard. Homesick for the cotton fields and scruffy towns of home, they encountered less sympathy than recrimination and ridicule. Other Americans (and in some cases, foreigners) rarely let pass an opportunity to belittle Georgia as the epitome of the South's "benighted" image. Discovering that one's home state defined "bad government" and "backwardness" in the minds of other Americans was a humbling experience that few white veterans forgot.

The antics of former governor Eugene Talmadge, who had served several terms as governor in the 1930s and early 1940s, had long been synonymous with the reputation for corruption, provincialism, and high-handedness that Georgia politics had long enjoyed. Few would dispute that Talmadge had provided plenty of fodder to fuel national ridicule during his terms as agricultural commissioner and as governor. Not every politician, for example, could make political capital out of provoking an investigation into misuse of funds, but Talmadge did. As commissioner of agriculture in the 1920s, one of Talmadge's most infamous feats involved purchasing eighty-two truckloads of Georgia hogs from local farmers to ship to Chicago, all without any legal appropriation of funds for that purpose. In the ensuing imbroglio, Talmadge publicly asserted that "if I stole, it was for the farmer," an explanation that may have delighted his wool-hat followers but that left uptown Georgians writhing with embarrassment.[6]

As governor during the Great Depression, Talmadge reached new heights of absurdity and reaction. The "wild man from Sugar Creek" pastured a cow on the statehouse lawn, kept the capital in a state of martial law for months as he consolidated his control of state agencies, and declared the young men serving in the Civilian Conservation Corps to be "bums and loafers." Talmadge also called out the state national guard in a brutal suppression of Georgia workers in the great textile strike of 1934. These troops incarcerated thousands of strikers in barbed wire camps and even beat one worker to death in front of his family. The following year, Talmadge provoked an impasse with the Georgia General Assembly by vetoing old-age pensions, seven constitutional amendments, and hundreds of local measures. State legislators subsequently adjourned in late 1935 without having appropriated money to operate the state government in 1936. Talmadge then defied state law and political convention (at least to those outside Georgia) by having the adjutant general physically remove the state treasurer from his office in order to force open the state vault.[7]

Such capers, and there were plenty of others, drew national attention to Georgia's "banana republic" political style. With Talmadge publicly bragging about having read *Mein Kampf* seven times just as war broke out in Europe, more and more observers drew a connection between his style of governing and that displayed by totalitarian and militaristic regimes overseas. Newspapers remarked, for example, that Talmadge "is getting to be worse than Hitler or Mussolini" and that he was a "paper-mache dictator" who administered "lynch law" in Georgia. Talmadge's response was not to deny these charges but to embrace them: "I'm what you might call a minor dictator. But did you ever see anybody that was much good who didn't have a little dictator in him?"[8]

Georgia's servicemen and women entered the armed forces with Talmadge's reputation already well established. His reckless attack on the University Board of Regents in 1940 and 1941, however, provided a new source of embarrassment. Petty political jealousies brought to Talmadge's attention two professors and administrators who were working to improve the education of white and black students in Georgia. Walter D. Cocking and Marvin D. Pittman, both hired from outside the state, had reputations as progressive educators, which meant, among other things, that they advocated improving facilities and training for students and teachers irrespective of race. Cocking had been hired to rebuild the University of Georgia's College of Education, and as part of his effort he had accepted money from the liberal Rosenwald Fund. He then recommended building a new school to train both rural white and black teachers, without specifying any provisions for segregated attendance. In response to this, and to Pittman's reputation for similar "infractions," Talmadge demanded that the University Board of Regents refuse to reappoint either professor. When the Board of Regents dutifully fired both men, the Southern Association of Colleges and Secondary Schools revoked its accreditation of ten Georgia colleges and universities for "unprecedented and unjustifiable political interference" in the administration of higher education. "Here in the heart of Dixie," cried the *Saint Louis Times-Dispatch*, "has developed a prize specimen of full-blown American fascism."[9]

Many Georgia GIs in service in 1941 and 1942 cringed at this latest display of classic Talmadgism. "At least forty of my company are Northerners from New York, Pennsylvania, Ohio, and New Jersey," all of whom watched Talmadge's feud with the Board of Regents unfold "with great interest," wrote one soldier at the Augusta Air Force Base to his friend James Setze in Atlanta. "What could I say about my home state after such a farce was enacted," he lamented, adding "small wonder that Northerners have such views about the South."[10] Filipinos in Manila put Sergeant Norman Tant of Georgia on the spot by questioning him about the racial implications of Talmadge's behavior. "I was ashamed and I could give no adequate explanation," he recalled; to Tant, as well as to many other soldiers, Talmadge's "actions stank 10,800 miles from Georgia."[11]

Nonsoutherners not only took shots at Georgia's political practices, they also pointed out the state's persistent economic and social shortcomings. Recalling that no one had "greater regard for Georgia" when he entered the service, Lewis Adams of Carrollton found himself "shocked and awakened" by "the many unfavorable but true things" his friends and shipmates knew about his home state. Adams grew too embarrassed to even claim his place of birth because he "grew tired of hearing how low Georgia stood in comparison to other states in education, how high it stood in illiteracy, physical unfitness, syphilis, murder, etc."[12] A Georgia soldier stationed in Orlando, Florida, remarked that a soldier away from home liked nothing better "than being able to brag to his buddies about conditions at home." However, "he likes to do it honestly and nothing is so irritating as having to 'take it' when somebody launches an attack on his state which he knows is justified."[13] Confronting this barrage of criticism and wisecracks, more than one Georgia soldier came to regard his home state less with nostalgia than with embarrassment. Military service taught them, often for the first time, just how different from the rest of the nation Georgia and the South really were.[14]

Not surprisingly, many veterans found Talmadge's reactionary campaign for governor in 1946 to be an unpleasant reminder of the unflattering attention Georgia had attracted during the war. As a serviceman, Thomas Y. Lovett of Athens complained, "I had an opportunity to see Georgia from the outside. I had the humiliation of being constantly reminded that my state was one of the most backward in the nation, and we Georgians were often called the electors of dictators and demagogues for governors." A soldier at Quantico, Virginia, similarly admitted that Georgia's servicemen and women had taken a lot of "wisecracks" from "people of other states concerning Georgia and her political leaders of the past."[15] J. C. Huddleston from LaGrange similarly remarked, "you would be surprised at the things that have been said by people from other states about the kind of rule the state of Georgia [has had]." In fact, "what they know and say about Talmadge would fill several volumes of books. Most of them classified him alongside of Hitler." "Hitler, Mussolini, and Tojo are gone," noted E. G. Wilkes of Atlanta, and soon, he predicted, "Eugene Talmadge is joining them." No one had done more "to retard the progress and growth of a state." "Men from all sections of the nation during my six-year cruise in the Navy . . . couldn't understand why the people of Georgia would elect a man like Talmadge," Wilkes observed. As far away as Japan, embarrassed GIs were "sick and tired," explained Captain Frank

Morrison, "of being ragged and ribbed about '[the] loud-mouthed, demagogic and dishonest government we have in Georgia.'"[16]

For many white veterans, the saving grace appeared to be Talmadge's defeat and Ellis Arnall's victory in the gubernatorial election of 1942. The image of poverty, backwardness, and reactionary, corrupt politics that dogged Georgia's servicemen and women in the early years of the war began to recede as the new governor demonstrated a more businesslike and democratic administration of state government. Arnall's accomplishments included the installation of a new state constitution, the passage of the first soldier voting law, the lowering of the age of voter eligibility to eighteen, the abolition of the poll tax, the allocation of increased expenditures for education, the establishment of a teacher retirement plan, the liquidation of the long-standing state debt without raising taxes, and a successful legal battle against the freight-rate differential. Suddenly, the Empire State now seemed the embodiment of modern and urbane government rather than its antithesis, and Georgia's servicemen and women appreciated the difference.[17]

Bill Boring, a war veteran and *Atlanta Constitution* reporter, first heard of Arnall in Egypt, where the accolades for the new governor surprised him. Used to hearing his peers say, "from Georgia, huh? It's a great state but how does a man like that Talmadge get elected Governor?," Boring "got a big lift in Cairo" when someone spoke well of Arnall, "particularly since all my life I had been accustomed to listening to indignities heaped upon my Governor."[18] Lewis Adams found that with Governor Arnall "to lead Georgia out of its backwardness," he finally could "lift [my] head and proudly say, 'I'm from Georgia.'" To James M. Stewart, "the progressive years" under Ellis Arnall made up for Georgia's previous "bad crops," while a "Cracker in Service" decided that Arnall "has really made a name for Georgia, and brought her forward from the lowest depths of corrupt government to a democracy admired by 47 states." Lieutenant P. D. Cunningham, stationed in Walla Walla, Washington, breathed a sigh of relief that Georgia had "finally rid herself of Talmadge" because now "us boys away from home can stop apologizing for Ol' Gene's antics."[19]

Talmadge's capriciousness, the constant criticism and ridicule about Georgia, and their own observations of the world outside their home state underscored for many white veterans what Georgia's political, social, and economic shortcomings really were. What created an actual sense of entitlement to a better future, however, was the act of serving in the war. Like other black and white ex-servicemen, good government veterans found their sense of political and male identity—their understanding of themselves as male citizens uniquely entitled and obligated to participate in political and civic affairs—magnified by serving in the war.[20]

Moreover, while survival may have been the driving force for most soldiers during the war, defending democracy and "good government" against dictatorship and "bad government" became the meaning many southern white veterans drew from their participation once they returned. This "recovered" sense of mission defined the war as a fight against governments removed from popular influence and unrestrained by concerns for political honesty and community betterment. The lessons of the recent war, Georgia's good government veterans came to believe, demanded vigilance against "bad government" at home.

Not surprisingly, the reemergence of former governors Eugene Talmadge and Eurith D. Rivers in the gubernatorial race of 1946 especially alarmed veterans who were by then well acquainted with the poor image both governors' previous administrations had foisted upon Georgia.[21] "Veterans are interested in building up and protecting the good name of Georgia," declared Sergeant Harry Baxter of Ashburn; "They fully realize how the shameful practices of the Talmadge and Rivers administrations blacken the name of Georgia." James Stewart warned Georgians "to look out again for these forces that want to destroy our land" and urged citizens to "join forces as good neighbors to keep Georgia that 'green pasture' so we will be proud to live in this famous state."[22]

In addition to opposing Talmadge and Rivers, veterans clashed with entrenched local county rings and urban machines, which they believed limited a community's postwar potential for development and growth. Military service enhanced veterans' sense of civic obligation and possibility and weakened the habits of deference that had helped to sustain these local dynasties, sometimes for generations. Men once regarded as the political "betters" of local communities, or at least tolerated as necessary evils, now stood as virtual national enemies. "Evil men made evil government in Germany and Japan," declared veterans in Gainesville. "It was for this reason alone that ninety-nine Hall county youth now lie buried in foreign lands . . . with hundreds more grievously wounded and maimed." And, they warned, "evil men can make evil government in Georgia. It has happened before . . . . It must not happen again."[23] Sergeant Harry Baxter agreed that veterans who "have made sacrifices in the name of democracy to overthrow dictators and tyrants in Europe and Asia" will not "return to power in their home state men who have shown beyond a doubt that they have all the characteristics and instincts of would be dictators." Henry McLemore, a newspaper editorialist and Georgia veteran, vowed to vote against Talmadge "for every boy who died in this war" because his "'enlightened'" program for Georgia was little more than a recapitulation of *Mein Kampf*. In fact, McLemore concluded, "there are men under the sands of Okinawa, who . . . were killed fighting against the things Mr. Talmadge says he stands for."[24] Veterans in Savannah lauded the local youth who had "answered the call to the colors . . . to 'stop dictatorship'" abroad, and then they denounced the local political machine for perpetrating the same thing "in our own backyard."[25] Why bother to defend democracy, freedom, and opportunity abroad, veterans wondered, if citizens tolerated undemocratic and corrupt regimes at home?

Although many white veterans came to interpret the war as a "democratic mission," they also articulated a more pragmatic and self-interested understanding. Fighting to defeat dictatorships abroad translated for many of Georgia's veterans, black or white, into a battle to ensure a better way of life, not just for those victimized by the Germans and Japanese, but for themselves as well. Participation in the war should and would, one way or another, bring about a better standard of living after the war. "Just what opportunities will [veterans] have when they return?" brooded Private Lake Upchurch of Carrollton, Georgia. "Will they get what they are fighting for?" Veterans have returned to home and families "to try to fulfill the way of life which they dreamed of and planned for during the war years," stated James W. Green of Atlanta, and they "want to be assured of a way of life which will warrant their having fought the most costly war in history." Thus, reminded Green, "let us not forget the purpose behind these four years of sacrifice and death."[26] C. W. Carver of College Park, an Atlanta suburb, spent 3½ years in the Pacific theater "fighting for a better place to live," while H. P. Dasher and his "buddies" passed the war "in their foxholes, dodging bullets, [and] dreaming of home and what they could come back to."[27]

Unfortunately, dreams of postwar abundance, immediate employment, and comfortable, affordable housing quickly fizzled amid the reconversion problems of the first postwar years. The war had boosted Georgia's economic growth significantly but not enough to guarantee a better standard of living to everyone right away. Whereas black veterans also confronted racial discrimination and injustice when they returned, white veterans were most discouraged by the myriad economic dilemmas and difficulties that still plagued many Georgia communities.[28]

New and higher paying industries followed the southward flow of government capital and military contracts during the war, but the Georgia economy remained fundamentally low wage and labor intensive in 1946. Even as late as 1960, a large majority of working men and women labored for incomes that fell at or below the national poverty level of $3,000 per year, despite the growth of the white- and skilled blue-collar sectors.[29] In addition, the opportunities the war did produce helped to accelerate what the boll weevil and the Great Depression had already begun, namely, the demise of sharecropping-tenancy agriculture. The lure of war jobs rapidly depopulated Georgia's rural counties and hamlets and overpopulated the state's larger towns and cities, a trend that continued after the war.[30] Thus, between 1940 and 1950, ninety-six Georgia counties registered significant population losses, some as large as a 20 to 35 percent decline.[31] As the rural South lost population, cities and towns grew seriously overcrowded, straining limited urban services and underdeveloped infrastructures and testing the ability of parochial leaders to respond. From a lack of suitable work to inflated prices for substandard housing, postwar life in Georgia seemed a disappointment, at least initially, after years spent anticipating the return home.[32]

The complaints white veterans posted in Georgia's newspapers revealed a smoldering frustration with these conditions, particularly regarding employment and housing. "We expected to find things a little tough," remarked "Ex-Sarge" in Atlanta, "but little did we dream how things could have gotten in such a rotten state of affairs."[33] Highlighting the fact that her husband had served in the army for five years, including almost two years overseas, Mrs. W. R. Lewis expressed her "thorough disgust" at the treatment meted out to returning veterans. Laid off only two months after his military discharge, Lewis's husband searched fruitlessly for comparable work. "At 36 he's told he's too old to work," Mrs. Lewis complained, though, she pointedly noted, "he wasn't too old for the Army." Even firms participating in the GI Bill's on-the-job training program preferred veterans with relevant experience. "Human memory is short-lived," Mrs. Lewis bitterly concluded. World War II veterans were "being given the 'run-around' just as veterans were after the last war."[34] Other veterans blamed the labor disputes that brought important sectors of the economy to a standstill shortly after V-J Day. "GIs returning to 'civilization' are having difficulty in finding 'on-the-job' training in this strike-ridden land," proclaimed a "$20 GI" to the *Atlanta Journal*. Veterans in Valdosta went so far as to petition the federal government to open plants shut down by strikes to veteran employment, "if the strikers refuse to resume work."[35]

While not all of Georgia's white veterans experienced the same problems with employment, virtually all struggled to find affordable, decent housing. Overcrowding, the repeal of federal price controls, inflation, and profiteering landlords prompted some of the bitterest complaints from white veterans who were finding it difficult to locate homes and apartments to buy or rent. War veteran W. F. Powers of Newnan, Georgia, for example, told the story of an ex-GI in Atlanta who was evicted when his wife became pregnant. "My friend has worried himself sick looking for an apartment," Powers lamented.[36] "JBC" of Atlanta was lucky enough to obtain a GI Bill housing loan, but he ended up with a substandard dwelling that afforded more problems than comfort. Despite its cracked ceilings, lumpy floors, leaks, and missing gutters, he paid $4,290 for the house an Atlanta engineer claimed "could not have cost $2,000 to build." Thus, "JBC" bitterly concluded, "look what they have sold . . . to a GI who stopped 23 pieces of shrapnel and three bullets."[37] A local landlady's refusal to sell a house under the GI Bill loan program because, she claimed, "we cannot sell our houses that cheap because we want to make money," outraged Jewell Richardson. Having spent over three years "dodging brass, kitchen police and fatigue details," and two years overseas "dodging everything from small-arms fire to the terrible German V-1 and V-2," Richardson now felt "absolutely sure there is no hope for . . . the lonely, weather-beaten, houseless veteran."[38]

The job and housing situation seemed so dire, in part, because of the inflation that followed the repeal of wartime price controls. Theodore S. Courtney, an ex-Marine from Sunnyside, for example, wondered why the state and federal government allowed "large manufacturers of the essentials of life . . . to quibble [and] hoard back material things" in order to get a higher price, while "the marine, sailor or soldier that was lucky enough to get back is unable to get the bare necessities." After all, he concluded, "if the government can force a man to give up his life for fifty dollars a month, why can't they do something about prices and hoarding?" J. H. Bottoms lamented, "Unless you're in politics [in Georgia] you haven't got a chance. Why doesn't this state get on the ball?"[39] For many of Georgia's white veterans, housing shortages, inflated prices, and menial jobs called into question the whole purpose behind the war. Why had the oft-heralded growth touched off by the war, they wondered, fallen so short of their dreams of postwar abundance and prosperity?

Postwar conditions brought home in very personal terms the cost of maintaining a long tradition of civic apathy and political exclusion. Complacency, these veterans believed, had left Georgia's communities to languish as opportunities to capitalize on the growth touched off by the war passed by. Meanwhile, local administrations, machines, and factions throughout the state routinely stuffed ballot boxes and defrauded even white voters at the expense of democracy and clean government. Disgusted veterans concluded that the reactionary parochialism of most county seat and statehouse cliques rendered these incumbents ill-suited to govern in the modern and prosperous future veterans envisioned. White veterans throughout the state subsequently invaded the postwar political arena, fighting for a vision of "good government," honest elections, and economic opportunity nurtured in the war. Out-of-touch incumbents, mossback factions, self-appointed courthouse rings, and corrupt urban machines ultimately paid the price.[40]

Veterans formed local political associations throughout the state to articulate their agenda and to offer slates of veteran candidates in Georgia's first postwar Democratic primaries. In virtually every county, veteran-led "good government leagues" rallied popular support. The gubernatorial race of 1946 attracted scores of white veterans to the candidacy of James V. Carmichael, who ran a moderate business progressive campaign against both Eugene Talmadge and Eurith D. Rivers. Veterans organized Carmichael-for-Governor Clubs in numerous counties and towns (as well as in Tokyo, Japan), appeared with Carmichael regularly on the stump, and made numerous speeches on his behalf at rallies and over the radio.[41]

In almost every Georgia community, moreover, white veterans targeted local incumbents and state legislative delegations for defeat. In Augusta a group of veterans organized the Veterans Political Reform League, which led the Independent League for Good Government against the long-standing Cracker Party headed by Roy V. Harris. In Savannah veterans formed the Citizens Progressive League. This group concentrated on the state legislative delegation fronted by the local political machine headed by John Bouhan, the Chatham County attorney and Democratic Party boss.[42] Similar organizations and campaigns emerged in communities throughout the state, including Gainesville, Americus, Rossville, Valdosta, and Waycross.

Like their progressive white and black counterparts in the Georgia Veterans League, the American Veterans Committee, or the GA-PAC, good government veterans recognized that breaking the hold of the past on the present first meant overcoming electoral tradition. The poll tax, black disfranchisement, and corrupt politics had for years combined to create a seriously diminished electorate in Georgia and enabled the old guard to maintain its hold on politics and power.[43] Years of low voter turnout, however, had also encouraged local machines and rings to maintain small political organizations, accustomed to dealing with only a handful of voters. Defeating Georgia's incumbents, good government veterans concluded, could be accomplished by increasing the number of registered voters to a level beyond what these organizations could control. That required capitalizing on the electoral changes induced by the war, including the demise of the white primary, the end of the state poll tax, and the lowering of voter age eligibility to eighteen years. With more black and white citizens than ever before eligible to vote in 1946, the time to strike seemed to be at hand.

Few good government veterans publicly endorsed the notion of black political equality or industrial democracy, but most recognized that expanded black and worker voter rolls could be useful. Political expediency dictated developing a loose cooperation with progressive campaigns to register and mobilize black citizens and workers. Thus, voter registration drives were the first shot fired by a multitude of veterans in a homefront battle to enact very different notions of what progress for postwar Georgia ultimately should mean.

Successful registration campaigns fed on the grievances of a relatively diverse group of disgruntled citizens. For example, businessmen and professionals in the Junior Chambers of Commerce, many of them returned veterans, often resented the political preferment and corruption that benefited some white citizens at the expense of others, something they believed damaged a community's reputation and hindered the growth of their own businesses. The League of Women Voters opposed electoral fraud and manipulation in principle, and black organizations as well as unions hoped to develop new political influence by helping oust regimes that had done very little for the majority of citizens, black or white, over the years.[44] Such broad-based support helped turn what could have been isolated and futile efforts into remarkably successful campaigns that registered an unprecedented number of new voters in 1946 across the state.

In the gubernatorial race, for example, the League of Women Voters, Junior Chambers of Commerce, African American organizations, and the Georgia CIO joined white pro-Carmichael veterans to encourage registration and voting. Three war veterans headed the Atlanta Jaycee's registration drive, and student veterans in the Student Voters League, the Student League for Good Government, and other groups worked to register high school and college students. The resulting surge of new voters made for an unpredictable election, and political campaigners across Georgia scrambled to lay claim to the flood of new registrants.[45]

Probably the most well organized and diverse voter drives occurred in Augusta and Savannah, where a tremendous boost in registration helped to overturn the Cracker Party and the Bouhan machine, respectively, in the spring and summer of 1946. In Augusta, where a "hard core of the dead and departed" regularly made it to the polls to vote for the Crackers, citizens affiliated with or sympathetic to the veterans' reformist Independent League for Good Government mounted energetic registration campaigns. John Bell Towill, an Independent candidate and war veteran, led a Rotary Club committee in cooperating with a Jaycee effort to register 20,000 voters. Local businessmen joined in, allowing employees to take off entire days in order to register; moreover, the League of Women Voters, the Augusta Women's Club, Typographical Union Local #41, and the rabbi of the Adas Yeshuron Synagogue all promised their support and cooperation. "If it's worth fighting for," declared the associated Veterans Political Reform League, "it's worth voting for."[46]

Having ruled virtually unchallenged for years, the Cracker Party provoked opposition in the war years and after with its high-handed treatment of local citizens, arbitrary tax hikes, and inflated city budget and by flaunting electoral laws

and regulations, all the while exhibiting an untrammeled enthusiasm for nepo-
tism and expropriating city funds. The road to revolt in 1946, however, actually
began with an incident four years earlier, when city officials arrested a local
printer for yelling "to hell with the Cracker party!" at a local football game. Popular outrage at such "Nazi tactics" generated the formation of the anti-Cracker
Augusta Citizens Union (ACU). Although it failed in its attempt to oust the party
in a local election the following year, the ACU nonetheless continued its campaign against Augusta's political machine by funding investigations into the electoral process and the operation of city and county government and by providing a base of information and support for veterans' antimachine efforts after the
war.[47]

The precipitating events that spurred veterans and citizens to form the anti-
Cracker Independent League for Good Government (Independents) in 1946, and
to enter veteran candidates in the upcoming state and local election, grew from
recent decisions passed by the Cracker-dominated city council. The council raised
the city tax rate in March 1946 to "a record high," passed a budget that exceeded
all earlier proposals, and accepted a state legislative directive allowing a 60 percent increase in the salary of John Kennedy, the safety commissioner and local
Cracker political boss. All of this, according to A. M. Lehmann, an opposition
leader and councilman from the Seventh Ward, seemed particularly suspicious,
given that the city budget had dramatically increased each year since 1940 without any obvious or significant outlays for paving or other public services. Meanwhile, property owners faced a tax hike in order to pay for street improvements.[48]

At the same time, even white veterans in Augusta struggled with unemployment, housing shortages, and an endless run-around when seeking information
on or assistance with obtaining veteran benefits. This bureaucratic inefficiency
persisted even though the city administration had received and used state funds
to build a one-stop center for veteran services. None of this inspired confidence
among Augusta's white veterans or citizens in the Cracker Party's fitness to rule.
Nor did the circumstances indicate the kind of modern, business-oriented, and
fiscally responsible administration of city and county affairs most believed crucial in order for a postwar community to attract industry. As a result, returning
white veterans such as John Bell Towill, Henry P. Eve, David Franklin, and James
P. Walker formed the anti-Cracker Independent League for Good Government
to challenge Augusta's incumbent machine in 1946.[49]

In Savannah the political machine headed by John Bouhan, Chatham County
attorney, matched the unsavory political habits of the Crackers both in spirit and
enthusiasm, spurring the formation of the Citizens Progressive League in 1946.
The CPL charged the incumbent city administration with failing to capitalize on

Savannah's advantageous coastal location and local resources to bring in new jobs to Chatham County. Furthermore, veterans charged, the Bouhan machine corrupted the political process and the administration of local government by manipulating elections and by colluding with the vice underworld through a local gaming racket. Meanwhile, the county school and recreational systems had fallen into abject disrepair. Savannah's government was "politically sick," charged CPL veteran John J. Sullivan, and citizens needed to "use your vote as a surgeon would use his scalpel to correct this illness."[50]

In 1946 several organizations kicked off registration campaigns aimed at ending the Bouhan organization's domination of local civic affairs. The Veterans Council Administration, a white veteran organization formed in 1944, met a Jaycee voter drive with their own intensive registration effort. Utilizing the slogan "Buddy, are you registered?" the Veterans Council Administration elicited veteran support by asking, "after having served your country in time of war, are you going to sit idly by and let everyone else run it but you?" The Savannah Trades and Labor Assembly joined in with its own "get-ready-to-vote-drive," alongside the enthusiastic registration campaign launched by the black World War II–Veterans Association.[51]

Through these strategic alliances, and despite the opposing efforts of both the Cracker Party and the Bouhan machine, veterans managed to push registration and voting in Augusta and Savannah and throughout the state to record levels during the Democratic primaries of 1946.[52] Augusta's citizens broke all previous records for registration in a single day when over seven hundred prospective voters turned up on April 3 at the county courthouse to register. Two weeks later, "old-timers" observing the large crowds turning out for political rallies remarked that Augusta had not experienced such "political hustings" in twenty years.[53] Long lines of citizens crowded the streets around the courthouse in Savannah in early May, with an average of three hundred blacks and three hundred whites registering on a typical day. Registration turnout consistently exceeded records set during the war, with around nine times as many African Americans and two times as many whites added to the rolls. In fact, on July 8 the *Savannah Evening Press* reported that voter registration had "smashed to smithereens all existing records," peaking at almost 60,000 registrants.[54] Statewide, voter registration in the gubernatorial primary of 1946 topped over one million citizens by the eve of the July 17 election, including over 150,000 African Americans.[55]

Registration alone, however, did not guarantee that these new voters would cast the "right" kind of vote. As opponents hustled to develop a response to what must have seemed to be a baffling wave of civic interest, pro-modernization veterans turned the moral force of their wartime participation and the emotional appeal of wartime rhetoric to their political advantage. In advertisements, broadsides, radio broadcasts, and public rallies across the state, white veterans linked their struggle against "bad government" at home with the recent fight against fascism overseas.

Much like their black counterparts, but for very different reasons, white veterans made a strong appeal to democratic patriotism. They aimed to overcome an historical reluctance to challenge the Democratic establishment or to jeopardize the solidarity of the white vote. By connecting their campaigns at home with the "Good War" in which most Americans took great pride, they tapped into the patriotic fervor of victory. Such rhetoric served to legitimate what actually constituted an unusual revolt against the established leadership of the Democratic Party in Georgia. If experience in administering state and local government and in controlling elections gave incumbents a political edge, veterans gambled that familiarity with "bad government" overseas gave them a moral advantage. By condemning their opponents as fascist-like dictators, white veterans assumed the lead in the rhetorical battle for "democracy" at home.

Good government veterans took pains to portray their opponents as homegrown variants of Axis despotism. "When Gene was governor, you wouldn't have known Georgia from Germany," declared veterans in the Student League for Good Government. Citing Talmadge's notorious incarceration of striking workers in "concentration camps" during the textile strike of 1934, as well as his propensity to resort to "bayonet rule" during his gubernatorial administrations, these veterans concluded that "no wonder this devotee of dictatorship bragged that he had read 'Mein Kampf' seven times," particularly as "Hitler and Nazism fascinated him." "Are these the workings of democracy?" asked Hoke Smith, a former navy lieutenant commander; "They are the worthy of Hitler, Mussolini, or Tojo; but they are not worthy of Georgia's governor."[56] Veterans employed the same rhetorical tactics in local insurgencies throughout the state. After observing "first hand" in Germany, Italy, and Japan "just what a one-man rule such as has threatened our city and county for years can lead to," the Veterans Political Reform League in Augusta trumpeted its determination to rip "out by the roots" the "cancerous virus" that the Cracker Party represented. After all, the veterans proclaimed, "we fought and many of us died to end dictatorship in the world and those of us who came back alive will be traitors to those who died if we permit the same thing to happen here that happened under Hitler, Mussolini, and Tojo."[57]

Despite these bouts of hyperbole, few white veterans actually expected to see the type of despotism that developed overseas establish itself in Georgia. What these white veterans really feared were undemocratic administrations removed from popular influence, but not because such regimes denied the rights of citizenship to black Georgians. Political chicanery and civic complacency hurt the state's national image and impaired the ability of local communities to attract new investment and industry. That was what good government veterans thought was most important. The reluctance of incumbent conservatives to develop aggressive programs of community betterment, along with their willingness to blatantly defraud even white citizens of their political rights, offended white veterans' finely honed sense of civic propriety and entitlement. Fighting to defend the American way of life abroad, good government veterans surmised, gave them a right to challenge these political practices at home.

These veterans fervently believed that the venality of mossbacked politicians accounted for a community's failure to thrive. Deteriorating streets, schools, and recreational facilities, financial scandals, and rule by personal favor and decree created an image of backwardness and provincialism that allegedly spooked industrial investors who preferred more "forward-looking" and business-oriented communities. The Carmichael campaign, for example, harped on the financial scandals, corruption, and political wheeling and dealing that characterized both of the administrations of former governors Talmadge and Rivers. After all, as Carmichael explained to voters throughout the state, unless the people elected a governor who could "assure business and industry that shake-down politicians and for-sale officeholders will not choke commerce in this state," the chance to create jobs and prosperity for all would be lost. Indeed, declared veteran Hoke Smith, "the people of Georgia are at a crossroads in the state's history," and re-electing Talmadge as governor would set Georgia back twenty years. Thus, pleaded war veteran George Doss Jr., president of the pro-Carmichael Student League for Good Government, "turn down the professional politicians who seek to drag us backward. Let's go forward with Carmichael."[58]

Veterans in the Independent League for Good Government in Augusta believed that their community had "failed to progress as it should" due to a political machine "more interested in perpetuating itself in office [than] in advancing the general welfare of the community." Potholed streets, a mismanaged University Hospital, substandard schools, neglected airfield facilities, and inequitable tax assessments—all the product of one-man rule, veterans believed—discouraged industry from locating in Augusta. At one rally, Scott Nixon, an Independent candidate and naval veteran, cited two instances in which large businesses allegedly had bypassed the city "on account of the Cracker party." Thus, trumpeted the Independents shortly before the election, "Are You the Citizen Who Wonders Why Augusta does not progress and why new industry has dodged politically dominated Augusta for the last twenty years and chosen to locate in our sister cities?"[59]

White veterans in Savannah also blamed the local political machine for the city's apparent lack of economic progress. "The Administration which has been in power for the last twenty-five years is not abreast of the needs of today," declared the CPL; "it has long since outlived its usefulness." While other southern cities comparable to Savannah in size twenty-five years ago, "and with far less natural resources and advantages, have forged ahead . . . in population, industrial expansion, public improvements and modern facilities," Savannah had lagged behind. Thus, veterans concluded, "misrule" had "severely retarded the progress of our city and county," contributing to inadequate recreational facilities, juvenile delinquency, deplorable school conditions, dirty, pockmarked streets, and limited opportunities for returned servicemen. CPL members chided the Bouhan-supported administration for "exchanging bouquets on industrial progress," while at the same time "for every plant Savannah had secured, cities less favorably located had secured three plants."[60]

Georgia's black and progressive white veterans pursued a politics of change in which racial and industrial democracy held the key to a prosperous and just future for all. In contrast, pro-modernization veterans expressed an unwavering faith that governmental efficiency and economic development would cure all of Georgia's political and economic ills. The Keynesian philosophy of the late New Deal, combined with the economic stimulus of war mobilization, had done much to move national policy toward an "accommodation" with capitalism that, according to one scholar, "established a new political religion devoted to the god of economic growth."[61] The priorities that good government veterans in Georgia outlined reflected this shift. "Progress" to these veterans meant modernizing the economy, making the administration of government more efficient and fiscally responsible, cleaning up ramshackle towns and overcrowded cities, and repairing and expanding old infrastructure. All of this seemingly promised to attract new industries, boost agriculture, and elevate per capita incomes, thereby resolving the state's social, economic, and political troubles. Racial and industrial democracy simply were not part of the equation.

The B-29ers-For-Carmichael-Club, for example, which included former employees of the Bell bomber plant in Marietta as well as returned veterans, spelled out a platform that James Carmichael and his veteran supporters articulated throughout the state. Their candidate pledged to keep Georgia out of debt, to never increase taxes unless with voter approval and for education, to improve veteran services as well as general health and pension programs, and to accomplish all this "within the Georgia income." Home rule promised communities control over local matters, while improved rural roads and agricultural markets extended a helping hand to the state's farmers. Governed by the maxim that "the very foundation of good government is economy," Carmichael promised to run the state "like you run your business" because good government was crucial to "create an atmosphere that will attract industry."[62]

The Independents in Augusta and the CPL in Savannah followed suit, pledging to improve education, roads, recreational facilities, and teacher pay through free, independent, and democratic government "of the people" sustained by honest elections and modern voting machines. They also planned to clean up Police Recorder Courts, usually bastions of corruption, indignity, and political patronage, and to institute civil service and merit systems for city and county employment. The Independents promised that "better government" would make "Richmond county . . . more attractive to new industries," while the CPL held that a well-developed harbor, slum clearance, and the recruitment of large and small industries would remake Savannah's image. "We believe that the administration of public affairs creates an atmosphere in which a community may flourish or stagnate," explained John C. Wylly, chairman of the CPL, because "it sets the stage for progress or reaction." In fact, "we believe that the misrule to which our people have been subjected has severely retarded the progress of our city and county."[63]

The call for new administrations committed to economic modernization and clean government apparently resonated with many citizens throughout the state. For middle-class whites, these campaigns provided an explanation for why their communities lagged behind and a solution for moving forward that avoided upsetting social and racial convention. For black southerners, good government campaigns that were willing to court black voters, to endorse black registration, and to eschew an extreme politics of racial division, if not actual reform, were preferable to the often reactionary candidates who were usually the only alternatives. To unionists, whose primary aim was to defeat incumbents with proven antilabor records, good government campaigns promised to elect new candidates, whose stances on organized labor might still be molded to the unions' advantage.

Thus, good government insurgencies attracted a diversity of support, which turned out record-breaking numbers of voters in the state's first postwar primaries. On July 17, around 700,000 voters went to the polls in Georgia, roughly a third of the potential black and white electorate. The Independents in Augusta and the CPL in Savannah swept state and county offices, broke the back of both the Cracker and Bouhan political machines, and immediately began implementing their programs for change. In the gubernatorial race, however, James V. Carmichael won a popular majority of 307,126 votes but lost to Talmadge because of the county unit system. Eurith D. Rivers siphoned off 18 county unit votes, and Carmichael's 128 units could not overcome the 236 units Talmadge won in Georgia's rural-agricultural counties. The curious results of this election, according to one scholar, proved that "the forces of reaction could not attract a majority of voters even within Georgia's truncated electorate, while the forces of 'progress' could not achieve a county unit majority."[64] Local elections, however, did not occur under the county unit system, and in communities throughout the state even white citizens directly experienced machine rule and the economic stagnation it allegedly perpetuated. Here, pro-modernization crusades after the war did often defeat conservative incumbent regimes.

The success veterans' good government insurgencies enjoyed demonstrated, once again, the war's disruptive impact on the stability of political relations throughout the state. In Savannah, Augusta, and dozens of other communities, Georgia's political establishment faced an unusual mobilization of disaffection led by veterans convinced of the need for new leadership in a new age. This coalescing of disgruntled Georgians into a nascent constituency for modernization reflected the shifting foundations of the postwar political South, as the demands of a newly engaged citizenry with a perspective broadened by the experience of going to war challenged the certainties of the past. As such, good government veterans represented an opening shot in a much longer campaign to modernize Georgia's political economy in the wake of the war.[65] Their activism reflected a growing realization among many white southerners that prosperity lay within the country's economic mainstream, not counter to it. These veterans were the immediate precursors to the neo-Whig southern politicians of the 1950s and later, as one scholar has described them, who found that political success increasingly demanded advocating active programs of industrial recruitment and soliciting federal military spending and research contracts.[66]

In 1946, however, the issue of race could not remain separate from the quest for modernization. Veterans who challenged the right of conservative rings, machines, and factions to maintain an exclusive political hegemony in Georgia confronted a race-baiting response designed to invoke the loyalty of white citizens by arousing their racial fears. From Talmadge in the gubernatorial race to Roy V. Harris and the Crackers in Augusta to opponents of the CPL in Savannah, race became the rhetorical ploy old guard defenders enlisted to offset the moral advantage that good government veterans enjoyed in challenging the incumbents' right to rule. Veterans' response to these tactics revealed a basically conservative foundation to their vision of progress, a fact that further underscores the contradictory nature of the war's political impact.

Georgia's crusading white veterans found themselves in a difficult position when their opponents injected the issue of race into state and local campaigns. As proponents of law and order, industrial progress, and democracy, they felt compelled to pledge to obey federal law on the question of black voting. This promise often earned good government campaigns important black support, but it also rendered them vulnerable. Candidates such as Eugene Talmadge and Roy V. Harris seized the opportunity to attack pro-modernization veterans as the first step on the road to racial Armageddon.[67] This pressure encouraged good government veterans to adopt a Janus-faced approach to reform. They rejected the practices and customs that allegedly impeded economic and governmental modernization but also affirmed an allegiance to those southern traditions that promised racial stability.

Veterans chose this approach for a number of reasons. First, they somehow had to deflect their opponents' racial attacks without losing the support of white voters. Second, they could not imagine any peaceful transition to racial change in the midst of the racial tensions that permeated the postwar period. Real racial reform promised to create a level of chaos and instability that modernizers believed would scare away new industry and investment. Finally, few, if any, good government veterans construed black equality as a desirable or worthy goal as they continued to labor under the weight of their own traditional racial prejudices.

James V. Carmichael's struggle to respond to Talmadge's race-baiting attack suggests how difficult this balancing act could be. Carmichael pledged to obey a federal court decision allowing blacks to vote in Georgia's Democratic primary in 1946, prompting Talmadge to smear his opponent as an integrationist and to market himself as the last and best defense of white supremacy.[68] The Carmichael campaign tried to combat this strategy by combining an assault on the resurgent Ku Klux Klan and the kind of racial extremism that Talmadge represented with a strong defense of Georgia's county unit system, meant to affirm Carmichael's white credentials in the public eye.[69]

Thus, pro-Carmichael veterans took to the stump to proclaim both their candidate's southern loyalties and the durability of Jim Crow, despite their professions of faith in majority rule and democracy. Lon Sullivan, a veteran of both World War I and II, dismissed the importance of the race issue by reminding Georgians that "no negroes go to white schools in Georgia, and they never will." "We have no Negro sheriffs, policemen, or congressmen," he added, "and we never will." Veteran George Doss Jr. and the Student League for Good Government agreed. Talmadge had been predicting for twenty years that blacks would "take over" Georgia, Doss argued, yet that had not happened. Still, rather than offer a positive program, Talmadge "screams 'Nigger, Nigger, Nigger'" to cloak the real issue: good government versus his own past record as governor. In fact, Doss explained, "we all know that letting the Negro vote in our primary will not bring the results that [Talmadge] claims." "You know Georgians well enough to know that whites and Negroes are never going to mix in schools, restaurants, picture shows or other public places and institutions," Doss assured white voters, and "in every county in Georgia there are far more whites than Negroes registered." Thus, "there is no county where the Negro can possibly gain control."[70]

The Independents in Augusta also found themselves on the defensive when confronted with Cracker leader Roy V. Harris's racial tirade shortly before the local spring election. The Crackers assured Augustans that a vote for the Independents meant a vote for integration, intermarriage, and interracial warfare, consequently defining veterans' agenda for change in the political arena as a challenge to the racial sanctity of the domestic sphere. "The principal issue in this race," Cracker incumbent Roy V. Harris insisted, was whether "you [will] turn your county and state over to . . . Ellis Arnall and the Negroes'" While Arnall (whom the Crackers regularly linked to the Independents and any campaign for change in Georgia) wanted to end the white primary, Harris claimed, the Crackers promised to "continue" the fight to preserve it.[71]

The Independents responded by noting that "some of the Crackers are putting out the bunk that if you elect the independent candidates, the Negroes will go to school with the white children, will go to the same shows, will sit in the same seats on the buses." However, wrote "WW Veteran" to the *Augusta Herald*, this claim was "absolute bunk." Affording black citizens the right to vote, this veteran explained, "does not mean that we will give them the right to attend our schools, our churches, etc."[72] Although they pledged to treat Augusta's black citizens with fairness, the Independents expressed a peculiar definition of what this meant, taking great pains to point out that "we Independent candidates bow to no one in their love for and loyalty to the traditions of the South." In fact, "we are opposed to the FEPC, as is every man and woman in Richmond county," and "we are southerners through and through." The Independents stood for "honesty, decency, and clean government," they assured white citizens, not "mingling and mixing of the races."[73]

The contention that the only real issue in 1946 was the perpetuation of bad government versus establishing good government and progress, however, proved to be wishful thinking. Carmichael lost the gubernatorial race in part because of the fraud the Talmadge faction practiced, but also because not enough rural white Georgians were willing to abandon Talmadge's race-baiting campaign. Soon after the election, Carmichael admitted that "selling out" on the

county unit system had been a mistake.[74] More than one citizen who participated in or supported his campaign apparently agreed. A white veteran who
headed an Atlanta political consulting firm that handled Carmichael's campaign, for example, blamed the candidate for allowing Talmadge's race-baiting
to "rattle him." Rather than stick to the "propaganda line laid down" by his con-
sultants, Carmichael talked "about his grandfather's having fought in the Civil
War." This response put the campaign on the defensive. Thus, as a political observer confided in another interview, "Mr. Carmichael was guilty of grave bad
judgement in conducting the kind of campaign which he did."[75]

John J. Flynt accurately described most of Georgia's white veterans as neither
"radicals" nor "reactionaries." Like many white southerners, they regarded economic and electoral reform, not integration and black civil rights, as the only
answer to Georgia's most pressing problems—underdevelopment, poverty, and
corrupt governance. Yet some good government veterans also saw the wisdom
in opening Georgia's primary elections to African American voters, at least in
1946. In order to break the grip of local machines and courthouse rings, good
government veterans also needed as many votes as they could get. It proved ex-
pedient to pledge to obey federal policies mandating black participation in the
Democratic primaries of 1946. A few other veterans even endorsed the notion of
black voting in principle. As participants in the war, and as American citizens,
more than one white veteran surmised that black Georgians had a valid claim to
political rights, if not social equality. "The colored people of this state have just
as much right to vote as do the white people," stated Arthur W. Melton, while
stationed with the navy at Augusta: "I did not decide this . . . . [T]he highest
court in the land decided the issue."[76]

In fact, white veterans in the CPL in Savannah demonstrated a relatively moderate attitude toward the city's black political community. As W. W. Law, a war
veteran and black political activist recalled, the CPL not only refused to race-bait
during the campaign, it also met with black leadership, publicly promised to
rule in the interests of all citizens, and opposed the reinstatement of the white
primary. In addition, once elected, the CPL's candidates promised and delivered
concrete benefits for Savannah's African American communities and neighborhoods in exchange for their support.[77]

With its long tradition of black political organization and activism, however,
Savannah proved to be more of an exception than the rule.[78] Few good government veterans were of the same ilk as the reactionaries in the KKK and the Columbians. The premium they put on growth and development as the sum of progress, however, had a significant blind spot on race that could not be ignored. By
and large, these veterans still thought of black equality as inconceivable, and

some even applauded black powerlessness. As white veterans reiterated again and again, segregation stood as an immutable southern tradition that both blacks and whites, allegedly, preferred to maintain. "We don't want to go to school with Negroes, and they don't want to go to school with us," proclaimed white veteran George Doss Jr.: "it will never happen regardless of who is governor."[79] The Independents, so determined to end the "tyranny" of the Crackers in Augusta, proved less than farsighted when it came to black citizens' demands for racial reform in the 1950s and 1960s. Independent leader Scott Nixon, for example, urged the Richmond County School Board in 1963 to seek a way around desegregation. Berry Fleming, ACU leader and anti-Cracker reformer, even suggested segregating classes by gender rather than comply fully with court-ordered integration.[80]

Service in the war fostered among many white veterans a desire for economic development and clean, honest government, as well as a deep aversion to the civic apathy, political corruption, and economic stagnation that plagued communities throughout Georgia and the South. These were goals important enough to moderate the racial attitudes of some veterans, as in the case of Savannah's CPL, and to compel others to neglect the needs and demands of black southerners in favor of maintaining white support, as in the case of veterans who campaigned for James V. Carmichael and Augusta's Independents. The vision of progress that motivated most white veterans set industrial development, not racial democracy, as the region's foremost postwar political goal. Nor would workers and unionists fare any better under the politics of "conservative modernization" that these veterans pursued. Despite their conviction in good government, despite their occasional alliances with progressive campaigns, and in direct contrast to their paean to the principles of majority rule, Georgia's good government veterans moved quickly after 1946 to exclude both blacks and unionists from the program for change they envisioned as the foundation for their state and region's future.

Hitler Is Not Dead but Has Found Refuge in Georgia

The General Assembly of 1947 and the Limits of Progress

AS GOOD GOVERNMENT veterans elected throughout the state in 1946 prepared to embark on new postwar political careers, Eugene Talmadge passed into the twilight of his own. Haggard and wan even before the primary election that summer, the intensity of the campaign ruined Talmadge's already fragile health. Proud of his victory, Talmadge nonetheless confided to a friend that the 1946 race "cost me ten years of my life."[1] Indeed, Talmadge died in December 1946 before his formal inauguration, leaving open the question of who could legitimately claim to be governor. A storm of protest erupted when Eugene's son, Herman, already in control of the Talmadge faction, took the initiative in answering this question by seizing the gubernatorial office by force. Herman justified this action on the basis of a suspicious tally of write-in votes for him from Telfair County in the general election and a dubious decision by the state legislature to endorse his claim. Outraged citizens organized mass meetings across the state to denounce what many regarded as a usurpation of the people's right to choose a new governor. Veterans, in particular, condemned the younger Talmadge's tactics and the legislature's apparent rubber-stamp decision as all too reminiscent of both his father and Nazism.

The Georgia General Assembly "made the government of the state of Georgia a dictatorial government and . . . violated all the rights of the citizens of our state," cried William H. Gunn and A. C. Lindstedt, along with fourteen other veterans. Moreover, they pointed out, "we veterans have fought to prevent the very thing that you have done."[2] S. L. Cox of Atlanta agreed. "I have just returned from overseas in a fight to rid the world of dictatorial government," he commented, but "I return to my native state to find that we have it here." "In Germany Hitler ruled," he bitterly concluded, but "here in Georgia the General Assembly and a few hand-picked cutthroats rule."[3]

However outraged these veterans were, their protest was remarkable more for what it failed to address than for what it did in fact condemn. Many white citizens and veterans opposed the decision made by the General Assembly and by Herman's subsequent strong-arm methods. However, very few attacked the platform he promised to implement. Herman Talmadge had played a pivotal role in crafting his father's race-baiting campaign tactics in 1946, and he promised to reinstate a white primary as his first act as governor. Yet, white veterans who were repulsed by this blatantly undemocratic seizure of power in 1947 were silent on what that turn of events meant to black Georgians.

That silence, however, was not surprising. Throughout the earlier campaign season, good government veterans were much more likely to trumpet their southern white heritage to offset an opponent's race-baiting attack than to decry such smear tactics as an affront to the principles of democracy. Amid the political controversies and challenges of the following years, Georgia's newly elected good government proponents perpetuated this pattern. By backing Herman Talmadge's bid for governor, disfranchising measures aimed at black voting, and two anti-union, so-called right-to-work measures, white veterans in the Georgia General Assembly of 1947 played out the politics of race and modernization that they had earlier crafted as the war's most important political legacy. The cost of that legacy became immediately apparent through the racial terror and anti-unionism that characterized the Georgia political landscape in 1948. Even as it pointed toward the state's economic and governmental modernization in the following decades, the vision of majority rule and economic progress that good government veterans put forth offered little of either to the state's black citizens and unionists, underscoring the contradictory nature of the politics of change wrought by the war.

THE "THREE-GOVERNORS CONTROVERSY" that erupted after the elder Talmadge's untimely demise stemmed from conflicting interpretations of the constitutional provisions for gubernatorial succession. Supporters of Ellis Arnall argued that the newly elected lieutenant governor, Melvin E. Thompson, should assume the governorship. Supporters of Herman E. Talmadge—who had assumed the de facto leadership of the Talmadge faction even before his father's passing—insisted that the state legislature should choose the governor from among the candidates who had received write-in votes in the general election. This approach would provide the only opportunity for Herman to become governor in 1947 without calling a special election. Both arguments had a certain constitutional justification.[4] However, the events were unique enough and the constitutional language was vague enough to make any solution highly controversial. The ensuing public spectacle was a fitting end, perhaps, to the elder Talmadge's cantankerous political reign.

After intensive wrangling, the General Assembly chose Herman Talmadge as governor on January 15, 1947, on the basis of the write-in votes he had received in the general election.[5] Given the allegation that many of these ballots appeared to be penned in the same handwriting and included the names of Telfair County's best dead citizens, Ellis Arnall and Lieutenant Governor–elect Melvin Thompson naturally refused to accept the assembly's decision. Armed with the legislature's endorsement, however, Herman had already begun consolidating his power. On January 16, backed by his control of the national guard and state troopers, an armed Talmadge seized the gubernatorial offices by force, ousting Governor Arnall, who then set up a makeshift office in the rotunda of the state capitol.[6] On March 19, 1947, the state supreme court overturned the General Assembly's decision and named Thompson governor. Talmadge dutifully relinquished the office and began planning his successful gubernatorial campaign of 1948. Thus ended a peculiar episode in Georgia political history that was, nonetheless, all too characteristic.[7]

As the gubernatorial controversy developed, media attention had focused particularly on what position the veterans elected to the state legislature in 1946 would take. The arbitrary nature of the legislature's decision and Talmadge's subsequent actions offended many white veterans' sense of civic propriety. Nonetheless, some veterans supported Talmadge's claim. Both sides tended to articulate their positions in reference to the war. No one, however, questioned what Talmadge's assumption of office on the same white primary platform espoused by his father would mean for the political and civic rights of Georgia's black citizens.

Prior to the vote in the General Assembly, several freshman legislators who were veterans called for a special election to determine the people's choice for governor.[8] Pierre Howard, a naval veteran from DeKalb County, John J. Flynt, a lieutenant colonel from Spalding County who had served in the European theater, Rhodes Jordan of Gwinnett County, also a naval veteran, Country Johnston of Lowndes County, who had served as a private in the war, Benjamin Garland of Butts County, who served in the Eighty-fifth Infantry, and Buford Ingle of Gordon County, a lieutenant colonel who served for six years on an antiaircraft battery in the South Pacific, all hoped a special election would avoid the "factional strife and discord" that would result if the legislature named the governor.[9] A few political pundits regarded a special election as an underhanded ploy aimed simply at bettering Talmadge's chances, but these veterans denied any such ulterior motive. "It matters not to . . . us who is the next governor of our beloved state," Howard explained, "except that he be [the] duly elected and unmistakable choice of the people of Georgia." A special election, first and foremost, was about the people's right to choose, an "inalienable right" for which veterans had "fought under enemy gunfire during the immediate past war." After all, Howard continued, "we have seen our comrades-in-arms die on the beaches of Norman[d]y and on the sands of Okinawa and by the eternal God we are determined that they shall not have died in vain." Thus, "we are in this fight for a free election of a Governor of Georgia and we intend to do our part to see such a democratic move through to the bitter end."[10]

As it turned out, those veterans who had been elected through some of the least contested campaigns of 1946 were more likely to voice support for Talmadge. Culver Kidd and Sibley Jennings of Baldwin County, Garland Byrd of Taylor County, and J. E. Briscoe of Walton County, for example, won office through relatively quiet campaigns of little controversy. They announced their support for Talmadge's claim in early January.[11] Veterans who won office against entrenched machines or county seat rings through hotly contested campaigns tended to support Thompson's claim. This group generally viewed Talmadge's appointment by the legislature as an end run around the democratic and legal electoral process, a type of tactic that many had campaigned against in their home counties. Malberry Smith and R. E. Evans, elected through the CPL campaign in Savannah, and Henry P. Eve and John Bell Towill, elected through the Independents' insurgency in Augusta, for example, sided with Thompson.[12]

What really disturbed many white veterans, however, was the manner in which Talmadge had assumed power. Smashing through the outer door to the governor's office, changing the locks on the office doors, ousting Arnall from the governor's mansion, and imposing immediate control over the national guard and state troopers reeked of Nazi storm trooper tactics. A cacophonous torrent of outrage erupted, particularly since not everyone agreed that Talmadge even had a legitimate legal claim to the office. White veterans participated in organizing mass meetings in communities across the state to confront state representatives who had voted for Talmadge. These so-called indignation meetings, organized by the "Aroused Citizens of Georgia," as they designated themselves, adopted resolutions and issued angry statements condemning the legislature's action and Talmadge's tactics.

In Cleveland, Georgia, citizens elected war veteran C. C. Blalock as chairman of a mass meeting that denounced this "flagrant use of storm troop methods."[13] Indeed, wrote Russell J. Brooke to the *Atlanta Constitution*, "the same thing was done in Italy by the Fascist Party, in Germany by the Nazi Party and in Japan by the Military Party." In fact, "we have just fought a terrible war because the law-abiding citizens of those countries and the rest of the world did not take it seriously until it was too late."[14] Almost two hundred Georgia Tech students who were veterans condemned Talmadge for "applying himself in true 'Heil Hitler' fashion" and for violating the principles for which they believed they had fought.[15] Hugh Henderson even advised the governors of the surrounding states to fortify their borders against "the horde of storm troopers now on the march in Georgia." He lamented further, "I never dreamed when I was advancing through the N. Apennines and Po Valley with the 701st Tank Destroyer Battalion . . . that if I were lucky enough ever to get back to Georgia that I would ever see the disgraceful situation that exists today." "I wonder," Henderson concluded, "did some of my best friends and buddies die in vain in their fight for democracy?"[16] Approximately one thousand college students from eight different institutions held a protest rally on the statehouse steps on January 22. Many of the students were veterans, and many of the protestors carried derogatory signs that read "Heil Herman," "Down With Dictatorship!" and "We'd Rather Have Kilroy!" The students even hung an effigy of Talmadge, complete with red suspenders, from a statue of Tom Watson, while two Emory students sported a genuine swastika flag.[17] H. C. Dever of Atlanta summed up the sense of frustration and irony that many veterans felt when confronted with the gubernatorial debacle. "To many veterans, besides myself," he explained, "it seems ridiculous that we should have been sent 1000s of miles to fight a long and bloody war against the same form of government now attempting to take control of Georgia." He asked, "Could it be that Hitler is not dead but has found refuge in Georgia? Or can it be that Hitler is dead and Georgia is honoring him by adopting his principles?"[18]

Not all veterans, however, interpreted Talmadge's election by the General Assembly, or even his subsequent actions, as a usurpation of the people's rights. Those veteran legislators who voted for Talmadge defended their actions when confronted by the "Aroused Citizens of Georgia." Pierre Howard of DeKalb, for example, explained that he had grown disenchanted when Thompson refused to agree to a special election. As a result, Howard voted for Talmadge because his election came closest to fulfilling what he believed the state constitution allowed.[19] Almost seventy overseas veterans from Thomas County voiced their support for the legislature's choice of "our buddy" as governor and condemned Arnall's and Thompson's intransigence as "un-American."[20] Over three hundred Floyd County veterans signed a petition calling for "fairness and justice" in the gubernatorial dispute, expressing their support for Talmadge and their hostility to the "biased press in Atlanta."[21] Ultimately, of the legislators identifiable as World War II veterans who cast votes on the question of gubernatorial succession in 1947, around 55 percent voted to make Herman Talmadge governor.[22]

Clearly, many of Georgia's white veterans did not believe that the younger Talmadge's "banana republic" political style squared with their sense of what the war had been about. Yet, these veterans did not raise a similar hue and cry as the elder Talmadge race-baited his way across Georgia in 1946, or in response to the wholesale purges of black registrants in county primaries that followed, or even in reaction to the terrible lynching in Walton County that same summer. Few condemned Herman Talmadge's election in 1947—including the blatant electoral chicanery in Telfair County that allowed it to take place—in terms of what it meant to black Georgians. Talmadge, in fact, had taken the lead in crafting his father's 1946 campaign platform that promised to uphold the white primary and to defend the county unit system. Good government veterans attacked the younger Talmadge's tactics as undemocratic, but they stopped well short of condemning the white supremacy program he endorsed from the start. The controversy that arose around the white primary bill, introduced by Talmadge as the legislature's first order of business in 1947, further illustrated this contradiction.

After the *Primus King* decision ended the white primary in Georgia early in 1946, Eugene Talmadge had campaigned enthusiastically on behalf of its restoration. When the elder Talmadge died, both Herman Talmadge and Thompson pledged to follow through on this promise. In his inaugural address immediately after the legislature's vote on the governorship, in fact, the younger Talmadge promised to send a white primary bill to the state legislature as his first official act as governor. Similar moves occurred in several southern states in the wake of the earlier *Smith v. Allwright* decision, as southern conservatives scrambled to maintain restrictions limiting the black vote. First in South Carolina, then in Alabama, and finally in Georgia, conservatives passed measures that removed the Democratic primaries from all state laws and regulations, thus converting the state Democratic Party to the status of a private club that could determine its own membership and process of election.[23] In early 1947 Talmadge introduced a bill "to revise the election laws and to repeal all laws or parts of laws providing the method and manner of holding primary elections by any political party," in order to "divorce the state of Georgia from having anything to do in any manner . . . with the holding of primary elections."[24]

Controversy over the white primary bill (designated as House Bill 13, or HB 13), however, did not develop because it threatened to eradicate black participation in the Democratic primaries. Rather, many white Georgians, including a number of veterans in the state legislature, interpreted the measure as an effort by the conservative Talmadge faction to wrest control of state government and politics permanently from the pro-modernization Thompson-Arnall faction. Roy V. Harris, the Democratic boss of the Cracker Party in Augusta, supported Eugene Talmadge in 1946 and endorsed his son thereafter. He also drafted much of the white primary bill. This fact disturbed the many veterans who associated Harris with the Cracker Party's domination of political and civic life in Augusta and Richmond County. Coming on the heels of an election year in which machine politics, corrupt incumbency, and provincialism had played as prominent issues in numerous local campaigns, HB 13 naturally proved controversial right from the start. Removing primary elections from the regulation and protection of all state laws, many believed, left wide open the door to fraud, corruption, and minority rule by whichever faction managed to control the Democratic Party machinery.

Like their reaction to the gubernatorial squabble, white veterans' responses to HB 13 reflected little concern about the political rights of black Georgians. In fact, many white veterans supported the white primary bill. In January the State of the Republic Committee voted unanimously to recommend HB 13 favorably to the House. Committee members included veterans J. Julian Bennett of Barrow County, Sibley Jennings of Baldwin County, Country Johnston of Lowndes County, and Howard Overby of Hall County.[25] Bennett conceded that "the Negro has a moral right to vote," yet apparently he did not believe such a right included participation "in a Democratic white primary."[26] Harold Willingham, a veteran elected to the legislature in 1946 from Cobb County, agreed: "thousands of my people have asked me to vote for this bill," and "I told them many months ago that I would vote for the white primary bill." Moreover, he complained, "I'm sick, tired and disgusted of certain northern elements trying to tell us, through devious methods of pressure and coercion, how to run our great and sovereign state of Georgia."[27] Representative John J. Flynt actually looked forward to voting for HB 13 because then "when we go home, we can say we have put on the statute books the greatest piece of legislation ever introduced."[28] Sibley Jennings and Culver Kidd, also veterans elected to the statehouse in 1946, proudly displayed for Atlanta reporters a list of some two thousand citizens who had written to congratulate them for supporting HB 13.[29]

Many other white veterans, however, particularly those from the larger, urban, six unit counties, where many citizens had long felt disfranchised by the county unit system, condemned the white primary measure as a machine bill designed to foist minority rule on all Georgians. HB 13, remarked Representative Muggsy Smith, a veteran elected in 1946 from Fulton County, would "put the state into the hands of a political group." Representative Leroy Jenkins of Bartow County similarly opposed the bill, stating "I fought Hitlerism in Germany, and I don't want to have to fight it in Georgia." Not only legislators objected. A group of veterans from twenty-five Georgia counties threatened to organize a new political party to combat the Talmadge faction if HB 13 passed. The white primary bill, they argued, threatened to "rob white people" of the franchise. Rather than be subjugated by a Talmadge-Harris political machine, these veterans pledged to seek recognition as a new Democratic Party of Georgia. After all, explained John Sammons Bell, whose pledge made on the shores of a Pacific island during the war led him to campaign enthusiastically for James V. Carmichael, "We have got to out-rat the rats here in Georgia like we did the Japs in the Pacific."[30]

Most opposition to the white primary bill among veterans in the state legislature derived from their conviction that repealing state regulation of Georgia's primaries would subject the state to perpetual machine rule. Many had won office in the first place as a result of insurgent campaigns against a similar state of affairs in their home counties. Not surprisingly, the representatives from Chatham and Richmond Counties assailed HB 13 as an attempt by the "Harris machine" to take over the state.[31]

Even those legislators who did note the deleterious impact the bill would have on black voting, however, proved less than averse to some other measure that would still limit black participation without removing all state regulation of primary elections. Several favored a bill drafted and submitted by John Bell Towill, a veteran elected from Richmond County in 1946 as part of the Independents' defeat of the Cracker Party. The Towill bill promised to enforce the electoral restrictions already in the state constitution, thereby circumscribing the black vote without simultaneously eliminating all protections against fraud and corruption in primary elections.[32] In order to register, a citizen would have to read or write a paragraph of the constitution "correctly" or demonstrate a good moral character and an understanding of the duties of citizenship. White schoolteachers would sit on the Board of Registrars and administer tests to prospective registrants. Veterans who opposed the Harris bill generally favored the Towill

TABLE 1. Comparison of Veteran and Nonveteran Voting on the White Primary Bill (HB 13), 1947

	Veterans	Nonveterans	Total
Yes	22 (56%)	111 (68%)	133 (65%)
No	16 (41%)	46 (28%)	62 (30%)
Absent	1 (3%)	7 (4%)	8 (4%)

Source: Georgia Department of Archives and History, *Journal of the House of Representatives of the State of Georgia*, January 13, 1947.

measure. Marvin Kemper of Bibb County, a veteran of the Army Air Force elected in 1946, for example, admitted that blacks paid taxes to a government in which they were not allowed to participate, but he still considered the Towill bill to be a favorable alternative to HB 13.[33]

Veterans essentially condemned HB 13 for going too far in trying to fulfill the apparent "mandate" for electoral restrictions that the people ostensibly had endorsed by electing Eugene Talmadge as governor. Richard Kenyon of Hall County, for example, another veteran elected in 1946, described the white primary bill as "a step backwards in solving the problem of the minority." "The people of Georgia have not given us a mandate to wipe out the state laws it took them twenty-five years to pass," he explained; rather "they have given us a mandate to protect the county-unit system."[34] Bernard Nightingale, a representative and veteran from Glynn County, agreed: "This is not the white primary bill that the people gave us a mandate to pass. This will not accomplish what the people want."[35] Of the thirty-eight veterans in the state legislature who voted on HB 13, more than half voted to pass it.

Fewer veterans supported the measure compared to nonveteran legislators, but the nature of their objections had little to do with its threat to black political participation. Indeed, by referring to the white primary as a mandate from the people, they appeared to forget—or ignore—the fact that Eugene Talmadge won in 1946 because of the county unit system, *not* because his white supremacy platform had received a popular majority of votes. These veterans had won election by decrying dictatorship at home, by courting newly registered black voters, and by condemning the reactionary conservatism represented by Eugene Talmadge. Yet they did not really relate the political and civic rights of Georgia's black citizens to the democratic imperative of the war as they understood it. These veterans' racial conservatism was not of the same ilk, perhaps, as that of veterans who joined the KKK or who fervently supported Eugene Talmadge's campaign in 1946. Yet, protection of the civic rights of *white* southerners, they believed, should be the real priority. Only then could a new generation of Democratic leaders begin to modernize the state and fulfill the civic and economic ambitions many white veterans brought home from the war.

African Americans, however, were not the only ones excluded from the program for change pursued by Georgia's good government veterans. Organized labor and, by extension, any notion that unions had legitimate political or economic demands had little place in the good government vision of a modern and prosperous future. Herman Talmadge's extralegal assumption of the governorship and the subsequent white primary bill had disturbed at least some white veterans in the state legislature. The antilabor import of two "right-to-work" measures introduced during the same session, however, troubled these veterans far less.

Operation Dixie officials had anticipated a hostile response to the postwar drive to organize the South. The backlash against organized labor in postwar Georgia came not just from rural reactionaries, however, but also from those pro-modernization advocates who regarded successful industrial recruitment, not economic democracy, as the sort of change the state most needed. Veterans in the state legislature lent their broad support to right-to-work laws that effectively sealed Operation Dixie's fate in Georgia.[36]

Nationally, the postwar backlash against organized labor that began shortly before the war ended culminated in the Taft-Hartley Act of June 1947. This legislation overturned many of the protections afforded organized labor through the earlier pro-labor Wagner Act, an important provision of the New Deal.[37] The Wagner Act had included key union security measures such as the closed shop, which required all workers hired in a mill or plant to join the union. Taft-Hartley cleared the way for a wave of state "right-to-work" laws, however, that allowed workers to eschew union membership in a mill even when the majority had voted for certification. These laws consequently crippled all southern organizing drives by "dividing workers, destabilizing union membership," and providing "companies an opportunity to discriminate against union members."[38] For once, the Georgia General Assembly anticipated, rather than countered, a national trend when it passed two antilabor bills months before Congress enacted the Taft-Hartley measure. White veterans elected to the state legislature in 1946 strongly supported House Bills 72 and 73, which outlawed the closed shop and other union security measures and severely restricted the right of workers to picket and demonstrate.

Legislators introduced these bills at the beginning of the General Assembly's regular session in January 1947. House Bill 72 (HB 72) prohibited the use of force, intimidation, violence, or threats to "restrict or otherwise interfere with the right of any person to work or refrain from working, or to peacefully conduct business, or for other purposes." Both its opponents and advocates regarded the bill as a measure outlawing mass picketing. House Bill 73 prohibited making any mandatory requirements, such as union membership or paying dues, a condition of employment or contract, and it provided penalties for violations of these provisions, including affording "individuals whose employment is affected by violations of this act" to enlist injunctions "in certain cases."[39] This statute became known as the "open-shop" bill.

White veterans in the legislature strongly supported both the spirit and substance of these measures. J. L. Webster, a farmer who served as a lieutenant in World War II and was first elected in 1945, sponsored a measure to obtain a constitutional amendment that permanently outlawed the closed shop.[40] Representative Charles "Buddy" Battle of Schley County, also a farmer and World War II veteran elected in 1946, introduced HB 72 for its third reading and passage in February 1947. Moreover, veterans consistently voiced their support of both measures as each traveled through House procedures and debate. For example, the Committee on Industrial Relations reported unfavorably on both bills in early February, which led to a discussion of the committee report on the floor. Representative and World War II veteran George B. Ramsey Jr. called members' attention to the allegedly improper presence of a Hall County labor organizer on the House floor during the debate. According to one report, Ramsey later explained his support of the two bills by citing the alleged disgust of servicemen who "read of strikes at home while they fought in enemy territory."[41]

The clear division between veterans who supported or opposed Herman Talmadge's election or the white primary bill—and between veterans and nonveterans in both cases—was far less evident in the vote on HB 72. On the question of placing the bills on the House calendar and on the actual passage of HB 72, veteran representatives voted in support of both measures, largely conforming to the pattern of votes by nonveteran legislators. Seventy-two percent of the representatives identified as veterans voted to reject the committee's unfavorable report and to place the bills on the House calendar. Seventy-eight nonveterans voted the same way. Similarly, 74 percent of identified veteran representatives voted for the passage of HB 72, as amended to incorporate both anti–mass picketing and open shop provisions; 78 percent of nonveterans also voted for HB 72. Fourteen percent of the representatives, veteran and nonveteran, voted against HB 72.

A few veterans voted against both antilabor measures, including Representa-

TABLE 2. Comparison of Veteran and Nonveteran Voting on Right-to-Work
Measures, 1947

	Veterans	Nonveterans	Total
Reject report; place on calendar	31 (72%)	126 (78%)	157 (77%)
Accept report; leave off calendar	7 (16%)	21 (13%)	28 (14%)
Not voting	5 (12%)	15 (9%)	20 (10%)

Source: Georgia Department of Archives and History, *Georgia Official and Statistical Register,* 362–63, 466–68.

tive George Talmadge Bagby, a criminal investigator and navy veteran from Paulding County, who requested that his vote of opposition be specified in the House
record. In general, those who opposed the measures came from counties with a
strong organized labor presence. Paulding County, for example, was in the Seventh Congressional District, the heart of organized labor's postwar strength in
the state. Veteran Jack R. Wells, described by one reporter in 1946 as "a practi-
cally unknown recently discharged war veteran" who had spent two years in the
navy during the war, hailed from Athens, home of the longest running textile
strike in Georgia history at the Athens Manufacturing Company. Miles Walker
Lewis, an attorney from Greene County who served as a captain in the Army Air
Forces during the war, came from Greensboro, where a TWUA local had long
wrangled with the management of the Mary Leila Cotton Mills. R. E. Evans of
Chatham County, a veteran and member of the CPL, which had overturned Savannah's Bouhan machine in 1946, came from a county with established AFL
and CIO locals, particularly among waterfront workers.[42]

The presence of organized labor in some constituencies, however, seemed more
often to have the opposite effect on their veteran representatives. Of the six veterans elected to the statehouse from counties in the Seventh Congressional District in 1946, for example, four voted in support of the antilabor measures while
one abstained. Even Representative Dean Covington of Floyd County, which
had one of the strongest and most politically active CIO unions, TWUA Local 689
of Rome, voted to pass HB 72. Likewise, Richard Kenyon and Howard Overby,
representatives from Hall County, both elected as part of a local veteran-led
"good government" crusade in Gainesville, voted for both measures. Gainesville

TABLE 3. Comparison of Veteran and Nonveteran Voting on the Open Shop Bill (HB 72), 1947

	Veterans	Nonveterans	Total
Yes	32 (74%)	125 (78%)	157 (77%)
No	6 (14%)	22 (14%)	28 (14%)
Absent	5 (12%)	14 (9%)	19 (9%)

Source: Georgia Department of Archives and History, *Georgia Official and Statistical Register*, 362–63, 466–68.

was the site of several postwar labor disputes. And in Savannah, Malberry Smith, the other veteran elected to the legislature as part of the CPL insurgency, voted for the bill. Moreover, veterans elected from counties in the Third Congressional District, where several bitter labor disputes and postwar organizing campaigns had developed in and around Columbus, also supported HB 72.[43]

The importance of white veteran support of these antilabor measures lies in what that endorsement actually meant. Good government veterans won election in 1946 on platforms that emphasized the need for economic modernization and growth. This program for change had little place for crusades to unionize workers or to augment their political influence. Little evidence existed at the time to prove that right-to-work laws, specifically, influenced why industry moved South after the war.[44] Nevertheless, postwar industrial promoters, including good government veterans, believed that organized labor threatened the only virtue many communities had to offer to new industry: an absence of or hostility to unions.[45] As one pamphlet published in 1947 by the Associated Industries of Georgia explained, "tolerating unionism amounted to 'throwing banana peels on the pavement of the road to industrial progress.'"[46]

The war drew some white veterans into the postwar labor movement, galvanizing Operation Dixie and making organized labor a real issue on the immediate political landscape. Yet, the war also made bolstering industrial recruitment a priority among many more white veterans, who used their newfound influence in local and state government to help quash what organized labor in Georgia had hoped to accomplish. The actions taken by the Georgia General Assembly and its veteran members in 1947—the passage of HB 72 was the only significant legislation to emerge from that troubled session—devastated the attempt of Georgia's labor organizers and unions to continue in the face of declining national CIO support for the southern organizing drive.

What happened in the Georgia General Assembly in 1947 further demonstrated the contradictory impact of World War II on Georgia and the South. On the one hand, the war disrupted the state's postwar political stability by focusing the political disaffection held by a variety of Georgians toward the state's incumbent old guard. This broad disenchantment with politics-as-usual pointed to a political culture in transition. Fewer southerners, black or white, wanted to continue to accept a leadership more inclined to work only for its own perpetuation in power by any means necessary than to develop active and dynamic programs for community betterment. On the other hand, as the diversity of veteran activism in Georgia indicated, the war also generated conflicting understandings of what "community betterment" should mean. And the racial, social, and economic changes accelerated by the war strengthened rather than weakened many white southerners' attachment to racial and anti-union tradition.

Amid the politics of race and modernization that followed the war's end, the liberal vision of a progressive reconstruction of the postwar South lost out to this conservative notion of progress and political change. Good government veterans rode to power on the wave of political disaffection induced by the war, but then dispensed with the needs and interests of both black citizens and unionists as they looked to the future. A politics of change *would* come out of the war for Georgia and the South. But veterans such as those in the 1947 Georgia General Assembly made sure that the war's legacy would stay within the important boundaries of white supremacy and anti-unionism. Their vision of progress would sustain, rather than eradicate, a distinctive southern political pattern: it would dispense the benefits of modernization to some Georgians more than others.

The high cost exacted by this contradictory politics of change became all too clear to Georgia's black citizens, unionists, and progressives by the end of 1948. Terror and violence directed against black citizens and an insurmountable wall of opposition to organized labor continued to characterize the postwar political landscape. This resistance to progressive change proceeded in tandem with efforts by the state's new political and civic leadership to modernize the economy and government.

THE IRONIC FINALE to Georgia's postwar tragicomedy began in 1947, when the state supreme court set September 8, 1948, as the date of a special primary election to officially fill the gubernatorial seat.[47] Herman Talmadge immediately began planning his "restoration" to the Georgia throne.[48] His strategy focused, in part, on seizing control of the state Democratic Party machinery, which determined the rules for primary elections. Whichever faction controlled that structure had a significant advantage going into the September primary. The substance of Talmadge's reelection bid, however, lay in campaigning on a platform that promised both to modernize Georgia's economy and government and to keep black Georgians fast under the heel of Jim Crow.

Early in 1948 the state supreme court dealt a heavy blow to Governor Melvin E. Thompson's electoral ambitions by ruling that Talmadge operative James S. Peters held the legal and legitimate title as chief of the Georgia Democratic Executive Committee.[49] Whatever immediate advantage this afforded the Talmadge campaign was somewhat offset at first by the uncertainty of whether blacks would legally participate in the September primary. With an appeal of Judge J. Waties Waring's decision to prohibit a reconstituted white primary in South Carolina pending before the U.S. Supreme Court, the Talmadge camp finally announced in late March that the Georgia Democratic Party would comply with current state law and change its party rules to allow black voting in the 1948 primaries. Eager to make political hay on the issue, party chairman Peters publicly blamed this outcome on Governor Thompson's earlier veto of the white primary bill in 1947. The Talmadge camp duly pledged to reassert black disfranchisement in Georgia as soon as possible.[50] This set the race-baiting tone that afflicted the campaign season of 1948.

In fact, the political events of that year reflected many of the same elements as 1946. Black Georgians again braved an ugly racial climate in order to register and vote in communities across the state. From larger urban communities such as Savannah to small town crossroads such as Mount Vernon and Fort Valley, black citizens lined up at county courthouses to take advantage, once again, of their access to the state Democratic primaries.[51] Overall registration climbed quickly, exceeding even the unprecedented levels of the 1946 elections. By early September the state had a record-breaking registration, with almost 1.2 million Georgians registered to vote—almost 117,000 more voters than in 1946. This number included approximately 140,000 black registrants.[52]

White veterans also reappeared in both local races and in the statewide gubernatorial campaign. Veterans stood with both Melvin E. Thompson and Herman Talmadge on the stump in 1948, and several veteran insurgencies against local incumbents disrupted smaller communities, including the mill towns of Porterdale and Greensboro, and the county of Telfair, home of the Talmadges. Progressive reformers, again, took an active, if ineffectual role in 1948, campaigning fruitlessly for gubernatorial candidate and liberal veteran Joseph Rabun and presidential candidate and progressive favorite Henry A. Wallace. Organized labor in Georgia failed to coalesce entirely behind one candidate, with some local PACs backing Rabun, others favoring Thompson, and some even supporting Talmadge. Thus, much like the political season of two years earlier, the 1948 primaries witnessed the participation of an unusual number and diversity of Georgians, including veterans.

Moreover, the racial legacy of the war resurfaced as a central political issue.[53] The wave of violence, terror, and electoral fraud directed against black citizens in the South after the war, as well as the pressure generated by leading national liberal and black civil rights organizations, finally prompted President Harry S. Truman to appoint and charge a presidential commission in December 1946 with assessing "current federal, state, and local laws and determine in what ways they might be strengthened to adequately protect the civil rights of U.S. citizens."[54] The Civil Rights Commission, which included key black and white progressives, issued a strong report in 1947, entitled *To Secure These Rights*, that called for increased federal activism on behalf of black civil rights. Among its controversial proposals, the commission report called for the desegregation of the armed forces, federal antilynching legislation, and the prohibition of poll taxes. This report drew increased national attention to the state of southern race relations as the nation's "new" number one regional problem.[55]

President Truman followed up this report by sending to Congress in February 1948 a new civil rights program that included proposals to eliminate the poll tax, to legislate the creation of a permanent "fair employment practices commission," and to "end segregation in interstate transportation."[56] These legislative proposals provoked heated debate in Congress, within the national Democratic Party, and throughout the nation. The decision of the national Democratic convention to endorse Truman's civil rights program that summer, not surprisingly, upset many southern whites, disturbed racial conservatives, and quickly spurred an angry regional backlash. Southern Democratic conservatives began a reconsideration of their loyalty to the national Democratic Party. Their impending revolt in a presidential election year became the subject of much media speculation. Within the South, state politics further destabilized as southern Democrats split over whether to support the developing Dixiecrat revolt from the national Democratic Party or to remain loyal to the national Democratic ticket and President Truman in 1948.[57] Given this context, the politics of race permeated Georgia's political campaign season of 1948, even more than it had two years earlier.

Defending white supremacy clearly ranked at the top of the Talmadge campaign strategy. Condemning Thompson's veto of the white primary bill in 1947, Talmadge declared early and often that his bid for governor was essentially "a white man's fight to keep Georgia a white man's state."[58] He also recognized the political expedience of using the Truman civil rights program as a platform on which to register his racial stance for the voters. As the Dixiecrat revolt from the national Democratic Party took shape, however, Talmadge had to be careful in his campaign not to appear to be bolting from party ranks, given his fight with Thompson over control of the state party. Thus, Talmadge publicly declared his strident opposition to the Truman program without endorsing the Dixiecrat solution of challenging the national party ticket.[59]

Describing the national Democratic civil rights planks as the "most dangerous threat to Georgia's way of life since Reconstruction," Talmadge told audiences at campaign rallies that he was "unalterably opposed to every principle enunciated by the President's civil rights program." He also ran political advertisements that announced, "HERMAN TALMADGE TAKES HIS STAND WITH THE WHITE PEOPLE," which apparently meant defending segregation and white supremacy at all costs.[60] Voters could even sing the "Talmadge Victory Song," composed by Dr. Rayford W. Thorpe of Austell, Georgia, which noted that with Georgia's supposed favorite son as governor, "races and religion will all be treated right," but nonetheless "there will be segregation, for colored and for white."[61] At a rally in Fort Valley, Georgia, where a quarter of the registered voters were black, Talmadge explained to black citizens at a campaign rally what they could expect if he were elected governor. While promising that black Georgians would have nothing to fear from his administration, he also pledged to uphold segregation. "I want to help the Negroes," Talmadge explained, "but I don't believe it will help them to throw open the white schools, restaurants, theaters, streetcars, and swimming pools to mixed groups." After all, he continued, "the good Negroes don't want it and the good white people don't want it." And if any "good Negroes" in the audience felt inclined to take Talmadge's promise of "moderation" at face value, another speaker at the rally, Will Wallace of Roberta, Georgia, clarified Talmadge's meaning. "We hope to have white supremacy by peaceful means," he shouted from the platform, "but we'll have it by force if necessary."[62]

Governor Thompson attempted to deflect Talmadge's charges that he was "soft" on white supremacy by declaring his own opposition to the Truman civil rights program, his support for reinstituting the white primary, and his conviction that no real threat to white supremacy in Georgia existed.[63] "There is no issue about the supremacy of the white people," explained one Thompson aide; "nobody doubts that white supremacy is safe in Georgia and always will be safe."[64] Much like James V. Carmichael's ill-fated attempt to neutralize Eugene Talmadge's race-baiting in 1946, Thompson's response proved feeble and even naive in the racially charged climate of 1948. The racial direction of the campaign was crystal clear at the outset.

In a definite departure from the 1946 political season, however, most white veterans who voiced a public opinion now lined up behind the Talmadge campaign. Their willingness to support "Hummon," after so adamantly opposing his father, in part indicated the younger Talmadge's appeal as a veteran himself, as well as his developing reputation as a pro-development modernizer. Thus, in some respects, Herman Talmadge was not exactly the same candidate his father had been. Though he did run a blatantly racist campaign, he also appealed to the urban uptown interests who had vehemently opposed his father, promising, among other things, to revamp the highway department, to build many more rural hospitals, and to offer quicker responses on veteran services. As Roy V. Harris, who played an instrumental role in crafting both Eugene's 1946 campaign and Herman's 1948 gubernatorial bid, commented later, Herman, in consideration of the political controversies of 1946, adopted a pro-modernization platform in 1948, including policies "that were strange and different from what his father had advocated in the past," such as endorsing substantially improved funding for the state's public educational system.[65]

This was indeed a very different approach than Herman had crafted for his father's 1946 campaign, which had banked on ignoring the "uptown better element and unfriendly whites" with impunity, while enlisting racial appeals and purging black voters to capture enough rural county unit votes alone to win the governor's seat.[66] Herman's new two-pronged strategy tapped into the ambitions and frustrations that had fueled the good government insurgencies two years earlier, making him a more palatable candidate than his father had been to development-minded white veterans.

Nonetheless, if white supremacy did not constitute the only issue on which Herman Talmadge campaigned in 1948, it did end up as the most prevalent and damaging one. Moreover, white veterans clearly reflected the increasing importance of defending southern racial tradition to their understanding of the postwar politics of change. James V. Carmichael had offered good government veterans a chance in 1946 to oppose Eugene Talmadge's "anti-modernization" campaign, which had offered a politics of racial extremism rather than a concrete plan for economic and governmental development. Herman Talmadge now provided the opportunity to elect someone as governor who advocated at least a modest program of economic and governmental progress along with a defense of white supremacy. It was this combination that resonated with many white veterans and citizens in 1948, appealing to a broader constituency of voters than Herman's father had been able to recruit two years earlier.

Thus, in 1948 veterans lined up behind a candidate whose conservative notion of progress largely matched their own. As Talmadge race-baited his way across the dusty cotton fields, sweltering mill towns, and rural crossroads in the spring and summer of 1948, members of the American Legion and the Veterans of Foreign Wars served up barbecue at one Talmadge rally, while the Montgomery County Veterans Organization in Mount Vernon fried fish at another.[67] Members of the Veterans Committee of the Muscogee County Talmadge Club issued a letter to local veterans endorsing Talmadge for his experience in governmental affairs, his background as a farmer, businessman, and lawyer, his service record in the navy overseas during the war, and his active and sincere interest in veterans' affairs. They also applauded "his heritage of . . . staunch principles passed on to him by his father, the late Eugene Talmadge."[68] Other veterans appeared with Talmadge on rally platforms and often introduced him to local audiences, like Monroe Phillips from Baxley, Georgia, who praised "Hummon" for not only fighting three dictators overseas during the war (Hitler, Mussolini, and Tojo), but particularly for fighting three more "dictators" at home (Thompson, Arnall, and Rivers) in a "Battle for Individual Liberties for Georgians."[69]

By combining this unapologetic defense of white supremacy with a program for economic growth and development, Herman Talmadge weakened the opposition faction and diversified his base of support, attracting not only the rural and small town voters on which his father always counted, but also white veterans and business-minded Georgians from larger and more urban counties.[70] This strategy reflected the lessons of 1946: a campaign for modernization alone would be vulnerable on race in the highly charged postwar climate, but race-baiting alone might not mobilize the good government–minded white voters who had gone to the polls in droves to vote against Eugene Talmadge. Most whites in Georgia, including veterans, wanted a candidate who could promote dynamic growth and development *and* defend white supremacy without embarrassing the state's national image. Herman Talmadge rode that demand—one shaped and defined by the impact of World War II and the veteran insurgencies of 1946 —straight into the governor's mansion in 1948. Whereas his father won the governorship in 1946 without a popular majority, in 1948 Herman squeaked by with 45,000 popular votes over Thompson, carrying 130 counties overall, garnering the support of rural conservatives, uptown business interests, white veterans, and the many courthouse gangs who could still turn out the local white vote.[71]

Talmadge may have finally captured the governor's office formally, but he did not win that seat by most standards of "fair and square." The events of the 1948 primary indicated that Georgia's black citizens might in fact have plenty to fear from a Herman Talmadge administration and certainly little to hope for from a program of conservative modernization that defined economic growth and development alone, not racial justice, as the solution to Georgia's many ills.

Even as James S. Peters, chairman of the Georgia Democratic Executive Committee, promised in late March to keep the primaries open to black voting in 1948, he also busily schemed to subvert their participation. "Even if we cannot have a White Primary as such by name," he wrote to another Talmadge operative in April, "we can achieve almost the same results through educational qualifications for voters"—or, at least "in those counties where we can get the cooperation of the local election authorities."[72]

The local "cooperation" Peters hoped to enlist readily appeared by way of Ku Klux Klan chapters, which took an even more active role in the elections of 1948 than they had on behalf of Eugene Talmadge two years earlier. A campaign of intimidation and terror against black citizenry began in earnest in the early spring, when the Klan burned crosses in Swainsboro, Georgia, and left miniature coffins on the doorsteps of local black political leaders.[73] In March, over 300 hooded and robed Klansmen paraded through downtown Wrightsville, led by Grand Dragon Samuel Green in a jeep carrying one lighted cross, stopping at the courthouse to burn another. Of the 400 blacks registered in that county in 1948 (out of 4,500 black residents), none voted in the local election.[74] One hour before the polls opened in the local election in Jeffersonville, Georgia, the Klan burned two crosses at the local courthouse. Despite this threat, 150 brave black citizens voted anyway.[75] In Montgomery County, the Klan used more individualized tactics, mailing threatening leaflets to each registered black voter in Mount Vernon.[76] Finally, at a Klan rally at Stone Mountain in July 1948, Green openly endorsed Talmadge at a ceremony to initiate some 700 new members. Stetson Kennedy, who attended the rally, estimated an attendance of 10,000 people, drawn from several southern states, who arrived in charter buses and even a limousine or two. Amid the hot dog and lemonade stands, a large cross and several smaller ones burned at altars as the initiates marched or, according to Kennedy's account, staggered in a drunken stupor, to a central platform. Grand Dragon Green mounted the stage to deliver his "customary spiel," followed by an endorsement of Herman Talmadge for governor as "the only man in the race who believes 100 per cent in white supremacy." Green then warned that "blood will flow in the streets" if blacks' civil rights were to be "enforced with Yankee bayonets."[77]

"Yankee bayonets" never made an appearance on behalf of black voters or anyone else in Georgia in 1948, but blood flowed in the streets anyway. African Americans brave enough to actually cast a vote faced real danger, especially in rural and small town communities. Two families in Montgomery County, about two hundred miles south of Atlanta, discovered firsthand what the politics of race and modernization wrought by the war could bring. Local whites assaulted Dover Carter on the day of the 1948 September primary as he carried black voters to and from the polls in his car. They also murdered Isaac Nixon for voting in the election and drove both families from the communities in which they had lived for nearly all their lives.

The story of Dover Carter and Isaac Nixon reflected many of the political currents of the postwar era, from the leading role both men played in local black voter registration drives after the war to Nixon's status as a World War II veteran. Carter was a middle-aged black farmer who, with his wife, Bessie, and their ten children, ranging in age from a four-month-old baby to a seventeen-year-old teenager, lived on his father-in-law's farm in Montgomery County. On the heels of the *Primus King* decision prohibiting the white primary, Carter and several other black residents established the county's first NAACP chapter in 1946. Prior to that time, few blacks in the county voted or were even registered to vote, and the "primary function of the branch was to stimulate such registration." Under Carter's presidency, the chapter built its membership quickly to about a hundred black citizens, most of whom were farmers and sharecroppers. By 1948, around six hundred blacks had registered to vote.[78] Not long before the day of the primary, three local white politicos asked Carter to help transport black citizens into Alston to the polls to vote on election day, and he agreed.[79]

Along with this activism, not surprisingly, came harassment from the local Klan. In 1946 the KKK reportedly had paraded in full regalia in front of Carter's home on at least two occasions, and he continued to receive threats over the next two years: "the threats were of proposed beatings and in one instance there was a threat of death." Carter apparently reported these threats to the "good whites" and sheriff, indicating his political connections to a local white faction, but he also continued his registration activities.[80] Isaac Nixon and his wife, Sallie, lived less than three miles from the Carters, and the two families had been neighbors for eighteen years. Carter had persuaded Nixon and his wife to vote in 1948, and Nixon joined his friend as an active leader in the registration campaign.[81] Four days before election day in 1948, according to Carter, another Klan demonstration set out for his home; failing to catch him there, they happened to pass him along the streets of Alston on the way back. "As they passed me in Alston," Carter reported, "one man threw his hand out the car door and said there he is now," though they had apparently decided to leave him alone.[82]

Right from the beginning, Carter and other black citizens in the county confronted a barrage of intimidation orchestrated by local whites to prevent them from voting in the 1948 primary election. When Carter pulled up to the polls in Alston on election day, for example, he noticed a white man named Claude Sharpe, sitting in a light blue Ford, watching a group of blacks gathered near the door of the polling place. Sharpe apparently called one of the men, John D. Harris, over to the car, where they spoke for a few minutes. When Harris returned to the group, he reported that Sharpe had advised him not to vote but to go home, "if he knew what was best for him." Harris reportedly told Sharpe that "he didn't know what was best for him but he came out to vote and he reckon that['[]s what he would do." According to Carter, the group went into the building, voted, and departed. Carter then left to begin transporting other black voters to the polls. Events from this point onward quickly took a turn for the worse.[83]

As Carter set out to take a woman home after voting, a car pulled abruptly in front of him, forcing him to halt. A white man named Johnnie Johnson then reportedly jumped out, came to Carter's car door, and demanded that he get out. Carter replied that he needed to take his passenger home, to which Johnson retorted that Carter "could wait"—the men "were going to beat the hell out of [him]." Johnson then snatched open Carter's door and began beating him with a piece of iron that Johnson had strapped to his wrist. Exactly what happened next is not entirely clear, but Carter apparently tried to defend himself, possibly reaching toward the floor of his car for a shotgun. Then he heard another white man, Thomas Jefferson Wilkes, say, "don't do it or I will blow your damn head off." Carter looked over and saw that an armed Wilkes had drawn a bead on him as he walked toward the car. "I realized at this time that they were determine[d] to hurt me," Carter reported, "and there wasn't anything I could do." As Johnson continued to hit Carter, Wilkes poked the gun barrel through the passenger side window and told Carter to get out of the car, "stating that they were going to kill me." At one point, Johnson stopped hitting Carter long enough to take a breath and laughed as he saw Claude Sharpe drive by. "They continued to beat me," Carter explained, "until my head was bloody, my hands felt as though they were paral[y]zed." When Wilkes apparently decided that Carter had had enough, he ordered Carter to "turn the car around, go home, and not haul any more people to the polls nor be caught at the polls any more." As Carter reported, this tirade ended with a warning: "they had better not hear anything that I said about him."[84]

Carter, however, immediately returned to the polling place, reported these events to the poll manager, and "asked him to get me some protection." When the manager, Marvin McBride, asked Carter who was responsible, he exhibited an unusual courage and identified both men. McBride apparently told another white man, Guy Morris, "to go down town and get someone to call someone else," but apparently he took no other action in Carter's defense.[85] Carter then left the polls and returned home, later visiting a white doctor in Ailey, Georgia. He also reported these events to the national NAACP, which made arrangements for his family to stay in nearby Dublin. Carter, however, felt unsafe even there. "The reason I cam[e] to Atlanta," Carter explained, "was that I feared that another attempt might have been made on my life." "I don't know what to do now," a desperate Carter added in a handwritten note on his sworn affidavit, "I have no home anymore and no place to bring my wife and children. I don't understand—I didn't do nothing wrong."[86]

The beating he received was only one of the reasons that Carter feared for his life. That same day, Johnnie Johnson and his brother, M. A. Johnson, murdered Isaac Nixon, Carter's old friend and political compatriot. A World War II veteran, Nixon had actively encouraged other local blacks to register and vote in the September primary. When he went to the polls on September 9, he insisted on casting his ballot even though he was reportedly warned by whites at the polling place not to do so. That night, the Johnson brothers, who apparently worked as local loggers, lynched Nixon on his own doorstep, shooting him point-blank in the chest three times. He died some hours later that night at a hospital in Dublin. Nixon's wife and six children witnessed the brutal assassination.[87]

Sheriff R. M. McCrimmon clearly linked Nixon's murder to the primary election, possibly as a means of warning other blacks against voting in the future. The sheriff "was told that Nixon went to a polling place in Alston . . . and asked if he could vote . . . . Nixon was told . . . that he had the right to vote, but was advised not to do so . . . . Nixon had insisted, however, and was permitted to cast his ballot." The Johnsons shot Nixon later that evening, according to the sheriff, "because he had insisted on voting in Georgia's Democratic primary election."[88] Dover Carter, Nixon's neighbor and friend, apparently reached the hospital just in time to hear his friend's dying words, the only black person to do so. Reportedly, Nixon told Carter "that when the Johnsons drove up before his home, he came down off the porch to meet them because it was the 'only thing for me to do to save my family,' that is, 'to take it myself.' "[89] Like many southern black veterans, Nixon drew on the only mantle of protection he really had, his own manhood, and he sacrificed himself to protect hearth and home.

Sheriff McCrimmon arrested the Johnsons, who claimed to have fired in self-defense. The NAACP employed a local attorney to assist the prosecution in the case, in part because Nixon's widow lacked the means to employ legal counsel. Initially, there appeared to be "considerable white sentiment against the killers in that particular community," as the Georgia Conference of the NAACP reported. McCrimmon especially hoped that the prosecution would be able to proceed against the Johnsons, who had a reputation for terrorizing local blacks. He apparently linked Claude Sharpe, who had won the nomination for sheriff and who had harassed Carter on the day of the election, to the Johnsons and their reprisal against Nixon.[90] The Georgia and the Federal Bureaus of Investigation got involved in the case, and the Montgomery County grand jury did indict

M. A. Johnson for murder and his brother as an accessory. Both the Carter and Nixon families lived in considerable fear as the case moved forward. Ralph Gilbert, president of the Georgia Conference of the NAACP, privately wrote, "I must confess I don't like the looks of the community myself; it is typically one where trouble of a racial nature might easily be stirred." "I have little confidence in a jury around there returning a verdict of guilty," he mused, "especially when the man was killed over exercising his right of franchise."[91] A superior court jury in Mount Vernon, the same community where the Klan had mailed its threats to individual black voters in 1948, returned a "not guilty" verdict for M. A. Johnson, and both brothers were acquitted of all charges relating to the Nixon incident.[92]

Carter and Nixon embodied the real determination among many of Georgia's black citizens to claim what political rights they could within the racial constraints of the postwar era. That this activism incurred Carter's beating, Nixon's murder, and the fleeing of both families demonstrated the limited political choices black citizens in Georgia still faced. The program of modernization that white veterans heralded in the postwar 1940s, and that became a channel for Herman Talmadge's political success, would not be a foundation on which to build a future for racial justice—not until enough reason existed to break away from this absolute defense of white supremacy. From the Independents in Augusta who publicly announced their proud white southern loyalties in 1946 to the legislators who voted to reinstate a white primary in 1947, the vast majority of Georgia's white citizens, veterans included, either acquiesced to, accommodated, or even perpetrated the injustices that Georgia's black citizens continued to suffer. Dover Carter cooperated with local whites in 1948 out of political expedience; and even though he carried blacks to the polls at their request, he still faced harassment and beatings from other whites and little protection or support from the men who had solicited his participation. The consequences, of course, were even grimmer for Isaac Nixon, as well as for veteran George Dorsey in Walton County in 1946 and Robert Mallard, another black World War II veteran murdered by whites in Toombs County for voting in Georgia's Democratic primary in 1948.[93] The white veterans elected in the insurgencies of 1946 remained largely mute in the face of these gross violations of the democratic political rights they had purported to support. They did not see racial injustice as irreconcilable with the growth and prosperity they envisioned as Georgia's future. And the developing pressures within and outside the region that would eventually counter that assumption, such as a mass militant black protest movement or the regional dependence on outside investment and federal spending, were not yet powerful enough in the postwar 1940s to make them think otherwise.[94]

Nor would organized labor fare much better along the road to the future that good government veterans in Georgia had mapped out.[95] Indeed, the new right-to-work laws passed by the Georgia General Assembly in 1947 only compounded the difficulties that the CIO's postwar organizing drive had already encountered. Employers immediately took full advantage of the union-busting tactics these measures allowed, foreshadowing the impact the national Taft-Hartley Act would have on unions nationally. In the wake of the passage of HB 72, reported a CIO official in Atlanta, employer "opposition to unionism has become more and more arrogant." Violence against organizers had increased, mill communities passed blatantly unconstitutional ordinances limiting free speech and assembly, and management refused to agree to collective bargaining elections. Moreover, while employers insisted that "the union be responsible for the actions of all workers in a plant," this same CIO official noted that "these companies refuse to agree to any form of union security which will permit that responsibility." Thus, only a few months after passage of the laws, already "we can see how these bills will interfere with the process of peaceful collective bargaining and with the extension of union organization to the unorganized."[96]

The worsening climate for unions and organizing efforts in Georgia became especially evident during strikes that erupted after the General Assembly passed the measures and Governor Thompson signed them both into law. During the early days of the TWUA strike at the Athens Manufacturing Company in 1945, for example, Horace White, a white TWUA field representative, had successfully defended strikers from a court injunction that limited picketing. When the county Sheriff delivered the court order and ordered the pickets to disperse, White had objected. "Speaking so that all our pickets could hear," White announced that this order "meant absolutely nothing as far as our peaceful picketing the plant was concerned." "The Sheriff has no authority to order you to leave your lines," White assured the strikers; "we have our constitutional rights, one of them being our right to peacefully picket, and we will not permit any man, nor any group of men to deny us these rights." He then ordered the picketers to "return to your posts and ignore what this man has said."[97] The sheriff declined to arrest White for this bit of braggadocio, and the judge who issued the initial order ultimately struck out the provision limiting picketing at White's urging.[98]

Within two years such bravado was a rare thing. Indeed, the difference between 1945 and 1947 in Georgia was telling. A provision of HB 72 allowed the parties involved in a labor dispute to enlist injunctions, and employers immediately turned to sympathetic judges. Whereas White boldly declared the unconstitutionality of such court orders in 1945 and got away with it, veteran William Shiflett of Anchor Rome Local 787 ended up serving twenty days in the county jail in 1948 for violating a similar injunction. In fact, CIO officials believed that the unsuccessful Anchor Rome strike itself was, in part, a direct product of the passage of the Georgia statutes. At the time that employees sympathetic to management began circulating petitions to solicit union membership withdrawals, explained Joe Pedigo, manager of the Northwest Georgia Joint Board, "the Georgia statute had just become effective," undermining all union security measures. Immediately, "the company seemed to be taking advantage of the change in the law." The contract that Local 787 ultimately signed, and which Anchor Rome violated almost immediately, had no provisions for a closed shop or maintenance of membership in accordance with the new state law.[99] Thus, Pedigo condemned the "vicious state anti-labor legislation which, even more than Taft-Hartley, encouraged Celanese and Anchor Rome to force us into long strikes which sapped the joint board to the marrow."[100] Such sentiment led delegates at the TWUA's Southern Wage Conference in Atlanta in September 1947 to resolve that the handicaps created by the Taft-Hartley Act "have been aggravated by state anti-labor legislation, which in some instances is even more restrictive than national legislation . . . in a number of southern states."[101]

Though most scholars agree that Operation Dixie had largely spent its momentum by the time these antilabor statutes passed, numerous other organizing campaigns struggled on in Georgia throughout the postwar 1940s and into the 1950s. David Burgess, head of the Georgia CIO from 1951 to 1955 and a TWUA and Operation Dixie organizer before that, later recalled that "the right-to-work laws in both South Carolina and Georgia and the use of the Taft-Hartley Bill by both employers and their high paid lawyers greatly weakened existing union(s) and . . . our efforts to organize workers at textile mills and other manufacturing plants."[102] Nor did this situation soon improve. "The 1950s session of the state legislature," reported H. D. Lisk, state director of the Georgia CIO, "accomplished little or nothing in the direction of improving standards of the textile workers and their families." After all, "we still have the restrictive anti-labor laws in the state statute books [and] this year we saw eight of our own officers and members thrown into jail because of the unfair labor injunction law."[103]

As Operation Dixie organizers quickly learned, unionism continued to be a hard sell in the racially charged climate of the postwar era, particularly since the national CIO had adopted a policy of interracial membership. But industrial unionism represented a threat that went beyond its racial implications. The war had served to awaken many white veterans to the cost of homegrown civic complacency and political corruption. It did not eradicate, however, the conviction that selling a community to potential investors still depended on offering up a large pool of available cheap labor. Even as federal dollars poured into the state, and even as state and local boosters dreamed of attracting higher wage industries, the bread and butter of southern industrial recruitment, both before and after the war, remained marketing a community's labor as union-free.[104] Georgia's right-to-work laws had passed so easily in the state legislature in 1947 because good government veterans did not regard limiting the power of industrial unionism as a controversial or unwelcome issue. Georgia, and most of the South, continued to be strongholds for anti-unionism throughout the postwar 1940s and the following decades. Boosters eager to attract industry to employment-starved postwar communities often enacted local measures meant to deliberately impede union organization. In Sandersville and Baxley, Georgia, local laws required organizing unions to pay a $2,000 "licensing fee," followed by $500 for each local resident who signed up.[105] The road to progress that good government veterans followed bypassed industrial democracy, not only racial justice.

Despite these limits, political life in postwar Georgia was not exactly the same as it had been. Many southerners, black and white, moved from country to city within the South or left the region entirely, challenging local communities, as John J. Flynt had explained in 1946, to do better at creating reasons for residents to stay, such as expanded job opportunities. Thus, the imperative to develop dynamic programs of industrial recruitment and economic development increasingly animated local and statewide politics after the war and created, in turn, new political priorities. That departure from the past, however, still fell within the limits of change that good government veterans had mapped out. Few southern postwar leaders reflected a better understanding of this contradictory political legacy of the war, or were as successful in manipulating it, than Herman Talmadge.

Talmadge realized early on that the political times were changing. While his father had "followed the old Jeffersonian principle that the least governed people are the best governed" and "never raised taxes in his life," years later Herman Talmadge believed that "most people would say I was more progressive than my father." After all, "when I came along it was after World War II, and I think the people of Georgia had made up their mind that they wanted to see more progress in state government." As a consequence, the younger Talmadge "advocated what my father would have thought was a very progressive platform . . . . I spent a lot of money on education, and roads, and health, and things of that nature, not in accordance with what he'd done prior to that." Such changes were possible by his time, Talmadge noted: "the times and people had changed somewhat. World War II had intervened. The state was more prosperous than it would have been. Industrial development had started in Georgia."[106]

Ever the political opportunist, Governor Talmadge crafted a strong statewide political machine sustained by a program that offered unprecedented expenditures for education, public services, and industrial recruitment as well as a stalwart defense of white supremacy. As governor, Talmadge supported a 3 percent sales tax, which substantially increased state revenues. This money, in turn, funded the Minimum Foundation Program, which equalized expenditures between rural and urban schools in Georgia, effectively creating the state's first real public education system. In fact, Georgia spent more on education in Talmadge's six years in office as governor than had been spent by all previous administrations in the state's history.[107] In addition, Talmadge introduced a tax reform program in the early 1950s that was favorable to new industry and a constitutional amendment that finally allowed the state to spend more revenue than it took in. Over the course of Herman Talmadge's administrations, the state expanded the Georgia Port Authority to promote trade and industry, constructed or expanded twenty-eight farmers' markets, built 10,000 miles of new roads, and proposed or built sixty new hospitals. According to one scholar, Talmadge's programs produced over 15,000 new jobs in Georgia, along with $50 million in new plant construction.[108]

Yet Talmadge also continued to campaign on a Jim Crow platform and became one of the South's leading proponents of massive resistance to integration. He declared in 1950 that "as long as I am Governor, Negroes will not be admitted to white schools." Shortly thereafter he penned an epistle on regional resistance to integration entitled *You and Segregation*.[109] His contradictory program —one that blended all the dictates of white supremacy with the imperatives of economic and governmental development—proved to be a recipe for success for many more years. Talmadge served two terms as governor, then four terms as a United States senator from Georgia.[110]

Like Talmadge, good government veterans also believed a program of "conservative modernization" to be the state's only sure path to a better future. This notion reflected their conviction that economic prosperity alone, not racial justice or industrial democracy, meant progress. Those veterans, black and white, who believed that the war had meant something different—that the Four Freedoms did apply to the postwar South—lost out to this developing chamber of commerce ethos. Moreover, that ethos grew ever more central to the foundations of the modern political South, underscoring its importance as the most lasting legacy of World War II's contradictory political impact. "The dominant psychology of the South is no longer agrarian," remarked social scientist and regionalist Rupert B. Vance in 1955; "it is Chamber of Commerce."[111]

The politics of modernization pursued by good government veterans and the neo-Whig leaders who followed them did help to spur unprecedented growth and development in Georgia as the "rule of the rustics" declined. Federal court decisions in 1962 overturned the county unit system and malapportionment in Georgia, finally accomplishing what progressive black and white veterans had failed to achieve in the postwar 1940s. Popular voting assured the ascendance of metropolitan business-professional leaders over the rural county seat elites in statewide politics. From 1962 onward, Georgia governors by and large followed the ethos of change that good government veterans had articulated after the war: they exhibited a "growth-oriented ideology" that emphasized policies conducive to industrial recruitment, governmental efficiency, and racial stability.[112]

Development speeded the growth of the business-professional class centered in Atlanta, which, in turn, contributed to a smoother transition away from segregation than occurred in many other southern states and cities. Certainly, as the question of integration loomed in the 1950s, most Georgia whites preferred to keep the races separate, and most Georgia governors, including Herman Talmadge, continued to posture themselves as the last and best defense against black domination. Given the negative national publicity that Alabama and Mississippi's violent response to civil rights activities received in the late 1950s and early 1960s, however, the well-developed passion for recruiting industry to Georgia—rooted in Henry W. Grady's New South hustings after the Civil War and popularized by good government veterans after World War II—ultimately trumped no-holds-barred resistance to integration. Thus, in 1961 the state legislature appointed the Sibley Commission on Desegregation. Chaired by John Sibley, a well-known and respected Atlanta banker, the commission issued a moderate report that recommended local option, not wholesale rebellion, in response to federal mandates on public school desegregation. When school desegregation finally came to Atlanta, according to one scholar, it proved "anticlimactic and uneventful" compared to the "scorched-earth" policies of massive resistance that disrupted neighboring states and towns.[113]

Thus, the program of "conservative modernization" that good government veterans in the postwar 1940s had heralded eventually recognized that a community's prospects for the future would have to rely on at least a modicum of racial justice. But its proponents never drew the same conclusion about the need for a substantive redistribution of wealth and power. Neo-Whig politicians, following the example set by their good government predecessors, operated on the notion that the benefits of unregulated economic growth and industrial development would eventually "trickle down" of their own volition to all Georgians and resolve the state's economic and social problems.[114] Both good government veterans and the later political leaders of the Sunbelt South premised the politics of modernization on a fiscal and social conservatism that failed to eradicate the disparities between black and white, country and city, middle-class and poor, that had long defined southern life, even as their programs for change altered much of the region's physical and economic landscape.[115]

It was an ironic finale to the state's postwar political drama, one that reflected the peculiar contradiction at the heart of the war's political impact on Georgia and the South. The politics of change to come out of the war legitimized a conservative understanding of progress that still offered the Four Freedoms to some southerners more than others.

Conclusion

THE TURBULENT AND even curious political conflicts of the postwar 1940s wracked Georgia's postwar stability, leaving a political landscape undeniably marked by the impact of World War II. Challenges to a smooth reconversion to peace came from many quarters: from black citizens fed up with their second-class status and determined to assert their rights of citizenship whenever and however they could; from workers convinced that union membership represented the best ticket to higher wages and protection from the whims of management; from middle-class whites who demanded a more dynamic and rational response by state and local governments to the economic potential unleashed by the war; and even from reactionary whites who mobilized against the threats to white supremacy they saw developing around them.

For a time it appeared as if the plot to this postwar southern drama would take a surprising twist. In the number of newly registered black and white voters, in the CIO's postwar campaign to organize the South, and even in the willingness of so many white Georgians to line up behind a moderate alternative to Eugene Talmadge in 1946, the state appeared at first glance to be poised on the cusp of a progressive era. Georgia's postwar political life might actually have sustained a much broader and more diverse electorate—including an opening for black participation in civic affairs—as well as a seat for organized labor at the table of management and a state administration boasting a more forward-looking and moderate temper.

But if the political mobilization of blacks and organized labor stood as a signal landmark on Georgia's postwar landscape, so did the reactionary white back-lash that soon followed. In addition, the advocates of the campaigns for change that garnered the most support saw little contradiction in advocating a program of modernization bereft of racial or industrial democracy. Indeed, if any lesson could be drawn from World War II, it was that Georgia's political alternatives re-mained within the southern Democratic Party, positioned along a spectrum of conservatism, with scorched-earth reactionaries on one end and segregationist, anti-unionist, "but not a damn fool" modernizationists on the other.[1] The in-surgent white veterans who cooperated with blacks and organized labor to win election in 1946 easily dispensed with the interests of both parties when they sat in the state legislature in 1947. Good government veterans opposed Georgia's in-cumbents not because those officials oppressed blacks and labor, but because they manipulated white supremacy as a means to sustain corrupt, provincial, and reactionary governance to the detriment of Georgia's national image and future prosperity.[2] In the postwar 1940s many white Georgians, veterans in-cluded, still regarded toeing the southern line on race and anti-unionism a vi-able means to achieve modernization.

Herman Talmadge applied the lesson of 1946 quite effectively. He combined an unabashed defense of white supremacy that would have made his father proud with a program for urban, industrial, and educational progress that Eugene would have, no doubt, abhorred. In this way, Herman created a solid base of political support in the postwar years among ordinary whites, courthouse gangs, urban modernizers, and business interests. This "Talmadge blend" of change and tra-dition, according to one scholar, established a new foundation for political unity among white Georgians after the divisiveness of the immediate postwar years. That political "peace," however, came at the expense of blacks, organized labor, New Deal progressives, and any real redistribution of wealth and power.[3]

Yet it would be myopic to conclude that no significant change at all emerged from the complex matrix of events that defined Georgia's transition from war to peace. Veteran activism reflected a dynamic political tension building in Geor-gia and the South on the heels of the war's end. Black veterans demanding a po-litical voice, progressive white veterans fighting for democratic majority rule, and union veterans organizing against management exposed how destabilizing the economic, demographic, and social changes of the war years really were. In this sense, Georgia's veterans exposed the cracks that were developing in the foun-dations of the one-party South, and their insurgencies against the postwar sta-tus quo pointed toward the ruptures that would split the Solid South apart in later decades.

Doyle Combs, George Dorsey, and Isaac Nixon risked their lives not only to defend American interests abroad during the war, but to make that sacrifice have real meaning at home. Lacking a broad base of support or federal intervention on their behalf in the postwar 1940s, black veterans confronted a vicious racial backlash that prevented a new era for race relations in Georgia from emerging anytime soon. But their bravery, determination, and outright stubbornness presaged the black freedom struggle that eventually blossomed across the South, with black veterans of the Second World War once again at the helm.[4]

The white veterans in the Ku Klux Klan and the Columbians who rebelled against these currents of racial change, even to the point of terrorizing black citizens, indicated just how rocky the road to racial change in the South still would be. The war fostered a hardening racial line in Georgia and the South that hit the national political scene with the Dixiecrat revolt from the Democratic Party in 1948. Thus, reactionary veterans forewarned of the massive resistance to integration that would further destabilize southern politics in the following two decades.[5]

At the same time, however, good government veterans underscored the growing impatience of many southern whites with the conservative factions that still dominated their communities and the state at large. The broad support these campaigns enjoyed testified to the ambitions many Georgians held for a different sort of leadership, one that could banish the memory of the Great Depression for good. Veterans such as the members of the CPL in Savannah, the Independents in Augusta, and even Herman Talmadge were the predecessors of the "new Whig" governors and boosters who emerged in every southern state in the 1950s and 1960s, determined to lead their communities into the national economic mainstream. If this could be accomplished within the framework of segregation, as Herman Talmadge and good government veterans believed in the postwar 1940s, then so be it. Only when the price tag became too high—when massive resistance and civil rights protests threatened the image of stability these leaders believed was so crucial to continued growth and development—did movement toward moderate racial reform begin.[6]

Thus, World War II challenged the static nature of southern political life without inaugurating the new day that progressives had hoped to see dawn at the war's end. Georgia's white veterans wove a uniquely southern pattern into the postwar politics of change, sustaining the continuity of the South's political distinctiveness by accommodating rather than countering the weight of racial and anti-union tradition. Their vision of progress legitimized a politics of conservative modernization as the foundation of the Sunbelt future—a politics promising democracy and justice to some southerners far more than others. Georgia's veterans thus wrought a peculiar ending to a war most southerners, then and now, believed was fought in the best spirit of American freedom. The contradictory consequences of that war would reverberate in Georgia and the South for decades to come.

Notes

Abbreviations

ACSP   Alva C. Smith Papers, Archives, Schwob Library, Columbus State
          University, Columbus, Ga.
ACTWR   Amalgamated Clothing and Textile Workers Union of America,
          Northwest Georgia, Records, 1949–1976, Southern Labor Archives,
          Georgia State University, Atlanta, Ga.
CBP   Clarence Bacote Papers, Atlanta University Center, Atlanta, Ga.
CIOP-OD   Operation Dixie: The CIO Organizing Committee Papers (microfilm),
          Special Collections, Perkins Library, Duke University, Durham, N.C.
DPP   Daniel Powell Papers, Southern Historical Collection, Wilson Library,
          University of North Carolina, Chapel Hill, N.C.
GGDP   Georgia Government Documentation Project, Special Collections and
          Archives, Pullen Library, Georgia State University, Atlanta, Ga.
GSDECP   Georgia State Democratic Executive Committee Papers, Russell Library,
          University of Georgia, Athens, Ga.
GTHP   Grace Towns Hamilton Papers, Atlanta History Center, Atlanta, Ga.
GTRP   Glenn T. Rainey Papers, Special Collections and Archives, Woodruff
          Library, Emory University, Atlanta, Ga.
HTP   Herman Talmadge Papers, Russell Library, University of Georgia,
          Athens, Ga.
JSJP   James Setze Jr. Papers, World War II Miscellany Collection, Special
          Collections and Archives, Woodruff Library, Emory University,
          Atlanta, Ga.
JVCP   James V. Carmichael Papers, Special Collections and Archives, Woodruff
          Library, Emory University, Atlanta, Ga.

LRMP   Lucy Randolph Mason Papers (microfilm), Special Collections, Perkins
            Library, Duke University, Durham, N.C.

NAACPP   Papers of the National Association for the Advancement of Colored
            People (microfilm), Documents and Microforms, Hodges Library,
            University of Tennessee, Knoxville, Tenn.

NLRBR   National Labor Relations Board Records, RG 25, National Archives and
            Records Administration II, College Park, Md.

PPP   Prince Preston Papers, Russell Library, University of Georgia, Athens, Ga.

RG   Record Group

RMP   Ralph McGill Papers, Special Collections and Archives, Woodruff Library,
            Emory University, Atlanta, Ga.

RTBF   Robert Thompson Biographical File, Atlanta University Center,
            Atlanta, Ga.

SKP   Stetson Kennedy Papers (microfilm), Special Collections and Archives,
            Pullen Library, Georgia State University, Atlanta, Ga.

SPC   Southern Politics Collection, Special Collections and Archives, Heard
            Library, Vanderbilt University, Nashville, Tenn.

SRCA   Southern Regional Council Archives, Veteran Services Project (micro-
            film), Atlanta University Center, Atlanta, Ga.

TACR   Third Army Command, Domestic Intelligence Reports, RG 319, National
            Archives and Records Administration II, College Park, Md.

TWUAP   Textile Workers Union of America Papers, State Historical Society of
            Wisconsin, Madison, Wis.

Chapter One

1. Combs interview.

2. John Sammons Bell, Fulton County Carmichael-for-Governor Club, WSB Radio broadcast, July 11, 1946, transcript, Draft APR.1993.22.uc-M84–20/56b and 55b, GGDP. Also see *Atlanta Constitution*, July 12, 1946, 4.

3. Of the 16.3 million Americans who served in the Second World War, some 320,000 were Georgians. The first figure may be found in Millett and Maslowski, *For the Common Defense*, 408. The second figure is from Bartley, *Creation of Modern Georgia*, 180. The participation of Georgia's black and white servicemen and women ranged from being support troops at home and overseas to serving as occupation forces around the globe to fighting on the front lines in the European, Pacific, and African theaters of the war.

4. O'Brien, in *Color of the Law*, 102, 104–5, and 108, for example, notes the enhanced self-esteem experienced by black men who served in the war. Likewise, Tyson, in *Radio Free Dixie*, 140–41, quotes black civil rights militant Robert F. Williams, a World War II and Korean War veteran from North Carolina, as explaining that white male attacks on black women were an especial affront to black veterans "who had been trained to fight." Also see Brattain, *Politics of Whiteness*, 123–24. Marwick, in *Total War and Social Change*, xvi, concludes that "total war requires the involvement of hitherto underprivileged groups," who will expect certain "social gains" to reward their participation and who find in military service a new source of "consciousness and self-esteem."

5. For a variety of explanations of the connections between southern white racial attitudes, gender, and citizenship, see Kantrowitz, "Ben Tillman and Hendrix McLane, Agrarian Rebels," 498–501, 502–3; O'Brien, *Color of the Law*, 131, 133; Frederickson, "'As a Man I Am Interested in States' Rights,'" 260–74. In *Radio Free Dixie*, 140–41, Tyson notes the prevalence of a "racialized" sense of manhood among both black and white men in the South, in which each group's understanding of its own masculinity depended on the ability to protect women from the other. Manhood stood as an important "metaphor for citizenship" in the Jim Crow South, a connection only magnified by going to war.

6. On the racialization of both the domestic and political spheres by whites in the South after the Civil War and well into the twentieth century, see Williamson, *Crucible of Race*, 309–11; Brundage, *Lynching in the New South*, 58; Ayers, *Promise of the New South*, 153–57; Tyson, "Wars for Democracy," 262; Gilmore, "Murder, Memory, and the Flight of the Incubus," 74, 76–77; Kantrowitz, "Ben Tillman and Hendrix McLane, Agrarian Rebels," 498–99, 501, 524; and Frederickson, "'As a Man I Am Interested in States' Rights,'" 260.

7. The best treatment of Georgia during and after World War II is Bartley, *Creation of Modern Georgia*. For an eloquent, wide-ranging, and more personal assessment, see Cobb, *Georgia Odyssey*.

8. The county unit system of voting covered elections for governor, U.S. senator, "statehouse offices," state supreme court justices, and court of appeals judges. Key, *Southern Politics*, 119.

9. In an election under the county unit system, the unit votes went to whichever candidate had a plurality of the popular vote in that county. A candidate with only a plurality in the popular vote statewide could receive a majority of the county unit votes. The unit system also allowed a candidate to win without any popular majority of votes at all. V. O. Key concluded that the county unit system in Georgia was responsible for "deflating the popular vote of the larger counties and ballooning the influence of the smaller counties." This system, he surmised, accounted for the "accentuation of rural-urban differences in Georgia." Moreover, as "patently calculated to thwart majority rule," the county unit system was "unquestionably . . . the most important institution affecting Georgia politics" in the postwar 1940s and 1950s. Because this system heightened the political influence of rural-agricultural counties, and thereby sustained conservative hegemony statewide, progressive reformers targeted this political tradition as a fundamental impediment to real democracy and social change. They were not the only ones, however, to regard the county unit system as an obstacle to change. Proponents of economic development likewise viewed the county unit system as a barrier to Georgia's economic modernization. By perpetuating conservative Bourbon or reactionary rule in the state legislature and in local communities, these proponents argued, the system thwarted efforts to establish policies more conducive to industrial recruitment and development. Key, *Southern Politics*, 119–20; Bernd, *Grass Roots Politics in Georgia*, 4–6.

10. On the many voter registration campaigns that emerged in every southern state immediately after the war, see, for example, Lawson, *Black Ballots*; Dittmer, *Local People*, 19, 25–27; Sullivan, *Days of Hope*, 193–220; and Fairclough, *Race and Democracy*, 105, 112, 123–24, 129–34.

11. Disfranchising measures in the late nineteenth and early twentieth centuries in the

southern states excluded African Americans from participation in Democratic primary elections for local, state, and often national offices. Given that these elections were the only ones that really mattered in an essentially one-party region, these measures effectively barred African American participation in southern political life. The 1944 Supreme Court decision in *Smith v. Allwright* that such measures were, in fact, unconstitutional galvanized black civil rights activities in the late 1940s, heartened progressives within and outside the South, and unnerved many southern whites. In an effort to subvert the ruling, Democratic conservatives in Deep South states rushed to remove all state regulation of primary elections in order to claim that the Democratic Party had the status of a private club that could determine its own membership. In 1946 a federal court ruled in *Chapman v. King* that the *Smith* decision applied to Georgia as well, and not simply to Texas where the case originated. This decision allowed black participation in Georgia's Democratic primary for the first time in 1946. On the *Smith v. Allwright* and *Primus King* decisions, see Key, *Southern Politics*, 522, 621, 624–28, 632; and Harmon, "Beneath the Image," 37–38. For one of the classic treatments of black disfranchisement in the post-Reconstruction South, including the origins and impact of the white primary system, see Kousser, *Shaping of Southern Politics*.

12. The best treatment of these campaigns and the liberal-labor collaboration that sustained them may be found in Sullivan, *Days of Hope*, 133–248.

13. On the Augusta campaign see Cobb, "Colonel Effingham Crushes the Crackers," 507–16. For events in Savannah see *Savannah Morning News*, April 18, 1946, 2, 12, and April 25, 1946, 12. On the 1946 gubernatorial race see Bartley, *Creation of Modern Georgia*, 201; Sullivan, *Days of Hope*, 210–15; Key, *Southern Politics*, 106–29; and Brattain, *Politics of Whiteness*, 153–60.

14. On the campaigns of terror directed against African Americans in post–World War II Georgia and the South, see Grant, *Way It Was in the South*; and Burran, "Racial Violence in the South."

15. Studies that discuss Herman Talmadge's emergence as leader of the Talmadge faction in Georgia include Bartley, *Creation of Modern Georgia*, 204–7; Cobb, *Georgia Odyssey*, 56–57; Egerton, *Speak Now Against the Day*, 483, 521, 574; Frederickson, *Dixiecrat Revolt*, 107, 114, 162; Brattain, *Politics of Whiteness*, 161, 212, 217; Henderson, *Politics of Change in Georgia*, 210–13; and Pajari, "Herman E. Talmadge and the Politics of Power."

16. On the connection between the policies that good government veterans pursued and the later emergence of a "chamber of commerce" ethos of growth and development articulated by neo-Whig leaders in the modern South, see Bartley, *New South*, 398, 461, 467, 470; Cobb, *Selling of the South*, 128, 140, 142, 146–48, 155–59, 160, 162, 177, 270–71; and Schulman, *From Cotton Belt to Sunbelt*, 127–34.

17. Cobb, *Selling of the South*, 100, 122.

18. On the rise of Cold War liberalism and its displacement of New Deal liberalism, see Brinkley, *End of Reform*, 4, 7–8, 13, 269. On the increasing national focus on southern race relations after World War II, see Bartley, *New South*, 38–73.

19. For a sampling of the works that explore the importance of the World War II to the South, see Tindall, *Emergence of the New South*, 687–732; Bartley, *New South*, esp. chap. 1; Bartley, "Writing About the Post–World War II South"; Daniel, "Going Among Strangers"; Egerton, *Speak Now Against the Day*, 201–534; Cobb, *Selling of the South*, 35–63; Cobb,

Most Southern Place on Earth, 184, 198–200, 204, 208–11; Cobb, *Industrialization and Southern Society*, 50–67, 150, 153, 156; Schulman, *From Cotton Belt to Sunbelt*, 72–73, 80–85; and Sosna, "More Important Than the Civil War?" In *Lost Revolutions*, 1–3, Pete Daniel observes that in 1945 "at few times in southern history had the path to revolutionary change seemed so clear. The road into the 1950s, however, took unexpected turns. The South that evolved in the twenty years after the war emerged out of displacement, conflict, and creativity—not tranquility."

20. On the impact of the war in the South, see Tindall, *Emergence of the New South*, 687–732; and Daniel, "Going Among Strangers."

21. In "More Important Than the Civil War?" Morton Sosna argues that World War II had such a profound impact on southern society, economics, and culture that it might actually rival the Civil War as a promulgator of change for the region.

22. In *Emergence of the New South*, 731, Tindall notes the social and economic changes wrought by the war, but also that southern political leaders "embodied a curious paradox." While offering their wholehearted support for policies aimed at winning the war, "in domestic affairs they had retreated back within the parapets of the embattled South, where they stood fast against the incursions of social change." Also see Bartley who, in *New South*, 459, emphasizes the many changes brought on by the war, while also acknowledging that "as it turns out, the sweeping upheavals of World War II had little effect on southern politics, except in the short term to strengthen the position of Bourbon conservatives." Similarly, Harvard Sitkoff, in "African-American Militancy," 92, argues that while the "insurgent struggle for racial justice to come in the South would eventually draw sustenance from the many fundamental transformations in American life and world affairs catalyzed by the Second World War," African American militancy would not coalesce in the South in any significant fashion for another decade. Both studies, however, assess the region as a whole rather than focusing on specific events and developments tied to individual states and local communities. The immediate, pre–civil rights, postwar era did not, in fact, register as much change overall as the civil rights era itself. However, as the case of veteran activism and the level of political instability and turmoil in the postwar 1940s illustrate, the Second World War did have a notable effect. Coming on the heels of the Great Depression and New Deal, World War II disrupted the political stability of local, state, and regional politics, which produced the postwar political patterns from which the changes that wrought the modern South ultimately emerged. Moreover, Sitkoff bases his evaluation of the impact of the war on the black civil rights movement on an analysis of national organizations and institutions during the war years, ignoring the grassroots activism of black veterans and citizens that characterized the immediate postwar era.

23. See, for example, the finely textured arguments that balance in the middle of the continuity-versus-change spectrum in Frederickson, *Dixiecrat Revolt*; Frederickson, "'As a Man I Am Interested in States' Rights'"; Simon, "Race Reactions"; O'Brien, *Color of the Law*; Brattain, *Politics of Whiteness*, 86–131; and the essays in McMillen, *Remaking Dixie*.

24. Southern veterans appear briefly in the following works: Bartley, *New South*, 21–22, 135; Cobb, *Most Southern Place on Earth*, 203, 210–14; Haas, *DeLesseps S. Morrison*, 34–35, 39, 43, 49–50, 88; Lester, *Man for Arkansas*, 17–35; Dittmer, *Local People*, 9; Egerton, *Speak Now Against the Day*, 328, 340, 375, 377, 382, 385, 457, 468, 558, 604; Norrell, *Reaping the*

Whirlwind, 60–63; Key, *Southern Politics*, 198, 201–4, 436–37; Brattain, *Politics of Whiteness*, 123–24. More extensive treatments may be found in Cobb, "Colonel Effingham Crushes the Crackers," 507–16; Tyson, *Radio Free Dixie*, which explores the life and career of southern black militant Robert F. Williams, a veteran of both the World War II and the Korean War; and O'Brien, *Color of the Law*, which examines a 1946 race riot in Columbia, Tennessee, in which both black and white veterans participated.

25. I am indebted to Jane Dailey, Glenda E. Gilmore, and Bryant Simon, *Jumpin' Jim Crow*, for proposing this remolding of the traditional change-versus-continuity debate. These essays emphasize dissent from and resistance to the political and racial structures as a central theme in the history of the post–Civil War and twentieth-century South. See the introduction, 3–6, especially, for a well-written and precise articulation of this argument.

26. On the coalescing of white racial resistance in the postwar South that blossomed into massive resistance to integration, see Bartley, *Rise of Massive Resistance*, 3–46; and Frederickson, *Dixiecrat Revolt*.

27. On the role of black veterans in the later civil rights movement, see, for example, Dittmer, *Local People*, 1–18, 31; Tyson, "Wars for Democracy," 271; and Tyson, *Radio Free Dixie*, 29, 48–62. Also see O'Brien, *Color of the Law*, 102–5; and McMillen, "Fighting for What We Didn't Have," 93–110.

28. On the neo-Whig leaders who emerged in the South of the 1960s and 1970s, see Bartley, *New South*, 398, 461, 467, 470; Cobb, *Selling of the South*, 128, 140, 142, 146–48, 155–59, 160, 162, 177, 270–71; and Schulman, *From Cotton Belt to Sunbelt*, 127–34.

Chapter Two

1. *Atlanta Daily World*, March 28, 31, 1946.

2. "14 Points of Action of GVL, Inc.," December 1945, series VII:4, reel 190 (931), SRCA; *Atlanta Daily World*, March 31, 1946, 1, 2.

3. *Atlanta Daily World*, March 28, 31, 1946.

4. R. B. Dunham to *Pittsburgh Courier*, August 1946, pt. 4, reel 8 (188), NAACPP.

5. Heard interview. Few African Americans remained unaffected by war mobilization, but "it was the servicemen who were most conscious of the part they had played in the war, and so the most likely to have high expectations for change." Wynn, *Afro-American and the Second World War*, 21–37, 115. For further discussion on the role of African Americans in the military and in the war, see Dalfiume, *Desegregation of the United States Armed Forces*, 64–131; Blum, *V Was for Victory*, 182–220; Thomas, "'Double V' Was for Victory"; Buchanan, *Black Americans in World War II*; and Motley, *Invisible Soldier*. More recent works that emphasize the impact of military service in World War II on the black men who served include O'Brien, *Color of the Law*, 102, 104–8; Tyson, *Radio Free Dixie*, 29, 48–62, 141; Dittmer, *Local People*, 1–9; and McMillen, "Fighting for What We Didn't Have."

6. Heard interview. Alexander Heard was one of V. O. Key's primary researchers covering several southern states for *Southern Politics in State and Nation* in the postwar 1940s.

7. Flanagan interview.

8. Heard interview.

9. According to Neil Wynn, for example, "Army life, even with its racial restrictions, was better than life as a civilian. The uniform gave a measure of self-respect and a degree of authority. More important, black soldiers were taught skills and trades, given a certain amount of education, as well as being fed, clothed, and paid regularly. For a good number, it was the first semblance of economic security they had ever known." A black enlistee, he continues, "responded as an American with patriotism and loyalty," but this was at least, in part, "in the hope that his participation would be recognized and rewarded." At the same time, he "resented his treatment both in and out of the forces and was inclined to feel he had nothing to fight for." See Wynn, *Afro-American and the Second World War*, 28–29. In *Color of the Law*, 102, Gail O'Brien also notes the enhanced self-esteem black servicemen that derived from their military service during World War II.

10. See, for example, Marwick, *Total War and Social Change*, xvi.

11. On the notion of manhood held by southern black veterans that emphasized the obligation to protect hearth and home, see Tyson, *Radio Free Dixie*, 140.

12. On the development of the dynamic bond between political, racial, and gender identities and racial-sexual anxieties in the South from the late nineteenth century into the twentieth century, see Williamson, *Crucible of Race*; Brundage, *Lynching in the New South*, 58; Ayers, *Promise of the New South*, 158; Gilmore, "Murder, Memory, and the Flight of the Incubus," 73–94; and Tyson, "Wars for Democracy."

13. For a variety of explorations of the connections between southern white racial attitudes, gender, and citizenship, see Kantrowitz, "Ben Tillman and Hendrix McLane, Agrarian Rebels," 498–503; O'Brien, *Color of the Law*, 128, 130–31, 133; Tyson, "Wars for Democracy"; Tyson, *Radio Free Dixie*; Frederickson, "'As a Man I Am Interested in States' Rights'"; and Simon, "Race Reactions."

14. See, for example, O'Brien, *Color of the Law*, 102, 104, 105, 108, 246; McMillen, "Fighting for What We Didn't Have," 101–3; and Tyson, *Radio Free Dixie*, esp. chaps. 2 and 3.

15. Stouffer et al., *American Soldier: Adjustment During Army Life*, 495–97. From 1943 through the end of the war, the Army Research Branch conducted extensive interviews of soldiers' morale and their attitudes about the war, the military, Allied war aims, and the postwar future. Samuel Stouffer and his associates compiled and interpreted the data, separating the responses of black soldiers from those of white servicemen.

16. Ibid., 237.

17. The statistics are from Wynn, *Afro-American and the Second World War*, 115. Modell, Goulden, and Magnusson, in "World War II in the Lives of Black Americans," 838, reinterpreted Army Research Branch data to conclude that for most black men "the impact of military service influenced the structure of their aspirations in a way that contributed to their unwillingness to accept the prewar structure of racial dominance." This influence, according to the authors, served to foster personal ambitions to succeed in the postwar economy—an individualistic drive that allegedly undermined a traditional concern for black advancement as a group or community goal. While this interpretation helps explain why so many black GIs planned not to return to the South after the war, and why many left soon thereafter, it does not address the decision of many other African American ex-servicemen and women to remain in the South and to fight to increase black opportunity and freedom.

18. Bohannon interview.

19. Ibid. In Georgia the number of lower-level white-collar workers grew more rapidly during and after the war than the expanding business-professional middle class. Positions as clerks, salesmen and women, real estate agents, bank tellers, cashiers, and typists, Numan Bartley has concluded, were not especially lucrative, but they certainly created more purchasing power than tenant farming and sharecropping. Bartley, *Creation of Modern Georgia*, 183.

20. Stouffer et al., *American Soldier: Adjustment During Army Life*, 515–16.

21. Ibid., 515.

22. Ibid., 513, 517–18.

23. See O'Brien, *Color of the Law*, 105.

24. Law interview. Law never did receive overseas duty, although ultimately he felt "it was a blessing in disguise" because many of the men with whom he had trained never returned.

25. Both Wynn, in *Afro-American and the Second World War*, 29, and Dalfiume, in *Desegregation of the United States Armed Forces*, 81, note that black soldiers' reactions to the war and to discrimination in the service often fostered ambivalent attitudes. "On the one hand, [a black soldier] responded as an American with patriotism and loyalty in the hope that his participation would be recognized and rewarded," writes Wynn, but "on the other, he resented his treatment both in and out of the forces and was inclined to feel he had nothing left to fight for." Thus, concludes Dalfiume, a "profound cynicism" toward the war was often "accompanied by a widespread belief that conditions would be vastly improved after the war." Moreover, overseas service sometimes introduced African American soldiers to the possibilities of a life less encumbered by American and southern racism. For many, it offered the first real opportunity to be treated as Americans first and as blacks second, and to associate with people and cultures less imbued with racial prejudices against blacks. An overseas environment, pointed out a commander of a black supply unit, allowed black American soldiers to do "things they could not do at home," from frequenting local eateries and shops with ease to fraternizing with women of various races. Such an experience, he argued, was "something you can't expose a man to and expect him to forget overnight." For this quotation see Wynn, *Afro-American*, 32–34. For more information about the overseas experiences of African Americans in World War II, see Smith, *When Jim Crow Met John Bull*, 141–47. On the heightened racial consciousness that developed among many black GIs, see O'Brien, *Color of the Law*, 104; Tyson, *Radio Free Dixie*, chap. 2; and Dalfiume, *Desegregation of the United States Armed Forces*, 81.

26. Not surprisingly, black GIs often interpreted their dissatisfaction with army life in racial terms, even when describing the type of conditions that generally irritated all enlisted men. An entire history of discrimination and injustice, however, made comments such as "They treat us like dogs" or "Why don't they treat us like men?" mean something far different when articulated by black soldiers comparing their conditions to those enjoyed by their white counterparts. See Stouffer et al., *American Soldier: Adjustment During Army Life*, 503–5. Indeed, black soldiers resented this disparity in treatment and protested it whenever possible. In military encampments, airfields, bases, and communities throughout the South, black soldiers (two-thirds of whom were native to the region) talked back to racist military police officers, civilians, and local police; complained to white officers and officials as well as to the inspector general; helped each other evade ar-

rest; and in several notable examples, engaged in armed rebellion. For examples of African American soldiers engaging in mutiny and armed rebellion during the war, see Burran, "Racial Violence in the South," 152, 159, 162.

27. Combs interview. Several authors note comments by black veterans similar to those of Doyle Combs. "When I came out of the army I was determined to register to vote," recalled Tuskegee veteran Daniel Beasley. After all, he continued, "I had been in the army[,] . . . I had never been in jail[,] . . . [and] I just figured I ought to be registered." When Charles and Medgar Evers went to the Decatur, Mississippi, post office to register in 1946, they encountered recalcitrant whites who demanded to know "who you niggers think you are?" "We've grown up here," they explained; "We have fought for this country and we should register." Beasley quoted in Norrell, *Reaping the Whirlwind*, 60; Evers brothers quoted in Lawson, *Black Ballots*, 19, but also see Dittmer, *Local People*, 1–9.

28. Combs interview. This sense of earned citizenship endured despite the discrimination that black GIs encountered during the war. In fact, service in a segregated and discriminatory army ostensibly to defend American freedom and democracy exposed the moral bankruptcy and downright absurdity of Jim Crow, an experience that often served to heighten black soldiers' racial consciousness. When Amzie Moore of Cleveland, Mississippi, joined the service, for example, he ended up in a segregated unit in the Pacific where restrictions based on racial considerations made little sense when weighed against the exigencies of combat. "Here I'm being shipped overseas," Moore recalled, "and I have been segregated from this man whom I might have to save or he save my life." Nor did Moore hesitate to point this out to interviewers, noting "I didn't fail to tell it." In fact, the irony of his position grew even more apparent when Moore received the dubious assignment of persuading black troops that conditions in the United States would be improved after the war, in order to counteract the impact of Japanese propaganda harping on American racism. Moore quoted in Cobb, *Most Southern Place on Earth*, 211. Even the enemy could appear in a favorable light, as one former white POW discovered when he was assigned to address an audience of black servicemen. As part of the army's attempt to convince black soldiers of their importance to the war effort, the soldier, formerly a prisoner of the Japanese, described his encounters with the enemy and his observation of their treatment of prisoners of war. When he described Japanese soldiers shooting black GIs in order to demonstrate the barbarity of the enemy in a personal manner, however, he elicited an unexpected response. Did the Japanese shoot only black soldiers, his audience wanted to know, and did they keep black prisoners segregated from white POWs? To soldiers accustomed to mistreatment, discrimination, and injustice in their own military, an enemy who shot and imprisoned all POWs with little racial distinction seemed less than barbaric, and possibly even preferable. Thomas, "'Double V' Was for Victory," 155.

29. In the Mississippi Delta, as James C. Cobb has concluded, "irritated planters in desperate need of cotton pickers could hardly endure the sight of blacks driving about the Delta enjoying their new leisure and flaunting their new sense of independence." A few local planters, according to an Agricultural Adjustment Administration official, hoped for an "organization that would encourage Race Riots in Northern Cities to get a plentiful supply of labor around after the war so [they] can have two croppers begging for each tract and plenty of extra help around for picking." Quoted in Cobb, *Most Southern Place on Earth*, 198–99. In addition, black civic leaders reactivated voter registration drives, po-

litical campaigns, and reform movements in the wake of federal decisions that chipped away at segregation and disfranchisement. All of these developments appeared to many southern whites as dangerous transgressions of the paternalistic caste system that bolstered southern political and racial stability. Thus, "the major short-term impact of wartime upheaval," notes John Dittmer, in *Local People*, 114, "was an increased level of racial tension." For further examples of whites in the South and the North reacting against the wartime changes that tended to foster more black independence and opportunity, see O'Brien, *Color of the Law*; Burran, "Racial Violence in the South"; Shapiro, *White Violence and Black Response*, 355, 365; Corley, "Quest for Racial Harmony," 35–56; Daniel, *Breaking the Land*, 212–23; and Tindall, *Emergence of the New South*, 716. A discussion of African American activism during the war may be found in Blum, *V Was for Victory*, 182; Bartley, *Creation of Modern Georgia*, 201; Barnes, "Journey from Jim Crow," 117–19, 121; Autrey, "National Association for the Advancement of Colored People in Alabama," 179–82, 184; Wynn, *Afro-American and the Second World War*, 20–21; Dalfiume, "'Forgotten Years' of the Negro Revolution"; and Dalfiume, *Desegregation of the United States Armed Forces*, 61, 74–75.

30. Even more threatening were the so-called Eleanor Clubs of African American domestics who insidiously schemed, in the white mind at least, to "put a white woman in every kitchen" by taking higher paying jobs as laborers at military facilities. See Grant, *Way It Was in the South*, 359–60; and Dittmer, *Local People*, 14.

31. For the best treatments of the reactions of white farmers and planters, in particular, to the racial and demographic changes accelerated by the war, see Daniel, "Going Among Strangers," 889; and Cobb, *Most Southern Place on Earth*, 208–15.

32. See Bolster, "Civil Rights Movements in Twentieth-Century Georgia," 96–97. In Mississippi and Arkansas, planters and civic leaders not only persuaded local draft boards to defer good tenants and sharecroppers, they also manipulated local debt laws to keep workers on the farm. A Mississippi County, Arkansas, sharecropper, for example, told a Bureau of Agricultural Economics investigator that "a lot of colored people there couldn't leave [because] Sheriff keeps them there." Workers or sharecroppers who received a deferment, even if unsolicited, "do not feel free to leave the farm of the operator who requested their deferment." Quoted in Daniel, "Going Among Strangers," 891.

33. Horace Bohannon to George Mitchell, Fort Valley, Georgia, January 11, 1945, reel 188 (257), series VII:3, SRCA. After touring Mississippi extensively throughout 1946, SRC field agent and war veteran Harry Wright concluded that "Negroes are being weighed in the balance to determine that they are not trying to bring back to Mississippi some of the ideals of freedom that they helped to win for some of the other people of the world." Wary white southerners were watching "in every quarter to see that he still knows 'his place.'" See Harry Wright, "Wanted: A Square Deal for Negro Veterans in Mississippi," unpublished draft, reel 189 (794–97), series VII:32, SRCA.

34. In 1944 the United States Congress passed the Servicemen's Readjustment Act, which quickly became known as the GI Bill of Rights. This legislation aimed primarily to ease the transition of returning World War II veterans into homefront civilian life and to reward them for their years of service. Its passage represented the first time the federal government offered such formal and extensive compensation to soldiers and sailors for fulfilling their military duties. Veterans of the Civil War or World War I, for example, re-

ceived only a relatively small one-time bonus payment after their discharge. The GI Bill was the largest single piece of social legislation enacted by the Congress up to that time. Its provisions included unemployment benefits, the construction of veterans' hospitals, educational benefits, access to low-interest loans to start small businesses or to purchase homes, and occupational training. Widely credited with transforming many American institutions, especially higher education, the GI Bill "propelled millions of veterans into middle-class status in employment, education, and residence." Nonetheless, the access a veteran had to these benefits depended as much on location and race as it did on length of service. As my discussion here indicates, African American veterans in the southern states experienced widespread discrimination when attempting to claim the compensation they had earned. For a basic overview of this legislation and the quotation above, see Boyer et al., *Enduring Vision*.

35. "Statements by Teachers, Principals, and Administrators," Atlanta University Seminar, Summer 1946, reel 189 (1289–94), series VII:35, SRCA.

36. Ibid.

37. Ibid.

38. Ibid.

39. After a thorough examination of the records of the SRC's Veteran Services Project, David Onkst has concluded that the GI Bill of Rights did little to alter the economic situation of black veterans who stayed in the South. For a good discussion of the discrimination black veterans confronted in the delivery of veteran benefits and services, see Onkst, "'First a Negro . . . incidentally a Veteran.'"

40. Ibid., 9, 12.

41. Horace Bohannon to George Mitchell, Macon, Georgia, January 17, 1946, reel 188 (259), series VII:4, SRCA.

42. Horace Bohannon to George Mitchell, Savannah, Georgia, February 22, 1946, reel 188 (346), series VII:4, SRCA.

43. Horace Bohannon to George Mitchell, Augusta, Georgia, undated, reel 188 (346), series VII:4, SRCA. As one observer wryly concluded, "If a white man and a black man both walk up for an opening and it ain't no shovel in that job, they'd give the job to the white man, but if there's a shovel in it, they'd give it to the black man." Quoted in Cobb, "World War II and the Mind of the Modern South," 10; and in Jones, *Dispossessed*, 226.

44. Onkst, "'First a Negro . . . incidentally a Veteran,'" 18, 29–30; *Atlanta Daily World*, November 10, 1946, 4.

45. Twitty referred to Alabama specifically, but the same standard applied to Georgia and throughout the South. William B. Twitty to George Mitchell, Alabama, undated, reel 188 (1105–15), series VII:5, SRCA.

46. "Statements by Teachers, Principals, and Administrators," Atlanta University Seminar, Summer 1946, reel 189 (1289–94), series VII:35, SRCA.

47. Burran, "Racial Violence in the South," 200.

48. My account of the Walton County lynching of 1946 draws heavily on the very able work of Wallace H. Warren in "'Best People in Town Won't Talk.'" Also see Egerton, *Speak Now Against the Day*, 366–69; and Wexler, *Fire in a Canebrake*. Although Wexler's book is a detailed, eloquently written, and fascinating account of this event, it is a work of creative nonfiction. The many conflicting facts and confusing twists integral to the

Walton County lynching are well presented by Wexler but are difficult to verify due to the stylistic choices made by the publisher regarding the presentation of sources and citations. Therefore, I have chosen to rely on Warren's more scholarly article for the facts used here. However, I highly recommend *Fire in a Canebrake* to anyone interested in learning more about this tragic event.

49. Warren, "'Best People in Town Won't Talk,'" 273–75.

50. Ibid.; Egerton, *Speak Now Against the Day*, 367–69.

51. Warren, "'Best People in Town Won't Talk,'" 274.

52. Ibid., 283. On Clinton Adams, his story, and the problems with his account of what occurred, see Wexler, *Fire in a Canebrake*, 209–23.

53. Fear of reprisal, resentment of outside interference and media criticism, and a definite lack of white compassion for the victims or their families nullified the attempts of both the Georgia and Federal Bureaus of Investigation to crack the case. Warren, "'Best People in Town Won't Talk,'" 280–82.

54. Ibid., 280.

55. Egerton, *Speak Now Against the Day*, 369.

56. *Atlanta Constitution*, July 26, 1946.

57. In Alabama, though the war brought home 46 percent more industrial and commercial jobs by 1946, the percentage of African Americans among the state's population had declined 4 percent by 1950. Almost 3,000 black southerners fled Mississippi during the 1940s, and Georgia's black population declined 12 percent between 1920 and 1950. See Cronenberg, *Forth to the Mighty Conflict*, 75, 85. Also see Dittmer, *Local People*, 14; Sosna, "More Important Than the Civil War?" 150, 160 n. 18. Total black migration from the six plantation states in the South during the 1940s totaled over 6 million. See Mandle, *Roots of Black Poverty*, 84. While the superintendent of the Coahoma County, Mississippi, schools, Lillian Rogers Johnson, found that even some white veterans had expected to find "a more liberal state of mind at home, but find it just about the same," black veterans were especially "disillusioned and disappointed. They come in and say 'how do you do' and 'goodbye.'" "Both groups are leaving," she noted, "but mostly Negroes." *Washington Post*, May 7, 1946, clipping, reel 188, series VII:1, SRCA. On a previous visit to Clarksdale, Mississippi, Harry Wright found black veterans "hanging around," but in September 1946 he discovered that "this time they had gone . . . . [A]ll the dissatisfied veterans have left town, and the ones who could re-adjust themselves have found some way to make a living without going back to the cotton fields." Harry S. Wright to George Mitchell, Clarksdale, Mississippi, September 29, 1946, reel 190 (1800), series VII:49, SRCA.

58. Bohannon interview; Horace Bohannon to George Mitchell, Millen, Waynesboro, and Augusta, Georgia, February 14, 1946, reel 188 (274), and Bohannon to Mitchell, Brunswick, March 16, 1946, reel 188 (284), both in series VII:4, SRCA. Some black veterans chose reenlistment over staying in the South or migrating elsewhere. Reportedly "irked by what he considers a pronounced denunciation of the contributions members of his race played in winning the war," Corporal Nehmiah Leggett of Hemingway, South Carolina, reenlisted in the army. Representatives of the Negro Newspaper Publishers Association who toured army installations in Europe in 1946 concluded that many black soldiers were "wholly disgusted with conditions at home . . . and are re-enlisting." In fact, in the first six months after the war, 17 percent of army volunteers were black men even though they

comprised only 11 percent of the general population. Thus, concluded Samuel Stouffer, despite rampant discrimination in the military, "For more Negroes than whites, the Army was no worse and often much better than their civilian situation in the type of work it gave them to do, in the economic returns it made, and in the amount of individual status it accorded." See *Atlanta Daily World*, February 22, 1946, 2; *Birmingham World*, June 11 and 14, 1946; and Stouffer et al., *American Soldier: Adjustment During Army Life*, 542–43.

59. Modell, Goulden, and Magnusson, "World War II in the Lives of Black Americans," 839; Sosna, "More Important than the Civil War?" 160 n. 18; Bartley, *Creation of Modern Georgia*, 189.

60. In *Radio Free Dixie*, 54, Tyson similarly concludes that the postwar racial crisis that beset black veterans when they returned helped to forge a strong sense of community among them, one that sometimes translated into organizational activity and political activism.

61. Two recent assessments which adopt virtually opposite views on this question are Sitkoff, "African-American Militancy," and McMillen, "Fighting for What We Didn't Have." Differences in interpretation appear to depend upon differences in emphasis. Sitkoff, for example, focuses solely on black institutions during the war, which generally prioritized loyalty to the war effort over protesting ongoing discrimination. However, McMillen, who interviewed scores of black veterans in Mississippi, concludes that the war played a critical role in developing their racial consciousness. Other works, including my own, that focus more attention on the individual experiences of black veterans and southerners at the time, and less on the national organizations and institutions that channeled legitimized black protest, also find the war to be an important element in heightening the racial consciousness from which the civil rights movement eventually emerged. See, for example, Tyson, *Radio Free Dixie*, 29, 48–62; and Dittmer, *Local People*, 1–8. Both strongly emphasize the pivotal role of World War II in generating black veteran activism and the early beginnings of the black freedom struggle.

62. See, for example, O'Brien, *Color of the Law*, 249; and McMillen, "Fighting for What We Didn't Have," 106–7.

63. An excellent discussion of the importance of an expanded definition of what constitutes political behavior may be found in the diverse set of essays in *Jumpin' Jim Crow*, edited by Jane Dailey, Glenda Gilmore, and Bryant Simon. "The crucial political battlefields in this book are not the editorial page, the ballot box, and the smoky room," writes New South historian Edward L. Ayers in an afterword, 301, but "the household and the street. We see politicians not on the hustings or in the office but in failed crusades, vigilante groups, and photo ops." A perspective on southern power and politics from a vantage point beyond the ballot box and the regular channels of electoral competition, these authors argue, tends to reorient our thinking about southern history since the Civil War, bringing to light a persistent thread of protest and resistance that undermines the notion of a Solid South relatively impervious to political disruption and turmoil until the New Deal and civil rights eras. My treatment of the postwar 1940s mostly relies on the more conventional emphasis on regular electoral politics and political campaigns and activities, such as voter registration drives, as the realm of debate over the impact of World War II. However, I also focus on the efforts of ordinary citizens, black and white, to expand their political participation and the roles that a diversity of southerners of both

races and various political persuasions played in shaping the political legacy of the Second World War for Georgia and the region. This focus sometimes involves an expanded notion of political behavior by blacks and others, such as individual acts of rebellion or extralegal violence, that occurred outside conventional electoral channels.

64. Quoted in Thomas, "'Double V' Was for Victory," 85 n. 133.

65. For more on these federal actions, see Sullivan, *Days of Hope*, 194.

66. Isaac Woodward's case became a cause célèbre for liberal black and white organizations. See, for example, *Birmingham World*, May 7 and July 23, 1946. A thorough discussion of racial conflict on southern public transportation may be found in Barnes, *Journey from Jim Crow*, 38, 57, 59, 62; and Kelley, *Race Rebels*, 62–75.

67. *Atlanta Daily World*, March 19, 1946.

68. Ossie Davis quoted in Thomas, "'Double V' Was for Victory," 131–32 n. 3.

69. In North Carolina, for example, black veterans played a central role in the formation of the militant NAACP chapter in Monroe, under the leadership of black activist and veteran Robert F. Williams. See Tyson, *Radio Free Dixie*, 80–81.

70. *Atlanta Daily World*, February 10, 1946, C-17. Southern chapters of the mainstream and powerful American Legion and Veterans of Foreign Wars generally prohibited integrated membership. Rather than accept segregated posts, many black veterans opted for establishing their own organizations. In Mississippi, Tennessee, and Alabama, for example, veterans formed statewide organizations, often born out of mass meetings, to press for equal access to the provisions of the GI Bill, to petition against discrimination in state and local veteran services, and to call for fair housing and employment, improved educational opportunities, and equal medical care and hospital facilities. See *Birmingham World*, March 8, 1946, 1; *Atlanta Daily World*, October 1, 1946, 6; *Jackson Advocate*, September 7, 1946, 1; and *Memphis World*, August 23, 1946, 1.

71. Bohannon interview. Through its office established in Atlanta in early 1946, the GVL offered personal services and advice to veterans through the assistance of trained counselors. GVL members such as Charles Milton, the state commander who had studied veterans' work in Washington, D.C., for six months, James Williams, a civilian counselor at Fort McPherson's Separation Center, and Mrs. Lena Sayles, former counselor at the Fulton-DeKalb Veterans Service Center, assisted veterans in numerous ways, including filling out official papers and obtaining notary services. See *Atlanta Daily World*, February 10, 1946, C-17. Horace Bohannon, an active member, recalled that the GVL numbered two to three hundred members statewide, with sixty or so in the Fulton County chapter alone, and around four chapters across the state. The veterans who joined the GVL were usually high school graduates who had seen overseas service, men (and women) whom Bohannon recalled as "good guys" who would be "expected to succeed." Quotations and other information on the GVL may be found in Bohannon interview. Also see Bolster, "Civil Rights Movements in Twentieth-Century Georgia," 106.

72. Bohannon interview. In "14 Points of Action" the GVL pledged to seek equal pay for equal work, employment in all professions and occupations, equal school and other public facilities, equal justice under the law, and the hiring of black policemen and firemen. Promising to cooperate with organized labor, black-owned businesses, and any organization working to better the community, veterans of the GVL planned to use "every intelligent and honorable means," including the "ballot, publicity, picketing, parades, and

boycotts," to combat discrimination. "14 Points of Action of GVL, Inc.," December 1945, reel 190 (931), series VII:4, SRCA. The GVL worked to integrate Veterans Administration hospitals and protested police brutality. For more information on black veterans' postwar activities, see *Atlanta Daily World*, November 6, 1946, 1, 3; and *Jackson Advocate*, March 9, September 7 and 21, October 19, and November 9, 1946.

73. On the origins and impact of disfranchising measures in the South, see Kousser, *Shaping of Southern Politics*.

74. Key, *Southern Politics*, 624. For a comprehensive and clear explanation of the complex legal cases and maneuverings that led to the *Smith v. Allwright* decision and subsequent state actions to subvert it, also see ibid., 619–44.

75. Ibid., 625.

76. Ibid., 628–29.

77. My account of the *Primus King* case draws heavily from the very able discussion by Egerton, *Speak Now Against the Day*, 380–81, 406–7.

78. For more on the all-white Democratic primary, the *Smith v. Allwright* decision (321 U.S. 649 [1944]), and the *Primus King* decision (327 U.S. 800 [1946]), see Key, *Southern Politics*, 522, 621, 624–28, 632; and Harmon, "Beneath the Image," 37–38.

79. For an excellent recent assessment of postwar liberalism in the South that emphasizes the connections between national and regional organizations, see Sullivan, *Days of Hope*.

80. From poll taxes, the white primary, and the county unit system to electoral manipulation, fraud, and violence, whites in Georgia had long restricted black citizens' access to political power and public policy. During the 1930s, however, black Georgians used rallies, boycotts, labor strikes, and voter registration drives to encourage black political participation. These efforts generally met limited success, but they did produce a core of committed and experienced middle-class black leadership. New political organizations, such as the Atlanta Civil and Political League and the Savannah Young Men's Club, continued voter registration activities throughout the war. The best overall treatment of these political mechanisms of white control may be found in Key, *Southern Politics*, 3–12, 533–644; and Lawson, *Black Ballots*, 22, 35, 53, 56, 65, 67, 70, 74, 77, 84–86, 89. On these early black civil rights activities in Georgia, see Bolster, "Civil Rights Movements in Twentieth-Century Georgia," 85.

81. "14 Points of Action of GVL, Inc.," December 1945, reel 190 (931), series VII:4, SRCA; Bolster, "Civil Rights Movements in Twentieth-Century Georgia," 106. See Lawson, *Black Ballots*, 19, 93–97, 99–100, 107–9, 114; Dittmer, *Local People*, 1–2; Norrell, *Reaping the Whirlwind*, 60–63; and Sullivan, *Days of Hope*, 193–221; for other examples of black veterans pursuing voting rights in the postwar South.

82. The events that surrounded the black voter registration campaigns in Savannah and Augusta proved to be very similar. The Augusta insurgency, which involved a diversity of citizens, black and white, who challenged the local political machine, is discussed in more detail in chapter 5 here. It is also evaluated in Cobb, "Colonel Effingham Crushes the Crackers." Because Savannah has received far less attention from scholars, I examine black and veteran voter registration campaigns in this city in more detail.

83. Building on registration efforts in the late 1930s, a new civic campaign developed when black leaders and a few white supporters took advantage of the pending Primus

King lawsuit to renew efforts to gain a "participatory role in local politics" for Savannah's black citizens. In Savannah, one participant recalled, the NAACP and the Citizens' Democratic Club worked through established community leaders, including pastors, to spread the word about registration and to encourage a large turnout. Gadsen interview. Also see Law interview. The NAACP hoped to register 10,000 voters in the fall of 1945, and members of numerous civic organizations turned out in response. Tax collector John Cabell initially impeded these efforts, but a NAACP lawsuit weakened his resistance, and black citizens began registering with little trouble in early 1946. *Brunswick News*, April 2, 1946, 8.

84. On the CPL see *Savannah Morning News*, April 25, 1946, 12; *Savannah Evening Press*, April 25, May 27, 1946; and *Savannah Herald*, May 29, 1946, 1, 6. As black registration figures continued to climb, CPL leaders jumped on the opportunity to capitalize on African American frustrations by recruiting those "who were for kicking out the old rascals" to their insurgent campaign. Though putting forth a black candidate was out of the question, the CPL did run "a whole slate of people who, with a few exceptions, were decent and did not mind coming into the black community to campaign and to dialogue with blacks." From this dialogue emerged promises to hire black officers and to appoint a Negro Advisory Committee "that would begin to have them understand what things they needed to address to benefit blacks." Quotations from *Savannah Morning News*, April 18, 1946, 12, 2. On the CPL's appeal to black citizens in Savannah, see Law interview.

85. *Savannah Morning News*, April 21, 1946, 28; *Savannah Herald*, April 24, June 5, 1946.

86. *Savannah Herald*, May 15, 1946, 6; Bolster, "Civil Rights Movements in Twentieth-Century Georgia," 118–19.

87. *Savannah Herald*, June 5, 1946, 7; *Savannah Morning News*, May 12, 1946, 15.

88. During the war, the Fulton County Citizens Democratic Club encouraged black citizens to register, only to have many of them turned away at the polls during the 1944 primary. Harmon, "Beneath the Image," 29–36. As the *Primus King* case developed in 1945, however, black activists continued their registration activities through organizations such as the Negro Voters League, the NAACP, and the Atlanta Urban League. These efforts, particularly an organizing drive centered in Atlanta's Eagen Homes housing project in the Ashby Street precinct, succeeded in registering enough black voters in late 1945 and early 1946 to give Helen Douglas Mankin the margin of victory in the special election to fill the Fifth District congressional seat. As a special election with no primary, the usual restrictions under the Neill Primary Act—namely, the county unit system—did not apply. See Spritzer, *Belle of Ashby Street*, 66–67. According to Jacob Henderson, manager of Eagen Homes and an active participant in the earlier voter drives, this victory convinced many black Atlantans that voting paid off, and registration in black neighborhoods began to increase accordingly. See Henderson interview by Kuhn. On the ACRC voter registration campaign, also see Sullivan, *Days of Hope*, 193–221; Harmon, "Beneath the Image," 33–56; and Bolster, "Civil Rights Movements in Twentieth-Century Georgia," 116; on Mankin's election, see Spritzer, *Belle of Ashby Street*, 70–74.

89. Harmon, "Beneath the Image," 29–36; Henderson interview by Kuhn; McPheeters interview. Additional campaign material from the ACRC drive may be found in CBP; and Mss. 597, series 2, box 7, folder 1, GTHP.

90. Information concerning the structure of this ACRC campaign may be found in the

following: Harmon, "Beneath the Image," 29–36; Bolster, "Civil Rights Movements in Twentieth-Century Georgia," 116–17; Henderson interview by Kuhn; Wallace Van Jackson to Pastors, March 21, 1946, and Clarence Bacote to Pastors, April 12 and April 26, 1946, publicity letters, Mss. 597, series 2, box 7, folder 1, GTHP. Also see a file entitled "All Citizens Registration Committee" in CBP (although many of these documents duplicate those in GTHP); and *Birmingham World*, March 19, April 30, and May 7, 1946.

91. Memo to ward leaders, undated, Mss. 597, series 2, box 7, folder 1, GTHP; *Birmingham World*, March 19, 1946, 1; *Atlanta Daily World*, March 28, 1946, 7.

92. On January 6, 1941, President Franklin D. Roosevelt defined for Congress the "four essential human freedoms" that his war-preparedness policies "aimed at securing." These were "freedom of speech and religion, and freedom from want and fear." See Kennedy, *Freedom from Fear*, 469–70.

93. Veterans' division memo, Mss. 597, series 2, box 7, folder 1, GTHP.

94. Ibid.

95. As it grew increasingly obvious that Savannah's black citizens were registering in "droves," recalled black participant R. W. Gadsen, whites speeded up their own registration efforts as well. The end result was a voter registration list that swelled to almost 80,000 by the end of the year, far and above the 16,000 voters registered before the end of the war. Although white citizens also turned out in unusual numbers, black registration climbed proportionally higher. See Gadsen interview.

96. *Savannah Morning News*, May 1, 13, 1946; *Savannah Herald*, May 1, 1946, 2; *Savannah Evening Press*, July 5, 1946, 18; Gadsen interview; Bolster, "Civil Rights Movements in Twentieth-Century Georgia," 119.

97. *Savannah Morning News*, July 2, 14, 1946; *Savannah Evening Press*, September 20, 1946, 20, 17. There were good reasons for black veterans to choose the CPL candidates over the candidates supported by the Irish Bouhan machine. Savannah's black residents, black war veteran W. W. Law recalled, "were literally waiting for a chance to participate," and Johnny Bouhan's rise to power in the 1930s constituted a vivid and unpleasant memory for many. According to Law, the Irish machine "built itself during the Depression by taking away . . . public jobs from blacks and giving [them] to whites." Even in such "lowly tasks as sweeping the streets and gathering the garbage, blacks were fired and whites were [put] in their place." At the time the CPL campaign and black voter registration drive developed, Law believed, "streets were unpaved," and black Savannahians "realized that they were paying taxes and that the City was literally being run without them." Moreover, "the practice at police court . . . was one of: 'Nigger, get back,'" and police officers profited from the illegal gambling racket supported by the machine and resented by many middle-class black citizens. "With these kinds of things," Law noted, "there was a great desire for change." Quotations from Law interview.

98. Law interview. R. W. Gadsen also recalled deliberate delays on the part of poll managers and election officials. Poll workers refused to hand out more than one ballot at a time and schemed to keep black voters at the polls for ten to fifteen minutes each. Reporters for the Savannah papers found that at many polling places white citizens cast ballots in two to three minutes while black voters often took as long as ten to twenty minutes. Gadsen interview; *Savannah Morning Press*, July 18, 1946, 14.

99. Gadsen interview; *Savannah Morning News*, May 1, 13, July 2, 5, 14, 18, 19, 1946; *Sa-*

vannah Herald, July 25, 1946, January 30, February 6, 1947; Bolster, "Civil Rights Movements in Twentieth-Century Georgia," 123.

100. Harmon, "Beneath the Image," 47, 72; Bolster, "Civil Rights Movements in Twentieth-Century Georgia," 117, 122.

101. For details on the Augusta campaign, see chapter 5, and Cobb, "Colonel Effingham Crushes the Crackers."

102. Grant, *Way It Was in the South*, 363–65.

103. Ibid., 368–70.

104. Williams, "Mississippi and Civil Rights," 89–99, 108.

105. Lawson, *Black Ballots*, 128.

106. Ashmore interview.

107. On the implications of the developing Cold War anticommunist climate in regional and national politics for postwar southern liberalism, see Bartley, *New South*, 38–73.

108. In *But for Birmingham*, 14–16, Glenn T. Eskew emphasizes the conventional nature of the strategies used by black civil rights organizations in the 1940s, as well as their focus on recruiting mostly educated black southerners in voter registration drives. Such an approach also relied on the "process of petitioning white leaders for ameliorating reforms," rather than enlisting a mass-based grassroots movement aimed at direct confrontation and immediate wholesale change as in the 1950s and 1960s. In fact, historians of the black freedom struggle do not agree on what the connection between the activism of the 1940s and the later civil rights movement after 1954 really was. Eskew, for example, identifies discontinuity between these two eras, based on differences in strategy, membership, and tactics. Others, however, such as John Dittmer, in *Local People*, 1–9, and Timothy Tyson in *Radio Free Dixie*, 48, 51, and in "Wars for Democracy," see a more direct connection, reading the civil rights activism of black veterans in the 1940s as precursors of the later movement. The strategy and tactics may have been different, but black World War II veterans who had been active in the postwar 1940s often showed up in the later movement as well. In Mississippi Medgar Evers, Charles Evers, Aaron Henry, and Amzie Moore were active in both eras, emerging as leaders of both the more conventional tactics such as voter registration in the postwar 1940s and the more militant direct action protest activities of the later movement of the 1960s. Also see Cobb, *Most Southern Place on Earth*, 211, 214. For an excellent overview of this historiographical debate, see Eskew, *But for Birmingham*, 14–16.

109. In *Color of the Law*, 249, for example, Gail O'Brien emphasizes the importance of "meeting individual needs and not tackling structural problems" after the war to both black and white veterans. Similarly, Sitkoff, in "African-American Militancy," 92, stresses the exodus of black veterans out of the South after the war: "it appears that many of those southern African Americans most 'modernized' by military service soon left the South . . . to pursue their individual ambitions . . . or re-enlisted[,] . . . depleting the pool of potential southern black activists."

110. "Negro Vote in Southern States: 1946," Division of Research and Information, pt. 4, reel 8 (862), NAACPP.

111. In fact, black citizens throughout the South protested electoral discrimination after the war. In Birmingham, Alabama, for example, black veterans disputed voter registra-

tion denials through the federal court system, which ultimately overturned the disfranchising Boswell Amendment. Upon their return from the war, Arlington, Virginia, veteran Grant Clark and "his veterans" immediately began urging local citizens to register
and vote. Their efforts produced a "record number" of new eligible voters in 1946. Moreover, Arlington veterans also launched an "education campaign" for black bus riders in
Virginia to reduce interracial tensions. In Charleston, South Carolina, the Veterans' Civic
Organization opened an "intensive voter registration drive" in the spring of 1946. *Birmingham World*, June 14, 1946, 1, 8; Sheppard interview; *Savannah Herald*, July 4, 1946, 4;
Memphis World, March 12, 1946, 1. On South Carolina, also see Frederickson, *Dixiecrat
Revolt*, 109–10.

112. E. J. Jacobs to national office of the NAACP, July 18, 1946, pt. 4, reel 8 (187),
NAACPP.

113. R. B. Dunham to *Pittsburgh Courier*, August 1946, pt. 4, reel 8 (188), NAACPP.

114. "Negro Vote in Southern States," Division of Research and Information, pt. 4, reel
8 (862), NAACPP; *Atlanta Constitution*, July 14–16, 1946.

115. Grant, *Way It Was in the South*, 365; "Negro Vote in Southern States," Division of
Research and Information, pt. 4, reel 8 (862), NAACPP.

116. Warren, "'Best People in Town Won't Talk,'" 273.

117. Grant, *Way It Was in the South*, 366; Egerton, *Speak Now Against the Day*, 365; *Atlanta Constitution*, July 26, 1946.

118. M. O. Smith to national NAACP office, September 10, 1946, pt. 4, reel 7 (732),
NAACPP.

119. Lawson, *Black Ballots*, 129–33.

120. Grant, *Way It Was in the South*, 365–68.

121. Ibid., 365.

Chapter Three

1. *Atlanta Constitution*, February 7, 1947, 1, 6.

2. Ibid., February 16, 1947, A-10, February 7 and 9, 1947. See also Egerton, *Speak Now
Against the Day*, 423–24.

3. Quoted in Egerton, *Speak Now Against the Day*, 424.

4. Quotation from *Augusta Herald*, August 4, 1947, 3.

5. I use the term "progressive" generally to include white veterans who believed that the
principles of democracy and majority rule required the participation of black Americans
in political life. Although some opposed racial discrimination, few advocated integration
as an acceptable or likely goal, even if they generally refused to advocate segregation. Patricia Sullivan identifies two main currents in southern liberalism at the end of the war.
The first group, which included *Atlanta Constitution* editor Ralph McGill, was comprised
of traditional, more moderate, white liberals, who defended segregation even as they denounced violence and extremism and called for racial tolerance and cooperation. The
second group, to which this group of white veterans belonged, was a interracial coalition
of New Deal progressives who generally did not attack segregation directly but, nonetheless, regarded it as incompatible with their vision of political and racial democracy. This
latter group, which included a diversity of southern progressives and radicals, blacks and

whites, from Lillian Smith to Grace Towns Hamilton, believed that voter registration drives among southern blacks and workers eventually would enable the defeat of key conservative Democrats in Congress and in southern state legislatures and open the way to a permanent realignment of the national party. Organizations such as the Political Action Committee of the Congress of Industrial Organizations, the Southern Conference for Human Welfare, and the NAACP believed that "an organized campaign to enfranchise the disfranchised was essential to reaping the changes of the previous decade and resisting the conservative reaction that had already begun." Sullivan, *Days of Hope*, 188. For more on this interpretation of postwar southern liberalism, see ibid., 6–9, 162–68, 187–89, 191, 194.

6. For recent works on the goals and strategies of national liberal organizations in the wartime and postwar era, see Bartley, *New South*, 38–73; Zieger, *CIO*, 141–252; and Egerton, *Speak Now Against the Day*, 345–534.

7. I use the term "reactionary" to designate those veterans who were unalterably opposed to any reform benefiting African Americans and committed to defending Jim Crow. Some chose extreme measures, including violence, extralegal activities, and membership in organizations such as the Ku Klux Klan. Others opted simply to support political conservatives who pledged to defend white supremacy.

8. Scholars have noted the civic and political activism in local southern communities in the 1940s that complemented the efforts by national liberal organizations to make the region a "battleground" for the future direction of the Democratic Party and the New Deal agenda. See, for example, Sullivan's excellent treatment of the Southern Conference for Human Welfare in *Days of Hope*. Few historians, however, conduct an in-depth examination of what these local movements looked like on the ground, often preferring to understand them through the lens of the national organizations through which many operated. Even fewer scholars consider the role veterans played in assisting *and* hampering these efforts. For examples of works that do mention southern veteran activism, see Bartley, *New South*, 21–22, 135; Egerton, *Speak Now Against the Day*, 328, 340, 375, 377, 382, 385, 457, 468, 558, 604; Frederickson, *Dixiecrat Revolt*, 47; O'Brien, *Color of the Law*, 7, 10–11, 13, 16, 32, 67–68, 88, 97, 130–31, 133, 137, 249–51, 282–83; Kelley, *Race Rebels*, 64–65; Sullivan, *Days of Hope*, 197, 206–7, 213, 251; and Cobb, "Colonel Effingham Crushes the Crackers."

9. Such veterans often belonged to the national American Veterans Committee. See Egerton, *Speak Now Against the Day*, 375, 377, 382, 468, 558.

10. Quotation from Bartley, *New South*, 45. Also see Sullivan, *Days of Hope*, 78. On the origins of the "popular front" variant of American liberalism, see Kennedy, *Freedom from Fear*, 315.

11. Quoted in Sullivan, *Days of Hope*, 167–68.

12. Ibid., 168.

13. Zieger, *CIO*, 231; Gilbert, *Another Chance*, 11.

14. Sullivan, *Days of Hope*, 173, 187–89.

15. Quoted in Bartley, *New South*, 50, 73. Also see Sullivan, *Days of Hope*, 194.

16. For background information on a few progressive white veterans in Georgia, see "Personal Histories," Georgia Veterans for Majority Rule, August 1946, reel 190 (730, 733),

series VII:43, SRCA; Mackay interview by Kuhn, March 31, 1987; and Kytle and Mackay, *Who Runs Georgia?* ix–xxvii.

17. Quoted in Kluger, *Yank, the Army Weekly,* 265–66.

18. Ashmore describes his reaction to the black unit in *Hearts and Minds,* 71. For more on Ashmore, see Egerton, *Speak Now Against the Day,* 210–11, 527–28, 548; and Ashmore interview.

19. Texas sergeant quoted in Sosna, "More Important Than the Civil War?" 155; Captain Murrell quoted in Newberry, "Without Urgency or Ardor," 180.

20. *Atlanta Constitution,* July 17, 1946, clipping, scrapbook 7, JVCP.

21. Quoted in *Atlanta Constitution,* May 17, 1948, 7.

22. Fleming interview.

23. Ibid.

24. Ibid.; the last quotation is from an older interview reported in Fleming's obituary in the *Washington Post,* September 6, 1992. Also see Egerton, *Speak Now Against the Day,* 210, 435, 468, 527, 564–65, 605–6, 617.

25. Mackay interview by Cliff Kuhn, March 18, 1986. After the war, Mackay became an avid defender of the democratic political rights of all Georgians and developed a reputation as a maverick southern liberal in the state and national legislatures.

26. *Atlanta Constitution,* February 9, 16, 1947; Rabun interview.

27. On the American Veterans Committee, see Egerton, *Speak Now Against the Day,* 328, 340, 375, 377, 382, 385, 457, 468, 558, 604.

28. The first quotation is George Brown Tindall, cited in Jacoway, *Adaptable South,* 277. The remaining quotations are from an AVC pamphlet on the George W. Norris Award, in RTBF. In the South, one author has concluded, the AVC stood as "an activist organization with a biracial membership and a liberal agenda[,] . . . determined to right social wrongs at home." Egerton, *Speak Now Against the Day,* 468. A Mississippi chapter put it even more explicitly: " 'the A.V.C.' stands firm for the things for which we fought. We strive for survival of the righteous, liberation of the oppressed, and correction of the oppressor." *Jackson Advocate,* September 14, 1946, 3.

29. Quotation from *Atlanta Daily World,* November 14, 1946, 3; also see *Birmingham World,* May 10, 1946, 7.

30. Cited in Domestic Intelligence Summary #34, November 7–14, 1947, box 10, folder 000.24, TACR.

31. Calvin and Elizabeth Kytle interview.

32. Bohannon interview. Bohannon became vice president of the Atlanta AVC chapter, while GVL commander John B. Turner served as secretary.

33. Ibid. Italics reflect the emphasis in Bohannon's voice on the audio tape of the interview.

34. Ibid. So exciting, apparently, that the AVC attracted many other members from the GVL: "I think it had a lot to do with the fact that we may have left the Georgia Veterans League before the end of 1946 [and] were mainly active in the AVC."

35. The following towns and cities in the South appear to have had AVC chapters: Chattanooga, Memphis, Nashville, Knoxville, and Oak Ridge, Tennessee; Atlanta (Fulton County, Emory, Georgia Tech, and Atlanta University chapters), Emmanuel County, and

Savannah, Georgia; Forrest City, Arkansas; Miami, Florida; Louisville, Kentucky; Baton Rouge and New Orleans, Louisiana; Southern Pines, North Carolina; Columbia, Greenville, and Rockhill, South Carolina; Richmond, Virginia; and Lafayette County, and Jackson, Mississippi. This list, which is far from complete, does nonetheless illustrate how widespread the AVC was in the South. It is compiled from information culled from newspapers; records on the Atlanta AVC, box 5, folder "AVC, 1944–55," Gilbert Harrison Papers, Library of Congress, Washington, D.C.; the Chattanooga Area Labor Council Records, boxes 1090 and 1091, Southern Labor Archives, Georgia State University, Atlanta, Ga.; and the CIOP-OD.

36. *The Bellringer* 2 (October 20, 1947), in box 13, GTRP.

37. *Atlanta Journal*, May 31, 1946, 10.

38. Thompson interview. Annie McPheeters, a librarian at the Auburn Branch Public Library, recalled that the AVC conducted a letter-writing campaign and maintained contact with the board of trustees in an unsuccessful effort to desegregate the public library system in Atlanta. McPheeters interview. The Atlanta AVC chapter also endorsed the local campaign for African American policemen, noting that "our present petition for negro policemen will be endorsed by approximately a dozen other organizations." *The Bellringer* 2 (October 20, 1947), box 13, GTRP.

39. AVC pamphlet, RTBF. Activities such as these did not make the members of the AVC racial radicals committed to an immediate all-out assault on segregation. Nonetheless, through the AVC progressive white veterans acted on a desire to work directly with black southerners on a relatively equal footing for progressive social change, including fighting the racial hatred in Georgia that betrayed the war's meaning as they understood it. In the wake of violent attacks on black citizens by the neofascist Columbians in the fall of 1946, the Atlanta AVC chapter moved quickly to condemn the "Hitleresque" shenanigans of a group whose fondness for strong-arm measures, brown-shirt uniforms, and thunderbolt emblems closely parroted the Nazis. "Measures to counteract the Columbians, Inc., hate-mongering group," an AVC newsletter announced, "lead the docket of matters which will come before the Atlanta chapter" at the next meeting. The chapter's "Anti-Discrimination Committee" proposed distributing "healthy literature" and staging a "gigantic Freedom Rally," complete with speakers and music. Chairman Les Persells denounced Atlanta's inveterate hatemongers in a letter that gained national attention. "As veterans of World War II, the Atlanta chapter of the American Veterans Committee issued a call to veterans, organized and unorganized, to continue their fight against the Nazi menace," Persells proclaimed, because "the actions and ideas of the Columbians, Inc. and those of Hitler's party are the same." The Atlanta chapter supported state and local efforts to curtail the activities "of this hate preaching group" and requested that the state of Georgia revoke its charter for attempting to foist gang rule on "Atlanta and America" and "for admittedly sponsoring violations of the Constitution of the United States." See *The Bellringer* 1 (September 7, 1946), reel 190, series VII:4, SRCA.

40. On postwar trends in Georgia and the South, see Bartley, *Creation of Modern Georgia*, 179–207; Bartley, *New South*, 1–104; as well as Daniel, *Lost Revolutions*, 7–87.

41. See Egerton, *Speak Now Against the Day*, 423–24.

42. Fleming interview.

43. Ibid.; *Washington Post*, September 6, 1992.

44. On this southern focus see Sullivan, *Days of Hope*, 188; and Bartley, *New South*, 39–40.

45. Egerton, *Speak Now Against the Day*, 333, 521; Sullivan, *Days of Hope*, 203.

46. The national AVC forbade specifically political activities on the part of its chapters, but many veterans who belonged to the AVC were active in political causes.

47. Heard interview.

48. As a researcher for Gunnar Myrdal's seminal study, *An American Dilemma*, Stoney had become acquainted with Atlanta liberals in the SRC and the SCHW. "Josephine Wilkins and Maggie Fisher [of the SCHW's Georgia Committee]," he recalled, "suggested that I work for Helen Douglas Mankin." Stoney interview; Spritzer, *Belle of Ashby Street*, 98, 118, 121.

49. *Atlanta Journal*, July 12, 1946, 14.

50. *Atlanta Constitution*, July 9, 1946, E-1. Many of Mankin's positions paralleled those taken by the national AVC, including opposition to the Case antilabor bill, support for the minimum wage and the Wagner-Murray-Dingell Social Security Act, and favoring the continuation of price controls. See "Veterans Whirl," *Atlanta Daily World*, October 8, 1946, 3.

51. Mackay interview by author.

52. Mackay interview by Kuhn, March 18, 1986. The liberal Georgians who administered the research project financed by the Rosenwald Fund to discover "who runs Georgia" included Josephine Wilkins of the Georgia Committee of the SCHW, Grace T. Hamilton and A. T. Walden of the Atlanta Urban League, Alex Miller, Dorothy Tilly, and especially George Mitchell of the SRC. See Kytle interview; and *Atlanta Constitution*, August 11, 1946, 23. Although "Who Runs Georgia" was never published at the time, it did become, according to Calvin Kytle, "the most famous unpublished report of Georgia politics because the Talmadge people stole it" and enlisted it in the campaign. See Kytle interview. The unpublished manuscript of "Who Runs Georgia?" may be found in transcript series B, GGDP. The University of Georgia Press finally published this manuscript in 1998 as Kytle and Mackay, *Who Runs Georgia?*

53. Mackay and Kytle's interviewees included Roy Harris and James V. Carmichael, several new state legislators, racial liberal Lillian Smith, and reactionary Parson Jack Johnston.

54. "A group of veterans is out today to raise $40,000 in a month's time to wage a political battle against minority rule," announced the *Savannah Morning News*. Veterans in the GVMR set up a central office in Atlanta from which to coordinate their fund-raising efforts. *Savannah Morning News*, September 22, 1946, 27.

55. Sullivan, *Days of Hope*, 204; Egerton, *Speak Now Against the Day*, 435, 445.

56. The available records do not indicate why the GVMR's leadership appeared to be more heavily white than that of the AVC, to which many members also belonged. It may be that the charged racial climate that produced the Walton County lynching after Eugene Talmadge's election as governor led the GVMR to downplay its interracial nature. While the AVC pursued a variety of interracial activities, it could not, according to its charter, participate directly in politics as an organization. The entire purpose of the GVMR, however, was to attack the viability of Georgia's most unique political institution, one created specifically to disfranchise blacks. Members of the GVMR were well aware of just how provocative a challenge they were mounting. Thus, mostly white names

may have appeared in publicity documents in order to avoid alienating white citizens who were on the fence, politically, about the county unit system or to deflect the charges of racial amalgamation from racial conservatives. It may also be that fewer blacks were involved in this organization, possibly because of its domination by white liberals. Black citizens may not have felt as comfortable and welcome in the GVMR as they did in the GVL or AVC. More research is necessary to determine the actual composition of the GVMR membership. Records of this organization, however, remain quite scarce.

57. "Personal Histories," Georgia Veterans for Majority Rule, August 1946, reel 190 (730, 733), series VII:43, SRCA. According to James Mackay, the "Who Runs Georgia?" Rosenwald study generated the creation of the GVMR in particular because "when you figure out what's . . . really wrong with something that matters to you, you want to have a hand in seeing if it can be changed." Thus, "we believed it could be changed by relentless efforts in the courts." The GVMR coalesced from "just a bunch of us" who recognized the importance of developing a broad base of support. After all, as Mackay noted, the fact that the county unit system discriminated against all urbanites, black and white, provided a basis for mutual understanding and cooperation. "You do not understand another man's discrimination unless you've shared it with him," explained Mackay, "and we urban whites and blacks were locked in the same cage together." Thus, along with veterans, "we had professors, we had students, we had housewives, we had all sorts of people that understood that this thing was wrong." See Mackay interview by Kuhn, March 31, 1987.

58. *Atlanta Journal*, August 2, 1946, 1.

59. Ibid.; *Savannah Morning News*, August 11, 1946, 21; *Atlanta Constitution*, August 11, 1946, B-2; Mackay interview by author.

60. Georgia Veterans for Majority Rule, October 1946, series 5-1, reel 63 (413), LRMP; Georgia Veterans for Majority Rule, pt. 4, reel 7 (729–31), NAACPP.

61. Georgia Veterans for Majority Rule, October 1946, series 5-1, reel 63 (413), LRMP.

62. For more on the course of legal attacks against the county unit system, including in the 1950s and 1960s, see *Atlanta Journal*, October 28, 1946, 1; Lucy Randolph Mason to Mrs. McEachern, December 20, 1947, series 5-1, reel 63 (679), LRMP; Publicity letter for Baxter Jones, folder 76, DPP; David Burgess to Jack Kroll, March 17, 1952, folder 68, DPP; Burgess interview; Charles Bloch, undated memorandum, and Bloch to Senator Herman Talmadge, April 4, 1958, both in series II, subseries 2, box 317, folder 2, HTP.

63. On the specific importance of black voters in Georgia to this story, see Sullivan, *Days of Hope*, 218.

64. Scholars identify southern white liberalism in the 1940s as characterized by a New Deal ideology that emphasized the primacy of achieving economic and political reform as the best path to gradual racial change. They also cite the inability of many southern white liberals at the time to conceive of black social equality as a possibility or even as a desired goal. See, for example, Sullivan, *Days of Hope*, 163; Bartley, *New South*, 28–31; Reed, *Simple Decency and Common Sense*, 185–89; and Egerton, *Speak Now Against the Day*. Older treatments include Sosna, *In Search of the Silent South*; Kneebone, *Southern Liberal Journalists*; Ashmore, *Hearts and Minds*; and Stanfield, "Dollars for the Silent South," 117–38. In most of these interpretations, southern white liberals suffer from a lack of vision capable of confronting and surmounting the racial barriers that had long hindered all movements for progressive social reform in the South. Progressive white veter-

ans were part of this tradition. Few were driven by the war or anything else to challenge segregation head-on. Yet, if we try to understand the postwar 1940s on its own terms, recognizing the personal and political context in which all southern progressives were enmeshed at the time, we find that the war did have a revelatory impact on the racial attitudes of some white southerners and that these veterans did work to implement a notion of equal political participation that included black Americans.

65. See Sullivan, *Days of Hope*, 164, on southern popular front liberals' views about segregation, its incompatibility with American democracy, and the difficulties inherent in attacking it directly in the postwar era.

66. On these limits to the southern liberal vision of change, see Sullivan, *Days of Hope*, 164; and Egerton, *Speak Now Against the Day*, 470–71.

67. See Bartley, *New South*, 45, 50, 73, on the social and economic reformism of southern popular front liberals in the postwar era.

68. *Atlanta Constitution*, February 5, 7, 1947; Egerton, *Speak Now Against the Day*, 389.

69. On President Truman's postwar civil rights proposals see Frederickson, *Dixiecrat Revolt*, 57–58, 64–65.

70. Bartley, *New South*, 76, 95–97; Bartley, *Rise of Massive Resistance*, 32–37; Sullivan, *Days of Hope*, 258.

71. On President Truman's hostility toward southern liberals and his accommodation of southern Democratic conservatives, despite his simultaneous profession of support for black civil rights, see Bartley, *New South*, 95–97; and Sullivan, *Days of Hope*, 258.

72. Sullivan, *Days of Hope*, 229–30; Bartley, *New South*, 42–43, 46, 50, 54–57, 68.

73. "Summary of Subversive Activities in the Third Army Area for the Year, 1947," Domestic Intelligence Summary #34, box 10, folder 000.24, TACR. Another indication of these difficulties was the problem the AVC in Atlanta encountered in maintaining and attracting members. In October 1946 an AVC newsletter announced an all-out "Ring the Bell Campaign" to boost membership (nationally) to one million. In Atlanta, AVC members set up numerous booths in downtown hotels and office buildings to answer questions, distribute terminal pay blanks to ex-GIs, and solicit new members. *The Bellringer* 1 (October 8, 1946), reel 190 (787–88), series VII:43, SRCA. A year later, *The Bellringer* "urgently requested" each member to bring in one new enrollee in yet another drive "for new workers in our ranks to fight reaction and uphold true democracy." Amid the Cold War tensions and civil rights preoccupations of 1947, however, this call to arms apparently fell on deaf ears. Incoming president Johnnie Glustrom's acceptance speech in 1947 addressed "a spirit of defeatism about AVC growth and progress." The Atlanta AVC's peak of popularity and influence seemed to have been spent by the end of 1947 as concerns about the Cold War, anticommunism, and the Truman civil rights program took center stage. *The Bellringer* 2 (October 20, 1947), box 13, GTRP. For more on postwar responses to the Truman civil rights program, see Hamby, *Beyond the New Deal*, 189, 232–33, 243–44, 247, 250–51; Walton, *Henry Wallace, Harry Truman, and the Cold War*, 230–31, 237, 245; and Berman, *Politics of Civil Rights in the Truman Administration*, 79–136.

74. On the personal cost of attacking southern racial traditions for white liberals in the Deep South, see Egerton, *Speak Now Against the Day*, 406–9.

75. Fleming interview. On Judge Waring also see Egerton, *Speak Now Against the Day*, 407–9; and Frederickson, *Dixiecrat Revolt*, 55, 109, 145, 208.

76. Margaret Fisher had been "the key figure" in getting out the black vote during the July primary and, along with Wilkins, in "carrying the advisory work for the Georgia Veterans Committee for Majority Rule." See Lucy Randolph Mason to Eleanor Roosevelt, September 8, 1946, reel 63 (344); and Mason to Charlotte, September 5, 1946, reel 63 (341); Mason to Honorable Herbert Lehman, September 19, 1946, reel 63 (364); all in series 5-1, LRMP.

77. Lucy Randolph Mason to Barry Bingham, September 8, 1946, reel 63 (343); Mason to Eleanor Roosevelt, September 8, 1946, reel 63 (344); both in series 5-1,LRMP; Key, *Southern Politics*, 121.

78. Numan Bartley offers a detailed assessment of this Cold War battle among the left, middle, and right wings of American liberalism after the war. See *New South*, 38–73.

79. According to Sullivan in *Days of Hope*, 207, the "SCHW's success in establishing a regional presence was dependent in large part on the financial support of the CIO." The CIO, however, and particularly the Southern Organizing Committee, increasingly turned against the SCHW in its national effort to purge radicals and leftist unions from the organization amid the growing anticommunist timbre of the era. This alienated the SCHW, as well as other popular front and New Deal liberals, from an important source of financial and personnel support. This separation did not remain hard and fast on the ground, however. In Georgia, Lucy Randolph Mason of the SOC, which rebuked any alliance with the SCHW, nonetheless aided that organization's effort to support the GVMR and its lawsuit against the county unit system. On the CIO's hostility to the SCHW, see Bartley, *New South*, 48–50.

80. On this reactionary backlash see Sullivan, *Days of Hope*, chaps. 7–8; and Bartley, *New South*, chaps. 2–3. For comprehensive and creative assessments of the period as one of "lost opportunity" because of this backlash, see Egerton, *Speak Now Against the Day*; and Daniel, *Lost Revolutions*, 1–3.

81. Quoted in Harris, Mitchell, and Schechter, *Homefront*, 224. This account neglects to specify the Coverts' home state, but James's impression of the changes in his father and brother when they returned from the war is an apt description of the initial reaction many civilians articulated. For a popular examination of the war's general impact on veterans and others, see Brokaw, *Greatest Generation*.

82. Quotation from Kennedy, *Freedom from Fear*, 786. For a similar view see Polenberg, *War and Society*, 135–36.

83. Stouffer et al., *American Soldier: Adjustment During Army Life*, 598.

84. *Atlanta Constitution*, June 24, 1945, 1. On predictions of full employment, see *Atlanta Constitution*, August 19, 21, 22, 24, 26, 27, 1945; and *Savannah Evening Press*, April 27, 1946, 14.

85. *Atlanta Constitution*, September 6, 1945, 8; Address by Governor Herman Talmadge, January 30, 1947, in Georgia Department of Labor, "Tenth Annual Report," 2.

86. *Coffee County (Ga.) Progress*, May 16, 1946. On the developing unemployment that came with the end of the war, see *Savannah Morning News*, April 5, 1946, 14; *Atlanta Constitution*, September 6, 7, 1945, July 4, 1946; *Savannah Morning News*, January 24, 1946, 14; and *Atlanta Journal*, January 13, 1946, D-9. According to the Georgia State Department of Labor in February 1946, employment in the state dropped "from a peak" of "502,500 in

the third quarter of 1943" to 435,000 soon after V-J Day. "The drop was attributed to cut-backs in shipyards and war plants," reported the *Atlanta Journal*, as well as in "textile plants engaged in war production." *Atlanta Journal*, February 5, 1946, 6.

87. On industrial and employment trends in postwar Georgia, see Bartley, *Creation of Modern Georgia*, 180–81.

88. *Atlanta Journal*, April 29, 1946, 10; *Atlanta Constitution*, August 28, 1946, E-1.

89. In the Midwest, for example, returning veterans hoping to become independent farmers found it difficult to obtain good quality land at an affordable price. In addition, most wanted to start out as farm operators, not as hired hands or tenants. Thus, con-cluded one journalist, "Midwestern war veterans are returning to the farm much more slowly than they left it to see Paris and Tokyo." *New York Times*, April 28, 1946, IV-8.

90. For a discussion of these developments in Georgia, see Bartley, *Creation of Modern Georgia*, 179, 197–203. For the South generally, see Tindall, *Emergence of the New South*, 687–732; and Bartley, *New South*, 1–73; as well as Egerton, *Speak Now Against the Day*, 345–513.

91. My discussion of this notion of "racialized" and "gendered citizenship" draws on the excellent treatments of this political, racial, and cultural dynamic provided by Be-derman, *Manliness and Civilization*, 4–5, and chap. 1; Kantrowitz, "Ben Tillman and Hen-drix McLane, Agrarian Rebels," 501; Gilmore, "Murder, Memory, and the Flight of the In-cubus"; and Tyson, *Radio Free Dixie*, 140–41.

92. For additional examples of how this "psycho-sexual-social" dynamic that charac-terized southern white attitudes toward blacks manifested itself, see Brundage, *Lynching in the New South*, 58; Ayers, *Promise of the New South*, 158; Gilmore, "Murder, Memory, and the Flight of the Incubus"; and Tyson, "Wars for Democracy," 262.

93. See Kantrowitz, "Ben Tillman and Hendrix McLane, Agrarian Rebels," 501. This no-tion that white manhood depended upon excluding blacks from both the political and social spheres also explained the gendered language characteristic of the Dixiecrat revolt against the national Democratic Party in 1948. As Kari Frederickson has discovered, in re-sponding to the civil rights program initiated under the Truman administration in 1948, the Dixiecrats described themselves as "jilted lovers" and their changing fortunes within the national party as the result of "illicit liaisons" and a "broken marriage." Such rheto-ric, she concludes, demonstrated the "close interplay of race and gender in southern so-ciety and . . . how the potential loss of political power in the public sphere was intimately linked to concerns regarding the disruption of the private sphere." See Frederickson, "'As a Man I Am Interested in States' Rights,'" 260–62, 270.

94. Marwick, in *Total War and Social Change*, xvi, describes the dynamic in which par-ticipation in total war generates heightened expectations of "social gains"—a sense among the participants that recognition and reward will follow. "At bottom," he explains, "this is because those who are *in* demand are in a strong market position to press *their* de-mands." Moreover, "it may also be the case that governments will seek to reward essential workers, or maintain their morale by offering social reform."

95. Timothy Tyson, for example, has found that both black and white men in the post-war era shared an understanding of citizenship premised on a notion of "manhood" largely defined against the other. Both groups believed "manhood" meant the ability to defend

the domestic sphere and women from racial incursions by the other. Politics and the rights of citizenship were the avenue by which to defend this control. See Tyson, *Radio Free Dixie*, 140–41.

96. See the many examples of overseas conflict among black and white American soldiers during World War II in Smith, *When Jim Crow Met John Bull*.

97. O'Brien, *Color of the Law*, 129–34.

98. Allan Swimm, "Interview With Grand Dragon Samuel Green," October 19, 1945, reel 1, box 1, folder 3, SKP. After a large cross-burning at Stone Mountain, Green again maintained that "here in Georgia hundreds of men are clamoring to join the Klan." See "Interview with Grand Dragon of Georgia," *Greenville Piedmont*, November 19, 1945, reel 1, box 1, folder 5, SKP.

99. Wade, *Fiery Cross*, 279.

100. Reports on Atlanta Klavern #297, February 4 and 7, 1946; Report on Atlanta Klan, May 6, 1946; Report on Atlanta Klavern #1, September 23, 1946; all in reel 1, box 1, folder 3, SKP.

101. See *The Bellringer* 1 (September 7, 1946), reel 190, series VII:43, SRCA.

102. Article in unknown publication, 1946, clipping, reel 1, box 1, folder 6, SKP; Report on meeting of Columbians, Ned to AF, September 3, 1946, box 51, RMP; Ned to AF, August 27, 1946, reel 1, SKP; Report on Columbians, October 2, 1946, reel 1, SKP; Ned to AF, October 4, 1946, reel 1, SKP; Dudley, "'Hate' Organizations of the 1940s," 266, 270.

103. The other three were to "develop character," to "practice clannishness," and to show "a pure patriotism to the United States, its Constitution and its flag." See Swimm, "Interview of Grand Dragon Samuel Green," October 19, 1945, reel 1, box 1, folder 3, SKP.

104. Kennedy also cited the emerging national trend of conservatism and Klan ties to ultranationalist and isolationist groups. See "Facts About the Klan," reel 1, box 1, folder 13, SKP.

105. Information relative to Klavalier Klub, 1948, reel 1, box 1, folder 4, SKP.

106. In fact, the Columbians' objections to Jews, unionists, communists, and foreigners often centered on their alleged conspiracies with black Americans. As one observer noted, the Columbians not only disliked the CIO and most AFL unions, they especially resented black labor organizers and aimed to "kick [them] off the streets," leaving "the field clear for a Columbian gentile union." Hoke Gewinner accused "a Communistic Jewish block [of] regimenting the Negro vote," while Atlanta attorney and Columbian Vester Ownby blasted the Jews "on the grounds of Communism and promoting social equality between whites and Negroes." Finally, P. M. Adams put forth the ludicrous claim that "300,000 biological investigations . . . [have] discovered that the jews are a Negroid people." Although the informant reporting on this early meeting concluded that the Columbians seemed to be "90% anti-semitic and 10% anti-Negro," Adams nonetheless concluded the evening by urging the audience to "come on down and sign up if you are a white man." See "Atlanta Version of Mein Kampf," reel 1, box 1, folder 6, SKP; Ned to AF, September 3, 1946, box 51, RMP.

107. In addition to freeing "the American public from the clutches of Organized Jewry," members were to "fully understand that the fight being waged by the Columbians is to decide whether our country is to be the Anglo-Saxon nation of our dreams, or whether it is to be destroyed by Judaism, Foreignism, and Communism." See membership pledge card, box 51, RMP.

108. "Atlanta Version of Mein Kampf," reel 1, box 1, folder 6, SKP; Ned to AF, November 8, 1946, box 51, RMP.

109. Ned to AF, November 8, 1946, and September 3, 1946, box 51, RMP.

110. At one September meeting, veteran Homer Loomis reportedly launched a wild tirade "about how uniformed Columbians would patrol the streets in white sections and whenever they found a Negro . . . [they] would 'walk him out, throw him out or beat him up' and call the police who would lock him up for being drunk." Keeler McCartney to Ralph McGill, December 2, 1946, box 3, RMP. Scraps gleaned from a wastebasket at Columbian headquarters revealed that the Columbians fully intended to carry out these plans. Notes salvaged by Stetson Kennedy spoke of "Annie Jones" the "nigger that bought [the] house lives at 292 Ashby street" and the "nigger that house [is] in name of [is] Kennedy F. Jones." "Call smithwick at Cypress," the note continued, "and tell what the nigger is going to do." Another note instructed J. L. Kiser to "get leaders working in Western Heights and Exposition" as well as "Southside." These cryptic notes reveal that the Columbians closely tracked those black families who purchased or who planned to purchase homes in urban neighborhoods that the Columbians were concerned would lose their all-white identity. These notes are found in AF to Ned, January 3, 1947, reel 1, SKP.

111. Ned to AF, September 3, 1946, box 51, RMP.

112. "Atlanta Reporter Tells of Columbians' Meeting," November 1, 1946, reel 1, "Columbians," SKP.

113. "List of Real Estate Men" and "BEWARE! PROTECT YOUR COMMUNITY!"; both reel 1, miscellaneous documents, SKP.

114. "Atlanta Version of Mein Kampf," reel 1, box 1, folder 6, SKP; Grey to AF, October 1, 1946, box 51, RMP; *Atlanta Daily World*, November 1, 1946, 1. The Columbians promised "to encourage our people to think in terms of Race, Nation and Faith [and] . . . to build a progressive white community . . . bound together by a deep spiritual consciousness of the past and determination to share a common future." The "common future" they envisioned was a white society shorn of the influence of those whom the Columbians deemed "un-American," particularly blacks and Jews. *Atlanta Daily World*, November 1, 1946, 1.

115. Dudley, "'Hate' Organizations of the 1940s," 269; *Atlanta Daily World*, November 5, 1946, 1, 6; "Atlanta Version of Mein Kampf," reel 1, box 1, folder 6, SKP.

116. "Atlanta Version of Mein Kampf," reel 1, box 1, folder 6, SKP.

117. *Atlanta Daily World*, November 5, 1946, 1, 6; *Atlanta Journal*, November 3, 1946, 3, 12, 14; Dudley, "'Hate' Organizations of the 1940s," 270.

118. Ned to AF, November 2, 1946, reel 1, SKP. Not surprisingly, when a bomb exploded on the porch of another family in that area around the same time, the police and press immediately suspected the Columbians. The bombing at the home of Miss Minnie Sibley early one Thursday morning shook the house, broke two windows, and accelerated the police investigation into the rash of racial disturbances in the area. Like Jones's house, Sibley's home stood in a formerly white neighborhood on Ashby Street near Sells Avenue. Although Superintendent of Detectives E. L. Hilderbrand initially found "no evidence" linking the bombing to the Columbians, reports from informants suggested a direct connection. After an October meeting, "Grey" reported to "A.F." that the Columbians planned "to go to Sells Avenue where there has been trouble regarding Negroes moving into white housing developments." Grey to AF, October 1, 1946, box 51, RMP; *Atlanta*

Daily World, November 1, 5, 1946; *New York Times*, November 1, 1946, 2; Dudley, "'Hate' Organizations of the 1940s," 269. In early November the *Atlanta Daily World* reported, "real estate signs have been placed on certain property in the Northwest section . . . bearing the insignia of the Columbians, the lightning streak. In the windows of some homes are banners bearing the insignia." *Atlanta Daily World*, November 5, 1946, 1, 6; Dudley, "Hate' Organizations of the 1940s," 268.

119. The attraction that groups such as the KKK had for veterans of World War II was not unprecedented. Similar appeals and concerns drew large numbers of World War I veterans into the Klan of the 1920s amid the political, economic, and racial changes wrought by that war. For example, Nancy MacLean has found that in Athens, Georgia, the developing power of corporate capitalism as well as the emerging activism of African Americans frightened the average lower-middle-class white proprietor or farmer who felt under attack from both capital and labor. In addition, the militarism and martial style of the Klan, including the rigid hierarchy of leadership, masks and robes, elaborate ceremonies, and secret rituals and language, provided a strong sense of "us" versus the "world" for the disaffected. "Not surprisingly," MacLean notes, "the movement became a magnet for men imbued with martial values. Around the country, law enforcement personnel and military men joined the Klan in large numbers." On the Klan in the 1920s, see MacLean, *Behind the Mask of Chivalry*, xii, 17, 21; and Alexander, *Ku Klux Klan in the Southwest*, 11, 12, 18.

120. Albert Deutsch, "The Columbians," *PM Magazine*, December 12, 1946, reel 1, SKP. Both James Childers and Lanier Waller turned state's evidence after their arrests for illegal activities on behalf of the Columbians. Eventually, both Childers and Waller grew convinced that Homer Loomis and Emory Burke had manipulated them into breaking the law, and they subsequently worked with the New York Anti-Nazi League to put Loomis in jail and dismantle his reactionary organization.

121. Ibid.; "Atlanta Version of Mein Kampf," reel 1, box 1, folder 6, SKP; Keeler McCartney to Ralph McGill, December 2, 1946, box 3, RMP. Lanier Waller, a Texas veteran who claimed to have served two years with the Marines in the Pacific, boasted to an informant "of the anti-Negro sentiment in Texas" and his own participation in the zoot-suit riots in Los Angeles during the war. See "Western Union Press Message," ca. 1949, reel 1, box 1, folder 6, SKP.

122. Keeler McCartney to Ralph McGill, December 2, 1946, box 3, RMP. The scant information available on other Columbian veterans reveals backgrounds of modest but diverse means. Homer Loomis, secretary of the organization, was born in New York City to a wealthy family, then moved to Virginia, which he considered to be home. Loomis apparently served in the infantry in the European theater during the war and drew twenty dollars a week in unemployment compensation while directing the Columbians. Rumors circulated that he had spent as much as $1,500 of his own money on the movement. Report on Columbians, October 3, 1946, reel 1, box 1, folder 6, SKP. William Couch, an army officer on terminal leave who often appeared at Columbian meetings, was born in a rural county thirty-five miles outside Atlanta. He served as an officer bombardier in the Eighth Army Air Force, worked briefly as a clerk typist for the Atlanta Quartermaster Depot after the war, and lived with his wife in College Park. Couch claimed to have spent two years in a German POW camp where he learned and taught German. Report on Columbians,

October 3, 1946, reel 1, box 1, folder 6, SKP; Report of meeting with Homer Loomis, James Aiken, and William Couch, ca. December 1946, reel 1, SKP. Zimmerlee served as an officer in the Fifteenth Army Air Force and was probably a longtime resident of Atlanta. Born and raised in North Texas, Lanier Waller allegedly served with the Marines in the Pacific for two years for which he earned 100 percent service-connected disability. Report on Columbians, October 3, 1946, reel 1, box 1, folder 6, SKP; "Information on Lanier Waller," undated, reel 1, "Columbians," SKP. Clarence Knight, a Columbian veteran for whom little background information is available, described at one meeting an attack by a "black boy . . . whose job he had taken from Western Union after coming back from service," and his own attempt to hit the "nigger" with a blackjack. Untitled article, 1946, reel 1, SKP.

123. Quoted in Wade, *Fiery Cross*, 285.

124. Klan report, Atlanta, May 6, 1946, and report on Klavalier Klub, May 1, 1946, reel 1, box 1, folder 3, SKP; Klavalier Klub Activities, 1948, reel 1, box 1, folder 4, SKP. The CIO's drive to organize all southern labor, black and white, naturally drew the Klan's enmity as well. An April meeting of Atlanta Klavern #297, for example, heard one member relate his conversation with "some Negro men" who "said that if the Negro wanted the 65 cent minimum wage, [to] eat and sleep in the same cafes and hotels, work side by side with the white man, and draw the same salary, that he must join the CIO." See report by John Brown on Atlanta Klavern #297, April 18, 1946, reel 1, box 1, folder 3, SKP.

125. Report on Klavalier Klub, May 1, 1946, reel 1, box 1, folder 3, SKP.

126. See Frederickson, *Dixiecrat Revolt*, 58–59, 62. For a similar view, see O'Brien, *Color of the Law*, 130.

127. Report on Klavalier Klub, May 1, 1946, and report on meeting of Atlanta Klavern #1, April 29, 1946, reel 1, box 1, folder 3, SKP. On the Georgia Klan's many depredations against black citizens after the war, see Wade, *Fiery Cross*, 277, 282–83, 286, 289.

128. Bartley, *Creation of Modern Georgia*, 201–2; Bartley, *New South*, 173; Spritzer, *Belle of Ashby Street*, 70–74; Egerton, *Speak Now Against the Day*, 382. The Fifth District was composed of Fulton, DeKalb, and Rockdale Counties.

129. Thomas Jefferson first used this phrase to address the seriousness of the territorial dispute over slavery in the wake of the Missouri Compromise debates of 1820. See Tindall and Shi, *America*, 411.

130. On the conservative reaction to Mankin's election see Spritzer, *Belle of Ashby Street*, 74, 85, 87, 89, 92; Bartley, *Creation of Modern Georgia*, 201–4; Grant, *Way It Was in the South*, 363; and Harmon, "Beneath the Image," 39–40.

131. Representative Robert C. Word Ramspeck, whose unexpired term Mankin had been elected to fill, had managed to have congressional elections dropped from the regulations of the county unit system in 1932. Under the Neill Primary Act of 1917, however, the application of the county unit system to nomination of U.S. representatives was optional, to be decided by Democratic committees within the congressional district. On Eugene Talmadge's reemergence in 1946 due to the race issue, see Spritzer, *Belle of Ashby Street*, 89, 91–92, 95; Bartley, *Creation of Modern Georgia*, 201–3; Anderson, *Wild Man from Sugar Creek*, 215–33; and Henderson, *Politics of Change in Georgia*, 144–46.

132. Eugene Talmadge, WSB Radio broadcast, July 13, 1946, transcript, Draft APR.1992.1, GGDP. Also see Logue, *Eugene Talmadge*, 221–29, 279–84; and Anderson, *Wild Man from Sugar Creek*, 21–23, 27, 200, 210–12, 216, 219, 229–30. According to Spritzer, Helen Dou-

glas Mankin believed that James Davis and Eugene Talmadge specifically enlisted the Columbians to intimidate black voters before the November general election. Hoke Gewinner, Columbian and KKK member, was apparently a paid member of the Davis staff, and other connections existed as well. See Spritzer, *Belle of Ashby Street*, 116–19. In addition, the ouster of the Cracker Party and Roy V. Harris in Augusta in the spring of 1946 prompted "much disappointment" at an April meeting of Atlanta Klavern #297, and "this was used to good advantage by Exalted Cyclops Roper to show the necessity of getting the people registered to vote." Report by John Brown, Atlanta Klavern #297 meeting, April 18, 1946, reel 1, box 1, folder 3, SKP.

133. "Will They Dare to Finish the Job?" undated clipping, reel 1, SKP; Ned to AF, November 7, 1946, and September 3, 1946, box 51, RMP.

134. Report by John Brown, Atlanta Klavern #1 meeting, April 8, 1946, reel 1, box 1, folder 3, SKP.

135. Report by John Brown, Atlanta Klavern #297 meeting, April 18, 1946, reel 1, box 1, folder 3, SKP.

136. See Atlanta Klan, undated report, reel 1, box 1, folder 7, SKP.

137. Guy Alford to Prince Preston, July 31, 1946, box 33, PPP.

138. J. M. Jones to Muscogee County Talmadge Club, June 15, 1946, box 3, folder 8, ACSP.

139. *Douglas (Ga.) Weekly Enterprise*, May 9, 1946, 1; *Montgomery Advertiser*, May 7, 1946, 1; *Atlanta Constitution*, July 21, 1946, A-10.

140. *Atlanta Journal*, May 9, 1946, 14.

141. Ibid., August 20, 1946, 8.

142. Ibid., June 7, 1946, 18.

143. Christopher De Mendoza to Prince Preston, July 12, 1946, box 33, "Liberty" folder, PPP.

144. For a sampling of positions taken by candidates in the gubernatorial and Fifth District races, see *Atlanta Journal*, May 21, 1946, 4; and Spritzer, *Belle of Ashby Street*, 66–70.

145. *Atlanta Journal*, July 1, 1946, 10.

146. Clipping and statement, undated, Gubernatorial series, box 2, "1946 Campaign" folder, HTP.

147. W. W. Yergin, rally address, May 20, 1946, Draft APR.1992.6-M84–20/6a, tape recording, GGDP.

148. *Coffee County (Ga.) Progress*, June 20, 1946.

149. Ibid., June 20, July 4, 1946. While some veterans chose to voice their support of Georgia's political traditions through campaign advertising and letters to the editor, at least one decided that Talmadge's "call-to-arms" demanded a more direct response. Horace T. Scoggins, a former combat engineer from Stonewall, Georgia, who devoted most of his postwar time to his "hill-billy band, the 'Radio Rangers,'" pursued the Talmadge campaign's strategy of purging as many black voters as possible. He challenged some three thousand names on the Fulton County voter lists, offering criminal records of persons with the same names as registrants to challenge their eligibility. Although most of these challenges were directed at African American voters, Scoggins disclaimed "any attempt at racial discrimination" by declaring "he was having the inquiry made 'solely in the interest of more intelligent voting.'" "The fact that all of the first challenges were of

Negro voters," he disingenuously explained, "was 'a mere coincidence' and that it 'just happened' that he and his attorneys started inspecting the Negro lists first." *Atlanta Journal,* July 9, 1946, 4.

150. Paulding County citizens to Fred Hand and the General Assembly, January 24, 1947, box 1, folder 44, Fred Hand Family and Business Papers, Troup County Archives, La Grange, Ga.

151. *Atlanta Constitution,* July 16, 1948, 9.

152. "Veterans Back Talmadge," *Statesman,* February 13, 1947, 2, clipping, reel 2, folder 7, SKP; also in *Atlanta Constitution,* February 2, 1947, B-6.

153. Timothy Tyson, in fact, refers to World War II as a "watershed moment" in "Wars for Democracy," 10. An earlier but similar view is Sosna, "More Important Than the Civil War?" 145–61.

154. In *Local People,* 1, 9, John Dittmer identifies black World War II veterans, including Medgar and Charles Evers, as the "shock troops" of the modern black civil rights movement in Mississippi. Timothy Tyson examines the unusual and radical civil rights career of black veteran Robert F. Williams in North Carolina in *Radio Free Dixie*; and Cobb, in *Most Southern Place on Earth,* 211, 241, notes the key participation of black World War II veterans Aaron Henry and Amzie Moore in the civil rights movement in Mississippi.

155. On the faltering of southern white liberalism in the face of the increasing importance of the race issue after the war, see Sosna, *In Search of the Silent South,* 140, 156, 206–7. Sosna emphasizes the problems that southern white liberals faced as the social, economic, and racial changes accelerated by the Great Depression, the New Deal, and especially World War II made it increasingly difficult to avoid the question of segregation. The war, Sosna argues, did lead southern liberals to finally commit to ending Jim Crow, but that realization was a slow and often painful process that ultimately left them isolated in the region. Because of their failure to awaken a "silent South" for progressive reform after the war, Sosna argues, southern white liberals had minimal impact at the time. The Great Depression, the New Deal, World War II, and the civil rights movement, far more than their campaigns for racial reform, broke down Jim Crow. For other works in this vein, see the bibliographic citations in Bartley, *New South,* 479–80.

In my view, the case of progressive white veterans in Georgia underscores the importance of the progressive campaigns for political and racial reform that did exist after the war, but not because they managed to overturn segregation, which they did not. Rather, these campaigns added to the destabilization of the political and racial environment that both generated an intense racial backlash and exposed the developing cracks in the foundations of the one-party South, cracks that eventually widened into the campaigns that did transform the political South, such as massive resistance to integration, the black freedom struggle, and the rise of the neo-Whig, chamber of commerce ethos. Many southern white liberals, however, would play less of a role in these events after the defeats of the postwar 1940s, in part because some grew more defensive on race, or at least on a gradualist approach to reform, as real change loomed on the southern horizon in the 1950s and 1960s. In *Days of Hope,* 162–65, and passim, Sullivan discusses southern white liberals' evolving postwar stance on the question of segregation versus racial reform.

156. In *Dixiecrat Revolt* Kari Frederickson notes that the Dixiecrat presidential candidate in 1948, South Carolinian Strom Thurmond, was also a veteran of World War II.

Cobb, in *Most Southern Place on Earth*, 213, identifies several veterans as leaders and members of the reactionary White Citizens Council movement in Mississippi, including Robert Patterson, who founded the organization. Governor George Wallace of Alabama, who proclaimed "Segregation Today, Segregation Tomorrow, and Segregation Forever," also served in World War II. See Carter, *Politics of Rage*, 55, 60–61.

Chapter Four

1. William Shiflett, affidavit, July 27, 1947, box 209, folder 2, NLRBR. On the Anchor Rome campaign generally, see Brattain, *Politics of Whiteness*, 170–82.

2. Anchor Rome management focused on pressuring union workers to drop their membership because new right-to-work laws passed by the Georgia General Assembly allowed employers and workers to initiate union decertification. Brattain, *Politics of Whiteness*, 169. In *What Do We Need a Union For?* 70, Timothy Minchin notes that a common management tactic to forestall unionization in the postwar era was to refuse contracts that recognized union security. This issue, he concludes, was at the heart of virtually every TWUA strike in the postwar South. This pervasive conflict reflected the persistent lack of legitimacy held by the union and organized labor after World War II, as well as workers' militant defense of their rights to organize and to bargain collectively.

3. William Shiflett, affidavit, November 19, 1947, box 209, folder 2, NLRBR.

4. William Shiflett, affidavit, July 27, 1947, box 209, folder 2, NLRBR.

5. Notes of interviews with Anchor Rome workers, Mss. 396, box 218, "Anchor Rome Mills—Injunction" folder, TWUAP. All of the eight arrested picketers were accused of "being involved in clashes between workers and strikers." See *Atlanta Constitution*, May 12, 1948, 1; and Domestic Intelligence Summary #58, May 7–14, 1948, 6, box 10, folder 000.24, TACR.

6. Minchin, *What Do We Need a Union For?* 35, notes that the sort of support and protection afforded organized labor under the National War Labor Board during the war evaporated when the duties of that body were transferred to the NLRB with the advent of peace. As wildcat strikes, reconversion anxiety, and a conservative political resurgence shifted national policy and debate to the right immediately after the war, the NLRB proved to be an ineffectual partner, at best, for organized labor in the councils of the federal government. Confronted with this loss of federal support, unionists and workers such as Shiflett were disheartened by this change of fortune for organized labor's postwar cause. Thus, Minchin concludes, "the inadequacies of federal protection during Operation Dixie led to a strong sense of disenchantment and frustration with the NLRB."

7. William Shiflett to Paul Herzog, NLRB chairman, November 5, 1949, box 24, "Anchor Rome Mills, Rome Georgia" folder, NLRBR.

8. As one scholar of the southern labor movement has concluded, "World War II raised the stakes of the power game in the small-town South and made labor a legitimate contender in shaping the postwar order." See Flamming, *Creating the Modern South*, 235.

9. Zieger, *CIO*, 141. For a different and more negative view of the impact of World War II on the CIO, see Lichtenstein, *Labor's War at Home*.

10. Kennedy, *Freedom from Fear*, 783.

11. See Zieger, *CIO*, 230–31, on this developing southern focus toward the end of the war.

12. Ibid.

13. Ibid., 153–56.

14. Ibid., 230–31.

15. Ibid., 229. In some Georgia communities the demand for continuous production of war materiel actually boosted organizing drives. In Greensboro, Georgia, a bitter labor dispute erupted during the war between management and workers organizing a CIO local in the Mary Leila Cotton Mill, which held a federal war contract. When management's refusal to negotiate a settlement of a subsequent strike stalled the production line, the U.S. Army stepped in, taking over operations and recognizing the new TWUA local's right to exist. Federal intervention in wartime labor conflicts, of course, did not always favor unions, but the occasions when this did happen appeared to create a precedent of federal protection, on which organizations such as the CIO, the TWUA, and even the AFL hoped to build once the war ended. On the labor conflict in Greensboro, including seizure of mill operations by the U.S. Army, see "Mary Leila Cotton Mills Ignores the Order of the Labor Board," *Textile Labor*, May 1945, 4, and July 1945, 4, TWUAP. On the expectation of building on organized labor's wartime gains, see Zieger, *CIO*, 212.

16. Zieger, *CIO*, 227.

17. The most definitive assessment, if a somewhat dated one, of Operation Dixie is Griffith, *Crisis of American Labor*. For an older but very useful treatment of organized labor in the postwar South, see Marshall, *Labor in the South*, 254–56. More recent works include Bartley, *New South*, 40; Flamming, *Creating the Modern South*, 238, 248; Minchin, *What Do We Need a Union For?*; Simon, *Fabric of Defeat*; and Brattain, *Politics of Whiteness*.

18. Key, *Southern Politics*, 658.

19. On the centrality of the southern organizing drive to the CIO's postwar plans, see Griffith, *Crisis of American Labor*; Zieger, *CIO*, 227–41; and Brattain, *Politics of Whiteness*, 141.

20. Zieger, *CIO*, 227, 231. On the TWUA's strategy during the Operation Dixie drive, see Minchin, *What Do We Need a Union For?* 30.

21. Minchin, *What Do We Need a Union For?* 233–34.

22. Ibid., 234–35.

23. Ibid., 228.

24. Ibid.

25. Bartley, *New South*, 40. Also see Mason, *To Win These Rights*.

26. Zieger, *CIO*, 230–32.

27. Ibid., 228–34. On the focus on textiles in Operation Dixie, also see Minchin, *What Do We Need a Union For?* 26–47.

28. Statement of the CIO's Veterans Committee to President Murray and the Executive Board, April 12, 1945, Mss. 396, box 246, "Veterans Committee, 1945" folder, TWUAP.

29. On the 1945–46 wave of industrial strikes, see Zieger, *CIO*, 212–28, 232, 251, 320.

30. "Ex-Soldier Suspects Unions Are Lied About," *Southern Railway Journal*, November 1944, 2, clipping in reel 3, box 3, folder 5, SKP.

31. Corporal Odom Fanning to Lucy Randolph Mason, June 5, 1945, reel 63 (126), series 5-1, LRMP.

32. George Mitchell to AFL, August 29, 1945, reel 189, series VII:37, SRCA. For information on the decisions by the CIO and TWUA to waive initiation fees for returning veter-

ans, see the following: "Union Plans for After the War and Helps Protect Your Future," *Textile Labor*, November 1944, "Tubize, 1944–45" folder; and "Servicemen Not to Pay Initiation Fee," undated clipping, "Veterans TWUA Policy: World War II, 1944–45" folder; both in Mss. 129A, subseries 10A, box 22, TWUAP.

33. In fact, practical considerations dictated a consideration of the how the reemployment rights of veterans, established in the Selective Service Act and the Servicemen's Readjustment Act, might interact with the seniority rights most unionists regarded as critical to union security. In 1944, for example, the CIO Veterans Committee issued a comprehensive statement to the executive board outlining a program that focused particularly on veterans' reemployment and seniority rights. Indeed, the committee resolved that "our interest and activity [lie] in developing a constructive attitude and assistance to [all servicemen and women] as Americans with consideration that several million among them are members of Labor unions, including C.I.O. organizations." Such assistance included facilitating the delivery of veteran benefits to returned soldiers, protecting seniority rights in union plants, and waiving initiation fees for veterans applying for union membership. After all, stated the committee, "the returning serviceman [or] woman is not a detached member of our society; they are of us. Their interests are our interests; their needs are our needs." Merely supporting legislation to provide veteran benefits, however, was not enough: "it is the burden of the C.I.O. to further protect the veterans by helping to build a society in which all can be secure." Statement of the CIO Veterans Committee to President Murray and the Executive Board, by Clinton S. Golden, April 12, 1945, pp. 1, 2, 3, 6, box 693, folder 75, United Steelworkers of America, District 35, Papers, Southern Labor Archives, Georgia State University, Atlanta, Ga.

34. Ibid., 4, 6.

35. "Minutes of Conference held in Moultrie, Georgia," April 20–21, 1946, p. 7, Mss. 118, box 312, folder 4, United Packinghouse Workers of America Papers, State Historical Society of Wisconsin, Madison, Wis.

36. See Griffith, *Crisis of American Labor*, 30, 52, for evidence of this focus on veterans as important to Operation Dixie.

37. Van Bittner quoted in *Montgomery Advertiser*, May 5, 1946, 1. This strategy, notes Robert Zieger, aimed to counter "the inevitable charges of radicalism and carpetbagging." Zieger, *CIO*, 232.

38. George Baldanzi to Van Bittner, May 10, 1946, Mss. 396, box 40, "CIO Organizing Committee, Georgia, 1" folder, TWUAP.

39. See *Textile Labor*, December 1945, 10, TWUAP.

40. Dave Burgess, written survey response to author, November 18, 1999, in possession of author.

41. On the importance of in-plant committees to the SOC's strategy, especially in textiles, see Minchin, *What Do We Need a Union For?* 29.

42. "To All Field Representatives in North Carolina," from William Smith, director, CIO Organizing Committee, June 18, 1946, Mss. 396, box 40, "CIO Organizing Committee, Georgia, 1" folder, TWUAP. In *Crisis of American Labor*, 30, Griffith cites the same statement as coming from Van Bittner. Smith's apparent use of this same phrase regarding the recruitment of veterans probably indicates a memo written by Bittner and circulated for the use of the SOC staff.

43. Draper D. Wood, Southern Area Director, to William Smith, North Carolina Director, organizer's report, June 19, 1946, reel 8 (1158), series I:425, CIOP-OD.

44. The Operation Dixie records on microfilm are extensive for the states of Tennessee, Virginia, and the Carolinas, but not for Georgia, Alabama, Mississippi, Louisiana, Florida, or Arkansas. Apparently, these records were not saved for inclusion in the CIO-OD collection, as compiled by the AFL-CIO. A scattering of records on the postwar drive exists among other collections, however, most notably in the TWUAP and in the papers of the Northwest Georgia Joint Board in the Southern Labor Archives at Georgia State University. Most of the documents in this latter collection, however, are from a later period of the early 1950s. A small but useful collection of materials on the GA-PAC in the postwar 1940s and 1950s is the DPP.

45. Paul Christopher to John Neal, TWUA representative in Chattanooga, September 18 and October 1, 1946, reel 38 (320), series 3, CIOP-OD.

46. Weekly Reports, Nashville Area, Consolidated Vultee, reel 38 (359), series 3, CIOP-OD.

47. Paul Christopher to Meyer Bernstein, CIO Veterans Committee, August 7, 1946, reel 25 (561), series 3-37, CIOP-OD.

48. On the E. I. DuPont Company in Old Hickory, see Paul Christopher to Louis F. Krainock, area director, November 4 and November 12, 1946; on the Vestal Lumber Company and Miller Brothers in Knoxville, see Paul Christopher to T. C. Cole, August 21, 1946; and on the L. B. Jenkins Company of Greeneville, see Paul Christopher to James E. Payne, December 10, 1946; all reel 38 (320), series 3, CIOP-OD.

49. Ascertaining exact figures on the growth of union membership and locals during Operation Dixie in Georgia is difficult without a centralized accounting of membership records. The evidence that does exist, however, particularly in the records of the TWUA, indicates active organizing campaigns throughout the state, but particularly throughout the Tennessee and Chattahoochee Valley areas. TWUA records as well as those of the NLRB reveal the CIO and TWUA's involvement in numerous labor conflicts throughout Operation Dixie's tenure. See, for example, "Organization Progress in Ten Southern States," June 1, 1946–September 15, 1947, and Report to the Executive Council, October 4, 1947, Research Department, Mss. 129A, subseries 10A, box 21, "Southern Drive, TWUA, 1946–1950" folder, TWUAP. In January 1947 the CIO announced that 10,000 new members had joined in Georgia since May 1946, and Charles Gillman estimated that 7,500 of these members belonged to 50 new union locals. Only 5 of these locals were organized in textile mills, according to Gillman, while 18 were Mine, Mill, and Smelter Workers Union locals. Other locals included the United Autoworkers (3), Amalgamated Clothing Workers (6), United Packinghouse Workers (4), and the Wholesale and Department Store Workers (6). However, according to Gillman, organizing efforts were ongoing at several other textile mills, including the Macon Textile Mills and the Chicopee Mills in Gainesville. See *Atlanta Constitution*, January 19, 1947, A-10.

50. Scott B. Dollar, TWUA-CIO Office and Staff Employment Application, box 1613, folder 67, ACTWR.

51. On Doyle Powell see case 10-C-1868, box 5514, "Cedartown Yarn Mills, Inc." folder, NLRBR. On Eugene Parks see case 10-C-2017, 2, box 5516, "Thurman Manufacturing Company" folder, NLRBR.

52. H. D. Lisk to Emil Rieve, November 17, 1949, Mss. 129A, subseries 2A, box 6, "H. D. Lisk, State Director, Georgia," folder, TWUAP.

53. William Shiflett, affidavit, July 27, 1947, box 209, folder 2, NLRBR. On the Anchor Rome campaign see Brattain, *Politics of Whiteness*, 126, 128–29, 166–82, 191, 196. My account of both the Anchor Rome and Celanese locals and the strikes they waged after the war borrows heavily from Brattain's thorough, well-written, and excellent account.

54. Brattain, *Politics of Whiteness*, 174.

55. *Picket Line News*, October 13, 1945, and newspaper clipping, December 9, 1945, both in Mss. 129A, subseries 10A, box 20, "Strikes, 1945" folder, TWUAP. Veterans involved in a strike at the Industrial Mill in Rock Hill, South Carolina, formed a baseball team to entertain over four hundred strikers. See draft of press release, April 3 and 9, 1946, also in Mss. 129A, subseries 10A, box 20, "Strikes, 1945–46" folder, TWUAP.

56. R. S. Burgess, President of Athens Local Union, to A. G. Dudley, President, Athens Manufacturing Company, June 1, 1946, Mss. 396, box 156, "Athens Manufacturing Company, NLRB Case 10-C-1757" folder, TWUAP.

57. Quotation from *Textile Labor*, clipping, June 5, 1948, Mss. 129A, subseries 10A, box 3, "Athens Manufacturing Co., 1944" folder, TWUAP. Despite this victory, the strike ultimately broke the Athens TWUA local. See Minchin, *What Do We Need a Union For?* 80. Also see Kenneth Douty, Georgia State Director, to Emil Rieve, March 12, 1947, Mss. 129A, subseries 10A, box 3, "Athens Manufacturing Co., 1944," TWUAP; National Labor Relations Board, Petitioner, versus Athens Manufacturing Company, Respondent, 11852, Fifth Circuit Court of Appeals, May 7, 1947, Mss. 396, box 156, "Athens Manufacturing Company, NLRB Case 10-C-1757" folder, TWUAP; "Enclosure with Letter Addressed to Athens Manufacturing Company," October 24, 1947, Mss. 1664, box 14, folder 10-CA-106, Chicopee Manufacturing Company Papers, Special Collections, Hargrett Library, University of Georgia, Athens, Ga.

58. On the Anchor Rome organizing campaign, as well as the strike of 1948, see the well-researched account offered by Brattain, *Politics of Whiteness*, 129, 170–82, and passim. On the Celanese conflict in Georgia, see Brattain, "Making Friends and Enemies," 106–7.

59. According to Minchin, the tactics employed by management at Anchor Rome and the Celanese Corporation were typical throughout the textile South after the war. See Minchin, *What Do We Need a Union For?* 37, 39, 45, 70, 72, 75.

60. Zieger, *CIO*, 145–47. Flamming, *Creating the Modern South*, 248, also notes that union security was the key issue in the bulk of postwar textile strikes in Georgia.

61. William Shiflett, affidavit, November 19, 1947, box 209, folder 2, NLRBR.

62. On the use of racist and anticommunist propaganda by textile mill owners during postwar labor disputes in the South, see Minchin, *What Do We Need a Union For?* 37–47.

63. William Shiflett, affidavit, July 27, 1947, box 209, folder 2, NLRBR.

64. Ibid.

65. Ibid.; testimony of William Shiflett, in Senate Committee on Labor and Public Welfare, *Hearing on Labor-Management Relations in the Southern Textile Manufacturing Industry*, 221, 226–30.

66. The pattern that characterized postwar textile strikes in the South, as outlined by Minchin, describes the Anchor Rome example to the letter, from the initial conflict over

union security, the continual negotiating delays by management, and the reliance on racial smear tactics to undermine the local's legitimacy to the development of a back-to-work movement and the ineffectual and ultimately negative response by the NLRB to charges of unfair labor practices. See Minchin, *What Do We Need a Union For?* 37, 45, 70, 72–78.

67. Notes of interviews with Anchor Rome workers, Mss. 396, box 218, "Anchor Rome Mills, Injunction" folder, TWUAP.

68. All eight men sentenced were accused of "being involved in clashes between workers and strikers." See *Atlanta Constitution*, May 12, 1948, 1; and Domestic Intelligence Summary #58, May 7–14, 1948, p. 6, box 10, folder 000.24, TACR.

69. According to Minchin in *What Do We Need a Union For?* 79, violence between strikers and strikebreakers was a common feature of postwar textile disputes that usually damaged the union's credibility.

70. On these incidents see Domestic Intelligence Summaries #51, March 19–26, 1948, #55, April 15–23, 1948, and #56, April 23–28, 1948, in box 10, folder 000.24, TACR.

71. Eugene Ingram to the NLRB, undated, box 24, "Anchor Rome Mills, Rome, Georgia, 10-CA-84" folder, NLRBR.

72. Celanese workers walked out when the company refused a wage increase designed to equalize pay rates in the Rome mill with Celanese workers outside of the South. For an excellent examination of Local 689, the 1948 Celanese strike, and the reasons for its success, see Brattain, "Making Friends and Enemies," 91–138. Also see *Atlanta Constitution*, April 17, 1948, 2.

73. Quotations are from interviews conducted by Brattain for *Politics of Whiteness*, 122, 124.

74. Ibid., 124.

75. *Rome News-Tribune*, October 29, 1948, clipping in Mss. 129A, subseries 10A, box 6, "Celanese Strike" folder, TWUAP.

76. Brattain, *Politics of Whiteness*, 194.

77. Letter from [?] McCarthy, 1948, Mss. 129A, subseries 10A, box 6, "Celanese strike" folder, TWUAP.

78. Scott B. Dollar, TWUA-CIO Office and Staff Employment Application, box 1613, folder 67, ACTWR. William Shiflett also eventually joined the CIO organizing staff in Tennessee. This move came after serving as TWUA Local 787's president for five years. See *Textile Labor*, November 18, 1950, 5, TWUAP.

79. Shiflett is quoted in Senate Committee on Labor and Public Welfare, *Hearing on Labor-Management Relations in the Southern Textile Manufacturing Industry*, 226–30; Brooks is quoted in Brattain, *Politics of Whiteness*, 121–22.

80. For explanations of the notion of manhood as a framework for understanding claims to citizenship by both black and white men in the South, see Tyson, *Radio Free Dixie*, 139–49, on black World War II and Korean War veterans in North Carolina; and Kantrowitz, "Ben Tillman and Hendrix McLane, Agrarians Rebels," 498, on white farmers in late-nineteenth-century South Carolina.

81. Quoted in Griffith, *Crisis of American Labor*, 52.

82. This image appears in a photograph of the picket line in the Southern Labor Archives of Georgia State University. It is also included in Zieger, *CIO*, 201.

83. *Durham Sun*, November 10, 1945, clipping in Mss. 129A, subseries 10A, box 20, "Strikes, 1945" folder, TWUAP.

84. *Cedartown (Ga.) Daily Standard*, June 6, 1947, 3. Also see ibid., June 6, 9, 10, 1947. Even more pointedly, militant and mostly black veterans in a local of the Food, Tobacco, and Agricultural Workers, CIO, on strike at R. J. Reynolds Tobacco in Winston-Salem, North Carolina, carried picket signs in 1947 declaring, "We fought together in foxholes, why not here?" and "From the firing line to the picket line." As striker and veteran Haywood Davenport told a *Daily Worker* reporter, "We learned to stand up and take it when the going was toughest," and "we're not going to give up the fight for a decent life now. RJ Reynolds can't beat us where the Nazis couldn't." Quoted in Korstad, "Daybreak of Freedom," 302–3.

85. Quoted in exhibit 27, Senate Committee on Labor and Public Welfare, *Hearing on Labor-Management Relations in the Southern Textile Manufacturing Industry*, 138–39.

86. For examples of the weekly reports that organizers submitted to subregional offices and the SOC headquarters, see reel 8, series 1, and reel 38, series 3, CIOP-OD.

87. Bartley, *New South*, 48; Zieger, *CIO*, 236; Key, *Southern Politics*, 658.

88. Zieger, *CIO*, 236–39.

89. Quoted in Minchin, *What Do We Need a Union For?* 68.

90. Zieger, *CIO*, 235–38; Egerton, *Speak Now Against the Day*, 382; Bartley, *New South*, 48.

91. For more detail on the results of the postwar drive in textiles, see Minchin, *What Do We Need a Union For?* 31.

92. Brattain, *Politics of Whiteness*, 151; Zieger, *CIO*, 237.

93. Griffith, *Crisis of American Labor*, 162.

94. For discussions of why Operation Dixie failed, start with the first scholarly account evaluating the campaign, Barbara Griffith's *Crisis of American Labor*. Griffith identifies a host of problems that beset the southern organizing drive, from the increasingly conservative national political climate and the obdurate opposition met in southern mill communities, to the lack of understanding the SOC exhibited about southern workers and the southern context. She also notes the flawed strategy was rooted in lessons of the 1930s that never applied to the South, such as relying on organizing large "bellwether" textile plants. Most of all, as Robert Zieger has concluded, Griffith emphasizes the "culture of the mill communities and its contribution to defeat" as the real "heart" of Operation Dixie's failure. The long-standing pattern of employer dominance and worker subordination and dependence ultimately proved too strong to overcome. See Zieger, "Textile Workers and Historians," 40–41.

Later treatments include Bartley, *New South*, 39–48, which emphasizes the hostility of southern management, civic leaders, and the county seat establishment, the effective use of red- and race-baiting, divisions among southern liberals and within the CIO, and the developing politics of anticommunism; Sullivan, *Days of Hope*, 207–9, which focuses on the conservatism of the SOC's strategy, the division between the SOC and the southern PAC movement, and the limited tolerance of most white workers for the CIO's principles of racial egalitarianism. In *CIO*, 227–28, Zieger emphasizes all of these factors, as well as the "conflicting assumptions about the nature of the undertaking," then he concludes that the "bitter opposition of southern elites," the "uncertain response of white workers," and the "CIO's lack of resources and internal unity" proved to be the most devastating to

Operation Dixie's chances of success. Also see Barkin and Honey, "Operation Dixie"; and Brattain, "'Town as Small as That.'"

95. On this changing national climate and the impact it had on the southern organizing drive in textiles, see Minchin, *What Do We Need a Union For?* 77.

96. Quotation from Zieger, *CIO*, 212, 245–46.

97. On organized labor's struggles amid the domestic and international politics of anticommunism, see Zieger, *CIO*, 240, 244; and Bartley, *New South*, 42–43.

98. Bartley, *New South*, 42–47.

99. Ibid., 45, 40.

100. Zieger, *CIO*, 233–34.

101. Ibid., 234.

102. Sullivan, *Days of Hope*, 208.

103. Quoted in Griffith, *Crisis of American Labor*, 168.

104. Zieger, *CIO*, 233–34.

105. Bartley, *New South*, 69.

106. For a varied discussion on the question of race and labor relations in the South, see the essays in Zieger, *Organized Labor in the Twentieth-Century South*.

107. Zieger, *CIO*, 234.

108. Minchin notes that even the SOC staff grew increasingly critical of this cautious racial strategy, having recognized the need to develop a stronger core of support for the CIO's postwar agenda. See Minchin, *What Do We Need a Union For?* 39.

109. On the conservatism of the southern organizing drive, see Zieger, *CIO*, 227–28. Griffith, *Crisis of American Labor*, 164–66, notes that the SOC concentrated much of its effort on textiles, despite the fact that the TWUA actually faced the strongest opposition in the South, lacked a coherent organizing strategy, and faced an industry that was far more competitive than most others in the region.

110. The photograph may be found in Zieger, *CIO*, 201, and in the Southern Labor Archives at Georgia State University.

111. Minchin also notes that the efforts the SOC made to downplay race as an issue in the southern organizational campaign after the war were useless, even in the predominantly white textile industry. Employers used race to attack organized labor's local credibility anyway, sometimes to great effect in specific campaigns. See Minchin, *What Do We Need a Union For?* 39–41. In *Crisis of American Labor*, 39–40, Griffith barely mentions race as an important factor in the defeat of Operation Dixie or even as a significant problem organizers regularly encountered.

112. See, for example, Brattain, *Politics of Whiteness*, 142–43.

113. See Minchin, *What Do We Need a Union For?* 75–76, for more on the anti-union tactics that postwar textile mill owners used.

114. Minchin also notes the widespread use of the *Militant Truth* and other anti-union publications against organizing drives. See *What Do We Need a Union For?* 45–46.

115. Quoted in Brattain, *Politics of Whiteness*, 128–29.

116. On the prevalence of the Ku Klux Klan in particular organizing drives in textiles after the war, see Minchin, *What Do We Need a Union For?* 40–41.

117. See AF to Ned, September 12, 1946, and "Report on Columbians," October 30, 1946, reel 1, SKP.

118. Report on Atlanta Klavern #1, September 23, 1946, reel 1, box 1, folder 3, SKP.

119. See undated flyer, reel 1, box 1, folder 9, SKP; and Minchin, *What Do We Need a Union For?* 40–41.

120. In an all-white southern textile mill in Georgia at that time, these workers did not construe their struggles with management as putting their "white privilege" at stake. They understood threats that blacks would take their jobs if they voted in the TWUA as a management ploy: it simply would not happen. Understanding management methods to play the race card as the self-serving tactics they were did not, however, translate into endorsing the principle of racial equality. See Brattain, *Politics of Whiteness*, 128–29; and Kytle, "What has been the Popular Reaction to the Post-War Unionization of Industry in Georgia?" in box 8, "Georgia Project—V. O. Key—Personal" folder, SPC.

121. See Kytle, "What has been the Popular Reaction to the Post-War Unionization of Industry in Georgia?" in box 8, "Georgia Project—V. O. Key, Personal" folder, SPC; and Minchin, *What Do We Need a Union For?* 40–41.

122. Survey responses by David Burgess and Don McKee, November 18, 1999, in possession of author.

123. Timothy Minchin emphasizes the impact of the consumerist revolution and economic boom that came out of the war as a decisive factor in Operation Dixie's defeat in North Carolina. He also notes that the social and economic changes wrought by World War II not only boosted textile wages but also encouraged employers to sustain or expand these increases to counter any union appeal. This proved to be a key factor in the TWUA's difficulties in the postwar South. See Minchin, *What Do We Need a Union For?* 2, 3, 48–68. Also see Jones, "Some Aspects of the Opposition in Georgia to the CIO's Organizing Drive," 44–46, 83. From Cash, *Mind of the South*, to more recent works, studies have also emphasized the cultural flaws and peculiar character traits that allegedly explained southern textile workers' hostility or lackadaisical attitude toward unionization. Cash noted that "the fact about the Southern mill worker was plain. He was willing to join the union as a novelty, and to strike. It was a part of his simple childlike psychology and curious romantic-hedonistic heritage . . . that he was willing to join any new thing in sight" (243). Yet, as Cash continued, mill workers proved less than enthusiastic when it came to the long haul: "when it came to fixing a grievance continually in view and methodically preparing for a strike by regularly paying union dues, they were quite incapable of it" (244).

Other scholars have identified very concrete reasons why southern mill workers sometimes preferred a loyalty to management over any identification with the goals of industrial unionism. In the 1940s, particularly, southern textile mills used welfare capitalism to offset the appeal that union organizing might have. In his analysis of the southern labor movement in Georgia after World War II, Calvin Kytle, for example, cited the "strong paternalism of management," including voluntary wage increases and improved working conditions, as one reason for the CIO's failure to organize successfully in a number of Georgia textile mills. Kytle, "What has been the Popular Reaction to the Post-War Unionization of Industry in Georgia?" in box 8, "Georgia Project—V. O. Key—Personal" folder, SPC. Similarly, in *Politics of Whiteness*, 148–50, Brattain finds that "employer paternalism and local boosterism . . . posed the most significant obstacles to the organizing campaign" at the Pepperell Mill in Lindale, Georgia. At Cannon Mills in Kannapolis, North Carolina, workers "seemed to accept the paternalism and anti-unionism of their employer," including favorable wage rates. Zieger, *CIO*, 237.

124. This very apt comment is from Barkin and Honey, "Operation Dixie," 374. In Tallapoosa, Georgia, for example, Brattain finds that a number of factors explained the failure of the Operation Dixie drive, but "fervent local resistance"—not race or the "flaws" of southern workers—proved to be the most important. A "depressed economy" lent credence to management threats to shut down the American Thread Mill rather than allow it to be organized by the TWUA. With American Thread one of the only employers in town, mill workers "consistently voted the union down," while management demonized organizers as "Yankee outsiders" and beat union operatives with the complicity of local officials. Moreover, a conservative shift in the NLRB, the "indifference" of the federal government in the face of local abuse of labor organizers, and the passage of the Taft-Hartley Act in 1947 all contributed to the failure of the southern organizational drive. See Brattain, "'Town as Small as That.'" Also see Griffith, *Crisis of American Labor*, 39–42.

125. See Brattain, "Making Friends and Enemies," 93–94, 107, 116, for examples of how the connections among local civic, business, and political leaders in Rome and Floyd County, Georgia, added to organized labor's difficulties.

126. Flamming, *Creating the Modern South*, 247.

127. "Union workers" in Georgia were "remarkably active" politically in the postwar period. They especially hoped to "create a powerful labor coalition in Northwest Georgia." Ibid., 251, 253.

128. The history of the CIO-PAC is detailed in Foster, *Union Politic*, though this work does little with the southern PAC movement.

129. Zieger, *CIO*, 177–79. In practical terms, however, the CIO-PAC operated within Democratic Party councils, supported the reelection of Franklin D. Roosevelt as president in 1944, and gambled that a mobilized working-class electorate would offset a "conservative electoral tide" that had made significant Republican and southern Democratic conservative gains in Congress in 1942.

130. Ibid., 183, 186.

131. Ibid., 184–85.

132. Ibid., 230. The results of the CIO's political efforts in 1944 fell short of expectations. Although Roosevelt did win reelection, his popular showing was less than usual, and it was not at all clear what difference the CIO-PAC had made to that outcome. Some PAC voter drives did help elect more moderate or even progressive candidates, but many others failed to do so. Nonetheless, the successes that did come from the CIO-PAC efforts, combined with the ever increasing need to counter the growing conservative tide in the country, convinced the CIO to continue the PAC crusade, particularly when a spate of controversial postwar strikes further undermined labor's popular credibility. By the end of the war, politics had become organized labor's "crucial arena," with mobilizing voter registration and turnout its "No. One mission." On all of these points, see Zieger, *CIO*, 186–87, 241.

133. Frederickson, *Dixiecrat Revolt*, 34.

134. Ibid., 244–45.

135. Sullivan, *Days of Hope*, 208–9.

136. George Mitchell of the SRC and the CIO headed the southern PAC drive, but long-

time labor and liberal activist Palmer Weber of Virginia became its "primary strategist." Weber toured the South extensively in 1946, spreading far and wide the CIO-PAC message of black-white cooperation and political participation on behalf of progressive reform. Egerton, *Speak Now Against the Day*, 382; Sullivan, *Days of Hope*, 209.

137. Sullivan, *Days of Hope*, 209.

138. First quotation is in Zieger, *CIO*, 182; the second quotation is in Sullivan, *Days of Hope*, 210. Also see Bartley, *New South*, 46.

139. Zieger, *CIO*, 234.

140. Sullivan, *Days of Hope*, 210.

141. Ibid., 202–3.

142. Ibid., 209.

143. Quoted in ibid., 204.

144. Ibid., 204.

145. Spritzer, *Belle of Ashby Street*, 66–67, 70.

146. Sullivan, *Days of Hope*, 210–11; Anonymous, March 22, 1947, box 8, "Georgia Interviews, 1" folder, SPC. This is not a closed collection, but restrictions do require not publishing the name of this individual interviewed. Anyone interested in this identity, however, may locate it by consulting the collection.

147. On Helen Douglas Mankin, see Spritzer, *Belle of Ashby Street*.

148. In *Southern Politics*, 657, Key states that the CIO-PAC drive "almost certainly" accounted for Tarver's surprising defeat in 1946.

149. Brattain, *Politics of Whiteness*, 152–53.

150. Charles Gillman to Paul Christopher, September 21, 1945, box 1881, folder 3, AFL-CIO, Region 8, Papers, Southern Labor Archives, Georgia State University, Atlanta, Ga.

151. The delegates then passed resolutions directing Congress to extend the tenure of the Office of Price Administration, to pass the Wagner-Murray-Dingell Act, to increase the minimum wage to sixty-five cents, and to support new housing legislation. Delegates also called on Georgia's working families to register and vote. *Textile Labor*, June 1946, 2, TWUAP. Douty is also quoted in Brattain, *Politics of Whiteness*, 137.

152. Key, *Southern Politics*, 657; Sullivan, *Days of Hope*, 218.

153. Sullivan, *Days of Hope*, 127; Egerton, *Speak Now Against the Day*, 97; Brattain, *Politics of Whiteness*, 155. Also see Flamming, *Creating the Modern South*, 251.

154. Quoted in Brattain, *Politics of Whiteness*, 156.

155. Weekly report of Robert Hodges, March 31–April 6, 1946, series 1, folder 69, DPP.

156. Preparation for Seventh Congressional District PAC Convention, March 10–16, 1946, series 1, folder 69, DPP.

157. CIO membership, Georgia, 1946, folder 72, DPP.

158. Notes, Seventh Congressional District Race, 1946, folder 73, DPP.

159. Brattain, *Politics of Whiteness*, 156–58.

160. Quoted in ibid., 158. Also see 156–57.

161. Brattain, "Making Friends and Enemies," 128; Brattain, *Politics of Whiteness*, 155–56, 159.

162. Brattain, *Politics of Whiteness*, 161.

163. Ibid., 161, 133.

164. Ibid., 161.

165. Ibid., 153–55.

166. Ibid., 153–54.

167. Flamming, *Creating the Modern South*, 253, describes Carmichael as "strongly pro-labor," but as the rest of this discussion indicates, I do not find that to be the case at all.

168. See *Savannah Evening Press*, May 29, 1946; *Atlanta Journal*, May 30, 1946, 2; *Waycross (Ga.) Journal Herald*, June 5, 1946, 8; and Brattain, *Politics of Whiteness*, 154–56.

169. Telegram to Strickland-Rogers Motor Company of Columbus, June 3, 1946, box 3, folder 8, ACSP.

170. *Atlanta Journal*, June 8, 1946, 2, June 14, 1946, 13, and July 3, 1946, 22.

171. Tilford E. Dudley to Daniel Powell, June 17, 1946, folder 68, DPP. Maynard Smith joined the Carmichael campaign as manager in May 1946, shortly after his discharge from the United States Navy. *Atlanta Constitution*, May 14, 1946.

172. *Atlanta Journal*, June 2, 1946, 1. Troup County was a textile mill community dominated by the Calloway Mills family and a target for TWUA and CIO organizing campaigns at the time.

173. Herman Talmadge to C. L. Foster, June 26, 1946, and Herman Talmadge to C. L. Foster, June 27, 1946, both in box 3, folder 9, ACSP.

174. Sullivan, *Days of Hope*, 213–15.

175. In *Union Politic*, 1–2, Foster notes the failure of the CIO-PAC nationally after the war. Amid a developing conservative shift in the country, he concludes, the leadership of the CIO-PAC often ended up on the "wrong side" of controversial issues, hindered by the "1930s-thinking" that characterized the movement. Thus, in its twelve-year tenure, the CIO-PAC ultimately lost more elections than it won.

176. Flamming, *Creating the Modern South*, 259, finds in Dalton, Georgia, that Crown Mill's white workers in TWUA Local 185 kept focused on union organization and activities, so long as racial matters did not intrude. However, "once their world of civic involvement and political activism began to expand" after the war, and "once blacks began to re-enter southern politics, the 'race question' became central to the political world of Local 185." Thus, "for PAC leaders in the South," he concludes, "matters of race presented extreme difficulties in the late 1940s."

177. Brattain, *Politics of Whiteness*, 159–60.

178. See Brattain, "Making Friends and Enemies," 124, 128–29.

179. J. P. Mooney to Al Barkan, March 10, 1948, Mss. 396, box 479, "Georgia, 1948" folder, TWUAP.

180. For example, Flamming, *Creating the Modern South*, 251, finds that "working-class Georgians never had a chance to form a viable biracial alliance in the postwar decade, in part because the working people of the state were not tightly organized and also because white workers still saw blacks as problems, not allies."

Chapter Five

1. *Atlanta Constitution*, August 18, 1946, E-1.

2. For example, voter turnout for the gubernatorial election in 1946—over 690,000—

was more than twice the turnout in 1942 when Ellis Arnall was elected over Eugene Talmadge. See Anderson, *Wild Man from Sugar Creek*, 210–11; Bernd, *Grass Roots Politics in Georgia*, 66, 71; and Henderson, *Politics of Change in Georgia*, 50, 145, 166–68.

3. Bell interview (first quotation); *Atlanta Journal*, April 29, 1946, 10 (second quotation). Many observers at the time noticed, and hoped for, a change in the state's returning white soldiers. "Georgians . . . returning from lands all over the earth are bringing in new visions and ideas," reported the *Gainesville Eagle*, and having "seen and experienced many new things . . . they can do much to broaden the horizons of Georgia today." The *Augusta Chronicle* similarly remarked that "most, if not all, of these young men are quite different in their outlook and actions from the timid, apathetic, secure in the rut, average run of the mine citizen." *Gainesville Eagle*, May 9, 1946; *Augusta Chronicle*, March 9, 1946, 4.

4. *Atlanta Constitution*, July 21, 1946, A-14.

5. *Gainesville Eagle*, March 21, 1946, 2 (first quotation); *Atlanta Constitution*, August 7, 1946, E-1 (second quotation).

6. The state government lost almost $13,000 on this bogus deal worked out by Talmadge. See Anderson, *Wild Man from Sugar Creek*, 57–60, 73.

7. Ibid., 82, 89, 92, 110–11, 114–16, 147–50.

8. Ibid.

9. Ibid., 196–201.

10. Arnold to James Setze Jr., July 15, 1941, box 1, folder 1, JSJP.

11. *Atlanta Constitution*, May 15, 1946, clipping in scrapbook 6, JVCP. Frank, while in the navy in San Francisco, wrote to Setze about reading of "the Georgia students and Governor Talmadge in Life and Time. That sure is a mess." Larry wrote from Missouri: "It sure is a disgrace that Talmadge's meddling caused such a loss of prestige to the University of Georgia." See Frank to James Setze Jr., undated, box 1, folder 2, and Larry to James Setze Jr., January 11, 1942, box 1, folder 3, JSJP.

12. *Atlanta Journal*, May 22, 1946, clipping in scrapbook 6, JVCP.

13. "Georgia Soldier," Orlando, Florida, August 15, 1944, clipping in box 16, "Servicemen's reactions to Georgia" folder, Lamar Q. Ball Collection, Georgia Department of Archives and History, Atlanta, Ga. See also *Atlanta Journal*, May 10, 1946, 18.

14. For further examples of veterans recalling Georgia's reputation as a "laughingstock," see *Atlanta Journal*, February 13, 1946, 14; and *Atlanta Constitution*, July 16, 1946, E-1. When Mrs. George M. Kelly toured "as a pilot's wife" during the war, she tried to explain wherever she went "that Georgians do go to school and wear shoes and that most of us thought Stone Mountain was a place of scenic beauty and not a place for grown men to play 'ghosts,'" but veterans such as Lewis Adams, Norman Tant, and others found it difficult to frame a response to criticisms they knew were well founded. Mrs. Kelly's comment on Stone Mountain refers to its reputation as a haven for Ku Klux Klan gatherings. See *Atlanta Journal*, July 14, 1946, A-14.

15. *Atlanta Journal*, May 10, July 26, 1946.

16. Huddleston quotation from ibid., May 28, 1946, 10; Wilkes quotation from clipping, ca. 1946, scrapbook 6, JVCP; Morrison quotation from *Atlanta Constitution*, July 16, 1946, E-1.

17. Henderson, "Ellis Arnall and the Politics of Progress," 27.

18. "Talmadge has been my Governor for most of my life," Boring remarked, "and it

seemed that every time he opened his mouth, someone laughed." *Atlanta Constitution*, July 3, 1946, 1.

19. *Atlanta Journal*, May 22, 1946, clipping in scrapbook 6, JVCP; *Atlanta Constitution*, July 16, 1946, E-1; *Atlanta Journal*, May 14, 1946, clipping in scrapbook 6, JVCP; P. D. Cunningham to James Setze Jr., September 29, 1942, box 1, folder 6, JSJP. "All of the Georgians in my company were very happy over the results of the election," wrote Ensign Robert P. Lance in Massachusetts to James Setze in 1942: "It is certainly pleasant to see a governor of Georgia mentioned favorably by the press up here and in New York." See Lance to Setze, October 13, 1942, box 1, folder 7, JSJP. Ensign Doyle Butler told Setze, "I bet you are proud to have done your part in getting out that Sugar Creek Bastard," while W. Frank Bennett was "glad that the new governor is straightening things out in Georgia." Butler to Setze, October 24, 1942, box 1, folder 7, and Bennett to Setze, February 8, 1943, box 1, folder 9, JSJP.

20. On the notion of manhood as a source of civic and political entitlement for white men, see Bederman, *Manliness and Civilization*; Gilmore, *Gender and Jim Crow*; and Kantrowitz, *Ben Tillman and the Reconstruction of White Supremacy*. On the impact of military service in heightening the notion of entitlement, see Marwick, *Total War and Social Change*, xvi.

21. As governor during the peak of the Great Depression, Rivers tried to restructure the state government in order to take advantage of federal New Deal programs. His ambitious attempt to foster a "little New Deal" in Georgia, however, exceeded the state's capacity to fund the programs, due in large part to the hostility of the conservative state legislature. Rivers's administration ended in disgrace and financial crisis amid charges of corruption and incompetence. The Rivers debacle opened the door to Talmadge's reelection as governor in 1940. On Rivers's record see Bartley, *Creation of Modern Georgia*, 190–92.

22. Sergeant Harry Baxter, WSB Radio broadcast, July 2, 1946, transcript, Draft APR.1993.18, GGDP; *Atlanta Journal*, May 14, 1946, clipping in scrapbook 6, JVCP. "I'm afraid Talmadge will come back and disgrace the state again," wrote army veteran Frank Vinson to James V. Carmichael, and many other veterans apparently agreed. One pleaded with "Georgians" to not "let us down by electing Rivers or Talmadge. Let's continue to raise the standards of Georgia, so that the other states will continue to admire. Must we sacrifice her good name?" See Frank Vinson to James V. Carmichael, March 24, 1946, box 10, folder 4, JVCP; and *Atlanta Journal*, May 10, 1946, 18.

23. *Gainesville News*, July 11, 1946, 13; *Gainesville Eagle*, July 11, 1946.

24. Sergeant Harry Baxter, WSB Radio broadcast, July 2, 1946, transcript, Draft APR.1993.18, GGDP; *Atlanta Journal*, May 6, 1946, 11. Veterans Thomas Lovett and Henry Steadman regretted not only Talmadge's election as governor, but also that "more of the people of the state did not have the opportunity to see Germany after its defeat, as we did." Like Talmadge, the Germans "thrived on racial hatred and intolerance," and Lovett and Steadman wondered "if the people of this state realize that by this election we are in danger of having a form of government which so many of our native sons died fighting against?" *Atlanta Constitution*, July 23, 1946, E-1.

25. *Savannah Morning News*, May 10, 1946, 16. In Phenix City, Alabama, sister city to

Columbus, Georgia, veterans took issue with an incumbent administration apparently content with a city mired in gambling, political corruption, electoral fraud, and economic stagnation. "The men who gave their blood or their life on the battlefront . . . to put dictators out of business all over the world," proclaimed Phenix City veteran Shelby Johnson, "are hardly in the mood to admit now that they have lost the war, and submit to a local dictator within our city limits." *Columbus Enquirer*, September 15, 1946, A-4.

26. *Atlanta Constitution*, January 17, 1945; *Atlanta Journal*, October 28, 1946, 10.

27. *Atlanta Journal*, May 15, 1946, 12; *Atlanta Constitution*, August 23, 1946, E-1.

28. War mobilization inaugurated significant economic growth in Georgia and the South, boosting the region's overall industrial capacity by almost 40 percent. Along with new aircraft, munitions, rubber, and chemical industries came the expansion of traditional ones such as textiles, lumber, and mining. This growth, combined with increasing agricultural prices, generated new incomes that encouraged the development of a nascent consumer market in the South. In Georgia wartime development raised per capita incomes from 57 percent of the national average in 1940 to 73 percent in 1960. The arrival of over 1,600 new manufacturing establishments between 1930 and 1947 and the emergence of a burgeoning consumer market spurred a diversification and expansion of jobs in both the white- and blue-collar sectors of the economy. The prosperity induced by World War II seemed an abrupt change after years of unrelenting depression, a change that promised to eradicate the South's image as a "benighted" region burdened by its past and saddled with an unwelcome, though deserved, reputation as the nation's "number one economic problem." Much of this development, however, was uneven, favoring the Gulf Southwest within the South and larger cities within Georgia. In addition, with much of this development centered on war production, reconversion shut down plants that were important sources of wartime employment. Huntsville, Alabama, Columbia, Tennessee, Brunswick, Savannah, and Marietta, Georgia, for example, all suffered immediately after the war from the closure of war industries, which contributed to local racial tensions and political instability. See Tindall, *Emergence of the New South*, 694, 700–701; and Bartley, *Creation of Modern Georgia*, 187, 181–83.

29. Bartley, *Creation of Modern Georgia*, 186.

30. Ibid., 186–87; Bartley, *New South*, 122–31.

31. Bureau of the Census, *Sixteenth Census, 1940*, 240–43; and Bureau of the Census, *Seventeenth Census, 1950*, 11-9, 11-10.

32. On urban overcrowding and the strains it produced, see Bartley, *New South*, 132, 134; Bartley, *Creation of Modern Georgia*, 188; and Daniel, "Going Among Strangers," 894, 898–904.

33. *Atlanta Journal*, February 19, 1946, 10.

34. Ibid., July 23, 1946, 10.

35. Ibid., March 13, 1946, 10; *Atlanta Constitution*, February 10, 1946, A-15.

36. In fact, Powers warned, "profiteering landlords, real estate operators, private contractors and a slumbering Congress" should be prepared for the next war when "many ex-GIs . . . might stay at home and make a lot of money, or at least provide themselves with a roof over their heads, and let Congress find others to do the fighting and dying." *Atlanta Constitution*, August 28, 1946, E-1. In crowded cities such as Atlanta, office space was also at a premium after the war. A dentist who had served fifty-five months in the

war, including over two years overseas, found it difficult to renew his practice when he returned to Atlanta. "Since my discharge three months ago," he wrote to the Atlanta Journal, "I have been looking for office space. I have just about given up hope." *Atlanta Journal*, March 15, 1946, 18. War veteran Luther Alverson, who later served in the Georgia state legislature, encountered the same difficulty. "The war ended and I came back here," he recalled, "and I walked the streets of Atlanta for two months and . . . couldn't even rent desk space." Alverson interview.

37. *Atlanta Journal*, February 24, 1946, A-14.

38. Ibid., April 18, 1946, 16.

39. Ibid., April 29, July 16, 1946. "Since returning to the States I've been in quite a few states," remarked boatswain's mate J. H. Bottoms, "to find prosperity in all but Georgia. Elsewhere wages are triple and prices are under the best of control." Ibid., April 29, 1946.

40. On similar veteran revolts in other southern states, see Key, *Southern Politics*, 198, 201–4, 436–37, 453, 460–61; and Lester, *Man for Arkansas*, 8–35. On veterans in McMinn, Polk, Bradley, and Monroe Counties in East Tennessee, see Byrum, *Battle of Athens*; Lemond, "Good Government League and Polk County (Tennessee) Politics"; *Polk County News*, August 15, 22, 1946; *Sweetwater Valley (Tenn.) News*, May 2, 1946, clipping in Political Correspondence III, 1946 Political Files, Estes Kefauver Papers, Special Collections and Archives, Hoskins Library, University of Tennessee, Knoxville, Tenn.; and *Bradley County Journal*, June 13, 1946.

41. Veterans took leading roles in the Carmichael campaign, both in managing it and in appearing on the stump throughout Georgia. Soon after his discharge from the navy in 1946, G. Maynard Smith of Cairo, Georgia, became Carmichael's overall campaign manager. At virtually every rally on the campaign trail in rural and urban Georgia, white veterans introduced Carmichael, made speeches on his behalf, and/or sat with him on the speakers' platform. White veterans also organized Carmichael-for-Governor Clubs in counties across the state. *Atlanta Constitution*, April 28, May 14, 15, 1946, clippings in scrapbook 6, JVCP; *Atlanta Journal*, April 24, May 14, May 26, June 6, June 7, July 1, 1946; *Gainesville (Ga.) Eagle*, May 2, 1946; *Atlanta Constitution*, July 1, 1946, 12; *Waycross (Ga.) Journal Herald*, May 16, 1946, 1.

42. On the Veterans Political Reform League in Augusta, see Cobb, "Colonel Effingham Crushes the Crackers"; and on the CPL in Savannah, see *Savannah Morning News*, April 10, 1946, 2, 12.

43. On electoral and political trends in twentieth-century Georgia, see Bartley, *Creation of Modern Georgia*; Anderson, *Wild Man from Sugar Creek*, 210–11, 222; Henderson, *Politics of Change in Georgia*, 145, 166–68; and Key, *Southern Politics*, 106–29.

44. On the participation of these organizations in the postwar voter registration drives, see *Augusta Chronicle*, February 6, 1946, 1–2; *Savannah Evening Press*, April 19, 1946, 14; and *Savannah Herald*, May 1, 1946, 2.

45. Observers predicted that these new votes would largely go to Carmichael. Emory University political scientist Cullen Gosnell argued that this unprecedented registration made issues, not organization, the key to the statewide election, something that would serve to benefit Carmichael. After teaching American GIs at Shrivenham American University near London in 1945, Gosnell found them to be "hard to fool, callous to politicians' promises and demanding that a man deliver the goods." In fact, Georgia's soldiers

took great pride "out of the way those from other sections singled out Georgia under Mr. Arnall as a model of good government." And, he warned, "as veterans [they] won't easily forget what Georgia looked like from the perspective overseas." *Atlanta Journal*, June 6, 1946, 1. For more on voter registration during the 1946 Democratic primaries in Georgia, see *Atlanta Journal*, April 19, 24, May 5, 12, July 16, 1946; and *Atlanta Constitution*, July 1, 1946, 12.

46. Cobb, "Colonel Effingham Crushes the Crackers," 511; *Augusta Chronicle*, February 1, 2, 6, 1946, and April 7, 1946, 1.

47. Cobb, "Colonel Effingham Crushes the Crackers," 510–13.

48. *Augusta Herald*, March 31, April 1, 1946.

49. Ibid., March 31, July 9, 1946; *Augusta Chronicle*, March 3, 1946, 1.

50. Sullivan quotation from *Savannah Evening Press*, May 10, 1946, 9. For more on the CPL campaign, see *Savannah Morning News*, April 10, 18, 25, May 4, 10, 24, 1946; and *Savannah Evening Press*, April 19, 25, May 10, 27, July 10, 1946.

51. *Savannah Morning Press*, April 10, 1946, 12; *Savannah Evening Press*, April 10, 18, 19, May 12, 1946.

52. On voter turnout in the gubernatorial race of 1946 in Georgia, see Coleman, *Georgia History in Outline*, 101; and Bartley, *Creation of Modern Georgia*, 203.

53. *Augusta Chronicle*, April 4, 14, 18, 1946.

54. *Savannah Evening Press*, July 8, 1946, 14; *Savannah Morning News*, May 13, July 19, 1946.

55. *Atlanta Journal*, July 16, 1946, 1, 4; Bartley, *Creation of Modern Georgia*, 203.

56. Student League for Good Government, political broadside, reel 2, folder 5, SKP; Hoke Smith, WSB Radio broadcast, July 13, 1946, transcript, Draft APR.1993.18.uc-M84-20/42a, GGDP.

57. *Tri-County (Americus, Ga.) News*, October 3, 1946, 1; *Augusta Herald*, April 3, 1946, 1.

58. James V. Carmichael, WSB Radio broadcast, July 6, 1946, transcript, Draft APR.1993.19.uc-M84-20/49a and 46b; Hoke Smith, WSB Radio broadcast, July 13, 1946, transcript, Draft APR.1993.18.uc-M84-20/42a; Student League for Good Government, WSB Radio broadcast, July 6, 1946, transcript, Draft APR.1993.10.uc; all in GGDP.

59. *Augusta Chronicle*, March 31, April 14, 1946; *Augusta Herald*, April 12, 1946, 6.

60. *Savannah Evening Press*, May 27, 1946, 2.

61. Kennedy, *Freedom from Fear*, 359, 350–62. Also see Brinkley, *End of Reform*, 4, 7–8, 13, 269; Bartley, *New South*, 69; and Schulman, *From Cotton Belt to Sunbelt*, 127–28.

62. B-29ers-For-Carmichael-Club, WSB Radio broadcast, July 6, 1946, transcript, Draft APR.1993.20.uc-M84-20/49b and 46a, and James V. Carmichael, WSB Radio broadcast, June 15, 1946, transcript, Draft APR.1993.9.c-M84-20/29a and 29b, both in GGDP; *Atlanta Journal*, May 26, 1946, A-6.

63. *Augusta Chronicle*, April 7, 1946, 7; *Savannah Evening Press*, May 23, 27, November 13, 1946.

64. *Atlanta Journal*, July 16, 1946, 1, 4; Bartley, *Creation of Modern Georgia*, 203.

65. In *From Cotton Belt to Sunbelt*, 125, Schulman defines these veteran insurgencies as signaling the "emergence of a new breed of southern politician," the precursors of the business-progressive neo-Whigs of the Sunbelt era.

66. For a discussion of the specific impact of federal policies toward the South during

and immediately after the war in creating "a critical transformation in the character of southern political leadership," see Schulman, *From Cotton Belt to Sunbelt*, ix. He studies the emergence of a "group of politicians," or "new 'Whigs,'" who found that "their ability to win military spending, research contracts, and highway and airport funds proved essential both to their political success and to their region's development."

67. In announcing his campaign for governor in 1946, Talmadge minced few words in appealing to his constituency's southern and racial nationalism. Declaring that the white primary issue was the most important question facing the region and the state of Georgia, Talmadge then announced that "alien and communistic influences from the East are agitating social equality in our state." In fact, he alleged, "they desire negroes to participate in our white primary in order to destroy the traditions and heritages of our Southland." "If elected Governor," Talmadge promised, "I shall see that the traditions which were fought for by our grandparents are maintained and preserved[,] . . . unfettered and unhampered by radical Communistic and alien influences." Talmadge capitalized also on national controversies to imply that the outcome of the state gubernatorial race would have some sort of impact on issues that actually could be settled only in the halls of Congress. In a speech at Summerville, for example, Talmadge attacked "socialized medicine" and the "FEPC," purporting to explain how these questions could threaten white supremacy in Georgia. "If they get across the FEPC and the socialized medicine, too," Talmadge alleged, "if you apply for a doctor, they might send you to a Negro doctor right here in this county." See *Montgomery Advertiser*, April 7, 1946, 25; and Eugene Talmadge, WSB Radio broadcast, undated, transcript, Draft APR.1993.79.uc-M84-20/113a, GGDP.

Probably the only Georgia politician who could come close to matching Talmadge in racial hyperbole and demagoguery for political effect was Roy V. Harris of the Cracker Party in Augusta. As a state legislative incumbent opposed by the Independents, Harris led the Crackers in attacking their opponents as reincarnated "carpetbaggers" intent on eliminating the white primary in Georgia. Dubbing the white primary as the vehicle used by "the old Confederate veterans to wrest control of this state from the hands of the carpetbaggers, scalawags, and negroes," a political advertisement for the Cracker legislative candidates proclaimed the importance of maintaining a racially exclusive primary. The "colored people" who "vote as a bloc" and "take orders from Washington and New York" aim to defeat southern congressmen, pass a permanent FEPC bill, and end segregation in all public facilities, as well as promote intermarriage "of the races." The end result, the Crackers warned, would be "the end of Augusta's development and growth" because "we will either have race riots or the white people will leave the community." Having declared white supremacy to be the overarching issue, the Crackers then tried to put the Independents on the spot by challenging them to take a position on the white primary. "This is the most important election in Georgia since we got rid of the scalawags, carpetbaggers, and Negro government," trumpeted Roy V. Harris, yet "I have been asking this question [about the white primary] for two weeks but I have received no answer." *Augusta Chronicle*, April 12, 13, 1946.

68. Rather than attacking Carmichael directly, Talmadge often focused his most vitriolic efforts on his old rival, Ellis Arnall, who endorsed Carmichael. Talmadge's race-baiting attacks on Arnall—for refusing to defend the white primary, for example—labeled Arnall as the leader of the Yankee-liberal-union-black plot to overturn Georgia's racial

traditions, a conspiracy that Carmichael's election as governor would further. "Ellis 'Benedict' Arnall opened the breach in the dike that has protected Southern manhood, Southern womanhood, and Southern childhood for three quarters of a century," Talmadge charged, accusing Arnall of having gone "further than any white man in America to promote [racial equality] in America." Quoted in Henderson, *Politics of Change in Georgia*, 166–67. On Talmadge's racial antics during the 1946 gubernatorial campaign, see Anderson, *Wild Man from Sugar Creek*, 229–31; and Bartley, *Creation of Modern Georgia*, 201–3.

69. On Talmadge's racial extremism, Carmichael blasted "the doctrine of hate now being preached in Georgia . . . for the purpose of creating a shadow in which [Talmadge and Harris] can hide and attempt to steal this election." And, Carmichael warned, "if we permit the present forces stirring up race hatred in Georgia to continue[,] . . . we will have . . . four years of chaos, turmoil, and bloodshed in Georgia." See James V. Carmichael, WSB Radio broadcast, July 6, 1946, transcript, Draft APR.1993.19.uc-M84-20/49a and 46b, GGDP. Throughout the campaign Carmichael sought to make the Klan the only racial issue, linking both Talmadge, who was endorsed by the Georgia Klan, and Rivers, a former member, to the reconstituted KKK. In Vienna, Georgia, Carmichael flayed his opponents for allegedly affording the Klan significant influence during their former gubernatorial terms: "Georgia cannot have prosperity if the governor uses tax money to endow the imperial wizard of Ku Klux Klan." See *Jackson Advocate*, May 25, 1946, 1; and *Birmingham World*, May 24, 1946, 1. Carmichael often emphasized the need to obey the law and respect the courts as a way to deflect his opponents' attack on the white primary issue. "The welfare of any community . . . depends upon the maintenance of law and order, or respect for the courts, of reasonableness in dealing with one another," Carmichael stated; Talmadge's and Harris's antics aimed "to disturb the good relations that exist in Georgia between the races" by inviting a "disregard for law and . . . an invitation to lawless chaos." Thus, Carmichael continued, "my platform means that the county unit system will be preserved as a part of our law and that control of Georgia politics will remain with the people of our state and will not pass to Roy Harris and his stooges in what its leaders used to call 'occupied territory.'" The preservation of the county unit system and all other laws regulating primary elections, Carmichael promised, "means that the statutes against fraud, against ballot box stuffing, against fake registration lists, against the voting of dead folks on election day, will not be repealed in the interests of any political gain." See James V. Carmichael, WSB Radio broadcast, June 15, 1946, transcript, Draft APR 1993.9.c-M84/29a and 29b, GGDP.

70. Lon Sullivan and George Doss Jr., WSB Radio broadcast, June 25 and July 13, 1946, transcript, Draft APR.1993.14.uc-M84-20/32b and 59a, GGDP. The B-29ers also hurried to affirm Carmichael's southern "legitimacy" by delineating "Jimmy's stand" on race relations: "He adheres to southern racial traditions. [He] was born in, reared in, lives in, and expects to die in Cobb county, Georgia." B-29ers-For-Carmichael-Club, WSB Radio broadcast, July 5, 1946, transcript, Draft APR.1993.20.uc-M84-20/49b and 46a, GGDP.

71. *Augusta Chronicle*, April 9, 1946, 1. Harris and the Crackers usually linked the *Atlanta Journal* (owned by an Ohio native), Ellis Arnall, and the proponents of black voting together into one big Yankee-liberal-black conspiracy to overturn white supremacy in Georgia.

72. *Augusta Herald*, April 9, 1946, 4; Cobb, "Colonel Effingham Crushes the Crackers," 516–17.

73. *Augusta Chronicle*, April 13, 16, 1946. Also see Cobb, "Colonel Effingham Crushes the Crackers," 516–17.

74. In fact, Carmichael believed he did not deserve to be governor after defending a system he believed to be morally wrong. Carmichael interview.

75. Notes on an interview with anonymous, by V. O. Key, Atlanta, March 17 and 25, 1947, in box 8, "Georgia Interviews, 1" folder, SPC.

76. *Atlanta Journal*, April 16, 1946, 10.

77. Law interview. Also see *Savannah Evening Press*, May 27, 1946, 2; *Savannah Morning News*, October 27, 1946, 4; *Savannah Tribune*, November 28, December 5, 19, 1946, and February 6, May 8, 1947; and *Savannah Herald*, February 6, 1947, 1, 8.

78. The *Savannah Evening Press* ran an article by Bill Boring of the *Atlanta Constitution* analyzing Savannah's 1946 election. Boring noted that the large black vote that followed the *Primus King* decision and voter registration efforts in 1946 helped to defeat the Bouhan machine. He also pointed to the city's history of relative tolerance on racial matters, as well as the presence of an entrenched black political organization called the Hub. These factors made Savannah's black political community a more potent political force with real bargaining power at times, something quite uncommon in the rest of Georgia. *Savannah Evening Press*, September 20, 1946.

79. Student League for Good Government, WSB Radio broadcast, July 6, 1946, transcript, Draft APR.1993.11.uc, GGDP.

80. Cobb, "Colonel Effingham Crushes the Crackers," 519 n. 31.

Chapter Six

1. Quotation in Charles Myers Elson, "Three-Governors Controversy of 1947," *Atlanta Historical Bulletin*, series VI:A, box 65, "Three-Governors Controversy" folder, HTP.

2. *Atlanta Constitution*, January 19, 1947, clipping, reel 2, folder 7, SKP.

3. *Atlanta Journal*, January 20, 1947, 14.

4. Supporters of Herman Talmadge's claim to the governor's office relied on a state constitutional provision that awarded to the Georgia General Assembly the power to certify whichever candidate received a majority of unit votes as governor. If no majority existed, the legislature could choose the governor from the two candidates with the highest number of votes. In 1947 the Talmadge faction argued that the elder Talmadge's premature death, and James V. Carmichael's subsequent bowing out of the governor's race after his defeat in the primary election left no clear majority winner. Hence, the legislature had the constitutional right to choose the governor from the two candidates with the highest number of votes in the general election. These candidates were the Republican Talmadge Bowers and Herman Talmadge, who had received a number of write-in votes. The Thompson-Arnall faction disagreed with this interpretation of the state constitution. They relied on the constitutional provision that mandated that the lieutenant governor should succeed if a governor died while in office. Hence, Thompson, as the new lieutenant governor, should assume the office. The problem with this position was that Eu-

gene Talmadge had died before being sworn in; technically, he had been governor-elect only, not governor, when he passed. Moreover, since the office of lieutenant governor was new, no clear precedent on gubernatorial succession existed under the new state constitution. For an overview of this controversy, and the constitutional arguments behind it, see Bartley, *Creation of Modern Georgia*, 203–6.

5. A last-minute discovery of write-in ballots from Talmadge's home county of Telfair gave Herman a narrow margin of victory over James Carmichael and Republican contender Talmadge Bowers. This tally provided Herman's supporters in the legislature the means to legitimate his election, at least initially. Suspicions about these allegedly "lost" returns arose immediately, however, particularly when a reporter for the *Atlanta Journal* published an article claiming that the write-in votes for Herman included names of the dead and departed and were scribbled in the same handwriting. On this controversy and the nefarious political shenanigans in Telfair County, see *Atlanta Constitution*, January 15, March 3, 4, 1947; Kytle, "Long Dark Night for Georgia?" 60; Grant, *Way It Was in the South*, 366–67; and Anderson, *Wild Man from Sugar Creek*, 237.

6. These events are covered in detail in Charles Myers Elson, "Three-Governors Controversy of 1947," *Atlanta Historical Bulletin*, in series VI:A, box 65, "Three-Governors Controversy" folder, HTP. Also see Key, *Southern Politics*, 125; Bartley, *Creation of Modern Georgia*, 204–5; Egerton, *Speak Now Against the Day*, 386–89; and Brattain, *Politics of Whiteness*, 160–61.

7. For more details on this gubernatorial controversy, see Charles Myers Elson, "Three-Governors Controversy of 1947," *Atlanta Historical Bulletin*, 78–83, 91, series VI:A, box 65, "Three-Governors Controversy" folder, HTP.

8. The Georgia constitution provided for a special election to fill an unexpired term, and veterans relied on this clause to justify their demand.

9. *Atlanta Constitution*, January 7, 1947, 1, 5; *Atlanta Journal*, January 8, 1947, 6.

10. Quotation from *Atlanta Journal*, January 8, 1947, 10.

11. *Atlanta Constitution*, January 9, 1947, 5.

12. Ibid., January 14, 1947, 5.

13. *Atlanta Journal*, January 22, 1947, 1.

14. *Atlanta Constitution*, January 20, 1947.

15. *Atlanta Journal*, January 21, 1947, 11.

16. *Atlanta Constitution*, January 20, 1947.

17. Ibid., January 22, 1947, 1–2.

18. Ibid., January 27, 1947, 8.

19. Ibid., January 19, 1947, A-4; "Radio Speech by Honorable Pierre Howard," in box 6, folder 24, ACSP.

20. *Atlanta Constitution*, January 28, 1947, 1, 10.

21. Ibid., February 2, 1947, B-6.

22. This figure is derived from the roll call vote of the state legislature published in *Atlanta Constitution*, January 16, 1947, 7.

23. On efforts to circumvent the *Smith v. Allwright* decision in the Deep South, see Key, *Southern Politics*, 625–43.

24. Quotation from ibid., 636.

25. *Atlanta Constitution*, January 21, 1947, 7; Georgia Department of Archives and History, *Journal of the House of Representatives of the State of Georgia*, January 13, 1947.

26. Quotation from *Atlanta Constitution*, January 30, 1947, 1, 6.

27. Georgia Department of Archives and History, *Journal of the House of Representatives of the State of Georgia*, January 13, 1947, 166–67.

28. Quotation from *Atlanta Constitution*, January 30, 1947, 1, 6.

29. Ibid., January 28, 1947, 1.

30. Quotation from ibid., February 27, 1947, 1, 12. Also see ibid., January 27, 1947, 1, 11, and January 30, 1947, 1, 6.

31. Ibid., January 30, 1947, 1, 6.

32. Ibid., January 29, 1947, 2, February 9, 1947, A-14.

33. Ibid., January 30, 1947, 1, 6.

34. Ibid.

35. Ibid.

36. Zieger, in *Organized Labor in the Twentieth-Century South*, 4, notes the important role southern states played during and after World War II in "pioneering" right-to-work legislation.

37. On the Taft-Hartley Act see Zieger, *CIO*, 245–52.

38. On the Taft-Hartley Act and southern right-to-work statutes, see Foster, *Union Politic*, 49; Zieger, *CIO*, 212–15, 226, 246–47; Cobb, *Selling of the South*, 101; Marshall, *Labor in the South*, 323–31; and Bartley, *New South*, 49–50.

39. Georgia Department of Archives and History, *Journal of the House of Representatives of the State of Georgia*, January 13, 1947, 465–66. Legislators ultimately consolidated most of the provisions of HB 72 and 73 into one bill that included provisions against union security and picketing. The only enumerated roll call offered into the House record, however, was for HB 72, which is the emphasis here.

40. *Atlanta Constitution*, January 21, 1947; Georgia Department of Archives and History, *Georgia Official and Statistical Register*, 1945–1950.

41. *Atlanta Constitution*, February 19, 1947, 1, February 26, 1947, 10.

42. On these veterans and HB 72, see Georgia Department of Archives and History, *Journal of the House of Representatives of the State of Georgia*, January 13, 1947, 305, 361–69. For the state congressional districts see the maps in Georgia Department of Archives and History, *Georgia Official and Statistical Register*. Also see *Atlanta Constitution*, August 11, 1946, A-11.

43. See Georgia Department of Archives and History, *Journal of the House of Representatives of the State of Georgia*, January 13, 1947, 465–66.

44. On the reasons that industry moved South, see Cobb, *Selling of the South*, 102.

45. Zieger, *Organized Labor in the Twentieth-Century South*, 6, also notes that an important and continuous "prong" in the "southern anti-union strategy" was relying on a low wage and "union-free" environment to recruit new industry and retain existing enterprises.

46. Cobb, *Selling of the South*, 101–2, 104–5.

47. *Atlanta Constitution*, May 20, 1948, 1; Frederickson, *Dixiecrat Revolt*, 107.

48. On Talmadge's plans for the 1948 election, see Bartley, *Creation of Modern Georgia*,

204; on Talmadge's "royalist" pretensions, see Egerton, *Speak Now Against the Day*, 483. Also see *Atlanta Constitution*, February 8, 1948, A-2.

49. *Atlanta Constitution*, February 24, 1948, 1.

50. Ibid., March 30, 1948, 5.

51. On black registration during 1948, see Grant, *Way It Was in the South*, 368; *Atlanta Constitution*, September 5, 1948, 1; Shelby Myrick to James S. Peters, March 1, 1948, box 1, "Delegates to the 1948 Macon Convention" volume, GSDECP.

52. *Atlanta Constitution*, September 5, 1948, 1.

53. John Egerton refers to the "unmistakable rise of race relations as a primary and continuing social issue." In the late postwar 1940s, "it was to become the single most urgent and unyielding public issue—certainly for the South and eventually for the nation." See Egerton, *Speak Now Against the Day*, 487. On this heightened attention to the issue of race in Georgia and the South, also see Frederickson, *Dixiecrat Revolt*.

54. Frederickson, *Dixiecrat Revolt*, 57–58.

55. Ibid., 64–65.

56. Bartley, *New South*, 75.

57. For the most recent treatment of the impact of the Truman Civil Rights Commission and the Dixiecrat revolt, including in Georgia, see Frederickson, *Dixiecrat Revolt*.

58. Quoted in ibid., 162. For an example of the attack by the Talmadge campaign on Thompson for his veto of the white primary bill in 1947, see *Atlanta Constitution*, March 30, 1948, 5.

59. Frederickson, *Dixiecrat Revolt*, 158–64.

60. Henderson, *Politics of Change in Georgia*, 210; *Atlanta Constitution*, February 24, 1948, 1.

61. Herman Talmadge "Talmadge Victory Song," by Rayford W. Thorpe, in box 6, folder 15, 1948 State Democratic Primary, ACSP.

62. *Atlanta Constitution*, July 30, 1948, 7.

63. Frederickson, *Dixiecrat Revolt*, 162.

64. See comments by Senator Bill Dean, Thompson campaign aide and chairman of the state Democratic Rules Committee, in *Atlanta Constitution*, September 13, 1947, 1.

65. Roy V. Harris, transcript of interview, folder, Politics, 4, 5, AVA:86-1:3, Roy V. Harris Papers, Russell Library, University of Georgia, Athens, Ga. Also see *Atlanta Constitution*, August 22, 1948, A-15; and Bartley, *Creation of Modern Georgia*, 202, 206.

66. On the Talmadge strategy in 1946, see Bartley, *Creation of Modern Georgia*, 193.

67. On the barbecue see *Atlanta Constitution*, July 4, 1948, A-4; and on the fish fry, see ibid., August 22, 1948, A-15.

68. Muscogee County Talmadge Club to Veterans, August 18, 1948, box 6, folder 20, ACSP.

69. *Atlanta Constitution*, August 24, 1948, 3. On other veterans appearing with Talmadge in 1948, see *Atlanta Constitution*, August 22, 1948, A-14–15.

70. Henderson, *Politics of Change in Georgia*, 212–13.

71. On the outcome of the 1948 gubernatorial primary in Georgia, see ibid.

72. James S. Peters to T. Ross Sharpe, April 3, 1948, box 1, "Macon Convention, 1948" volume, GSDECP.

73. *Atlanta Constitution*, February 4, 1948, 1, and February 5, 1948, 6. Also see Grant, *Way It Was in the South*, 368.

74. *Atlanta Constitution*, March 3, 1948, 1. Also see Grant, *Way It Was in the South*, 367–68.

75. *Atlanta Constitution*, March 23, 1948, 6.

76. Grant, *Way It Was in the South*, 368.

77. Stone Mountain, July 23, 1948, reel 1, box 1, folder 4, SKP. This activism by the Klan prompted Governor Thompson to accuse Talmadge of using the extralegal order to issue "pre-vote" threats to keep blacks away from the polls in the fall primary. Most observers believed that the majority of black registrants supported the Thompson campaign. See *Atlanta Constitution*, March 25, 1948, 7.

78. Franklin H. Williams to Henry Lee Moon, November 26, 1948, reel 7 (883), pt. 4, NAACPP.

79. The men also offered to compensate Carter for his effort, and he apparently accepted, a fact that later NAACP investigators, bent on publicizing the Carter-Nixon case, privately decided was "less than pertinent to the issue at hand." Dover T. Carter, sworn affidavit, September 18, 1948, reel 7 (864), pt. 4, NAACPP; Franklin H. Williams to Henry Lee Moon, November 26, 1948, reel 7 (883), pt. 4, NAACPP.

80. Franklin H. Williams to Henry Lee Moon, November 26, 1948, reel 7 (883), pt. 4, NAACPP.

81. Ibid.; Press release, reel 8 (326), pt. 4, NAACPP.

82. Dover T. Carter, sworn affidavit, September 18, 1948, reel 7 (864), pt. 4, NAACPP.

83. Ibid.

84. Ibid.

85. Ibid.

86. Ibid.

87. On Isaac Nixon's murder see Grant, *Way It Was in the South*, 368; *New York Times*, September 12, 1948, clipping, reel 8 (288), pt. 4, NAACPP; and Austin T. Walden to Francis Williams, Assistant Special Counsel of NAACP, October 21, 1948, reel 8 (313), pt. 4, NAACPP.

88. *New York Times*, September 12, 1948, clipping, reel 8 (288), pt. 4, NAACPP.

89. Franklin H. Williams to Henry Lee Moon, November 26, 1948, reel 7 (883), pt. 4, NAACPP.

90. A. T. Walden to Francis Williams, October 21, 1948, reel 8 (313), pt. 4, NAACPP.

91. Ralph Mark Gilbert to Francis Williams, October 14, 1948, reel 7 (867), pt. 4, NAACPP.

92. Press release, reel 8 (326), pt. 4, NAACPP.

93. On Mallard's case see Grant, *Way It Was in the South*, 368. On George Dorsey's see above, chap. 2.

94. On the pressure exerted by the civil rights movement, federal intervention, and an increased regional dependence on federal revenues in the 1960s on the regional attachment to an absolute defense of white supremacy, see Schulman, *From Cotton Belt to Sunbelt*, 132. In *Southern Businessmen and Desegregation*, 3–6, Jacoway and Colburn conclude that the dependence on continuing industrial development and recruitment and the

pressures of the civil rights movement together eventually moved prominent white southern businessmen in the 1950s and 1960s away from massive resistance toward integration and toward an acceptance that change in racial matters was inevitable. Although they never became integrationists per se, and the desegregation they supported often was "calculated to preserve the image of progressiveness while yielding a minimum of desegregation," their efforts to lead their cities toward change did make a difference. A city such as Atlanta, which had a powerful business-civic elite who backed moderation and at least some compliance with *Brown*, found itself far less disrupted by massive resistance and civil rights protests than cities such as Birmingham, where a strong core of economic pragmatism was far less evident. Also see Hornsby, "City That Was Too Busy to Hate," 120–36.

95. In *From Cotton Belt to Sunbelt*, 164, Schulman also notes that the focus on industrial recruitment among state and local governments after the war in the South had a detrimental impact on union growth in the region. The "favorable business climate" that new industries allegedly loved, such as "right-to-work laws, low taxes, and industrial recruitment programs," went hand in hand with "anti-union legislation" that impeded unionization.

96. "Resolution on Anti-labor Legislation," September 21, 1947, Mss. 129A, subseries 10A, box 21, "Southern Wage Conference" folder, TWUAP.

97. Horace White to Isadore Katz, TWUA General Counsel, October 19, 1945, Mss. 396, box 156, "Athens Manufacturing Company Strike, 1945, Restraining Order and Injunction" folder, TWUAP.

98. Ibid.

99. *Atlanta Constitution*, May 12, 1948, 1; Joe Pedigo, affidavit, November 20, 1947, box 209, folder 2, NLRBR.

100. Report by Joe Pedigo to Emil Rieve, 1950, Mss. 129A, subseries 2A, box 6, "J. D. Pedigo—1950, Northwest Georgia Joint Board" folder, TWUAP.

101. "Resolution on Anti-labor Legislation," September 21, 1947, Mss. 129A, subseries 10A, box 21, "Southern Wage Conference" folder, TWUAP.

102. Dave Burgess to author, November 18, 1999. The immediate political impact of these provisions, however, was first to galvanize the GA-PAC and its constituent locals into action. As the GA-PAC chairman remarked, "passage of anti-labor legislation and anti-social laws in the state and Nation cannot be charged against lack of pressure in so far as the CIO workers of Georgia [are] concerned." PAC organizer Hugh Gammon, for example, conducted a furious house-to-house canvass, "securing petitions, letters, telegrams and telephone calls to representatives in the state and the Nation's Capitol." Workers in Georgia's textile communities, particularly Aragon and Cedartown, followed suit, obtaining "thousands of signatures on petitions urging state representatives to vote against anti-labor–anti-social legislation in the State." The Northwest Georgia Joint Board mailed copies of a publication entitled "Truth About Unions" to fifty state legislators, and the GA-PAC chairman and a large committee of Georgia unionists called on Governor Thompson to urge his veto. The failure of this grassroots effort, according to the GA-PAC chairman, could be attributed to the "past indifference of labor" and "should serve as a warning that we must re-double our political efforts so that the present cannot be blamed for indifference when the future comes." See Georgia State Political Action Com-

mittee, Report of Chairman, 1947, Proceedings, Annual Convention, Georgia State Industrial Union Council, Macon, September 26–28, 1947, folder 71, DPP.

That "redoubled" political effort produced some surprising victories in the local and state elections of 1948. The GA-PAC intensified its voter registration drives, particularly in counties with a labor presence. Labor-backed candidates for the state legislature won seats in Polk, Greene, Whitfield, Floyd, Haralson, and Walker Counties, replacing representatives who voted for passage of the antilabor bills. In Haralson County, for example, James R. Murphy, who had supported the bills, was defeated by "a new man who . . . will be a good state legislator man and friendly to labor." Georgia CIO staff reported that TWUA Locals 246 and 937 in Walker County similarly helped to defeat "two representatives who voted for state anti-labor legislation" by endorsing "two new ones that are favorable to us"; and Whitfield County gained two new representatives and a state senator who "is very good and friendly to labor." Moreover, TWUA representative J. P. Mooney reported that in Sumter County, "we was [sic] successful in unseating [a] Representative Jennings who introduced the anti-labor bill in the lower house of the state legislature last year." Several of these new representatives were World War II veterans. See Ken Douty to Al Barkan, September 10, 1948, Mss. 396, box 479, "Georgia, 1948" folder, TWUAP; Al Barkan to Emil Rieve, September 16, 1948, and report to Rieve and George Baldanzi, April 6, 1948, both in Mss. 396, box 480, "PAC Departmental Reports, 1948" folder, TWUAP; Staff Report, Mss. 396, box 479, "Staff Reports, 1948, Hugh Gammon" folder, TWUAP; J. P. Mooney to Al Barkan, March 10, 1948, Mss. 396, box 479, "Georgia, 1948" folder, TWUAP.

103. "NLRB Proceedings," 5, Report by H. D. Lisk, Annual Meeting of Georgia Local Unions, TWUA, CIO, December 9–10, 1950, Mss. 129A, subseries 2A, box 6, "H. D. Lisk, Georgia State Director, 1950" folder, TWUAP.

104. Cobb, *Selling of the South*, 98, 254.

105. Ibid., 103.

106. Talmadge interview. Numan Bartley also sees Herman Talmadge as an embodiment of the conservative approach to modernization produced by the war. See *Creation of Modern Georgia*, 193, 202–6, 211–12, 215.

107. Bartley, *Creation of Modern Georgia*, 206.

108. Pajari, "Herman Talmadge and the Politics of Power," 76, 81–85.

109. Frederickson, *Dixiecrat Revolt*, 219. Also see *New York Times*, June 6, 1950; and Egerton, *Speak Now Against the Day*, 574. Indeed, white veterans who had fought overseas against discriminatory and undemocratic regimes led the white South's massive resistance to integration in the 1950s and 1960s. Governor George Wallace of Alabama, a former World War II bomber flight engineer, called for "Segregation Forever" rather than allow the integration of the University of Alabama. See Carter, *Politics of Rage*, 55, 60–61. Governor Orville Faubus of Arkansas, also a World War II flight engineer, prompted the nationalization of the state guard in 1957 when he defied a presidential order to integrate the state's public schools. He ended up shutting down the entire school system for a complete year rather than bend to federal will. See Blair, *Arkansas Politics and Government*, 17; and Bartley, *Rise of Massive Resistance*, 142, 265–67. During Mississippi's civil rights movement of the 1950s and 1960s, a World War II paratrooper from Mississippi named Robert Patterson founded the segregationist White Citizens Council, while a former Ma-

rine veteran of the Pacific theater named Byron de la Beckwith murdered NAACP activist Medgar Evers. See Cobb, *Most Southern Place on Earth*, 213, 228; and Nossiter, *Of Long Memory*, 117.

110. For a brief biographical sketch of Herman Talmadge, see ‹http://wwwlib.gsu.edu/spcoll/collections/GGDP/talmadge.htm› (February 10, 2004).

111. Quoted in Schulman, *From Cotton Belt to Sunbelt*, 124.

112. Coleman, *Georgia History in Outline*, 103; Cobb, "Georgia Odyssey," 62–63.

113. On Georgia and Atlanta's transition from segregation to integration, see Cobb, "Georgia Odyssey," 50–55.

114. In *From Cotton Belt to Sunbelt*, 151, Schulman notes, for example, that the military defense spending that did so much to fill southern industrial coffers and build Sunbelt prosperity actually perpetuated social and economic disparities even as it turned the South into the nation's fastest-growing region. The defense establishment, he concludes, brought in the revenue to build highways, airports, "research facilities," and expansion in "higher education," but it neglected "welfare, job training, [and] primary education." Thus, "southern business progressives could develop their states without providing economic opportunities for blacks or the poor."

115. In the Sunbelt South, James Cobb has argued, "a surplus of underemployed, unskilled labor," a continued devotion to forestalling unionization, "depressed wages," and disparities in living standards among blacks and whites, middle class and working class, and city and country still characterized southern society, despite the significant economic growth and development that had also occurred since World War II. "The Sunbelt remained a paradox," he concludes, in that "its recent gains and excellent prospects for future growth, as well as many of its most serious deficiencies, were closely related to the policies that had shaped its economic development." See Cobb, *Selling of the South*, 260, 265. Also see Schulman, *From Cotton Belt to Sunbelt*, 174–205.

Conclusion

1. Quotation from remark by James C. Cobb in an E-mail to author, January 8, 2003. Originally quoted by Cobb in *Selling of the South*, 141, as a remark by Sunbelt Georgia governor Carl Sanders. Also see Bartley, *New South*, 256.

2. Many thanks to James C. Cobb, in an E-mail to author, January 8, 2003, for suggesting this portrayal of Georgia's Bourbon leadership at the war's end.

3. The divisiveness of the immediate postwar years among whites in Georgia began to recede, Bartley has concluded, but the Talmadge program also "propitiated business, opposed organized labor, courted outside investors, and denigrated black people." See *Creation of Modern Georgia*, 207.

4. See, for example, Dittmer, *Local People*, 9; and Tyson, *Radio Free Dixie*, 29, 48–62.

5. See Bartley, *Rise of Massive Resistance*; and Frederickson, *Dixiecrat Revolt*.

6. On the initial process of desegregation in Georgia, see Cobb, *Selling of the South*, 127, as well as *Georgia Odyssey*, 64. In *Selling of the South*, 142, Cobb also notes that significant differences existed between how Atlanta's economic, political, and civic leaders confronted the civil rights movement and how their counterparts in Mississippi and Alabama reacted. Although he concludes that a definitive relationship between the level of

industrial development in a southern state and its approach to desegregation is difficult to establish with certainty, nonetheless Atlanta's civic-business elites had more "clout" in Georgia, and desegregation there did proceed more smoothly and peacefully, however limited it might have been, than in Mississippi or Alabama. For a similar explanation, see the essays in Jacoway and Colburn, *Southern Businessmen and Desegregation.*

Bibliography

Manuscript Collections

Athens, Ga.
  University of Georgia
    Russell Library
      Georgia State Democratic Executive Committee Papers
      Roy V. Harris Papers
      Prince Preston Papers
      Richard B. Russell Papers
      Herman Talmadge Papers
    Special Collections, Hargrett Library
      Chicopee Manufacturing Company Papers
Atlanta, Ga.
  Atlanta History Center
    Grace Towns Hamilton Papers
  Atlanta University Center
    Clarence Bacote Papers
    League of Women Voters of Georgia Papers
    Southern Regional Council Archives, Veteran Services Project (microfilm)
    Robert Thompson Biographical File
  Emory University, Special Collections and Archives, Woodruff Library
    James V. Carmichael Papers
    Ralph McGill Papers
    Glenn T. Rainey Papers
    James Setze Jr. Papers, World War II Miscellany Collection

Georgia Department of Archives and History
  Lamar Q. Ball Collection
Georgia State University
  Southern Labor Archives
    AFL-CIO, Region 8, Papers
    Amalgamated Clothing and Textile Workers Union of America, Northwest
      Georgia, Records, 1949–1976
    Chattanooga Area Labor Council Records
    United Steelworkers of America, District 35, Papers
  Special Collections and Archives, Pullen Library
    Georgia Government Documentation Project
    Stetson Kennedy Papers (microfilm)
Chapel Hill, N.C.
  University of North Carolina
    Southern Historical Collection, Wilson Library
      Daniel Powell Papers
      Southern Oral History Program Collection
College Park, Md.
  National Archives and Records Administration II
    National Labor Relations Board Records, Record Group 25
    Third Army Command, Domestic Intelligence Reports, Record Group 319
Columbus, Ga.
  Columbus State University, Archives, Schwob Library
    Alva C. Smith Papers
Durham, N.C.
  Duke University, Special Collections, Perkins Library
    Lucy Randolph Mason Papers (microfilm)
    Operation Dixie: The CIO Organizing Committee Papers (microfilm)
Knoxville, Tenn.
  University of Tennessee, Knoxville
    Documents and Microforms, Hodges Library
      Papers of the National Association for the Advancement of Colored People
        (microfilm)
    Special Collections and Archives, Hoskins Library
      Estes Kefauver Papers
La Grange, Ga.
  Troup County Archives
    Fred Hand Family and Business Papers
Madison, Wis.
  State Historical Society of Wisconsin
    Textile Workers Union of America Papers
    United Packinghouse Workers of America Papers
Nashville, Tenn.
  Vanderbilt University, Special Collections and Archives, Heard Library
    Southern Politics Collection

Washington, D.C.
    Library of Congress
        Gilbert Harrison Papers

Government Publications

Georgia Department of Archives and History. *Georgia Official and Statistical Register.*
    1945–1950.
———. *Journal of the House of Representatives of the State of Georgia.* January 13, 1947.
Georgia Department of Labor. "Tenth Annual Report: To the Governor and the General Assembly, 1946." Microfilm, Box 17, Drawer 311, Record Group 16-1-1, Georgia
    Department of Archives and History, Atlanta, Ga.
U.S. Bureau of the Census. *Sixteenth Census of the United States, 1940.* Vol. 1, *Population.*
    Washington: Government Printing Office, 1940.
———. *Seventeenth Census of the United States, 1950.* Vol. 2, pt. 2, *Population: Georgia.*
    Washington: Government Printing Office, 1950.
———. *State and County QuickFacts.* ‹http://quickfacts.census.gov/gfd/states/
    13000.html›. February 7, 2004.
U.S. Congress. Senate. Committee on Labor and Public Welfare. *Hearing before the Subcommittee on Labor-Management Relations: Labor-Management Relations in the
    Southern Textile Manufacturing Industry.* 81st Cong., 2d sess., August 21–24, 1950.
    Washington: Government Printing Office, 1950.

Interviews

Alverson, Luther. Interview by Anne Larcom, October 11, 1990. Audio tape, Georgia
    Government Documentation Project, Special Collections and Archives, Pullen Library, Georgia State University, Atlanta, Ga.
Ashmore, Harry. Interview by John Egerton, June 16, 1990. Interview A-353, transcript,
    Southern Oral History Program, Southern Historical Collection, Wilson Library,
    University of North Carolina, Chapel Hill, N.C.
Bell, Griffin. Interview by Cliff Kuhn, September 19, 1990. Transcript Series B, transcript, Georgia Government Documentation Project, Special Collections and Archives, Pullen Library, Georgia State University, Atlanta, Ga.
Bohannon, Horace. Interview by David Onkst, June 16, 1989. MS 2854, audio tapes,
    Hargrett Library, University of Georgia, Athens, Ga.
Burgess, David. Interview by William Finger, September 25, 1974. Labor History Series,
    E-1, transcript, Southern Oral History Program, Southern Historical Collection,
    Wilson Library, University of North Carolina, Chapel Hill, N.C.
Carmichael, James V. Interview by James Mackay and Calvin Kytle, July 23, 1947, "Who
    Runs Georgia?" Transcript Series B, manuscript, Georgia Government Documentation Project, Special Collections and Archives, Pullen Library, Georgia State University, Atlanta, Ga.
Combs, Doyle. Interview by A. K. Umoja, October 13, 1989. Audio tape, Georgia Gov-

ernment Documentation Project, Special Collections and Archives, Pullen Library, Georgia State University, Atlanta, Ga.

Duke, Daniel. Interview by Peggy Bulger, February 2, 1990. Transcript Series K, transcript, Georgia Government Documentation Project, Special Collections and Archives, Pullen Library, Georgia State University, Atlanta, Ga.

Flanagan, Robert. Interview by Cliff Kuhn, January 9, 1989. Transcript Series E, transcript, Georgia Government Documentation Project, Special Collections and Archives, Pullen Library, Georgia State University, Atlanta, Ga.

Fleming, Harold. Interview by John Egerton, January 24, 1990. Interview A-363, transcript, Southern Oral History Program, Southern Historical Collection, Wilson Library, University of North Carolina, Chapel Hill, N.C.

Flynt, John J. Interview by James Mackay and Calvin Kytle, July 13, 1947, "Who Runs Georgia?" Transcript Series B, manuscript, Georgia Government Documentation Project, Special Collections and Archives, Pullen Library, Georgia State University, Atlanta, Ga.

Gadsen, R. W. Interview by James Mackay and Calvin Kytle, July 10, 1947. "Who Runs Georgia?" Transcript Series B, manuscript, Georgia Government Documentation Project, Special Collections and Archives, Pullen Library, Georgia State University, Atlanta, Ga.

Hagan, Booker T. Interview by Duane Stewart, October 14, 1989. Audio tape, Georgia Government Documentation Project, Special Collections and Archives, Pullen Library, Georgia State University, Atlanta, Ga.

Heard, Alexander. Interview by John Egerton, July 17, 1991. Interview A-344, transcript, Southern Oral History Program, Southern Historical Collection, Wilson Library, University of North Carolina, Chapel Hill, N.C.

Henderson, Jacob. Interview by Cliff Kuhn, July 24, 1992. Series L, video tape, Georgia Government Documentation Project, Special Collections and Archives, Pullen Library, Georgia State University, Atlanta, Ga.

———. Interview by Duane Stewart, June 8, 1989. Transcript Series E, transcript, Georgia Government Documentation Project, Special Collections and Archives, Pullen Library, Georgia State University, Atlanta, Ga.

Kidd, Culver. Interview by John Allen, October 3, 1988. Transcript Series B, transcript, Georgia Government Documentation Project, Special Collections and Archives, Pullen Library, Georgia State University, Atlanta, Ga.

Kytle, Calvin and Elizabeth. Interview by John Egerton, January 1, 1991. Interview A-365, transcript, Southern Oral History Program, Southern Historical Collection, Wilson Library, University of North Carolina, Chapel Hill, N.C.

Law, W. W. Interview by Cliff Kuhn, November 15–16, 1990. Transcript Series E, transcript, Georgia Government Documentation Project, Special Collections and Archives, Pullen Library, Georgia State University, Atlanta, Ga.

Mackay, James. Interview by author, July 22, 2000. Notes in possession of the author.

———. Interview by Cliff Kuhn, March 18, 1986, and March 31, 1987. Transcript Series B, transcripts, Georgia Government Documentation Project, Special Collections and Archives, Pullen Library, Georgia State University, Atlanta, Ga.

McPheeters, Annie. Interview by Kathryn Nasstrom, June 8, 1992. Transcript Series J, transcript, Georgia Government Documentation Project, Special Collections and Archives, Pullen Library, Georgia State University, Atlanta, Ga.

Rabun, Joseph. Interview by Calvin Kytle and James Mackay, [1947], "Who Runs Georgia?" Transcript Series B, Pt. 2, manuscript, Georgia Government Documentation Project, Special Collections and Archives, Pullen Library, Georgia State University, Atlanta, Ga.

Sheppard, Cornelius. Interview by Cliff Kuhn, October 14, 1989. Audio tape, Georgia Government Documentation Project, Special Collections and Archives, Pullen Library, Georgia State University, Atlanta, Ga.

Stoney, George. Interview by John Egerton, June 13, 1991. Interview A-346, transcript, Southern Oral History Program, Southern Historical Collection, Wilson Library, University of North Carolina, Chapel Hill, N.C.

Talmadge, Herman. Interview by Harold Paulk Henderson, July 17, 1987. Transcript Series A, transcript, Georgia Government Documentation Project, Special Collections and Archives, Pullen Library, Georgia State University, Atlanta, Ga.

Thompson, Robert. Interview by Duane Stewart, June 5, 1989. Transcript Series B, transcript, Georgia Government Documentation Project, Special Collections and Archives, Pullen Library, Georgia State University, Atlanta, Ga.

Newspapers and Periodicals

Americus (Ga.) Times-Recorder, 1946–47.
Americus (Ga.) Tri-County News, 1946.
Atlanta Constitution, 1945–49.
Atlanta Daily World, 1946–47.
Atlanta Journal, 1945–49.
Atlanta Journal-Constitution, 1998.
Augusta Chronicle, 1946–48.
Augusta Herald, 1946–48.
Birmingham (Ala.) World, 1946.
Bradley County (Tenn.) Journal, 1946.
Brunswick (Ga.) News, 1945–46.
Cedartown (Ga.) Daily Standard, 1946–49.
Coffee County (Ga.) Progress, 1946.
Columbus (Ga.) Enquirer, 1946.
Douglas (Ga.) Weekly Enterprise, 1946.
Gainesville (Ga.) Eagle, 1946–47.
Gainesville (Ga.) News, 1946–47.
Greensboro (Ga.) Herald-Journal, 1946.
Huntsville (Ala.) Times, 1946.
Jackson (Miss.) Advocate, 1946.
La Grange (Ga.) Life, 1946.
Memphis (Tenn.) World, 1946–48.
Montgomery (Ala.) Advertiser, 1946.
Nashville (Tenn.) Tennessean, 1946.

New Orleans (La.) Times-Picayune, 1946.

New York Times, 1946.

Polk County (Tenn.) News, 1946.

Raleigh (N.C.) News and Observer, 1996.

Savannah Evening Press, 1946–47.

Savannah Herald, 1946–48.

Savannah Morning News, 1946–47.

Savannah Tribune, 1946–48.

The (Ga.) Statesman, 1946–47.

Textile Labor, 1945–48.

Valdosta (Ga.) Daily Times, 1946.

Washington Post, 1946.

Washington Times, 1996.

Waycross (Ga.) Journal-Herald, 1946.

Books

Alexander, Charles C. *The Ku Klux Klan in the Southwest*. Lexington: University of Kentucky Press, 1965.

Allsup, Carl. *The American GI Forum: Origins and Evolution*. Austin: Center for Mexican-American Studies of the University of Texas, 1982.

Anderson, William. *The Wild Man from Sugar Creek: The Political Career of Eugene Talmadge*. Baton Rouge: Louisiana State University Press, 1975.

Ashmore, Harry. *Hearts and Minds: The Anatomy of Racism from Roosevelt to Reagan*. New York: McGraw-Hill, 1982.

Ayers, Edward L. *The Promise of the New South: Life After Reconstruction*. New York: Oxford University Press, 1992.

Barnard, William D. *Dixiecrats and Democrats: Alabama, 1942–1950*. University, Ala.: University of Alabama Press, 1974.

Barnes, Catherine Anne. *Journey from Jim Crow: The Desegregation of Southern Transit*. New York: Columbia University Press, 1983.

Bartley, Numan V. *The Creation of Modern Georgia*. 2d ed. Athens: University of Georgia Press, 1990.

———. *The New South, 1945–1980*. Baton Rouge: Louisiana State University Press, 1995.

———. *The Rise of Massive Resistance: Race and Politics in the South during the 1950s*. Baton Rouge: Louisiana State University Press, 1969.

Bass, Jack, and Walter Devries. *The Transformation of Southern Politics: Political Consequences since 1945*. New York: Basic Books, 1976.

Bayor, Ronald H. *Race and the Shaping of Twentieth-Century Atlanta*. Chapel Hill: University of North Carolina Press, 1996.

Bederman, Gail. *Manliness and Civilization: A Cultural History of Gender and Race in the United States, 1880–1917*. Chicago: University of Chicago Press, 1995.

Berman, William C. *The Politics of Civil Rights in the Truman Administration*. Columbus: Ohio State University Press, 1970.

Bernard, Richard M., and Bradley R. Rice, eds. *Sunbelt Cities: Politics and Growth Since World War II.* Austin: University of Texas Press, 1983.

Bernd, Joseph L. *Grass Roots Politics in Georgia: The County Unit System and the Importance of the Individual Voting Community in Bi-Factional Elections, 1942–1954.* Atlanta: Emory University Research Committee, 1960.

Bernstein, Alison R. *American Indians and World War II: Toward a New Era in Indian Affairs.* Norman: University of Oklahoma Press, 1991.

Blair, Diane D. *Arkansas Politics and Government: Do the People Rule?* Lincoln: University of Nebraska Press, 1988.

Blum, John Morton. *V Was for Victory: Politics and American Culture during World War II.* New York: Harcourt Brace Jovanovich, 1976.

Bolte, Charles. *The New Veteran.* New York: Reynal and Hitchcock, 1945.

Boyer, Paul S., Clifford Clark Jr., Joseph F. Kett, Neal Salisbury, Harvard Sitkoff, and Nancy Woloch. *The Enduring Vision: A History of the American People.* Vol. 2: *From 1865.* 5th ed. Boston and New York: Houghton Mifflin, 2004.

Brattain, Michelle. *The Politics of Whiteness: Race, Workers, and Culture in the Modern South.* Princeton, N.J.: Princeton University Press, 2001.

Brinkley, Alan. *The End of Reform: New Deal Liberalism in Recession and War.* New York: Alfred A. Knopf, 1995.

Brokaw, Tom. *The Greatest Generation.* New York: Random House, 1999.

Brundage, W. Fitzhugh. *Lynching in the New South: Georgia and Virginia, 1880–1930.* Urbana: University of Illinois Press, 1993.

Buchanan, A. Russell. *Black Americans in World War II.* Santa Barbara, Calif.: Clio Books, 1977.

Byrum, C. Stephen. *The Battle of Athens.* Chattanooga, Tenn.: Paidia Productions, 1987.

Carter, Dan T. *The Politics of Rage: George Wallace, the Origins of the New Conservatism, and the Transformation of American Liberalism.* Baton Rouge: Louisiana State University Press, 1995.

Cash, W. J. *The Mind of the South.* New York: Alfred A. Knopf, 1941.

Cecelski, David S., and Timothy B. Tyson, eds. *Democracy Betrayed: The Wilmington Race Riot of 1898 and Its Legacy.* Chapel Hill: University of North Carolina Press, 1998.

Cobb, James C. *Georgia Odyssey.* Athens: University of Georgia Press, 1997.

———. *Industrialization and Southern Society, 1877–1984.* Lexington: University Press of Kentucky, 1984; Chicago: Dorsey Press, 1988.

———. *The Most Southern Place on Earth: The Mississippi Delta and the Roots of Regional Identity.* New York: Oxford University Press, 1992.

———. *The Selling of the South: The Southern Crusade for Industrial Recruitment, 1936–1990.* 2d ed. Urbana: University of Illinois Press, 1993.

Cohodas, Nadine. *Strom Thurmond and the Politics of Change.* New York: Simon and Schuster, 1993.

Cole, Taylor, and John H. Hallowell, eds. *The Southern Political Scene, 1938–1948.* Gainesville, Fla.: Kallman Publishing Company, 1948.

Coleman, Kenneth, ed. *Georgia History in Outline.* Rev. ed. Athens: University of Georgia Press, 1978.

———. *A History of Georgia.* Athens: University of Georgia Press, 1977.

Cronenberg, Allen. *Forth to the Mighty Conflict: Alabama and World War II*. Tuscaloosa: University of Alabama Press, 1995.

Dailey, Jane, Glenda Elizabeth Gilmore, and Bryant Simon. *Jumpin' Jim Crow: Southern Politics from Civil War to Civil Rights*. Princeton, N.J.: Princeton University Press, 2000.

Dalfiume, Richard. *Desegregation of the United States Armed Forces: Fighting on Two Fronts, 1939–1953*. Columbia: University of Missouri Press, 1969.

Daniel, Pete. *Breaking the Land: The Transformation of Cotton, Rice, and Tobacco Cultures since 1880*. Urbana: University of Illinois Press, 1985.

———. *Lost Revolutions: The South in the 1950s*. Chapel Hill: University of North Carolina Press for the Smithsonian National Museum of American History, 2000.

Davies, Wallace Evan. *Patriotism on Parade: The Story of Veterans' and Hereditary Organizations in America, 1783–1900*. Cambridge, Mass.: Harvard University Press, 1955.

Dittmer, John. *Local People: The Struggle for Civil Rights in Mississippi*. Urbana: University of Illinois Press, 1994.

Eby-Ebersole, Sarah, and Zell Miller. *Signed, Sealed, and Delivered: Highlights of the Miller Record*. Macon, Ga.: Mercer University Press, 1999.

Egerton, John. *Speak Now Against the Day: The Generation Before the Civil Rights Movement in the South*. Chapel Hill: University of North Carolina Press, 1994.

Eskew, Glenn T. *But for Birmingham: The Local and National Movements in the Civil Rights Struggle*. Chapel Hill: University of North Carolina Press, 1997.

Fairclough, Adam. *Race and Democracy: The Civil Rights Struggle in Louisiana, 1915–1972*. Athens: University of Georgia Press, 1995.

Flamming, Douglas. *Creating the Modern South: Millhands and Managers in Dalton, Georgia, 1884–1984*. Chapel Hill: University of North Carolina Press, 1992.

Foster, James Caldwell. *The Union Politic: The CIO Political Action Committee*. Columbia: University of Missouri Press, 1975.

Frederickson, Kari. *The Dixiecrat Revolt and the End of the Solid South, 1932–1968*. Chapel Hill: University of North Carolina Press, 2001.

Garson, Robert A. *The Democratic Party and the Politics of Sectionalism, 1941–1948*. Baton Rouge: Louisiana State University Press, 1948.

Gilbert, James. *Another Chance: Postwar America, 1945–1968*. Philadelphia: Temple University Press, 1981.

Gilmore, Glenda Elizabeth. *Gender and Jim Crow: Women and the Politics of White Supremacy, 1896–1920*. Chapel Hill: University of North Carolina Press, 1996.

Goldman, Eric. *The Crucial Decade—and After: America, 1945–1965*. New York: Alfred A. Knopf, 1966.

Grafton, Carl, and Anne Permaloff. *Big Mules and Branchheads: James E. Folsom and Political Power in Alabama*. Athens: University of Georgia Press, 1985.

Grant, Donald. *The Way It Was in the South: The Black Experience in Georgia*. New York: Carol Publishing Group, 1993.

Grantham, Dewey. *Southern Progressivism: The Reconciliation of Progress and Tradition*. Knoxville: University of Tennessee Press, 1983.

Gray, Justin. *The Inside Story of the American Legion*. New York: Boni and Gaer, 1948.

Greene, Melissa Faye. *Praying for Sheetrock: A Work of Nonfiction.* New York: Addison-Wesley, 1991.

Griffith, Barbara S. *The Crisis of American Labor: Operation Dixie and the Defeat of the CIO.* Philadelphia: Temple University Press, 1988.

Gropman, Alan L. *The Air Force Integrates, 1945–1964.* Washington: Office of Air Force History, 1986.

Haas, Edward F. *DeLesseps S. Morrison and the Image of Reform: New Orleans Politics, 1946–1961.* Baton Rouge: Louisiana State University Press, 1974.

Hamby, Alonzo L. *Beyond the New Deal: Harry S. Truman and American Liberalism.* New York: Columbia University Press, 1973.

Harris, Mark Jonathan, Franklin D. Mitchell, and Steven J. Schechter. *The Homefront: America during World War II.* New York: Putnam, 1984.

Henderson, Harold P. *The Politics of Change in Georgia: A Political Biography of Ellis Arnall.* Athens: University of Georgia Press, 1991.

Henderson, Harold P., and Gary L. Roberts, eds. *Georgia Governors in an Age of Change: From Ellis Arnall to George Busbee.* Athens: University of Georgia Press, 1988.

Honey, Michael K. *Southern Labor and Black Civil Rights: Organizing Memphis Workers.* Chicago: University of Illinois Press, 1993.

Hyatt, Richard. *Zell: The Governor Who Gave Georgia HOPE.* Macon, Ga.: Mercer University Press, 1997.

Inscoe, John C., ed. *Georgia in Black and White: Explorations in the Race Relations of a Southern State.* Athens: University of Georgia Press, 1994.

Jacoway, Elizabeth, Dan T. Carter, Lester C. Lamon, and Robert C. McMath, eds. *The Adaptable South: Essays in Honor of George Brown Tindall.* Baton Rouge: Louisiana State University Press, 1991.

Jacoway, Elizabeth, and David R. Colburn, eds. *Southern Businessmen and Desegregation.* Baton Rouge: Louisiana State University Press, 1982.

Jones, Jacquelyn. *The Dispossessed: America's Underclasses from the Civil War to the Present.* New York: Harper Collins, 1992.

Kantrowitz, Stephen. *Ben Tillman and the Reconstruction of White Supremacy.* Chapel Hill: University of North Carolina Press, 2000.

Kelley, Robin D. G. *Race Rebels: Culture, Politics, and the Black Working Class.* New York: Free Press, 1994.

Kennedy, David M. *Freedom from Fear: The American People in Depression and War, 1929–1945.* New York: Oxford University Press, 1999.

———. *Over Here: The First World War and American Society.* New York: Oxford University Press, 1980.

Key, V. O., Jr. *Southern Politics in State and Nation.* New York: Alfred A. Knopf, 1949.

Kirby, Jack Temple. *Darkness at the Dawning: Race and Reform in the Progressive South.* Philadelphia: J. B. Lippincott, 1972.

Kluger, Steve. *Yank, the Army Weekly: World War II from the Guys Who Brought You Victory.* New York: St. Martin's Press, 1991.

Kneebone, John T. *Southern Liberal Journalists and the Issues of Race, 1920–1944.* Chapel Hill: University of North Carolina Press, 1985.

Kousser, J. Morgan. *The Shaping of Southern Politics: Suffrage Restriction and the Estab-*

lishment of the One-Party South, 1880–1910. New Haven, Conn.: Yale University Press, 1974.

Kytle, Calvin, and James Mackay. *Who Runs Georgia?* Athens: University of Georgia Press, 1998.

Lawson, Steven F. *Black Ballots: Voting Rights in the South, 1944–1969.* New York: Columbia University Press, 1976.

Lester, James E. *A Man for Arkansas: Sid McMath and the Southern Reform Tradition.* Little Rock, Ark.: Rose Publishing, 1954.

Lichtenstein, Nelson. *Labor's War at Home: The CIO in World War II.* Cambridge: Cambridge University Press, 1982.

Logue, Calvin M. *Eugene Talmadge: Rhetoric and Response.* New York: Greenwood Press, 1989.

Lumpkin, Katharine Du Pre. *The Making of a Southerner.* New York: Alfred A. Knopf, 1947.

MacLean, Nancy. *Behind the Mask of Chivalry: The Making of the Second Ku Klux Klan.* New York: Oxford University Press, 1994.

Mandle, Jay R. *The Roots of Black Poverty: The Southern Plantation Economy after the Civil War.* Durham, N.C.: Duke University Press, 1978.

Marable, Manning. *Race, Reform, and Rebellion: The Second Reconstruction in Black America, 1945–1982.* Jackson: University Press of Mississippi, 1984.

Marshall, F. Ray. *Labor in the South.* Cambridge, Mass.: Harvard University Press, 1967.

Marwick, Arthur, ed. *Total War and Social Change.* London: Macmillan, 1998.

Mason, Lucy Randolph. *To Win These Rights: A Personal Story of the CIO in the South.* New York: Harper, 1952.

McGuire, Philip. *Taps for a Jim Crow Army: Letters from Black Soldiers in World War II.* Santa Barbara, Calif.: ABC-CLIO, 1983.

McMillen, Neil R., ed. *Remaking Dixie: The Impact of World War II on the American South.* Jackson: University Press of Mississippi, 1997.

Milford, Lewis, and Richard Severo. *The Wages of War: When America's Soldiers Came Home—From Valley Forge to Vietnam.* New York: Simon and Schuster, 1989.

Millett, Allan R., and Peter Maslowski. *For the Common Defense: A Military History of the United States of America.* New York: Free Press, 1984.

Minchin, Timothy J. *What Do We Need a Union For? The TWUA in the South, 1945–1955.* Chapel Hill: University of North Carolina Press, 1997.

Mohl, Raymond. *Searching for the Sunbelt: Historical Perspectives on a Region.* Knoxville: University of Tennessee Press, 1990.

Moley, Raymond. *The American Legion Story.* New York: Meredith Publishing, 1966.

Motley, Mary Penick. *The Invisible Soldier: The Experience of the Black Soldier in World War II.* Detroit: Wayne State University Press, 1975.

Myrdal, Gunnar. *An American Dilemma: The Negro Problem and Modern Democracy.* New York: Harper and Row, 1944.

Norrell, Robert J. *Reaping the Whirlwind: The Civil Rights Movement in Tuskegee.* New York: Alfred A. Knopf, 1985.

Nossiter, Adam. *Of Long Memory: Mississippi and the Murder of Medgar Evers.* New York: Addison-Wesley, 1994.

Oberly, James W. *Sixty Million Acres: American Veterans and the Public Lands Before the Civil War.* Kent, Ohio: Kent State University Press, 1990.

O'Brien, Gail Williams. *The Color of the Law: Race, Violence, and Justice in the Post–World War II South.* Chapel Hill: University of North Carolina Press, 1999.

O'Neill, William L. *American High: The Years of Confidence, 1945–1960.* New York: Free Press, 1986.

Phillips, Cabell. *The 1940s: Decade of Triumph and Trouble.* New York: Macmillan, 1975.

Polenberg, Richard. *War and Society: The United States, 1941–1945.* Philadelphia: J. B. Lippincott, 1972.

Reed, Linda. *Simple Decency and Common Sense: The Southern Conference Movement, 1938–1963.* Bloomington: Indiana University Press, 1991.

Rogers, William W. *Alabama: The History of a Deep South State.* Tuscaloosa: University of Alabama Press, 1994.

Ross, Davis R. B. *Preparing for Ulysses: Politics and Veterans during World War II.* New York: Columbia University Press, 1969.

Ruchames, Louis. *Race, Jobs, and Politics: The Story of FEPC.* New York: Columbia University Press, 1953.

Rumer, Thomas A. *The American Legion: An Official History, 1919–1989.* New York: M. Evans, 1990.

Schulman, Bruce J. *From Cotton Belt to Sunbelt: Federal Policy, Economic Development, and the Transformation of the South, 1938–1980.* New York: Oxford University Press, 1991.

Shannon, Jasper Berry. *Toward a New Politics in the South.* Knoxville: University of Tennessee Press, 1949.

Shapiro, Herbert. *White Violence and Black Response: From Reconstruction to Montgomery.* Amherst: University of Massachusetts Press, 1988.

Shulman, Holly Cowan. *The Voice of America: Propaganda and Democracy, 1941–1945.* Madison: University of Wisconsin Press, 1990.

Siegel, Frederick. *Troubled Journey: From Pearl Harbor to Ronald Reagan.* New York: Hill and Wang, 1984.

Simon, Bryant. *A Fabric of Defeat: The Politics of Southern Carolina Millhands, 1910–1948.* Chapel Hill: University of North Carolina Press, 1998.

Sims, George F. *The Little Man's Big Friend: James E. Folsom in Alabama Politics, 1946–1958.* Tuscaloosa: University of Alabama Press, 1985.

Sitkoff, Harvard. *The Struggle for Black Equality.* New York: Hill and Wang, 1981.

Smith, C. Calvin. *War and Wartime Change: The Transformation of Arkansas, 1940–1945.* Fayetteville: University of Arkansas Press, 1986.

Smith, Frank. *Congressman from Mississippi.* New York: Pantheon Books, 1964.

Smith, Graham. *When Jim Crow Met John Bull.* London: I. B. Tauris, 1987.

Sosna, Morton. *In Search of the Silent South: Southern Liberals and the Race Issue.* New York: Columbia University Press, 1977.

Spritzer, Lorraine Nelson. *The Belle of Ashby Street: Helen Douglas Mankin and Georgia Politics.* Athens: University of Georgia Press, 1982.

Stouffer, Samuel A., et al. *The American Soldier: Adjustment During Army Life.* Vol. 1 of

Studies in Social Psychology in World War II. Princeton, N.J.: Princeton University Press, 1949.

―――. *The American Soldier: Combat and Its Aftermath*. Vol. 2 of *Studies in Social Psychology in World War II*. Princeton, N.J.: Princeton University Press, 1949.

Sullivan, Patricia. *Days of Hope: Race and Democracy in the New Deal Era*. Chapel Hill: University of North Carolina, 1996.

Tindall, George Brown. *The Emergence of the New South, 1913–1945*. Baton Rouge: Louisiana State University Press, 1976.

Tindall, George Brown, and David E. Shi. *America: A Narrative History*. 4th ed. New York: W. W. Norton, 1996.

Tyson, Timothy B. *Radio Free Dixie: Robert F. Williams and the Roots of Black Power*. Chapel Hill: University of North Carolina, 1999.

Wade, Wyn Craig. *The Fiery Cross: The Ku Klux Klan in America*. New York: Oxford University Press, 1987.

Waldron, Ann. *Hodding Carter: The Reconstruction of a Racist*. Chapel Hill, N.C.: Algonquin Books, 1993.

Walton, Richard J. *Henry Wallace, Harry Truman, and the Cold War*. New York: Viking Press, 1976.

Wexler, Laura. *Fire in a Canebrake: The Last Mass Lynching in America*. New York and London: Scribner, 2003.

White, William W. *The Confederate Veteran*. Tuscaloosa, Ala.: Confederate Publishing Company, 1962.

Williamson, Joel. *The Crucible of Race: Black/White Relations in the American South since Emancipation*. New York: Oxford University Press, 1984.

Wittner, Lawrence. *Cold War America: From Hiroshima to Watergate*. New York: Praeger, 1974.

Woodward, C. Vann. *The Origins of the New South, 1877–1913*. Baton Rouge: Louisiana State University Press, 1951.

Wright, Gavin. *Old South, New South: Revolutions in the Southern Economy since the Civil War*. New York: Basic Books, 1986.

Wynn, Neil. *The Afro-American and the Second World War*. London: Paul Elek, 1976.

Zieger, Robert H. *The CIO, 1935–1955*. Chapel Hill: University of North Carolina Press, 1995.

―――, ed. *Organized Labor in the Twentieth-Century South*. Knoxville: University of Tennessee Press, 1991.

Articles

Badger, Tony. "Fatalism, Not Gradualism: The Crisis of Southern Liberalism, 1945–1965." In *The Making of Martin Luther King and the Civil Rights Movement*, edited by Brian Ward and Tony Badger, 67–95. Washington Square, N.Y.: New York University Press, 1996.

Barkin, Solomon, and Michael Honey. "Operation Dixie: Two Views." *Labor History* 31 (Summer 1990): 373–85.

Bartley, Numan V. "Writing About the Post–World War II South." *Georgia Historical Quarterly* 68 (Spring 1984): 1–18.

Bernard, Richard. "Metropolitan Politics in the American Sunbelt." In *Searching for the Sunbelt: Historical Perspectives on a Region*, edited by Raymond A. Mohl, 69–84. Knoxville: University of Tennessee Press, 1990.

Brattain, Michelle. "Making Friends and Enemies: Textile Workers and Political Action in Post–World War II Georgia." *Journal of Southern History* 63 (February 1997): 91–138.

———. "'A Town as Small as That': Tallapoosa, Georgia and Operation Dixie, 1945–1950." *Georgia Historical Quarterly* 81 (Summer 1997): 395–425.

Cobb, James C. "Colonel Effingham Crushes the Crackers: Political Reform in Postwar Augusta." *South Atlantic Quarterly* 78 (Autumn 1979): 507–19.

———. "Georgia Odyssey." In *The New Georgia Guide*, edited by the Georgia Humanities Council, 3–104. Athens: University of Georgia Press, 1996.

———. "World War II and the Mind of the Modern South." In *Remaking Dixie: The Impact of World War II on the American South*, edited by Neil R. McMillen, 3–20. Jackson: University Press of Mississippi, 1997.

Dalfiume, Richard. "The 'Forgotten Years' of the Negro Revolution." *Journal of American History* 55 (June 1968): 90–106.

Daniel, Pete. "Going Among Strangers: Southern Reactions to World War II." *Journal of American History* 77 (December 1990): 886–911.

Dudley, J. Wayne. "'Hate' Organizations of the 1940s: The Columbians, Inc." *Phylon* 42 (no. 3, 1981): 262–74.

Edmundson, Charles. "How Kefauver Beat Crump: The Story of a Southern Victory." *Harper's Magazine*, January 1949, 81.

Finkle, Lee. "The Conservative Aims of Militant Rhetoric: Black Protest during World War II." *Journal of American History* 60 (December 1973): 692–713.

Frederickson, Kari. "'As a Man I Am Interested in States' Rights': Gender, Race, and the Family in the Dixiecrat Party, 1948–1950." In *Jumpin' Jim Crow: Southern Politics from Civil War to Civil Rights*, edited by Jane Dailey, Glenda Elizabeth Gilmore, and Bryant Simon, 260–74. Princeton, N.J.: Princeton University Press, 2000.

Gall, Gilbert J. "Southern Industrial Workers and Anti-Union Sentiment: Arkansas and Florida in 1944." In *Organized Labor in the Twentieth-Century South*, edited by Robert H. Zieger, 223–49. Knoxville: University of Tennessee Press, 1991.

Gilmore, Glenda E. "Murder, Memory, and the Flight of the Incubus." In *Democracy Betrayed: The Wilmington Race Riot of 1898 and Its Legacy*, edited by David S. Cecelski and Timothy B. Tyson. Chapel Hill: University of North Carolina Press, 1998.

Grafton, Carl. "James E. Folsom's 1946 Campaign." In *From Civil War to Civil Rights—Alabama, 1860–1960: An Anthology from the Alabama Review*, edited by Sarah Woolfolk Wiggins, 441–62. Tuscaloosa: University of Alabama Press, 1987.

Halpern, Rick. "Interracial Unionism in the Southwest: Fort Worth's Packinghouse Workers, 1937–1954." In *Organized Labor in the Twentieth Century South*, edited by Robert H. Zieger, 158–82. Knoxville: University of Tennessee Press, 1991.

Henderson, Harold P. "Ellis Arnall and the Politics of Progress." In *Georgia Governors in an Age of Change: From Ellis Arnall to George Busbee*, edited by Harold P. Henderson and Gary L. Roberts, 25–39. Athens: University of Georgia Press, 1988.

Hornsby, Alton. "A City That Was Too Busy to Hate: Atlanta Businessmen and Desegregation." In *Southern Businessmen and Desegregation*, edited by Elizabeth Jacoway and David R. Colburn, 120–36. Baton Rouge: Louisiana State University Press, 1982.

Kantrowitz, Stephen. "Ben Tillman and Hendrix McLane, Agrarian Rebels: White Manhood, the Farmers, and the Limits of Southern Populism." *Journal of Southern History* 66 (August 2000): 497–524.

Kohn, Richard H. "The Social History of the American Soldier: A Review and Prospectus for Research." *American Historical Review* 86 (June 1981): 553–67.

Korstad, Robert R., and Nelson Lichtenstein. "Opportunities Found and Lost: Labor, Radicals, and the Early Civil Rights Movement." *Journal of American History* 75 (December 1988): 786–811.

Kytle, Calvin. "A Long Dark Night for Georgia?" *Harper's Magazine* 197 (September 1948): 55–64.

Lee, R. Alton. "The Army 'Mutiny' of 1946." *Journal of American History* 53 (December 1966): 555–71.

"Manipulation in Memphis." *Economist*, August 21, 1943, 235–36.

May, Elaine Tyler. "Cold War—Warm Hearth: Politics and the Family in Postwar America." In *The Rise and Fall of the New Deal Order, 1930–1980*, edited by Steve Fraser and Gary Gerstle, 153–81. Princeton, N.J.: Princeton University Press, 1989.

McMillen, Neil R. "Fighting for What We Didn't Have: How Mississippi's Black Veterans Remember World War II." In *Remaking Dixie: The Impact of World War II on the American South*, edited by Neil R. McMillen, 93–110. Jackson: University Press of Mississippi, 1997.

Modell, John, Marc Goulden, and Sigurdur Magnusson. "World War II in the Lives of Black Americans: Some Findings and an Interpretation." *Journal of American History* 76 (December 1989): 838–48.

Nixon, H. Clarence. "The South after the War." *Virginia Quarterly Review* 20 (Summer 1944): 321–34.

Pajari, Roger N. "Herman E. Talmadge and the Politics of Power." In *Georgia Governors in an Age of Change: From Ellis Arnall to George Busbee*, edited by Harold P. Henderson and Gary L. Roberts, 75–92. Athens: University of Georgia Press, 1988.

Reich, Steven A. "Soldiers of Democracy: Black Texans and the Fight for Citizenship, 1917–1921." *Journal of American History* 82 (March 1996): 1478–504.

Seiber, Lones. "The Battle of Athens." *American Heritage* 36 (February/March 1985): 72–79.

Simon, Bryant. "Race Reactions: African American Organizing, Liberalism, and White Working-Class Politics in Postwar South Carolina." In *Jumpin' Jim Crow: Southern Politics from Civil War to Civil Rights*, edited by Jane Dailey, Glenda Elizabeth Gilmore, and Bryant Simon, 239–59. Princeton, N.J.: Princeton University Press, 2000.

Sitkoff, Harvard. "African-American Militancy in the World War II South: Another Perspective." In *Remaking Dixie: The Impact of World War Two on the American South*, edited by Neil R. McMillen, 70–92. Jackson: University Press of Mississippi, 1997.

Skates, John R., Jr. "World War II as a Watershed in Mississippi History." *Journal of Mississippi History* 37 (May 1975): 131–45.

Sosna, Morton. "More Important Than the Civil War? The Impact of World War II on the South." In *Perspectives on the American South: An Annual Review of Society, Politics, and Culture, Vol. 4,* edited by James C. Cobb and Charles R. Wilson, 145–61. New York: Gordon and Breach, 1987.

Spinney, Robert G. "Municipal Government in Nashville, Tennessee, 1938–1951: World War II and the Growth of the Public Sector." *Journal of Southern History* 61 (February 1995): 77–112.

Stanfield, John H. "Dollars for the Silent South: Southern White Liberalism and the Julius Rosenwald Fund, 1928–1948." In *Perspectives on the American South: An Annual Review of Society, Politics, and Culture, Vol. 2,* edited by Merle Black and John Shelton Reed, 117–38. New York: Gordon and Breach, 1984.

Stein, Judith. "Southern Workers in National Unions: Birmingham Steelworkers, 1936–1951." In *Organized Labor in the Twentieth Century South,* edited by Robert H. Zieger, 183–222. Knoxville: University of Tennessee Press, 1991.

"Trouble at Athens, Alabama." *Events and Trends in Race Relations, Monthly Summary* 4 (August/September 1946): 51.

Tyson, Timothy B. "Wars for Democracy: African American Militancy and Interracial Violence in North Carolina during World War II." In *Democracy Betrayed: The Wilmington Race Riot of 1898 and Its Legacy,* edited by David S. Cecelski and Timothy B. Tyson, 253–77. Chapel Hill: University of North Carolina Press, 1998.

"Veterans: Rule by Fist." *Newsweek,* January 27, 1947, 25–26.

"Veterans: Tennessee Siege." *Newsweek,* August 12, 1946, 30–31.

Warren, Wallace H. " 'The Best People in Town Won't Talk': The Moore's Ford Lynching of 1946 and Its Cover-up." In *Georgia in Black and White: Explorations in the Race Relations of a Southern State,* edited by John C. Inscoe, 266–88. Athens: University of Georgia Press, 1994.

White, Theodore H. "The Battle of Athens, Tennessee." *Harper's Monthly* 194 (January 1947): 54–61.

Woodman, Harold D. "Economic Reconstruction and the Rise of the New South, 1865–1900." In *Interpreting Southern History: Historiographical Essays in Honor of Sanford W. Higginbotham,* edited by John B. Boles and Evelyn Thomas Nolen, 254–307. Baton Rouge: Louisiana State University Press, 1987.

Zieger, Robert H. "Textile Workers and Historians." In *Organized Labor in the Twentieth Century South,* edited by Robert H. Zieger, 35–59. Knoxville: University of Tennessee Press, 1991.

———. " 'A Venture into Unplowed Fields': Daniel Powell and CIO Political Action in the Postwar South." In *Labor in the Modern South,* edited by Glenn T. Eskew, 153–81. Athens: University of Georgia Press, 2001.

Unpublished Works

Autrey, Dorothy. "The National Association for the Advancement of Colored People in Alabama, 1913–1952." Ph.D. diss., University of Notre Dame, 1985.

Barnes, Catherine Anne. "Journey from Jim Crow: The Desegregation of Southern Transit." Ph.D. diss., Columbia University, 1981.

Behel, Sandra K. "The Mississippi Homefront during World War II: Tradition and Change." Ph.D. diss., Mississippi State University Press, 1989.

Bolster, Paul Douglas. "Civil Rights Movements in Twentieth-Century Georgia." Ph.D. diss., University of Georgia, 1972.

Burran, James. "Racial Violence in the South during World War II." Ph.D. diss., University of Tennessee, 1977.

Corley, Robert Gaines. "The Quest for Racial Harmony: Race Relations in Alabama, 1947–1963." Ph.D. diss., University of Virginia, 1979.

Cunnigen, Donald. "Men and Women of Goodwill: Mississippi's White Liberals." Ph.D. diss., Harvard University, 1988.

Fosdick, Roger Barry. "A Call to Arms: The American Enlisted Soldier in World War II." Ph.D. diss., Claremont Graduate School, 1985.

Franco, Jere. "Patriotism on Trial: Native Americans in World War II." Ph.D. diss., University of Arizona, 1990.

Harmon, David Andrew. "Beneath the Image: The Civil Rights Movement and Race Relations in Atlanta." Ph.D. diss., Emory University, 1993.

Horowitz, Roger. "Our Desire for Peace and Home: The Postwar Visions of World War II's Working-Class Veterans, 1944–1946." Paper presented at the American Historical Association annual meeting, January 1995, Chicago, Ill. Copy in possession of author.

Jones, Bartlett Campbell. "Some Aspects of the Opposition in Georgia to the CIO's Organizing Drive, 1946–1953." M.A. thesis, Emory University, 1956.

Korstad, Robert R. "Daybreak of Freedom: Tobacco Workers and the CIO, Winston-Salem, North Carolina, 1943–1950." Ph.D. diss., University of North Carolina at Chapel Hill, 1987.

Lemond, Thomas Addison, Jr. "The Good Government League and Polk County (Tennessee) Politics, 1946–1965." M.A. thesis, Vanderbilt University, 1970.

Leonard, Kevin Allen. "Years of Hope, Days of Fear: The Impact of World War II on Race Relations in Los Angeles." Ph.D. diss., University of California, Davis, 1992.

Manns, Adrienne Lynette. "The Role of Ex-Servicemen in Ghana's Independence Movement." Ph.D. diss., Johns Hopkins University, 1984.

Newberry, Anthony Lake. "Without Urgency or Ardor: The South's Middle of the Road Liberals and Civil Rights, 1945–1960." Ph.D. diss., Ohio State University, 1982.

Onkst, David. " 'First a Negro . . . incidentally a Veteran': Black World War II Veterans and the G.I. Bill of Rights in the Deep South, 1944–1948." Paper delivered at the Hagley Museum and Library "Aftermath" Conference, October 27, 1995, Wilmington, Del. Paper in possession of author.

Skinner, Byron D. "The Double 'V': The Impact of World War II on Black Americans." Ph.D. diss., University of California, Berkeley, 1978.

Thomas, Joyce. "The 'Double V' Was for Victory: Black Soldiers, the Black Protest, and World War II." Ph.D. diss., Ohio State University Press, 1993.

Williams, Kenneth. "Mississippi and Civil Rights, 1945–1954." Ph.D. diss., Mississippi State University, 1985.

Index

Christopher, Paul, 83, 93, 104

Citizens Progressive League (CPL), 28, 30, 31, 125, 127, 128, 131, 132, 133, 136, 137, 142, 150, 151, 171

Civil rights movement, 11, 15, 33, 36, 39, 73, 74, 162, 167, 171

Cold War: and anticommunism, 32, 33, 53, 54, 73, 82, 94, 107; and liberalism, 8, 9, 53, 54, 56, 95, 131. *See also* Liberalism: and Cold War

Columbians, Inc., 39, 62, 63, 64, 65, 66, 67, 69, 97, 136, 171

Columbus, Georgia, 5, 27, 35, 84, 97, 109, 151

Combs, Doyle, 3, 4, 18, 19, 25, 171

Congress of Industrial Organizations (CIO), 41, 47, 49, 50, 55, 59, 74–111 passim, 148, 150, 151, 163, 164, 169; defeat of, 8, 93, 94, 95, 98, 99, 107, 109, 110, 111, 148, 151, 163, 164, 165; and Georgia, 7, 47, 74, 76, 79, 80–111 passim, 126, 151, 164; and right-to-work bills (HB 72 and 73), 8, 164; and southern postwar progressivism, 7, 78, 79, 100. *See also* Congress of Industrial Organizations Political Action Committee; Operation Dixie; Organized labor

Congress of Industrial Organizations Political Action Committee (CIO-PAC): in Georgia, 7, 49, 56, 76, 100–111 passim, 125, 153; national organization, 7, 41, 49, 56, 71, 76, 80, 100, 101, 102, 103, 104, 105, 106, 107–8; in South, 7, 41, 49, 56, 76, 80, 100, 101, 102, 103, 104, 105, 106, 107. *See also* Congress of Industrial Organizations; Operation Dixie; Organized labor

Conservative modernization, 9, 10, 130–68 passim, 170

Conservatives, southern Democratic, 4–16 passim, 27, 37, 38, 40, 56, 57, 59, 60, 77, 78, 79, 93, 94, 96, 101, 103, 121–32 passim, 144, 154, 155, 156, 157, 159, 160, 161, 162, 166, 169, 170; and anti-union backlash, 8, 10, 75, 78, 79, 81, 93, 94, 96, 97, 99, 103, 107, 108, 109, 148, 164, 165, 170; and backlash against African Americans, 8, 10, 14–27 passim, 33, 34, 35, 36, 37, 38, 39, 47, 53–74 passim, 79, 133, 134, 144, 153–62 passim, 166, 169, 170, 171, 182 (nn. 29, 30, 32); and racial violence, 22, 23, 24, 25, 33, 34, 35, 154, 157, 158, 159, 160, 161, 162. *See also* Racism, southern white

County unit system, 6, 31, 33, 38, 39, 49, 50, 51, 52, 53, 56, 68, 72, 100, 103, 134, 135, 144, 146, 147; challenges to, 36, 38, 49, 50, 51, 52, 53, 56, 174 (n. 9); and Neill Primary Act, 6

Cracker Party, 125–37 passim, 146

Davis, James C., 31, 49, 50, 69

Democratic Party, national: and New Deal coalition, 53, 77, 154, 155, 171; and Truman civil rights program, 53, 154, 155

Dixiecrats, 9, 154, 155, 171, 199 (n. 93)

Dorsey, George, 22, 23, 35, 162, 171

Dorsey, Mae Murray, 23, 35

Doss, George, Jr., 51, 130, 134, 135, 137

Emory University, 51, 143

Fair Employment Practices Commission (FEPC), 38, 40, 59, 61, 78, 95, 101, 109, 135, 154

Fleming, Harold, 43, 44, 45, 47, 48, 55, 73

Flynt, John J., 113, 114, 136, 141, 145, 165

Georgia, 5, 6, 7, 8, 9, 10, 77, 79, 82, 83, 84, 93, 102, 114–25 passim, 129, 140, 144, 152, 165, 166, 167, 169, 170, 220 (n. 28); and boosterism, 151, 165; conditions in, 5, 6, 9, 10, 19, 21, 22, 34, 35, 47, 58, 59, 77, 114–25 passim, 130, 131, 140, 144, 165, 166, 167, 169, 170; Democratic Party in, 153, 157, 158; Minimum Foundation Program in, 166; Supreme Court of, 152, 153; and textile belt, 77, 79, 83, 84, 102, 103, 104